A BIOGRAPHY

POLLY
FARMER

REVISED & UPDATED

The Slattery Media Group Pty Ltd
1 Albert St, Richmond
Victoria, Australia, 3121

First published by Fremantle Arts Centre Press 1994
This edition published by The Slattery Media Group Pty Ltd 2014
All images reproduced with permission.

National Library of Australia Cataloguing-in-Publication entry

National Library of Australia Cataloguing-in-Publication entry

Author: Hawke, Stephen, 1959- author.

Title: Polly Farmer / Steve Hawke.

ISBN: 9780992363154 (paperback)

Subjects: Farmer, Graham, 1935-

            Australian football--Western Australia--Biography.

            Australian football--Victoria--Biography.

            Football players--Western Australia--Biography.

            Football players--Victoria--Biography.

Dewey Number: 796.336092

Group Publisher: Geoff Slattery
Editor: Bronwyn Wilkie
Creative Director and design: Kate Slattery

Printed and bound in Australia by McPherson's Printing Group

To the best of our knowledge, the information in this book was correct at the time of publication. The opinions are those of the author.

Every effort has been made to verify the source of each photo.
Inquiries should be made to the publisher.

slatterymedia.com

THE GRAHAM FARMER (POLLY) FOUNDATION
MAKE YOUR MARK

A BIOGRAPHY

POLLY
FARMER

REVISED & UPDATED

STEVE HAWKE

slattery
MEDIA GROUP

visit *slatterymedia.com*

As a young boy growing up in a home for Aboriginal children, Graham 'Polly' Farmer set himself the goal of reaching the very highest echelons of Australia's most popular home-grown sport.

Through hard work and sheer determination, with a leavening of pure natural brilliance, he made it to the top, and stayed there. Not only did he claim a position among the greatest footballers of all time, he changed the very nature of the game.

Polly Farmer, the first full-length biography of the national football hero, traces his sometimes tortuous path to national stardom and vividly re-creates the crowning achievements of his 20-year playing career.

DEDICATION

The first edition of this book was published 20 years ago, in 1994. When I first approached the Farmers about the idea in the early 90s, Graham and Marlene were initially reluctant. But Farmer had been harbouring a different dream which worked to my advantage as a would-be biographer.

His greatest attribute as a footballer was an unparalleled ability to create openings and opportunities for those around him—to bring them into the play. In 23 seasons of football, from the suburban leagues of Perth through to the elite levels of the game, this was his hallmark. The idea he had in mind was to continue this tradition in a different way, and on a different field. He wanted to use his name and standing to create an organisation that would provide opportunities for young Indigenous people to make the most of their own skills in the sporting and academic arenas.

We struck a deal. In parallel with my research and writing of the book, I worked with Graham to establish the Graham (Polly) Farmer Foundation, shaping the objectives and a structure, recruiting a board, and getting the organisation up and running.

Twenty years on, it is a source of pride and pleasure to the Farmer family that the Foundation has survived and thrived, and continues to deliver for young people around the country under its banner of 'Make Your Mark'.

The Honourable Fred Chaney has been an inspirational presence for the Foundation since its inception, remaining on the Board throughout. Its chairs have been the eminent legal figures and High Court judges, Sir Ronald Wilson and John Toohey, and Indigenous magistrate Sue Gordon. Its programs are supported by an impressive array of corporate, government and community partners.

Very early on the Foundation decided that as a relatively small organisation, it should focus on programs providing direct support and encouragement for secondary school Indigenous students, assisting and supporting academic achievement and job readiness. It has developed a program it calls 'Follow the Dream / Partnerships for Success' that it first implemented in the Pilbara in the late 1990s. This and other programs have now spread to 26 communities in four states and territories, supporting many hundreds of students each year. The results for its program graduates in terms of Year 12 completion, training and apprenticeship outcomes, and employment participation are clearly documented and impressive.

To quote Fred Chaney:

> I have been involved in a lot of organisations over the years including the National Native Title Tribunal, Reconciliation Australia, Desert Knowledge Australia, but I can say that at a personal level this has been the most satisfying because I can see in a direct way that it has changed the life of some of the kids for the better. That is what is important and what catches my heart. The beauty of the Foundation is that it is an example of how a small group of people, both Aboriginal and non-Aboriginal, can work together to pursue a worthwhile objective.

This book is dedicated to the Graham (Polly) Farmer Foundation, and to Fred and the other Board members and the staff and supporters who have helped to realise Graham's dream.

Graham and Marlene asked for nothing for themselves for their participation in the biography project; they used it as an avenue to create opportunities for others. This book is not only a tribute to one of Australia's greatest sporting sons, but has also helped contribute in a small way to realising one of his dreams.

I urge the readers to help the Foundation continue its great work in Graham Farmer's name.

Steve Hawke
February 2014.

The Graham (Polly) Farmer Foundation
pff@pff.com.au
PO Box 388, Osborne Park, Western Australia, 6917

Abbreviations used in photo captions:
WAN—West Australian Newspapers Ltd
HWT—Herald and Weekly Times Ltd
GA—Geelong Advertiser

POLLY FARMER

CONTENTS

THE BEST EVER

Graham Farmer is the greatest player to have played the great game of Australian Football. There, I've said it.

I played with him for four seasons at Geelong, and against him in interstate footy. There was nothing he couldn't do for the greater good of his team; there was little he wouldn't do either, in an era in which pretty well anything went. This was a brutal time, and Polly answered fire with more fire.

He was competitive beyond the call; he was sophisticated at a time when most of us were hillbillies; and most importantly, he is the only player to have changed the game.

Polly could see opportunities in space where others could only see conflict in close. His use of handball as an offensive weapon, in a time when it was used as a last resort, was years ahead of the pack.

He was a conundrum as well. He was selfish, yet selfless. Selfish, in that he knew that nobody could handle a moment better than he could, nobody could battle an opponent better than him, and nobody could get the ball more easily than him, and then provide it to the best purpose for the team.

Thus the conundrum: he needed to get the ball not for himself or his stats, or any sense of self-aggrandisement, but so he could deliver to the best advantage of his team. He knew what he could do, and he did it, week in, week out. He was selfish, and selfless.

I remember the first time I saw him play; I was with my late father, and we'd come from the Barwon River, at the end of the Head Of The River, a lively little public school jaunt for boats and boaters. It was early in 1962, and we strolled from the river to Kardinia Park to watch Geelong in an intra-club match.

The hype about Farmer was already huge—he had reached legend status in Perth, and Geelong coach Bob Davis and secretary Leo O'Brien had pulled off something of a coup to drag him across the Nullabor.

We had gone to see whether the hype matched the reality. I remember saying to my father, as we took our places in the outer: "Now which one is Farmer?" At that moment, there was a boundary throw in, and this great arm reached to the sky, grabbed the ball, and in a blink of the eye the ruckman had done something I'd never seen before: he swivelled, and in the same action, handballed ahead of the play, to a running teammate. I turned to my father, and said: "That's him. That's Farmer."

Little did I know that I would be playing with him a couple of years later. Little did I know what an influence he would have on me, and my career: not via words, but by his actions.

Polly was never one to set a teammate aside and say, 'this is how you do it'. He expected his teammates to observe closely, and to learn from watching him. He never said to his smaller players—notably Billy Goggin, or Tony Pollinelli or Wayne Closter—'be there' or 'run there'. He had this inner sense that he would choose the best option, and soon enough these guys knew to run to space, to get ahead of the pack, to take the easy way forward—Polly's way. Wherever they were, he'd find them.

It's sad that we can follow every moment of every one of today's players— full games, highlights, training routines, up close, multiple camera angles— but there is only limited vision of Farmer in action.

Fortunately for me, and those who played with him, and in his era, we have retained indelible images of him in action, impregnated in our mind's eye. It's an exhilarating view, as bright in my mind as that first day I saw him, more than 50 years ago. I hope many more will be able to gain some of that magic and joy reading Steven Hawke's superb summary of Polly's life, his game and his eternal legacy.

Sam Newman, August 2014

I

SISTER KATE'S

One of Graham Farmer's best known characteristics is the rolling gait that makes him seem a little off balance when he walks. It is caused by the fact that his left leg is slightly shorter than his right. This quirk has become a part of the Farmer legend, reported in countless feature stories. It tends to be seen as a handicap, yet another obstacle he has overcome on his climb to the very pinnacle of his chosen field. Our sporting champions are expected to be perfect physical specimens.

No one, least of all Farmer himself, is sure how to account for the phenomenon of the uneven legs. There were no childhood accidents or illnesses that provide an explanation. Farmer does have a theory, though. Every doctor with whom he has discussed it has dismissed his theory as ridiculous. Plausible or not, it tells us something about Farmer the boy.

Like the other boys and girls at the Sister Kate's Children's Home, he spent most of his schooldays in bare feet. He can recall walking barefoot in the snow to school one winter's morning. The Home relied on donations and cast-offs to clothe the children, and shoes were a rare commodity. However, at one stage young Graham did manage to get hold of a left shoe without its right partner. He wore it regardless "because I'm a left-footer, and I wanted to kick the footy with a shoe on."[1] He believes that because he got around for so long in one shoe, perhaps at the time of one of the rapid growth spurts that saw him shooting up above his contemporaries, his right leg may have outgrown the left to balance things up. An early example perhaps of the boy's dedication to football literally shaping the man.

S ister Kate's Children's Home began as the Children's Cottage Homes in Perth's beachside suburb of Cottesloe in 1933, two years before Graham Farmer was born. It was established by an English nun already well beyond retirement age who could not walk away from a lifetime's mission of work with poor and abandoned children, and a long-serving bureaucrat obsessed by racial theories.

Sister Kate—Katherine Clutterbuck—belonged to the Sisters of the Church, an Anglican order devoted to the education and care of children, which came to Perth in 1901 to establish a girls' school. Sister Kate and a colleague followed shortly afterwards with a brief to establish a Home to care for "delicate, sick and destitute"[2] children. They brought 22 English orphans with them. After some early hostility from the authorities, and a series of short-term stays in locations around Perth, the Home was established in 1903 at Parkerville, in the hills east of the town. Sister Kate soon became well known in Perth, forming friendships and attracting support from many prominent citizens. Her kindly nature and progressive policies inspired loyalty and love from the children of the Home. She helped many of them to find homes and work after they left the Home, and some stayed on as workers. Sister Kate remained at Parkerville until 1932, when she was retired at the age of 72.

Sister Kate's desire to keep on working in her chosen field resulted in a letter to A O Neville, then entering the third decade of his tenure as Western Australia's Chief Protector of Aborigines. "I have always been interested in the half-castes and natives," she wrote, "and I should very much like to work among them."[3] She offered to find premises to establish a home for children referred by the Department, and to run it herself with a volunteer staff, if the government would provide a subsidy for each child. She was motivated by charity and social conscience, as indicated in a later letter to Neville: "We would, of course, like to have the poorest and most neglected children, not those who have mothers who love and care for them ... those who are the most unwanted in the State."[4]

One of Neville's major preoccupations was the future of part-Aboriginal children. He was a leading proponent of "biological assimilation" which aimed at the "breeding out" of colour by controlled racial intermarriage. The legislation of the time gave him extensive powers over every aspect of the lives of Aboriginal people and placed him in a position to put his theories into practice. In essence, his aim was to remove part-Aboriginal children from their families, in the hope that they would become "good citizens" and merge into the wider society. The smaller the proportion of Aboriginal blood, and the paler the skin, the more important it was that the child be removed from the Aboriginal milieu.

Neville had no qualms about enforcing these policies, and throughout Western Australia there are stories of children taken from grief-stricken mothers by policemen and others acting on behalf of the government. At a practical level, Neville's problem was placing and caring for such children within his limited budget, so Sister Kate's offer was a heaven-sent opportunity. These mixed motives on the part of the two main figures were to cause confusion and tensions in the years to come.

By 1933 the first cottage was established, and the first 10 children, mostly under five years old, were selected by Neville from the Moore River Native Settlement on the basis that "they are so White [they] should be given the benefit of the doubt."[5] The subsidy for each child paid by the Department was half that paid by the Child Welfare Department to institutions caring for non-Aboriginal children, but Sister Kate was able to draw on her network of contacts and supporters to obtain the facilities and funds she needed. Her lieutenant was Ruth Lefroy, who had been with her at Parkerville. The Lefroy family were prominent in the West Australian pastoral industry and business circles. The cottage mothers and other workers were mostly ex-Parkerville kids who knew Sister Kate as 'Mum'.

Once her operation was established, Sister Kate was keen to enlarge it. She was inclined to act on good intentions, and rely on the Lord and her fundraising skills to provide later. Within a year, through the Lefroys, a two-hectare property was acquired amid the market gardens at Queens Park. Funds were found to build one cottage, and then more.

Neville continued to send children to the Home from Moore River and other places, while Sister Kate began admitting children who had not been sent by the Department, and did not, therefore, attract the subsidy payment. Some of them were "of more than quarter-caste blood", which contravened Neville's policy for the Home. Relationships between the Home and Department deteriorated, with Neville unable to exercise the level of control he had expected. Sister Kate continued to go her own way, and was not averse to taking her complaints against Neville to the newspapers at times.

To some degree the Home was caught in a cleft stick. Its primary income from the subsidy payments, and a large part of its public profile and support, was based on the children being Aboriginal, yet the Home was trying gently to remove the children from the status, or stigma as most saw it, of being Aboriginal. Sister Kate would have preferred to end her connection with the Aborigines Department and its successor, the Department of Native Welfare, and come under the Child Welfare Department with its higher subsidies and different connotations, but she could not do so unilaterally.

She would refer to the children as being "to all intents and purposes White."[6] Over the years the Home complained to the press about stories that spoke of "dusky children" and "half-castes". In 1949, the superintendent wrote to the *Women's Weekly* following a feature it ran on the Home stating: "There is not and never has been an Aboriginal or a half-caste child in this home. They are all quarter-castes. We are very sensitive of this line of demarcation."[7]

But all the politics and manoeuvring that occurred were of no consequence to the children of the Home. At times the finances were severely stretched, but they always managed to battle through and put wholesome if plain food on the tables.

Graham Vivian Farmer arrived at Sister Kate's in December of 1936 at the age of 21 months. His birth certificate shows that he was born at the Salvation Army's Hillcrest Hospital in North Fremantle on 10 March 1935. His mother, Eva, was 25 at the time, and living in North

Perth. His father is listed as unknown, and remains so to this day, as do the other details of his life before Sister Kate's and the circumstances of his admission there.

The Farmer family comes from the Wheatbelt town of Katanning. The matriarch was Emily, born a Coyne at Bremer Bay on the south coast. She met and married a surveyor by the name of William Farmer, more commonly known as 'Peg'. He did much of the original surveying work in the Albany and Katanning districts around the turn of the century. Emily was a prominent and respected local identity. She worked as a midwife both in her own right, and as an assistant to the town doctor. She and Peg had 13 children between 1895 and 1915, of whom Eva was the 11th. Four of Graham's uncles fought in the First World War, two of them dying in France. Larry Farmer was buried with full military honours, and was awarded medals for outstanding service. Surviving photographs of the Farmers show signs of the big build and firm, square face bequeathed to Graham.

It seems likely from what is known that young Graham was one of the children admitted to Sister Kate's voluntarily, outside the auspices of the Aborigines Department. Farmer assumes that his mother was unable to look after him, and took him to the Home to ensure that he would be raised well. Most of the children sent to Sister Kate's by the Department were from the rural regions, not Perth. It is easy to imagine a young single Aboriginal mother in Depression-wracked Perth falling on desperate times. Farmer has never been inclined, as some others have, to search out the details of his past. There is no anger at his fate, nor hidden angst. This is probably because during his time at the Home under the direction of Sister Kate herself, and then Ruth Lefroy, he was provided with a loving and caring environment. Farmer accepts Sister Kate's as his home, and regards himself as fortunate to have been there.

Sister Kate's was no Dickensian workhouse. The cottage homes were modelled on the style Sister Kate had developed at Parkerville, using theories and attitudes that were progressive for their time, as an unpublished history of the Home records:

The environment aimed to reassemble family life as much as possible. No corporal or 'degrading' punishment was allowed... No silences were inflicted... The fact that the children were part Aboriginal was of no relevance to her because she believed in the importance of socialization rather than in hereditary traits. To Sister Kate the children were simply disadvantaged children. All that was needed was to give them an opportunity. An appeal leaflet of 1935 declared the aims of [the] Home: "...to give the girls and boys the best possible chance in life ...we believe that freedom within the law brings the best results. To give the children a happy childhood in happy circumstances and surroundings, not harassed by restriction and unnecessary rules they should lead the happy, healthy life of normal childhood."[8]

The children like Farmer who arrived at a young age started out in the nursery, then graduated to live in a series of cottages based on age groups, each with a cottage mother. In these early years of the Home most of the cottage mothers were young women who had grown up at Parkerville. They were great supporters and admirers of their 'mum', Sister Kate, and knew what she wanted of them. Also—an important plus given the continuing fragile state of the Home's finances—they were willing to work for their keep and a little pocket-money. Sister Kate asked for, and received from Neville, some older girls and boys to help with the heavy work around the Home, and as they moved on out of the institution, younger children grew to take over their chores. The children went to the local Queens Park primary school, where Farmer did his first year of schooling in 1941. The children all had chores to do, but these were not onerous or excessive by all accounts. They also attended church on Sundays, and prayed before meals, but the religion was not overzealous, nor forced upon them. There was plenty of time to play and an abundance of playmates, even if they had to improvise their own toys and games. Farmer recalls little of these early years at Queens Park except the "tremendous fete at least once a year... and the holidays at Cottesloe and Point Walter."

From a modern perspective, the one jarring note in this relatively benign picture is the Home's connivance with Neville in removing the children from their families and their Aboriginal heritage. There was no suggestion of denying their origins, but every attempt was made to downplay and discount them. With the best of intentions the Home aimed to prepare the children for a life in which their families would play no role. Contacts outside the Home were with the white world; some children were sent for holidays with white families in the suburbs. On the other hand, contact with their own families was discouraged. This attitude hardened as the years passed, to the extent that in correspondence with Neville's successor F I Bray in 1941 Sister Kate wrote: "I am afraid with the older girls and boys, they will revert back to their relations," and later, " ... the mothers and relatives come to see the children and keep the remembrance always before the children that they belong to them ... I think it is a real difficulty, will the girl in service like it when her brown mother or aunt comes to see her?"[9]

Bray instructed her to discourage such contact, and to "dispose" of any letters that might arrive from relations. He went so far as to ban all relatives from Sister Kate's annual November fete. Farmer can dimly remember a couple of visits from his mother during his early years at Queens Park. There is one account of her supplying "a beautifully worked set of clothes" for him.[10] It is enough to suggest that she had not forgotten her child. It is pure speculation, but one cannot help wondering whether a more enduring connection might have been made between mother and son were it not for these attitudes, and the fact that Farmer left Perth to live in the country.

About 50 girls and boys from the Queens Park home made the move down to Greenbushes in March 1942, the month of Farmer's seventh birthday. Concern at the course of the war with Japan was one of the reasons behind the move, but it had just as much to do with the now chronic overcrowding of the Queens Park cottages. It was a big move in more ways than one. Except for those who could still remember the reserves and stations where they had started life, it was the first experience of country life. It meant a change from the cottage system they were used to. It was a scattering of the Sister Kate's family, and it removed the children from the direct presence of Sister Kate herself. They were in the care of two women, both ex-Parkerville girls, Nan Holt and Nurse Thomas.

They travelled down by train and had to walk two kilometres into town from the station. They were given a welcoming lunch at the community hall, and then made their way to a former hotel next to the post office. The building has since been removed, there is only a vacant block that slopes back up the hill.

Behind the hotel there were orchards, and late on that first afternoon the action began from that quarter. The town boys decided to test out the newcomers, and a fruit fight erupted between the Sister Kate's kids and "the outside kids." It must have been quite a battle, for it is still well remembered by Farmer and others who were there, with the orchards pillaged for the ammunition they provided and the green fruit flying back and forth over the back fence of the hotel. All insist that there was nothing vindictive, nothing racial about the fight—it was merely the inevitable confrontation between the new kids on the block and the locals to test each other's mettle. However, it did establish a local tradition. Farmer recalls:

> At various stages in the period I was there, there were a tremendous number of fights between the locals and the older Sister Kate's boys. They were actually ging* fights out in the woods, and they were amazing—they were amazing scenes … But the interesting thing about these ging fights was that there were also some of the locals who were on the side of the boys from Sister Kate's Home. They weren't all the town kids against Sister Kate's there were two different groups … They were really interesting fights out in the middle of the forest … like all the things people do during war, but with gings and stones.

At the old hotel the children were crowded into the former guestrooms and on the verandahs, and all ate together in the dining room. It was a particularly difficult time for the Home financially, with public charity directed to the concerns of the war. The children owned nothing.

> You lived in the clothes you had, and then if you were lucky enough and you had those washed, you had another set to change into—but it wasn't every day … all that was required was a pair of pants and a shirt or jumper. They were the basics of the living standards of the kids in the Home.

But they felt no sense of poverty or deprivation. As Farmer pointed out,

---

* A child's slingshot.

the Sister Kate's children were not the only ones turning up at school in bare feet.

It was at the school that Farmer got an early lesson on the social rewards of sporting prowess. He and Ted Kilmurray, with whom he went through the Home, both recall that one of the main reasons for the acceptance of the Sister Kate's children into the local community was the fact that they turned Greenbushes into the sporting champions of the region, overcoming the traditional winners from the bigger schools at Bridgetown and Manjimup. At one of the annual athletics carnivals three of the four titles for girls and boys senior and junior champions went to Greenbushes. The all-round junior boys champion in the running races and jumping was young Graham Farmer.

After a while an ex-Parkerville boy, Mr Mack, came to work at the Home, bringing with him a T-model Ford with a gas producer, and his ferrets. Each Saturday he would pile a dozen of the boys and the ferrets into the T-model and go rabbiting. At times, the boys would also go out on their own. Farmer remembers the ferrets as smelling terrible:

> ...and they were great biters. You knew they would bite you but they were great at getting rabbits, the old ferrets. We did a fair amount of rabbit chasing in those days. It was quite a big business. You'd bring them back and eat them and sell the pelts. What happened to the money I don't know.

The boys would also set traps and check them in the mornings before school.

Nurse Thomas became Mrs Mack not long afterwards, and the new couple departed. There was a succession of supervisors and workers, and an Italian stonemason who was given a room at the back in return for maintenance work about the place. Farmer remembers one couple as stern but good, another as:

> ...a good guy, but if for some reason you spoke to his wife in not what he called an accepted manner, without warning he would lose control and whack you with a big stick ... It only occurred occasionally but ... he would go off and lose control. I know at one stage he eyed me up and I ran for my life and kept out of his way until he got over it ... You'd have to say he was a

decent enough man but when he lost it he didn't know how to go about it, and so it was just brute strength.

This particular story of Farmer's is the only one that brings a note of disapproval in his memories of Sister Kate's, or recalls any fear of those placed in charge of him. The spirit of the Home children is indicated by the way they dealt with the man. "The kids ended up ganging up on him to tell him to cut it out ... some of them were old enough to do that, they took the stick off him." The girls had returned from Greenbushes to the Queens Park cottages when the war ended, and it was a relatively small group of boys that remained. They "had the run of the town ... the opinion of the townsfolk, whatever it was, we never knew it as negative ... and we were never made to feel any less of a person than anyone else." They were able to make some pocket-money from odd jobs around the town:

> I used to go and work at a woman's place for the morning and she would give me sixpence for it ... I remember coming from her place back to the hostel and losing the sixpence. I reckon I cried for a day losing that sixpence ... at that time it was such a precious amount of money.

His first real day's work earned him 4 shillings, for a full day of potato picking for an Italian market gardener near the town.

Farmer and the other boys spent five years at Greenbushes. With their home dismantled now, the only tangible reminder of the time is the avenue of trees in the main street they planted one Arbor Day. But the memories linger. Farmer and Kilmurray see those years as the high point of their childhood. "From my point of view Greenbushes was a great experience in my lifetime," says Farmer.

At Greenbushes Farmer also acquired something that has lasted as long as the memories. Sometime during these years he picked up the nickname 'Polly'. Legend has it that the name was bestowed because of his incessant parrot-like chatter. If so, he has certainly changed with the years. Kilmurray, who got his nickname 'Square' around the same time, has a different theory. As he puts it: "Pol was always good on the tooth." He suspects the parrot connection might have more to do with the way the bird is forever pecking at its seed.

S ister Kate died in 1946, working with "her children" until her death at the age of 86. There had been some doubt as to whether the institution could continue without her, but her long-time colleague, Ruth Lefroy, took over as principal, with the Minors, an elderly couple who had previously been involved as honorary officials of the Home, moving in as assistants.

Without wishing to be harsh to those who followed, it seems fair to say that some of the heart went out of the institution with Sister Kate's death, and it entered into a long, slow decline. Certainly those who passed through it in later years hold the place much less dear, and their accounts tell of a regime that was nowhere near as warm. Farmer, Kilmurray and others attribute this to the fact that "they didn't know her [Sister Kate]."

At a more practical level, the Home stood outside any of the official government, church or charitable networks. It had been Sister Kate's creation, and had relied on her capacity to attract support. From 1946 until it eventually came under the auspices of the Presbyterian Church in 1956, the eternal struggle for financial survival was more fraught than ever. Greenbushes had become a financial drain, and apparently the Home had been seeking alternatives for the boys down there ever since it had moved the girls back to Queens Park. When the boys did leave Greenbushes, it was not to return to the familiar cottages at Queens Park.

A new property was acquired in Kenwick, eight kilometres from the Queens Park complex. In 1948, Kenwick was very much on the outskirts of the city, a semirural suburb of market gardens and vineyards. A surplus wartime hospital building was acquired and transported to the property, which fronted onto the Canning River. The 'Sister Kate's Memorial Farm' was open for business.

The Home had never held high career expectations for its children. Both boys and girls were expected to go out to work as soon as they could, usually in domestic service for the girls, and manual work or farm labour for the boys. This was not unusual for children's institutions, but in the case of Sister Kate's an element can be detected of an attitude that the children should accept their limited horizons as natural for their race. Certainly the Home, and the Department that looked over its shoulder, wanted to assimilate them into the wider community, but they were expected to enter, probably remain, and be happy at the lower levels.

Ruth Lefroy, presumably due to her family background in the pastoral industry, often spoke of the great debt society owed the man on the land. She seemed to regard it almost as a duty that the children of the Home go out to work on farms and sheep stations. The Memorial Farm was established with the intention of training the boys in suitable agricultural skills for the life that lay in store for them. There was the added bonus of a potential supply of free food for the Home, for it was run as a market garden. There was a resident instructor and supervisor, Mr MacDonald, with his wife in the role of cottage mother. Farmer had just turned 12 when he and the rest of the Greenbushes boys moved up to become the first batch of children at The Farm.

The work on The Farm was not overly demanding, taking up about an hour a day, as Kilmurray recalls. There was still plenty of time afterwards for play. In summer it was cricket, or swimming and catching marron in the Canning River. In winter it was football in the vacant paddock beside The Farm.

By now the football games were getting more serious. Farmer and Kilmurray also began to play their first organised games at the Kenwick primary school they were now attending. Once again their sporting prowess helped bring acceptance. Kenwick did not lose many games with The Farm boys on their team, and, like Greenbushes, won the regional school sports. The Farm boys would walk back home from school for their lunch each day. Before long some of the neighbourhood kids were accompanying them, and then coming round after school because they knew there would always be a game of footy or something else going on.

Farmer did two years at Kenwick Primary before graduating to high school in 1949. There was no high school in the district at that stage, so it was a matter of catching the train each morning to the Forrest High School at Mount Lawley, just out of the city. His school reports for 1949 show a very able student. The final report shows that he progressed to second in the class on his results, and earned high praise from his teacher.[11]

The good results did not inspire any academic ambitions, but did contribute to a gradual realisation that he wanted something other than the farm worker's life that seemed to lie in store for him. Looking back now, he regrets that he did not take his education further than the two years at high school, and he is critical of the school system of his day for its lack of individual attention and encouragement.

His world and his experiences were beginning to broaden beyond the confines of Sister Kate's. Travelling into school on the train took the boys out of the local environment, and gave them more of a sense of independence and worldliness. Some of them were going to the local youth club on Thursday and Friday nights, where they learned boxing and gymnastics. Farmer got a job on a property two doors down, inheriting it from one of the older boys who had left The Farm and gone out to full-time work:

> In the morning and night I was working for a Mr Wild who was a member of parliament—Gerry Wild—and his wife ... I used to go and milk a couple of cows for them and feed their chickens and poultry. I used to get 12 and six a week for it or something like that. And I used to bring it back and give that money to Mrs Mac[Donald] and never saw a penny of it. But you know, that's the way things were. It really didn't worry me one way or the other, but it was my money.

He and the other Farm boys also worked at times driving tractors, planting, picking and ploughing at a large vegetable farm run by the Packer family across the river. They enjoyed the work because they felt the family took a genuine interest in them. One of the brothers would take them for boat rides down the Canning into the Swan River. "He left a good impression on me because I think he was basically very compassionate and understanding of our situation, and obviously wanted to do his best for us," says Farmer.

With the wider experience and his growing years, Farmer was beginning to find more questions to ask about what was happening to him, and what the future held. He denies any dissatisfaction, but does say that, "at Greenbushes we were younger, and as young kids you seem to enjoy your life better. I think because you may not be aware of what's going on around you, whereas as you get a bit older it may be more noticeable." Emerging into adolescence in the institutional atmosphere cannot have been particularly easy, and there is the impression that the MacDonalds, while being good providers and carers, were not especially sensitive to the boys' needs, or any problems they might have had.

School football continued at Forrest High, with Farmer playing at centre half-forward in his school team on Friday afternoons. But he is dismissive of his efforts and abilities at that stage, saying: "I didn't have the ability to read the game very well." He had just turned 14, Kilmurray was going on 15, but in the 1949 season they played in their first adult competition, with Kenwick in the South Suburban B Grade. Farmer was tall for his age, but very lightly built, and there was nothing at all to Kilmurray, but they played against the local men and loved it, revelling in the rough-and-tumble, and the thrill of competition.

> I was probably the 16th or 17th or 18th player for the side, just battling to get a game. We were making up the numbers and being grateful for the game … In those days, it was having fun, but with ambition … the thought was just: 'Try to become a good footballer.'

Farmer played on a half-forward flank and wing, and did well enough to hold his place in the Kenwick team. He garnered his first-ever press report in the suburban paper that covered the games. In a rundown of the winning Kenwick side midway through that 1949 season, it reported: "Good scouting; two nice goals Polly." Kenwick went on to win the B Grade premiership that year, and repeated the success in 1950. A pattern of playing in successful teams was established early.

At the time he celebrated this second success Farmer was 15 years old. He was nearing the end of his last year of compulsory schooling, and was also of the age when The Home started to look for farm jobs for its boys.

2

INTO THE
ADULT WORLD

Farmer was already showing many of the qualities that he would carry
through life, and his sporting prowess was merely the most obvious.
He had an able mind, and was willing to apply his intelligence, along
with his fierce determination and competitiveness, to achieve a desired
result. But he kept his own counsel as to just what his aims might be, where
he saw his dreams taking him. Kilmurray's wife, Elsie, who lived near
The Farm in Kenwick and knew all the boys at this stage, remembers
Farmer as if he were saying even then: "'I'm going down that way, and I'm
in control ...' But he did it quietly, he didn't do it with a lot of fuss."

Some of the first batch of Farm boys of 1947 had already been sent out to
distant farms and country towns in keeping with the Sister Kate's tradition.
One such was a big tough lad named Jack Hunt. He was to rejoin Farmer
and Kilmurray in years to come, but by 1949 he was working on a property
in the Mukinbudin district. But the success with the Kenwick football team
in 1949 and 1950 seemed to have settled the boys into the district, and won
them acceptance in the local community. A quiet resistance to the notion of
being banished to the bush began to build, and for a short period the Home
seemed prepared to accommodate some of them.

Despite his good performance at school, Farmer had no ambitions to continue his studies beyond the compulsory stage. He had no particular career in mind, but like many adolescents he was clearer about what he wanted to avoid: "the only thing I didn't want was to be farming." What he wanted was a job, a job in Perth. Through Mr Minors at the Queens Park base of Sister Kate's, he secured an apprenticeship as a motor mechanic at Winterbottom's, starting in 1951, the year he turned 16.

Winterbottom's was the biggest car dealership in the state at that time. As well as a salesroom fronting St Georges Terrace in the central city, there was a large workshop occupying the length of the Mill Street block that sloped down towards the Swan River. Here they not only serviced and repaired cars, but assembled and prepared for sale Austin, Chrysler, Dodge and De Soto vehicles, for which they held the franchise. It was a large enterprise, and Farmer was one of almost 50 apprentices on the shop floor.

There were few, if any, boys with Aboriginal blood in apprenticeships at the time. Two years later it was still unusual enough for the *West Australian* to run a feature story and picture of a young lad from Carnarvon when he came down to Perth for a stint at technical college as part of his printing apprenticeship, pointing out that he had only been given a chance after no suitable white boys could be found. The manager at Winterbottom's, Russell Miller, must have been prepared to take Farmer on face value, without such preconceptions, for Farmer recalls Miller querying his wish to be an apprentice, and saying: "Your marks are good enough for you to study accountancy." But young Farmer wanted a job, not years at school.

Previously it had always been the policy of the Home that once its children had found or been placed in work, they should make their own way and move out of the Home. But this too seems to have been relaxed for a year or two, perhaps because the numbers at the Memorial Farm remained small. Farmer was allowed to stay on despite having found full-time work. This arrangement lasted for almost two years, with Farmer travelling into the city each day by train. It enabled him to make a gradual transition from child to adult, student to worker, institution boy to independent young man; much easier than the radical departure to a remote farm that most of the Home children made.

It was not all easy going for the young lad in the new environment at Winterbottom's though. It was here that he learned how to deal with those who sought to establish their superiority with the tried and tested method of racial abuse. "If you got into a fight about every stupid comment that was made you would have four or five fights a day," he says. "It just wasn't worth it." His response was to either ignore the taunts, or to reply in similar terms. Those who called him 'boong', 'darkie' and 'nigger' got 'ding', 'dago' or the like in return.

> And if you were an Australian—how do you put an Australian down? You call him a poofter ... The point is, I'm not saying that I was any better than them for the things that I may have said, because if there was an opportunity to put the boots in I did, too. I learned to handle it without wanting to physically fight back, and sort of get around the issue or be smart with my replies ... All it probably did was harden me.

It was from this environment and this experience that Farmer largely developed his thoughts and attitudes on issues of race and how to handle it. At a personal level, the important thing was not to let it get to him, to get in the way of what he was trying to do, be it his work or his football. "Whatever a person is saying about me, I don't have the problem. He is the one saying it, so I've just got to go on living."

Nor did he become embittered towards those who tried it on him, seeing such actions as an inevitable, almost normal facet of society.

> I didn't think any less of the people for doing it ... [I] did not think that I was being singled out for any worse than anyone else ... Australians were noted for putting people down, and it never changes ... [It] is because of the hierarchy scale of going up a ladder. Someone is always putting someone down below them.

He does note, however, that each new wave of arrivals to Australia, the Greeks and Italians, the Slavs, and more lately the Asians, have slotted in not at the bottom of the ladder, but just above the eternal dwellers on the bottom step, the Aboriginal people.

The apprenticeship was just a job to Farmer, a means to an end.

It provided a regularity to his life and security for the five-year duration of the indentures that would keep him in Perth. There was one day a fortnight at Perth Technical College, plus occasional night courses in particular skills, such as welding. His workbook from the five years at tech is stamped each year by the Department of Motor Mechanics and Aircraft Engineering, and inscribed with the word "excellent". Farmer eventually completed the apprenticeship and became a qualified tradesman, but he had no passionate interest in machines or motor cars, and no dreams of opening up his own garage or anything of that sort. The dreaming was reserved for football.

It was around this time that Farmer began to imagine his own career. He confided in no one, not even Kilmurray and the others at The Farm. They would have laughed if he had. Making it into a West Australian League team was merely the first step. It was not until he had made the boyhood dreams come true that he ever felt free to reveal them.

> I always had secret ambitions long before I went to play League football, when I was playing out at Kenwick and Maddington. Those ambitions were I wanted to play with East Perth, I wanted to play in a premiership side, I wanted to play for the state, and I wanted to play in Victoria. And I wanted to play in a premiership side in Victoria, and also for the state … I always thought they were going to come true. It was just a matter of how long it took.

The first step along the path was the move up from B Grade to A Grade in the South Suburban League. Following its two wins in the B Grade, in 1951 Kenwick applied to make this transition as a club in its own right. But the bid was rejected, they were told to remain where they were, as an affiliated feeder club of the A Grade side, Maddington. The powers at Kenwick were dissatisfied with this, and left the South Suburban League to join the lower grades of the Amateur League. However, a number of the players, including the Sister Kate's boys, led by Kilmurray who had already tried out with Maddington the previous year, went along to pre-season training at Maddington in 1951 to see if they could get a game.

In that era there was no strict hierarchy among the local competitions that existed below the main Perth competition, then called the Western Australian National Football League (WANFL). The A-Grade Amateurs were probably the strongest of the second-tier competitions, at a standard somewhere below the League's seconds teams. Then there were a number of the regional leagues, such as the South Suburban; the senior levels of these regional leagues and the Amateurs were the main recruiting grounds in the city for the major League teams.

In the regional leagues the clubs had strong local identities and followings. "If you lived in Maddington, you played for Maddington." A crowd of 2000 at the Sunday game at Maddington Oval was not unusual. The club was also a social focus with its barbecues and fundraisers on top of the games. The football was serious, and willing.

Maddington had acquired a new coach in 1950, Steve Jarvis, who had played League for Perth just before and after the war. He had started with Maddington as a player in 1947, when after getting married and moving to Armadale he had been unable to continue the necessary level of time and commitment to training at Perth. But he was both passionate and knowledgeable about his football. He also had an eye for a good footballer. When he was asked to take over as coach in 1950, he was less than happy with the casual attitude some of the older fellows at Maddington had in regards to their training: "I said bugger it, and took on all these young blokes." In 1950, Maddington crashed from runners-up the year before, to second last in the six-team competition. Jarvis told his critics to give him three years and he would win a premiership.

When the Sister Kate's boys turned up at the beginning of the 1951 season it was like manna from heaven to the coach. Jarvis still has the faded, tattered exercise book he used back then to record statistics and comments. There, after the second game of the 1951 season, dated 13 May, are his first written comments about Farmer the footballer: "Polly Farmer lived up to early promise and should go a long way in the game."

Farmer was one of four boys from The Farm on the Maddington side. The others were Edward Lockyer, Kilmurray and Bruce Ashwin. From the beginning Jarvis believed three of the four had the potential not just to play League, but to be footballers of the top order. Kilmurray and Farmer proved him right, but the third, the one Jarvis believed was the best of the lot, never made it.

Farmer had started the season on the right half-forward flank. He was already over six-feet tall, but only about 10 stone, and Jarvis thought he would be too light to handle the ruckwork against the tall, heavy men of the opposition. But within a few weeks he had forced his way into the only position he wanted, and by July Jarvis was writing: "Polly Farmer gave another excellent exhibition in ruck, coolness being his best feature."

Kilmurray started in the forward pocket but soon graduated to full-forward, and sometimes centre half-forward. He was more of an eye-catcher than Farmer. He was starting to fill out his small frame and ride the knocks and bumps better. He was already a strong, at times sensational, mark for his size, and had the ability to kick freakish goals.

Bruce Ashwin played in the centre. He was older than both Kilmurray and Farmer. He had superb skills, a nuggety build, and was a tough, aggressive player. Even at 17, Jarvis says Ashwin "was the best hip and shoulder bumper I've ever seen in my life. A chap would be running with the ball, and he'd run flat out—he was very fast—flat out alongside him, and hit him as they were running. And the chap would go up. His eyes to the ceiling and spread out."

Word was starting to get around about the budding young stars. Before too long, a regular among the cars parked round the boundary line was the big expensive Packard of George Sweetapple. Sweetapple was a bachelor and man about town, with a flat in the city. He owned a sweet factory, and was prominent in trotting circles. He was also, at that time, the vice-president of the East Perth Football Club. Sweetapple knew he was on to something good. He cultivated the boys; and they were not hard to impress, the Packard alone made a lasting impact on them. He would come with packed lunches of chicken that appeared from the Packard's boot, and bestowed small gifts, largesse and bonhomie. The smell of something bigger was in the air.

The boys' heads were not totally turned, though. Late in the season Sweetapple arranged with Jarvis to treat them to a day at the football as the guests of East Perth. He would meet Jarvis and the lads outside the

Shaftesbury Hotel in the city and then take them to the game. All agreed, but Jarvis was nervous. The Sister Kate's kids had not been satisfied by the Sunday football with Maddington, through the season they had continued to play on Saturdays with Kenwick, now in the lower grades of the Amateurs. Kenwick had been sadly depleted since their move to the Amateurs, and were getting thrashed every week, but the boys played with them anyhow for the love of it. Jarvis frowned upon this practice, but tolerated it because he could not stop them. It was not strictly proper, players were supposed to be registered with one club and one competition only, but more to the point, Jarvis was worried about injuries, because the Amateurs was a rougher, less disciplined competition at the level they were playing.

This particular Saturday, as well as the arrangement with Sweetapple, he had an additional worry. Sunday was second semi-final day, and Maddington was in it; he wanted his young stars fresh and injury free for the big game. He extracted solemn promises that they would miss the Kenwick game, catch the train in, and meet him outside the Shaftesbury. He is still angry when he remembers it. "I get down to the corner there, and this Sweetapple's there in his huge imported car; and we wait and wait and wait. And they didn't turn up." Their loyalty to Kenwick had overcome the lure of a day at East Perth. Sweetapple took Jarvis to the game anyway where "we are supposed to be guests of honour [and] they're saying where are these so-called champions. I felt absolutely disgusted."

Worse was to come on Sunday when he discovered that Farmer had been injured in the Kenwick game, and would not be able to play. Many years later, when Farmer was playing at Geelong and the club came to Perth for an end-of-season trip, they played a game against the South Suburban League at the Gosnells Oval. At the function afterwards Farmer recalled the dressing-down he received from Jarvis that Sunday as his first lesson in football discipline.

The second semi was a draw. Maddington lost the replay, and then were eliminated in the preliminary final. Jarvis had seen the writing on the wall after the loss in the semi-final replay when he wrote: "We have too many youngsters, who play well when the game flows in our favour, but fall away when we have our backs to the wall." But he was satisfied with the progress made during the year, and had high hopes for the 1952 season. Ashwin won the club fairest and best for the 1951 season from Kilmurray, with Farmer back in equal fifth place.

By 1952, Ashwin and another of The Farm boys had also secured apprenticeships. Kilmurray's determination to stay in Perth had been increased by a short spell he did in Geraldton at a photographer's studio, filling in for another former Home boy who had fallen ill. On his return he had moved out of the Home, after managing to secure a job locally. But the job was not a good one, and did not last. Kilmurray was still only 17, and as principal of the Sister Kate's, Ruth Lefroy was still his legal guardian for another four years. She stepped in and announced that she was going to secure a farm job for him.

Kilmurray would not have dreamed of openly defying Miss Lefroy, but it was obvious to all that he was far from happy. He was the most personable and most popular of all The Farm boys around Maddington. He had neither Farmer's reserve, nor Ashwin's brashness. No doubt it was also relevant that the football season was just beginning. Steve Jarvis organised a coalition of locals, mainly from the Maddington and Kenwick Football Clubs, who rallied around young Square. They organised a plan to keep him in Perth. Accommodation was arranged with the brother of one of the Maddington players and a better job was found, as general hand and rouseabout at a factory in town. When Miss Lefroy turned the proposal down, Jarvis approached the local member of parliament—Farmer's former employer, Gerry Wild. Wild got in touch with the *Sunday Times*, and an interview was organised at Sister Kate's headquarters at Queens Park. The story that ensued took the form of a debate between Miss Lefroy and the spokesman for the local coalition, Jack Lynn, who was the father of the Farm boys' captain-coach at Kenwick.

Lynn outlined the arrangements that had been made, and told the *Sunday Times*: "There is no reason for the boy to be sent to the country if he doesn't want to go. It smacks of slavery ... I can get 150 people in the district to sign a petition backing me up ... I won't hesitate to take legal action if the lad is sent away."[1] Miss Lefroy held firm: "All young men should go on the land for a period. That has always been the policy of myself and Sister Kate. We owe so much to the men on the land ... When he is 21 he may do as he pleases. For the time being, as I am his guardian he must do as I say. I have only his welfare at heart. I am arranging a job for him, possibly at Bencubbin."[2] Kilmurray himself "shyly" commented: "My whole family have been brought up at the Home and I feel grateful to Miss Lefroy. Guess what she says must go. But I'd be happier at Maddington with a job in the district or in town. I don't want to go away, I play football out there and know everyone in the district."[3] The *Sunday Times* called on readers to send in letters with their thoughts, saying that both sides had "agreed to take no action until readers' opinions are known."[4]

In the paper the next Sunday opinion was overwhelmingly in favour of letting Square stay in the city. One writer even offered to adopt him. The weight of numbers was partly due to the handiwork of Steve Jarvis, who had spent "a small fortune" on stamps and envelopes, and dragooned all his workmates at the factory where he worked, and anyone else he could badger, into sending letters off. There was no public back down by Miss Lefroy, but the talk of sending Kilmurray to the country quietly faded, and he started in his new job and kept playing football at Maddington.

Farmer had kept his head down through this storm, secure in his apprenticeship, and still living at the Kenwick Farm. Though he was still skinny as a rake, another year's growth and the work at Winterbottom's had toughened him further, and his football was coming along well at Maddington. In the second game of the season the Jarvis notebook reports him "rucking well", and in the third game, "brilliantly". In this same game— as if to reward his coach, for it was the day his story broke in the *Sunday Times*—"Kilmurray was outstanding at full-forward", kicking eight goals. In fact he started the season in sensational form, kicking 35 goals in the first five games. The unfortunate one was Ashwin; he turned his knee on the cricket pitch in the middle of the Armadale ground in the fourth game. The injury proved to be serious. He missed 12 games, and never recovered his full fitness.

Jarvis was trying to do the right thing by his old club, Perth, and thwart Sweetapple's attempts to secure the boys for East Perth. He got the Perth coach, George Bailey, and a selector and committee member, Jack O'Dea, to come out and watch them play. On the day they came, Kilmurray turned on one of his blinders. It must have been his eight-goal game, or perhaps his nine-goal haul the following week, when Farmer does not get a mention in Jarvis' notes, for it was Kilmurray that took their fancy.

They were not alone in this judgement. Many who saw the two in this era comment that Kilmurray was more advanced, more accomplished, or more noticeable. While also enthusiastic about Kilmurray, Jarvis was confident of his own judgement about the relative prospects of the two:

> They saw this other strong robust lad—Kilmurray was a year older, more filled out. Farmer was long and gangly. Kilmurray was getting twice the kicks that Farmer was at that stage. It was just what Farmer did with it when he got it ... He had tremendous reflexes, which is very, very important for a footballer ... He was always thinking, always a thought ahead of you ... There was just something special about him. You know how a horse trainer can go into a yard full of horses and he'll look around and he'll pick one out— he was special, he was like that.

Jarvis continued to sing Farmer's praises to O'Dea, and got him to come out to a couple more games. Perth remained uncertain, but had enough respect for Jarvis' judgement to heed his urging. O'Dea worked in St Georges Terrace near Winterbottom's, and he approached Farmer at work. Farmer agreed to train with the club, so each Tuesday and Thursday O'Dea began to pick him up after work, and take him down to the WACA ground where the Perth club trained and played. He was getting closer and closer to the first step on the ladder of his dreams, training with a League team that included Merv 'Big Mac' McIntosh, a Sandover medallist, and the premier ruckman of the League. But Farmer resisted all the persuasions of O'Dea and others as they attempted to get him to play a game with the Perth reserves. If they had succeeded he would have been bound to the club. O'Dea recalls that: "He gave the impression in a very friendly way that he was just having a bit of a look around to see what made us tick."

There were other forces at work. Sweetapple had prevailed on Kilmurray to play a game for the East Perth reserves. Square was now tied. Once O'Dea heard about it, he realised that he had been outmanoeuvred by East Perth, and held little hope of getting Farmer. Nevertheless, the friendly training arrangement continued, and it was all grist to Farmer's football mill.

Farmer and Kilmurray were both chosen in a South Suburban League representative team. Through the 1952 season they were the dominant players in the Maddington team. Farmer was growing in confidence as well as ability. Jarvis, while anxious to stress that he did not use the word in a derogatory sense, described him as an arrogant footballer: "Shy in his normal way, but as far as his football went, arrogant ... He knew he was good, and he wanted everybody around him to be the same. Farmer taught himself. [He] taught more to coaches than coaches ever taught him."

Jarvis also says that Farmer became difficult to play with because he was always a thought ahead of everyone else in the team. He illustrates this and Farmer's self-confidence with the story of an incident in a game when he took to the field himself as a reserve. Farmer knocked the ball to him from the ruck, but he did not anticipate quickly enough and fumbled, then lost the ball. He found himself being "blown up" by his 17-year-old protégé telling him: "What the hell do you think I'm getting it down to you for?"

Farmer's one disadvantage was still his comparative lack of weight. Kilmurray and others recall that he was often knocked off balance. But they also remember that he hated to waste the ball, even then. If he was getting into trouble the ball would still be shot out to a teammate, if the player was quick enough to anticipate. And handball was the weapon he used. "Backwards, sideways, everywhere," says Jarvis.

Farmer and Kilmurray were coming in for plenty of attention from the opposition by now, both physical and verbal, which more often than not was racial. Farmer survived well though, and did not miss a game through injury that year. "He was that agile, he would ride everything that was coming," says Jarvis, "his reflexes would have made him a champion boxer." Kilmurray tended to cop more on both scores. Jarvis recalls one game where he was almost blinded by a mud clod thrown deliberately in his face as he kicked for goal.

Maddington cruised into the finals. Jarvis brought Ashwin back into the team, even though he was not fully fit. In the Grand Final, when

Cannington put the pressure on, Jarvis was glad to have Ashwin. Their full-back was putting Kilmurray off his game with dubious tactics. Jarvis called Ashwin in, and broke his own rules. He sent Ashwin to full-forward, saying, "If he does that to you, you've got my okay to whack him, and hit him hard." "You don't need to tell me," was Ashwin's response. He ran straight over and shirt-fronted the Cannington full-back, who gave no further trouble for the course of the game. Maddington won by 16 points, and Jarvis kept his promise to the club committee one year ahead of schedule, thanks, more than anything, to the Sister Kate's boys. This year Farmer won the fairest and best, relegating Kilmurray to second place once again. Jarvis realised it was time for them to move on. He knew they were ready for it. He also knew that they were still playing Amateurs on Saturdays, and was growing increasingly concerned that they might suffer serious injuries as the tough ex-Leaguers playing out their days in the Amateurs targeted the rising young stars more and more.

With Kilmurray now tied to East Perth, Jarvis knew that Farmer would not go to Perth on his own—he had resisted the pressure all year to play with them. Jarvis went into East Perth and looked up their coach, Mick Cronin. He told Cronin it was time to come and get the boys. Sweetapple's groundwork had paid off.

Sweetapple offered to pay for an operation on Ashwin's knee, in the hope of getting all three. But happy-go-lucky Bruce did not take the offer up. Not long afterwards he left his apprenticeship, and wandered off to a life of casual work on the farms and timber mills of the southwest. According to Jarvis, Ashwin was last heard of "playing at Forest Grove down near Margaret River. He was going grey then, and had both his knees gone, both bandaged up. And they said he was still playing all right." One wonders what might have been, what a talent was lost. But two of the trio who had made such an impression at Maddington were poised to make their mark in senior football in 1953.

Between the 1952 and 1953 seasons Farmer's prolonged stay at the Sister Kate's Farm came to an end, when he was finally told he had to move out. His first move, for want of any alternative, was to a boarding house in the city. His apprentice's wage of 34 shillings a week did not go close to covering the house's basic charge of £3. After a short but frantic period of casting around for a more sustainable alternative, he was rescued by the old boy's network of Sister Kate's.

Doug Lockyer was the older brother of Farmer's Maddington teammate, Eddie. He had been through Sister Kate's a few years ahead of Farmer, and by this time had married and found work driving a truck in Perth. He had a house on Scarborough Beach Road, on the other side of town from Kenwick, and offered to put Farmer up in a spare bedroom. He was to stay with the Lockyers for the next three years. The greatest advantage from his point of view was the proximity to Perth's northern beaches, which he came to know well.

Like Kilmurray, Farmer was still technically under the guardianship of Ruth Lefroy until the age of 21, but his childhood was now irrevocably gone. At one level he was more than ready to step out on his own. He was two years into the apprenticeship. He had been playing football against men for four years, and mixing in the rough-and-ready milieu of the football clubs at Kenwick and Maddington. But he was fortunate to find a room at the Lockyers, for with the friendships and triumphs that he found at East Perth still in the future, he was very much on his own in the world, with naught but his innate talents and determination to call on.

Farmer emerged from Sister Kate's with a self-protective shell that is not surprising given his institutional upbringing. He was open to the world, indeed eager to learn and to acquire knowledge, but he always held something in reserve. He was ready to accept offers of help and friendship, but did not expect them as a right. His habit was to absorb all he could in terms of experience and understanding of the world around him, and then to work out quietly by himself, and for himself, what it all meant and what lessons there might be for him. In one sense he was a fatalist, accepting of whatever came his way with little inclination to hanker for what might have been. This was balanced, though, by an awareness that he had it in his power to influence, indeed mould his own future.

The window of opportunity was the world of football. He had great faith in his own abilities; the determining factor would be his capacity to get the best out of himself. He might not have put it in these words, and would not have dreamed of saying it out loud if he had, but all the elements were there. He was a complex and thoughtful young man. Most of those he came in contact with sensed something unusual about Farmer, without being able to quite pin down what it was.

3

EAST PERTH—
THE CRONIN YEARS

League football in Perth in 1953 was moving towards the end of an
era dominated by the returned soldiers of the Second World War.
While the Victorians had played on, Perth had been restricted to
an underage competition from 1942 to 1944. The full-scale 1945 season
had started just as the war was winding down. The players of this time
give the impression that it was hard to take combat on the football field too
seriously in the aftermath of the war. There was a joy in being home and
playing footy, and a camaraderie between the players that transcended club
rivalries. The creed seemed to be to play hard on Saturday afternoon for
sure, but don't get too worked up over training, and enjoy the keg laid on at
the clubrooms on Sunday morning.

The League's traditional powerhouse club, East Fremantle, had won
the 1945 and 1946 premierships, but then their humbler co-tenants at
Fremantle Oval, South Fremantle, had emerged as the dominant force
in the competition, winning four of the six flags between 1948 and 1952.
South Fremantle was a great combination, led by the stylish centreman,
Clive Lewington, who became captain and then coach through most of this
golden period. Their stars were the prolific full-forward, Bernie Naylor,

a master of the fast lead and a prodigious and accurate punt kick for goal, and Steve Marsh, a fiery and deadly rover who won the 1952 Sandover Medal for the League's best and fairest player. Souths' great rival was West Perth, which had pipped them for the 1949 and 1951 premierships. The Souths versus Wests games were attracting record crowds to football. The quiet star of the competition was Merv 'Big Mac' McIntosh, a gentle giant who carried the Perth club on his ample shoulders, and invariably led the West Australian ruck in the quest to beat the Victorians. His hero status had been confirmed by his dominant role in the West's two defeats of Victoria in 1948—victories that had to sustain the parochial pride of Perth for another 13 years.

East Perth was among the also-rans. In the eight-team competition, its post-war results were three sixths, four fifths, and a best of fourth in 1952, following a first semi-final defeat by fellow struggler Claremont. At the end of 1952 their star player, Frank Sparrow, left the club to go to Swan Districts as captain-coach. East Perth's coach was Mick Cronin, who had taken on the job in 1951. His arrival had been a steadying influence after a turbulent period had seen five coaches at the helm in three seasons.

Cronin was a favourite son of the club, and a man whose life revolved around football. He had played 164 games between 1930 and 1941. He was the captain of the 1936 premiership team, the club's only success since 1927 when East Perth's glory run of seven premierships in nine years came to an end. In 1937, he had won the inaugural Tassie Medal for the best player at the national carnival. He had also had an earlier stint as the East Perth coach from 1939 until the competition closed down at the end of the 1941 season. Until he started his second coaching stint, Cronin had been a League umpire. He was known as a scrupulously fair player and a quiet man—like McIntosh, he was regarded as one of the game's gentlemen.

Farmer and Kilmurray had seen very little League football before they arrived as players in 1953. Playing every weekend as they did, the only games they occasionally got to were the Fremantle derbies between East and South that were traditionally held on the Monday of a long weekend. Farmer had had his year training with Perth, and Kilmurray his one game with the East Perth seconds, but:

... we were young footballers who needed to be taught the fine arts of the game. We had raw skill and we loved the game and we were anxious to get the ball, but as far as learning to kick and handle the ball correctly, tackle properly and read the game, know where to go and what was expected of you—that was all in front of us ... Our expectations were to probably get a game in the seconds, and then hope that sometime we would play well enough to get into the firsts.

The young pair were eager to impress, and under Cronin's watchful eye they breezed through the early pre-season training sessions, where the potential players are sorted from among the hopefuls, and made it on to the senior squad. Already they were seen as something more than reserve-grade battlers, but of the two, it was Kilmurray who stood out. Cronin had previously confessed to Steve Jarvis that he was rapt in Kilmurray, but could not see much in Farmer, and for a time this was the conventional wisdom at East Perth.

The player East Perth desperately wanted to groom as the understudy to their lead ruckman, Ray Perry, was a 19-year-old who lived on the border of their city recruiting zone. He was a burly, confident lad by the name of Ray Gabelich. But Gabelich was determined to play with West Perth, the team he had always followed. The League authorities ruled that he was bound to East Perth, and the club refused to provide him with a clearance, hoping he would relent and join them. Gabelich held firm, played the season out in the Metropolitan Junior League, and eventually moved to Victoria to join Collingwood.

East Perth started the season with a comfortable win against the cellar dwellers, Subiaco, then were thrashed by West Perth. When the team was announced for the third game—a tough one against East Fremantle at Fremantle—Farmer was named as Perry's offsider in the first ruck. It was a foul day for a debut, with gale-force winds and almost two centimetres of rain falling. There is nothing to suggest that Farmer did anything to distinguish himself in his first League game, but the side did well, bringing off a rare victory at Fremantle after pulling away in the last quarter of a low-scoring game.

In his third game, against South Fremantle, he led the ruck in the absence of an injured Perry. It was another foul day, bad enough this time for the Saturday race meeting to be abandoned. Easts were beaten by 24 goals to 12, with South's goal spree in the conditions showing just what a powerful team it was. But Farmer played well enough to make the best player lists for the first time in his career. The *Football Budget's* commentator picked up on the traits which were to become hallmarks of his game. "Graham Farmer at times dominated the ruck with clever knocking and good handball ... he is showing vast improvement in his play and he'll be a name in the league before the season concludes."[1] He played well again the following week in a one-point win over Claremont, but was unable to hold this form, and was dropped back to the reserves after nine games. His replacement was the other young ruckman at the club, Gus Kikiros. Farmer's own assessment of his ability and performance in that first year is harsh:

> I didn't deserve my games. [I played] very average football. I got picked on the basis that there was a chance, not on any basis of quality ... I was just very lucky to be at East Perth because it was a battling side, and every person that showed some interest in football was given a chance.

This could be dismissed as modesty, except the assessment seems to be shared by those who were coming up through the ranks with him. "He was just another footballer in 1953," is a typical comment from among those who played with him in both the firsts and reserve teams.

After a solid start to the season that had them perched in fourth, Easts went into a severe mid-season slump that saw them lose six straight games and eight out of 10 altogether. With three games to go, they still had a faint hope of sneaking into fourth spot ahead of East Fremantle, if everything went right. But the next game was against the runaway leaders, South Fremantle, which had suffered only one loss in 18 games, and East Perth had been hit by a spate of injuries. Farmer was one of a number of reserves players promoted for the game against the reigning premiers. The impossible happened, with the undermanned Easts winning by seven points. The euphoria was short-lived though, as an eight-goal loss to seventh-placed Claremont the following week sent them tumbling out of contention. Farmer held his place in the team, and finished off the season with a mention in the best player list rucking against big Merv McIntosh in the final game.

South Fremantle went on to win another premiership, beating West Perth narrowly in the second semi-final and easily in the Grand Final, where Steve Marsh picked up the Simpson Medal for his best-on-ground performance. Bernie Naylor had his best-ever year, kicking a record-breaking 156 goals in the home and away round, and a total of 167 for the year. Merv McIntosh also had a phenomenal season, at least in terms of the awards he reaped. He won the Sandover Medal by one vote from Geoff Burton, who, like Farmer, was in his debut year with East Perth, and he picked up a Simpson Medal for the best West Australian, and the Tassie Medal for the best player of the carnival at the national championships held in Adelaide. Another star of the Adelaide carnival who won selection alongside McIntosh in the All-Australian team was a farmer from Jennacubine by the name of Jack Clarke. Clarke was in his second season of driving the 120 kilometres down from his family farm every Saturday morning to play for East Fremantle. The consensus in Perth was that he would soon emerge to take McIntosh's place as the state's premier ruckman.

East Perth was not unhappy with Farmer's progress. He was one of 16 players to make their debuts during the year under Cronin's policy of introducing new blood to the team. Of this group, Burton at centre half-back had been the undoubted star, closely followed by centreman and forward, Tommy Everett. This pair had finished third and fourth in the club fairest and best. Kilmurray had also had a creditable season, playing mostly in the forward pocket or on a half-forward flank. Farmer was seen as the best of the rest—a player who might well have a future, but still with a long way to go. Farmer knew that he did still have a long way to go, but there were no mights and maybes in his mind. He regarded 1953 as "an extreme learning process" that would form a springboard to reach greater heights.

The best thing to come out of the year for Farmer was his absorption into the club itself. It became almost the family he had never had:

It was the centre point of my life. It was probably more important to me than my apprenticeship. It was a place to go, for fellows like me. You made friends with a lot of people ... In footy clubs people go out of their way to help people. There's a tremendous amount of good mateship in a footy club. The whole basis of the game is dependent on that because people can't survive on their own in football. It's a question of each person helping each other without expecting something in return ... if you were in a position to help a teammate or back him up, you did it because that's what was expected of you in a very normal way. That's what a football club was based on—that sort of selflessness.

George Sweetapple was still his particular mentor, but there is no doubt that many at the club went to special lengths to look out for the boys from Sister Kate's. One such was Jack Lalor, a railway worker who had played 50 games back in the 1930s and now served on the selection committee with coach Cronin and captain Jim Spencer. The whole Lalor family was involved with East Perth; brother Jim was the honorary solicitor, Jack's wife was active in organising the club socials and the regular players' teas, and his sons played in the local junior leagues. Soon Jack was bringing Farmer and Kilmurray home for dinner after training on Thursday nights.

At Winterbottom's one of Farmer's tasks as a junior apprentice was that of lunch boy. He would take the orders around to the delicatessen in Milligan Street run by Mick Cronin and talk football while the lunches were being prepared. More often than not Kilmurray would be there, doing the same. After work he would run to a tram stop in Barrack Street, and then from the East Perth terminus to the ground to be among the first there, and get in on the kick-to-kick sessions that preceded the serious training.

Using the analogy of the family, Kilmurray was the favourite son, charming all with his easy-going personality, while Farmer was the precocious one, capable of irritating at times. Frank Allen was a senior player at the club, a wingman with a hundred games under his belt. "Pol wanted to learn," he says. "He would go to any extreme to get information on how to improve." Not all players were willing to share their secrets, figuring that they had had to learn the hard way, and so should the young fellows. But "Polly had a very persuasive way, he wouldn't take no for an answer, he would just keep asking."

Allen and another senior player, 'Bomber' Brown, were in the habit of playing table tennis in the clubrooms. They were 10 years older than the young recruit. "Polly used to come and watch us play. You could see that he was itching to have a game … he said to me later he plucked up courage to ask if he could have a game with us. He started to be included in a group of three." His table tennis improved rapidly. By the following year he had a regular weekly meal with Allen and his wife. He insisted on doing the dishes afterwards, then the two men would go and play for the rest of the night. Allen, who took his table tennis seriously, was soon struggling to break even with Farmer in their games.

The club had begun to fill Farmer's life well beyond the ordinary demands of playing and training. In the little slack time that was left he was comfortable at the Lockyers, or out and about, reading, watching other sports, talking to sportsmen, always looking for knowledge he could utilise in his own quest for improvement.

The one sad note in the year was the sudden and premature death of George Sweetapple in October. Before he died he had given Farmer a watch to mark the completion of his first season. It was the first watch Farmer had owned. If there was one man who would have enjoyed the phenomenal football career that began to really blossom in 1954 it was Sweetapple, who had brought him to the club, and been his greatest advocate.

In the early months of 1954 Farmer underwent a compulsory three-month national service training with the army. He lived at the Swanbourne Barracks by the sea and trained with the Electrical and Mechanical Engineers. He was not particularly impressed by army life. The only thing that he came away from the army with, that he valued, was a truck driver's licence. His main memory of the period is lining up in uniform on the streets of Perth as part of the guard of honour for the young Queen Elizabeth during the triumphal tour of Australia that concluded with her visit to Western Australia in March.

Less than two weeks after watching the Queen go by, Farmer lined up once again against Merv McIntosh in the final practice match of the season. East Perth rolled Perth by a single goal. The report in Monday's paper cited Farmer as: "an outstanding follower for East Perth."[2] Club officials were said to be "jubilant", with Cronin claiming: "for the first time in years there will be keen competition for places in our side."[3]

In fact the club had lost six experienced players, including the versatile Jimmy Washboume, who many regarded as one of the best and most underrated players of the era. But Cronin had his crop of 1953 recruits and another bunch of youngsters coming through, plus a couple of more experienced additions. Cronin believed the club was ready to improve, and perhaps threaten for a place in the finals.

In 1954, East Perth and South Fremantle played the opening game of the season a week before the first full round of fixtures. This was done to enable the two clubs to have a two-week break for mid-season trips when the other six sides had one week off for interstate fixtures. The two sides lined up at Subiaco on Easter Saturday, 17 April. Perth was still basking in the glory of the royal visit, and the papers were dominated by the unfolding sensations of the Petrov defection from the Soviet embassy in Canberra. With these goings-on, the build-up to the football season seemed a little more subdued than usual. The weather might have had some impact too—the Saturday just did not seem like football weather with a maximum temperature of 83 degrees on the Fahrenheit scale (28°C).

Perry was not available for East Perth, and Farmer led the ruck. He did well enough to earn his first best on ground award at senior level from the *Football Budget's* reporter. His dominance in the ruck was not enough to lift his side though. South Fremantle carried on where it had left off in the 1953 Grand Final, kicking 20 goals—nine of them to Naylor—and winning comfortably.

East Perth went on to lose six of its first eight games, and there were clearly problems at the club in spite of Cronin's pre-season optimism. There were problems with injuries and some players were unavailable. Farmer was one of the few performing consistently. According to the *Budget's* reports, in the second game against Claremont he: "was the only East Perth ruckman who looked the part. He took a battering but was still playing on strongly at the finish."[4] Then, against Subiaco, "Farmer and Gus Kikiros were East Perth's two best players, carrying the ruck."[5] The East Fremantle followers "for the first time this season met their match."[6] And in a win over Perth, his "second half display was a match-winning game for his team. Farmer surprised everyone with his long-distance kicking with either foot. He was a worthy opponent for McIntosh whenever he clashed on the ball with the big Perth ruckman."[7]

The team rallied to beat fourth-placed Swan Districts 13 goals to five, but this was followed by another three losses. The team languished in seventh place, with no prospect of reaching the finals, even with a barn-storming finish. The more immediate lure of a place in the touring party might have provided the spur for better performances in the next two games, which produced the first consecutive victories of the season. One of these wins was against Perth, and Farmer was East Perth's best, again producing a big game opposed to McIntosh.

The tour was Farmer's first interstate trip. He remembers it as "an adventure ... a thrill ... a great experience", and in the club's report and the participants recollections, it has the ring of a "boy's own" story. There were 26 players, eight officials and five club members who came along for the fun. The train trip to Melbourne covered four days, and three boisterous nights. The drinkers in the party did not hold back, the card games went on through most of the nights, practical jokes and singing en masse were the order of the day. After a training session to loosen up long confined limbs at the Richmond Football Club, it was on to Albury. There was a game here against the strong Ovens and Murray League, and another three days later in Shepparton against the Goulburn Valley League, interspersed with social functions from 'high teas' to dances and picture shows and sightseeing trips. Then it was back to Melbourne for four days that included watching a VFL game on the Saturday, and official visits for functions of various kinds to five of the 12 VFL clubs.

Farmer's long-time friend, John Watts, regards this tour as a turning point in his career. He remembers Farmer's performance against some tough opposition as dazzling. He was able to test himself against a different standard in the country games, and get something of a feel for the Melbourne competition, which until then could only be the subject of dreams. It all made his hopes for the future seem a little bit closer, and a little more likely.

After returning from the tour, East Perth split the last six games of the season, with three wins and three losses, improving its position on the ladder to fifth, two games behind fourth-placed Perth. Farmer finished the season strongly, making the team's best player list in each of the games, and being nominated best player against Perth and South Fremantle. Perth was the only side that East Perth beat in all three meetings for the season, and on each occasion Farmer turned in a top game, clearly lifting himself to combat McIntosh. The last of these clashes, which Easts won by five points, was probably his best game of the season:

> Graham Farmer was the outstanding player in the game at the Perth Oval. His ruckwork opposed to McIntosh was faultless. He closely contested the ball with 'Big Mac' throughout the game, and his stamina was something to marvel about. Farmer and Gus Kikiros were given the job of curbing McIntosh. Kikiros gave Farmer able support. However, it was Farmer who, at the turning point of the game, found that little extra effort to help give his team the initiative and victory after it had lost the lead in the last 10 minutes of play. A brilliant effort Farmer, and one we'll remember.[8]

The quality of these three personal victories over McIntosh is underlined by the fact that the Perth ruckman that year won his third Sandover Medal by a runaway 22 votes to the runner-up's 14, and was generally regarded as the dominant player of the competition.

The icing on the cake of this very satisfying year for Farmer came when he ran out a comfortable winner in the club's best and fairest award with 108 votes, well clear of another second-year player, Ray Webster, on 86. In the Sandover Medal count he picked up six votes to be the top-polling player for East Perth, but well back in the pack overall.

In his second year he had progressed from the status of a fringe player with potential to become an integral member of the senior team, and a rising star. He had certainly escaped the 'second-year blues' notorious among young sportsmen, but in reality it had been his first full year, and the true test would be to see how he backed it up in the next season. In terms of the career goals he had set himself though, he was no further down the track. Step two after making it as a League player was playing in a finals series, and winning a premiership. He was a spectator again for the 1954 final round.

Although Bernie Naylor was down on form in his last year of League football—he only managed 133 goals—South Fremantle finished off a comparatively indifferent season that saw it finish third on the table with a series of comfortable wins against Perth in the first semi-final, West Perth in the preliminary final and East Fremantle in the Grand Final, to extend its run to three premierships in a row and six out of the last eight. During the year South also capped a run of earlier victories over interstate sides by defeating a South Australian second team, and VFL giants Collingwood and Carlton. They could justifiably claim to be the best football side in the country. This was the sort of success that Farmer craved.

At the end of the 1954 season Mick Cronin stood down as coach, and was elected vice-president of East Perth at the December general meeting. The club was looking for a playing coach, and thought they had found one in Don Scott, a ruckman defender who had played for West Perth until 1949 before going east to play for South Melbourne. However, "with final arrangements being almost completed and only the contract to be signed"[9], he was stolen away by his old club and became captain-coach of West Perth. With the season rapidly approaching, Cronin resigned the vice-presidency and stepped into the breach.

East Perth won its three practice games, including a victory over South Fremantle. The pre-season speculation had it as a good bet to make the four, with some pundits even suggesting them as outsiders to upset red-hot premiership favourites South Fremantle. The major player loss was the hard man of the club, centre half-back Col Pestell, who moved to the country to run a pub at Yarloop. Ray Perry had also retired, and Charlie Walker, a vigorous six-footer who had played nine games in the back pocket in 1954 despite a run of injuries, decided not to come back up from Manjimup for a second year. Young Johnny Watts moved up from the reserves to claim a permanent slot in the defence. There were no other notable newcomers, but the earlier crop of youngsters was maturing in years, strength and playing experience.

Farmer's practice match form was no small factor in the pre-season hype. In the preview of Easts' opening game against South Fremantle the *Budget* hyperbolised: "The tall Farmer has developed into one of the most polished followers seen on a football field in this state for many years."[10] More than anything else this game was notable as the debut for South of a sensational 16-year-old from Manjimup by the name of John Todd. From the East Perth perspective a 17-point loss to South at Fremantle Oval was seen as a creditable performance. The team continued to play reasonably well, but nothing would go right for them. They lost the first five—in three of them they led during the second half, but went down by 10 points or less—and once again were out of the finals race early in the season.

The fifth loss was by just one point in an away game at East Fremantle. By all accounts it was a desperate, high-class game of football. At times different reporters' accounts of a game of football leave the reader sure that they were all attending different matches, but this time all the press reports picked up on one particular feature. The *West Australian*:

> Farmer showed exemplary courage and stamina and was the driving force behind East Perth's gallant but unavailing bid to upset East Fremantle. [His] duel with East Fremantle's rangy ruckman Jack Clarke was the highlight of the game. Neither man spared himself in an effort to swing the game in his side's favour. Farmer had slightly the better of the heavy exchanges and Clarke was an inspiration to—and often a saviour for—East Fremantle with his classic high marking.[11]

The *Football Budget*:

> Farmer played easily his best game for East Perth because he practically played a lone hand against powerful opposition. For a time in the last quarter he was virtually "out on his feet" with exhaustion. [In fact he had "collapsed in the hands of the trainers" according to another report.] However he battled [and] never let up. At all times he was the team player and never the individualist ... Clarke started brilliantly, and was best on the ground for the

first 10 minutes ... but the further the game went, the more Farmer asserted his superiority until Clarke became a defending player.[12]

The *Daily News:*

Farmer, by his sheer grit and determination, finished on to win a narrow verdict from half a dozen other stars at East Fremantle Oval. His duel with Jack Clarke was a highlight.[13]

The two ruckmen had opposed each other in the previous two seasons, but this was the first of their classic encounters that were to become the highlight of West Australian football over the next seven years.

The performance against East Fremantle galvanised the team and it won the next two games comfortably to climb off the bottom of the ladder. In fact at the end of the first round of games, despite its two-win, five-loss record, it had the healthy percentage of 107—a clear indication that it should have been higher than sixth on the table.

The East Perth camp was sending out signals that panic would not take hold. They had had a cruel run with injuries. The other factor that was causing them to fade away in the close encounters, according to the *Budget,* was their youthful make-up—the average age of the team was under 20.

While all the East Perth players of the era are quick to defend Cronin, and to give him credit for building the side that went on to such success after his departure, there is an impression that frustration was starting to set in by this stage. The signs were there that Cronin was nearing the end of his use-by date as the senior coach. He had perhaps reached the same conclusion himself when he tried to stand down at the end of the previous season.

Farmer's first-round performance was solid. Apart from the clash with Clarke, he broke even with McIntosh in the Perth game, and was regularly in the best player lists. He was a hot fancy for selection in the state team to go on tour for matches against Victoria and South Australia, with some of the pundits selecting him ahead of Clarke as their preferred partner to McIntosh in the first ruck. Kilmurray was under notice too, after a great start to the season saw him leading the League's goalkicking list at this stage. Their performances were rewarded when, along with Tommy Everett, they were selected to make their debuts for the state team.

Between their selection and departure, though, East Perth's woes continued, with two more defeats sending it back to the bottom of the ladder. In another sign of things to come, and of Farmer's growing stature, reports of the defeat by South Fremantle have him "battling hard against heavy odds in the ruck", with five South players named as his "chief opponents".[14]

Stage three of the boyhood dream—playing for his state—was achieved before stage two. The side flew in a chartered plane to Melbourne, and encountered the worst that Melbourne's infamous winters could offer. In Farmer's first appearance on the hallowed ground the Melbourne Cricket Ground was an abysmal mud heap. The West could manage only 3.7 (25) for the entire game, but Victoria's 6.18 (54) was not all that much better.

> From my point of view it was tremendous to be picked for your state and play on the MCG. There was a tremendous amount of pride. But in those days, as it is even now, it was an almost impossible proposition to win in Victoria ... I suppose because it was a low-scoring game, we probably would have been quite pleased with our performance, because we didn't get really slaughtered.

The expectation of losing made the reality a little easier to bear:

> Losing is always a terrible feeling and it will never change, but the thrill of playing over there was also a very good experience ... You went over there to beat Victoria if you could, but it had never been done before and it was a dream. But it wasn't a dream where it was fight for your life. It wasn't a dream where if you couldn't win you would die. It wasn't that type. You did your very best and if you didn't win, bad luck—that's all it amounted to.

This was the closest Farmer came in many, many hours of talking to conceding that defeat in any circumstances is acceptable.

Another loss to South Australia in a closely fought game in Adelaide brought an unsuccessful tour to a close. Farmer did little to distinguish himself in the two games. Everett was one of the team's few good players in the Melbourne game. Kilmurray had a disastrous trip, getting pulled from the ground against the Victorians and dropped for the Adelaide game.

The best player for the West Australians in both games was Jack Clarke. By the end of the trip the local paper's travelling reporter was writing that the mantle of the state's greatest ruckman of the post-war era would soon be passing from Merv McIntosh to Clarke.[15]

Farmer bounced back in the first domestic game after the tour. Despite West Perth full-forward Ray Scott kicking 11 goals, Farmer won a £5 prize from the *Sunday Times* as the player of the week for one of his best games of the season. Over the next five weeks he continued to perform solidly, if not quite so spectacularly. East Perth had picked up enough wins to move up to fifth on the ladder, but the gap between the top and bottom four was unbridgeable. Farmer was also moving up the lists in some of the media awards, including the high-profile *Daily News* Footballer of the Year, in which he was lying equal third with young Todd of South Fremantle, two votes behind the Claremont captain-coach, John Hyde. The domestic season was then interrupted again for a return visit by the South Australian side.

Once again, the West Australians did not perform to capacity. Normally they expected to beat the South Australians at home, but the two games were split one each. This time Farmer was the star. In the first game he made all the best player lists and was the only ruckman to perform for the West, with Clarke and McIntosh unsighted. In the second game he won the Victor Penrose Trophy for a best-on-ground performance.

In the run down to the end of the season Farmer held his form from the interstate games. The last game of the year would be his 50th with East Perth. With the line-up for the semi-finals already a foregone conclusion, all the public attention was focussed on the East Perth-Claremont clash— Hyde and Farmer had cleared out from the field in the *Daily News* award, with Hyde holding a one-vote lead. Going head-to-head, if one of them could turn in a big game, he would secure the £100 prize.

Hyde had been the centre half-back in the brilliant Geelong side that won back-to-back VFL premierships in 1951 and 1952. He was in his first year with Claremont, and was unable to lift the team above seventh place, but had dominated at full-back and centre half-forward. He continued this form in the first half of the game against East Perth, as Claremont held Easts against a strong wind in the first quarter, and led at half-time.

Farmer "didn't open up like a German band, but he finished on a high note. He dominated the ruck, and ... lifted his side's general pattern of play."[16]

The Saturday evening report in the *Daily News* gave both players a big wrap. When the Monday issue came out with the votes, Farmer had got three, and Hyde one. Farmer had pipped Hyde by a single vote to win the title of "Footballer of the Year" and £100. He repeated the success in the other major award that carried a similar prize. For a young man still on an apprentice's wage of around £8 a week it was a startling windfall. On this form he was obviously a fancy for the League's official award, the Sandover Medal, but here he had to settle for second on 21 votes, four behind John Todd. Todd was just 17 years old, and the youngest winner of the medal except for the years of the underage competition in the war.

East Perth's fifth position finish was creditable after their shocking start to the season, but they were six games behind fourth-placed West Perth. Cronin had formally announced his retirement three weeks before the end of the season, and an era was over at East Perth.

The final series of 1955 will always be remembered as a triumph for Merv McIntosh in his farewell to League football. Perth had only won the premiership once, back in 1907. For the past eight years it had been a contender, making the finals seven times, and losing two Grand Finals. This year it won the first semi comfortably against West Perth, then confounded the experts by defeating South Fremantle in the preliminary final, to bring the port club's phenomenal run of success to an end. In the Grand Final Perth was only two points down at three-quarter time, but had to come home against a strong wind. East Fremantle went further ahead early in the last quarter, but McIntosh inspired his team in a fight back that has become one of the legends of West Australian football. Perth's two-point win was hugely popular in football circles as a fitting end to McIntosh's career and Perth's long drought and run of near misses.

With McIntosh's retirement, the League's heavyweight title of premier ruckman was open for contenders. Despite the glowing reports of Clarke in the wake of the Eastern States tour, Farmer's strong finish to the season edged him ahead as the popular choice, and he was now being referred to in a range of reports and publications as the state's "number one follower", and "leading ruckman". At East Perth he was now the undisputed club champion, winning the fairest and best award for the second year in a row with 144 votes, way ahead of club captain Jimmy Spencer on 108.

Farmer had not reached the zenith of his powers yet, but he had certainly moved beyond the status of a developing player to become an established star of the competition. In football terms the world was at his feet. It had been a meteoric rise for the lonely young lad who had left Sister Kate's Farm for a city boarding house less than three years earlier.

Farmer was still living with the Lockyers at Scarborough, but his life was so full it can have been little more than a friendly and familiar bed and breakfast. He was getting about on an old motorbike that he had bought with the winnings of a visit to the racetrack. His contemporaries laugh at the memory of him tearing about on the bike wearing an old army greatcoat, which flapped about him. There were the normal work and football commitments, and the regular evenings still with Frank Allen and the Lalors and other club stalwarts. By now though there was a circle of young fellows from East Perth whose friendships extended beyond the world of the club.

There were Polly and Square, Johnny Watts, young Kevin McGill, and his mate from the East Perth juniors, Laurie Kennedy, who was yet to break into the senior team. They attended the big dances on Wednesday and Saturday nights at the Maylands town hall, and the Canterbury Court and Embassy Ballrooms. Maylands on a Saturday night in particular used to be 'the big thing around town', and they would often run into Jack Clarke and other young players from opposing teams, but the rivalries of the day seemed to be forgotten easily enough at the dance.

With his apprenticeship at Winterbottom's due to finish in January, life must have been fairly sweet for Farmer as he looked forward to the summer of 1955-56. With his prize money he shouted some of his friends to celebratory dinners. He cannot remember at this distance what he did with the rest of his money, but "it didn't last long". With McGill and Kennedy he planned a summer holiday down at Bunbury. But before that eventuated, he became embroiled in a controversy that underlined his growing status in the football world.

Farmer got a phone call from the president of the Richmond Football Club, Harry Dyke. Richmond were interested in recruiting him, he was told. Would he like to fly over, all expenses paid, to talk to them? Without telling anyone at East Perth, Farmer got a week off work and flew to Melbourne on the Monday after Perth's triumph in the Grand Final.

Although it had yet to reach the scale of later years, the Victorian clubs were notorious, and hated, even then for poaching the stars of the West Australian League. Through press reports, interstate games, and an informal network of talent spotters, they kept close tabs on the Perth scene. Richmond's man in the West was Col Pestell, the East Perth centre half-back, now at Yarloop. Pestell had played for a state second eighteen against a visiting Richmond team in 1949, playing on the man reputed to be the toughest footballer of all, Jack 'Captain Blood' Dyer. Frank Allen recalls that: "Colin was a pretty tough sort of guy too, and Col never gave [Dyer] a kick. So Jack made him Richmond's representative over here, and told him: 'any good footballers you've got here, send them over to Richmond.'"

Although Farmer has no recollection of the details, circumstantial evidence points strongly to Pestell's hand in what unfolded. Dyke was quoted as saying he had received a phone call in Brisbane two weeks earlier telling him that Farmer was interested in playing in Victoria. Two weeks before he left for Melbourne, Farmer had been on an East Perth end-of-season trip to Collie that had included a visit to Pestell's hostelry in Yarloop. The East Perth officials might have been less effusive in their thanks and praise to Pestell as they presented him with a gift of a framed photo if they had known what was going on.

Farmer stayed at the Vaucluse Hotel in Richmond, run by the club's captain, Des Rowe. They moved quickly, and convinced him to sign up. The form bound him to Richmond for the next two years if he came to play in Victoria. The story was broken by Alf Brown in the Melbourne *Herald*, with a picture of Dyke and Rowe with Farmer wearing a Richmond tie. Farmer is quoted as saying: "If I can make the grade in Melbourne I would be as happy as a cricketer who got into a Test side."[17] The same afternoon it was the front-page headline in the *Daily News* in Perth: 'Ruck Ace Stuns

East Perth By Going East'.[18] It was announced as a fait accompli. Farmer would come back to complete his apprenticeship in January, and then move to Melbourne.

It was not quite as simple as that. He was contracted to East Perth until the middle of 1956, and had signed another agreement with the WANFL demanded from all interstate representatives. The WANFL document bound him not to seek an interstate clearance for two years, and would not expire until June 1957. The *Daily News'* Len Owens—the man who had given Farmer the three votes in the final round that won him the Footballer of the Year prize—spoke to Farmer, who was still in Melbourne, and in another front-page story reported him as saying that the only way he would play for Easts was if they guaranteed him a clearance for the 1957 season, and that he was "prepared to stand out of football for 12 months and take his application on appeal to the national body, [the Australian National Football Council]. I'm looking after myself. I've got the chance to make something of my future and I'm taking it."[19]

There was an added irony to the situation. East Perth had been trying to lure Richmond's Roy Wright, a dual Brownlow medallist who at that stage was regarded as the best ruckman in the country, to come to the club as Farmer's ruck partner. Cronin had actually tried to see Wright on a trip to Melbourne just two weeks before Farmer went over, but Wright had been in Brisbane with Dyke on Richmond's end-of-year trip.

East Perth was furious at Richmond for ignoring the protocol of speaking to a player's club first. There was also a great deal of resentment against Farmer for the way he had gone about the affair, and in some quarters a feeling of having been betrayed. Some liked to think that the club had made Farmer, and that he still owed them something. The precocious child had now well and truly grown-up; he was ready to leave home, and a family fight was brewing.

Len Owens ran a story in the *Daily News* with the weighty tones of an editorial, predicting that Farmer would be at the centre of a showdown between the Victorian and West Australian Leagues over clearances, and suggesting ominously that Farmer would come out the loser:

Farmer faces the prospect of having to play all his football in WA, or of retiring from the game altogether, for the interstate war will probably be fought over his case. He does not expect a clearance from WA, but does expect to win his clearance on appeal to the ANFC after 12 months out of League football ... [but] the ANFC is unlikely to interfere unless Farmer can convince them—in a year's time—that he is on legitimate transfer to Melbourne. Which all means that unless someone changes their minds, Farmer will play with East Perth—or not at all.[20]

4

THE RUCKMAN

Australian Rules football is the most unpredictable and free-flowing of sporting contests. A coach may theorise, exhort, demand and threaten in the quest to get his team playing to a pattern—to have each player knowing what to expect from the others, which way to move, where to deliver the ball. But without the offside rule of other football codes to lend the room to manoeuvre, and with footy's emphasis on direct man-to-man contests, the set-piece play is a rarity, and if the opposition is halfway up to scratch the coach's ideal will remain a dream.

The full-forward and full-back will spend the afternoon stepping on each other's toes and trying to outguess each other, never quite knowing how each play will unfold. The wingmen and flankers may check each other just as closely, or may play wide, striving to get into the game. There are almost as many ways to play centre half-forward and centre half-back as there are players in these positions.

There is one certainty in a game of football. The play will start, and restart, and restart again from a bounce down in the centre of the ground. The ruckmen from each team will strive to give their side the first advantage as the game returns to the starting point. At its best this contest is a ritual that embodies most of the great arts of the game; the ability to leap, manoeuvrability, ball control, pure strength, and the ability to apply that strength against your opponent.

The commentators have always argued over the relative importance of ruckmen to the game. 'Big men win big games' is the preferred cliché of the pro-ruckman brigade in Western Australia, while in Victoria they say 'a good big man will always beat a good small man'. 'It doesn't matter who wins the knock, what matters is who comes away with the ball when it hits the ground,' is the favoured response. The two arguments show the tendency of romance on the side of the ruckmen, and science in favour of the on-the-ground ball-getters; and in the modern era of statistics and scientific analysis the trend is in favour of the latter.

But the clash between the ruckmen is also bound up in the psychology of the game. Like no other position on the field, there is a personal and physical confrontation between the two lead ruckmen who contest the opening bounce. There is the formalised combat of the ruck contest which demands that the two confront each other over and over again in a direct, head-on clash. To quote football writer Garrie Hutchinson:

> Bounce of the ball. The ump's got the footy, he's got his whistle, he raises his right hand ... he bounces it on that special flat spot in the centre of the ground ... and up she goes. Nugget brown in the blue sky. In they come and up they go. Consider the opposing giants, pawing the ground, slightly crouched, staring deep into each other's soul. Does the one feel stop marks on the upper thigh, or a knee in the belly? Can he stand his ground at the boundary throw-ins, or will he wilt when tapped on the shoulder and kneed in the back?[1]

If one of the big men can dominate the other, psychologically or by sheer class of performance, or both, not only is there the obvious advantage in play, but a tone is set. For the ruckmen are seen by themselves, and to a large extent by the other players, as setting the standard for the strength and toughness of the team. If your man succumbs in this duel, there will be a spillover effect on the rest of the side. It may not necessarily spell disaster, but in this game, that is at least as much about attitude as skill, every edge counts.

Psychology aside though, it is also logical that a dominant ruckman will give his side a significant advantage on the field of play, even before any contribution he might make around the ground with his marking and general play. As well as the centre bounce downs to start each quarter and after each goal, the ruckmen go head-to-head at boundary throw-ins and each time play halts on the field and the umpire does not award a free kick. Depending on the scores and the nature of the particular game, this may be anything between 50 and 100 times in a match. And each time the umpire takes the ball the play is evenly poised—barring a scrimmage or a knock-back over the boundary line, one side or the other is going to come away in possession and start to make the play.

Assuming the game is poised in this way only fifty times in a match, a 60-40 split of the breaks gives one team ten more possessions than the other—10 more opportunities to create a score, ten times the opposition must try to counter them and wrest back the initiative. A 70-30 split increases the advantage to 20 extra possessions, with this number increasing with every additional bounce or throw-in. Of course the mere fact that a ruckman gets to the ball before his opponent does not guarantee that his team will take the ball away. He must direct the ball to a teammate, not an opponent. The teammate must have the time and space to pass the ball on in turn before he is swamped. Only then is the break achieved, and the ball being used to advantage.

All this theory assumes that the ruckman is trying to use the ball creatively if he gets to it first. There has always been the hit-and-hope school of ruck-play which relies on the big fist thumping the ball from the centre down towards the half-forward line to gain territorial advantage if nothing else, with everyone taking their chances from there. But Farmer was never a hit-and-hope man, that style was the very antithesis of his attitude to football.

Farmer had an instinctive understanding of the science and psychology of ruck-play, but he was never content to rely on instinct and raw talent. He single-mindedly honed his natural abilities to maximise his effectiveness in the art of the ruck contest, to ensure that it would be his hand that reached the ball first as it floated back down from the apex of the umpire's bounce, or arced back into play from the boundary throw. He developed his powers of endurance and concentration to ensure that this effectiveness would last all day every day. And most importantly—the feature that made his contribution to football unique—he single-handedly developed strategies and techniques to use the ball better than any ruckman had before him.

Beating his opponent to the ball was not enough in its own right. Palming the ball towards his rover was good, but he could do better. He wanted the man that received the ball from him to be in the clear, and on the move in the direction of goal. This is the basic principle of attacking football in the modern era. It is a principle that only began to gain general acceptance in the 1970s. Farmer had worked it out as a 20-year-old, 50-game player back in 1955. He saw his role in a team as the playmaker; his job was to gain control of the ball under contest in the ruck or in a pack, and deliver it to a player moving forward.

It is one of the truisms of football that big men, and ruckmen in particular, tend to mature slowly—25 to 27 is considered the prime age. Gleaning the experience that only years can bring is one reason for this. The other is one of physical maturity; for the ruckman the solid strength of a hardened adult's physique is worth more than youthful exuberance. But here was a fellow just out of his teens being promoted as the state's best and most skilful ruckman. How did he get so far so fast?

As we have seen, Farmer's first year of League football was nothing out of the ordinary. In the good games that brought him under some notice, the comments pick up on important facets of his style of play: "clever knocking and good handball", "with his quick thinking and clever handball escaped from many a difficult situation". He exhibited a natural football intelligence and a desire to use the ball effectively from the outset. But in that first year he lacked the experience to exploit this properly, and was unable to perform consistently.

One of the jokes that did the rounds at the time at East Perth was that 'Pol was the best man on the ground—he was never off it.' The problem was still largely one of size. With no weight on his lanky frame, he was easily knocked off his feet. He was also still very much a learner; he had no hesitation about leaping early and leaping high, but would often land on his back, or sprawled on the turf when nudged out of position by an opponent. Kilmurray remembers: "Even though he was fairly nimble, he was falling over a fair bit ... he lost his balance sort of, but he always got rid of the ball, he never lost it." It is the last half of the statement that is important—the Farmer style was developing. The prime objective was to get control of the ball, not just knock it on. Go to ground if you must, to get the ball, or keep control of it as you come under pressure, and look for a way to feed it out.

The other impediment in the early years was getting the chance to show his prowess. Opportunity in the shape of an opening in a side as other players come and go is a critical factor in a footballer's career. Farmer's class was such that he was bound to win through eventually, but none of his rivals were going to make it any easier for him. Initially he was contending with two other knock ruckmen at East Perth. Ray Perry had been playing since 1945. He had represented the state, and in his day was in the leading echelon of ruckmen in Perth. John 'Gus' Kikiros had made his debut in 1952. He was two years older than Farmer, more strongly built, and an eye-catcher with a good leap.

There were other big men and followers who could fill in, but these three had the class or the potential to make the running, and Perry was top dog. Just as there is a battle on the field to establish supremacy over the opposing ruckman, there is intense rivalry within the club for the status of leading the first ruck. Frank Allen remembers that: "When Polly first came to the club, Ray let him know in no uncertain terms that he was the number one ruckman. You had to get in the queue and wait for him." Farmer and Kikiros vied for the right to play in the forward pocket and change with Perry.

When Farmer was in the team, he had to wait on Perry's whim to get a run on the ball. "Every time he kicked a goal, if he'd been in the ruck for 20 minutes he'd go in for another five minutes because it picked him up." He never knew how long he might get to stay on the ball either, for it was Perry's prerogative to call him back to the pocket. "But that was the way it was. That wasn't a problem for me. I was only trying to make my way so I had no rights."

With Perry unavailable at the beginning of the 1954 season, Farmer's real opportunity came. At that point he and Kikiros were sharing the ruckwork, and vying for the leading role, which was very much up for grabs. But Farmer's early season performances, from his best on ground in the opener against South Fremantle, quickly put him ahead of Kikiros and marked him as the rising threat to Perry. One press report described his improvement in the space of a year as astonishing.

This observation is endorsed, and to some extent explained by his teammate Tommy Everett. The previous year, Everett says he had no sense of Farmer as anything special, but "he blossomed pretty quick", and in 1954: "He just improved day by day, week by week. He used to sleep with a footy. If you were going out to lunch somewhere he'd have a footy with him. He just lived and breathed it, and realised that his life was going to be football, and more or less set about making sure that he was going to be the best—which he did."

There was method, or at the very least an objective, in what some tended to regard as the madness of the ever-present football. Everyone who followed the Farmer career has heard the stories of him constantly handling the ball, practising his handball through partly opened car windows, or any other available target. It is a habit he tried to instil in his players as a coach. The idea behind the habit went beyond the mere practising of skills though. It was a matter of feeling the ball as an extension of himself, as something totally familiar and natural. He had seen and admired the ball skills of the Harlem Globetrotters, and wanted to be able to handle and control the oval footy with the same ease they showed with the more accommodating round basketball.

East Perth stalwart Gus Glendinning still remembers the pointed way in which Farmer explained it to him:

> Now you drink Gus. Some mornings you wake up not feeling very well, yet you sit at the table with your knife and fork, and because you use them so often, you eat quite normally. You use your knife and fork as if they were part of you, even though you are ill from your night out. A football to me must feel like that at any time.

Farmer's absolute dedication remained a hallmark throughout his career, but in those early years when he was raw, still learning, still establishing himself, it seems to have had a special intensity. To Farmer himself it was simple; not only did he want to develop his game, he was in a hurry to do it, to compress the timetable as much as possible. His intensity did set him apart, but evoked admiration, not scorn or jealousy from his young club mates. The kick-to-kick sessions before training were regarded by many as a warm-up, and a chance for a bit of fun and lairising, but not by Farmer. Kevin McGill, who started roving with East Perth as a 16-year-old in 1954, remembers the sessions well:

> Polly was building his game up in those years. He was lean. He could spring. At training, if we had a new football for kick-to-kick, Polly would claim that new ball every time. They'd be kicking for high marking, so there was no way the small fellows would have a chance, all the taller fellows would be trying to mark it. Polly would probably get 85 per cent of that—everybody else struggling around while Polly was taking his speccies.

But, although he delighted in them just like any other footballer, Farmer was not just taking speccies. He was consciously using these congested contests to practise new variations and techniques of the bodywork that was so important to his trade as a ruckman; how to time his leap, how to get the best ride, how to maximise the lift he could get from an opponent's own jump, how to evade a knock, or turn a clash of bodies to his own advantage. He never trained just for training's sake, with the single-mindedness of a fitness fanatic. He was always observing, thinking, looking for something new, a technique or an idea he could adapt and use.

Nor did he confine his quest for useful knowledge to the football club, where his questioning would at times irritate the elder statesmen among the players:

> I asked a lot—about life. I thought people had the right to say no, and a lot of them did, but I think everything is available to everyone if you find the right people to see. But in those days secretness seemed to be paramount, about football, about everything in life. The people who had it didn't want other people to know ...
>
> I didn't think anything was a secret [and] was not embarrassed about asking about everything. I was a very inquisitive person who wanted his

questions answered in a positive way. It seemed easy for people to tell you to pull in your head and mind your own business, but that didn't stop me. Most things are available, and if no one tells you, you can go and find it in the books anyway. I loved reading ... I always worked on the basis that you should listen to everyone, not say "Well he's not a footballer, how would he know."

He spent his spare hours watching other sportsmen in competition and training. He wanted to improve his leap, and from high jumpers and long jumpers he picked up that the keys to improvement were greater speed and power in the first few strides off the mark, and strength in the thigh muscles. So he undertook the exercises and practice that were necessary. This might sound commonplace today. Football clubs employ teams of experts to devise such exercises and drill the players. But in the early 1950s the phrase 'sports science' was yet to be coined.

Walking the streets he would leap at anything that seemed slightly out of reach, striving for that extra inch. He would jump at walls to practise the art of pushing himself off, extracting the maximum lift, then hanging in the air before he landed. There are echoes of that ultimate sporting champion, Don Bradman, and the legend of the lonely boy, endlessly throwing a golf ball against a fence and hitting it on the rebound with a stick, honing his natural eye and his reflexes to razor sharpness.

He watched soccer, and noted the way the players ran and ran to make position, and back into defence to cover, whether they were near the ball or not. From them he learned the value of endurance, and of reading and anticipating the play. He decided he needed to put extra miles in his legs and took up jogging. He loved to do this on the northern beaches and the dunes that backed them near his Scarborough home, because he could go for miles and work harder at it in the heavy sand, and there was always the option of a swim at the end. This was before Percy Cerrutty had become famous for his torture camps for elite athletes in the sand dunes of Portsea, and in an era when many players and some coaches still believed it was time to stop training when you raised a sweat.

He was still far from fully matured in a physical sense. He was much lighter than most of the opposing ruckmen, and could still be outbustled in a direct physical confrontation. But the training he did was putting the muscle on him, and he was fitter than any of his opponents. He knew from his nights at the WACA ground with Perth that for Merv McIntosh a training night consisted of a couple of leisurely laps of the oval. McIntosh relied on his inherent stamina and willpower. Farmer had these qualities as well, but chose not to rely on them solely. He developed the capacity to keep on running, keep on coming back for contest after contest. And the more time that passed, during the course of a particular game, and from week to week and month to month through the seasons, the more of the contests he won.

He took the honours against the benchmark player Merv McIntosh in their three clashes of 1954, and by the end of the season Farmer had clearly established himself in the position of lead ruckman at East Perth. Ray Perry had never got into rhythm after missing the first few games, and finished up being dropped towards the end of the season.

In 1955, with Perry retired and Kikiros falling by the wayside with a knee injury early in the season, the full burden of leading the East Perth ruck fell on Farmer's shoulders, and he thrived on the challenge, going from strength to strength. He was playing consistently well by now, making the East Perth best player lists in the *Budget* in 16 of the 19 games he played. The long series of classic encounters with Jack Clarke of East Fremantle began, and during the course of the season he overtook Jack Clarke as the inheritor of McIntosh's mantle of premier ruckman.

This was the year, too, in which the descriptions of his better games began to reach for superlatives beyond even the usual generous prose of sports writers. There was a growing sense that Farmer might be something more than the latest in the line of champion ruckmen; when his game clicked he might be capable of rising to a new level of excellence.

The mid-season game against West Perth that won him a £5 award drew this praise from the *Sunday Times* reporter:

> His display against the strong West Perth ruck was one of the best ever seen from an individual player. From the first bounce he was opposed by the much taller Foley and the older West Perth rucks, and although he received little assistance from his teammates he seldom missed the knock ... [He] was

brilliant in the air and outmarked all who flew against him. Apart from top scoring for his side, he gave one of the most courageous and determined exhibitions of purposeful football seen in this state for some time.[2]

By this time Farmer had developed the technique that enabled him to dominate and frustrate his opponents. Being able to leap high was one thing, but there were others who could leap just as high, some who had a natural height advantage that could counter his spring, and others again who had the body weight to muscle him away from the ball in mid-air—the leap itself was not enough. It was just as important to eliminate or at least neutralise your opponent's attempt to get to the ball as well.

Farmer was always a master of bodywork. In his earliest days at Maddington he could always ride the bumps and land on his feet. But the science of bodywork requires not only that you maintain your own balance and position, but wherever possible you use leverage and strength to put your opponents off balance and out of position. Time and again in photographs of Farmer this is apparent. He is reaching to one side of his body for the ball, with a hip thrust in the other direction, and his opposite number hopelessly out of the contest. His mastery of the art came through a combination of instinct, theory, and practice, practice, practice. At a bounce Farmer's favoured technique was to position himself close in and opposite the umpire—at right angles to his opponent instead of head on—and to leap early, just a fraction before his opponent. And he jumped into his opponent. When he timed it correctly, as he learned to do, he would land with a knee on the other ruckman's thigh or hip. He would gain lift from the other man's own jump, and simultaneously put him completely out of position, as Farmer himself rose to the ball. "He would leap on to you like one of those jumping spiders and hang up there for the ball," is John Watts' evocative description. Ray Montgomery, an umpire at the time, described it as "the cannon off the cush" technique.

Jack Clarke is as well qualified as anyone to describe what it was like on the receiving end:

He brought a style into the game that no one else had ever done. He developed a style where he jumped early and unbalanced his opponent. Just as you were going to prepare to jump, he'd hit you with his bum ... I played the old-fashioned style, I was more the McIntosh style I suppose. I liked a clear run at the ball, and he'd get between me and the ball and give me the backside ... He used to run more or less side on to you, he wouldn't run straight at you; he used to run at a bit of an angle to you, and then he'd turn his back.

Clarke felt that the style was unfair, because it deliberately impeded his run at the ball, and he would often appeal for free kicks. But as he concedes, Farmer's eyes never left the ball during these exchanges. Interpretation of the rules is one of football's delights, and the rules on interference are among the most difficult to adjudicate. Umpires tend to watch a player's eyes to assess whether his object is the ball or the other player. And they tend to accept bodywork as legitimate where they will penalise the use of arms that push. Generally, the umpires let Farmer's style go.

There was much more to this technique though than merely putting the opponent out of position. It became extremely punishing on the other man to have the jumping spider coming down hard on top of him all day. Farmer's opponents would come off the field with more than their normal share of corked thighs, bruised torsos and raking stop marks. Keith Slater of Swan Districts—no shrinking violet—remembers well his first League game against Farmer in 1955. At half-time, he says, he was in tears, with hardly any skin left intact from his chest to his knees.

The physical punishment was a by-product rather than an objective of the technique though. The style evolved into a fluid movement that enabled Farmer to achieve all of his aims of winning the ball, and feeding it out to a teammate on the move.

One possibility was that he would draw a free kick in his own favour. To quote Clarke again: "He'd hit you with his bum. You'd put your hands up automatically to sort of stop him bumping into you, and he'd get a free kick for it. I remember Lenny Gardiner was the top umpire at the time. I'd say: 'Len, he's interfering with me and you're giving him a kick for it.' But to his credit, he was getting away with it." As both Clarke and Farmer agree, the only real rules on the field are defined by what a particular umpire will let you get away with. Both used whatever tricks they could, and if they did not work on a particular day, they would adapt as necessary.

If, as was more common, there was no free kick, Farmer would be on top, with the choice according to the relative position of himself, the ball and his rovers, of palming with his left hand across his body, or flicking it back to the other side. But as time went by, he increasingly used another variation that devastated the opposition.

The secret of it lay in his half-turn in mid-air, which presented his back to Clarke and the others. He would grab the ball in mid-air, and land facing away from his own goals. Quick as a flash, sometimes even before he had hit the ground, the handpass would be fed out. More often than not, the handpass would go back across his body with the left hand, to Paul Seal dashing down the left wing. The whole technique was revolutionary, but one of the keys to it was this reversal of direction. The opposition would expect a left-handed ruckman to be knocking the ball forward and across his body towards the right flank. Suddenly the ball was in the hands of a man 180 degrees away, racing towards goal. It was as if a cricketer had invented an entirely new stroke, or a completely original bowling variation like Bosanquet and the googly. The opposition took a long time to even comprehend it, let alone develop counter strategies.

Some claim that Farmer only developed the grab and handpass from 1956 on, but he insists it was always part of his armoury, and Kilmurray testifies that it was in use back in the Maddington days. It just became more noticeable, and better executed as he grew in experience and stature.

Of course Paul Seal down the left wing was not the only option. Farmer had an uncanny ability to know where his men were positioned, whether they were in front of him or behind, and to assess whether they were in the clear or not. He would always pick the man with a clear path towards goal, and direct the ball his way, with the knock or handpass. With his constant practice he had developed a dozen different types of handball with either hand: short, flat and fast; long and low; long and looping; on the full; on the bounce. Always it was delivered out in front of the player, not directly to him. Farmer wanted the man to be on the move as he received the ball.

This was yet another new concept at the time. Until then the receiver had been used to making position, waiting to receive, then taking off. Once they adapted, and knew what to expect, they found that by the time they laid hands on the ball, they were three or four steps further away from their man than they used to be.

It did not work every time, nothing in a sporting contest does. But Farmer was turning the split of possessions from half-and-half, to 60-40, and much better on his good days. And he was turning those 10 and 20 extra possessions into quality possessions that put East Perth into a scoring position. And on top of this quality ruck play, he was winning the ball over and over in the air, taking strong and often spectacular marks. He won the hard balls, and won the admiration and respect of his teammates and his opponents for it.

This was the player that Richmond and East Perth were preparing to go to war over.

5

THE GOLDEN YEAR

During the break between the 1955 and 1956 seasons East Perth had reason to be well pleased with its off-field work. Not only did they convince Farmer to stay, but they lured Jack Sheedy across from East Fremantle as playing coach. In the six years to come, East Perth would be the dominant club in the competition, playing in all six Grand Finals, and winning three. During these golden years for the Royals, the story of the club revolves around these two pre-eminent figures, Farmer and Sheedy, often described respectively as the greatest footballer, and the greatest character ever to play football in Western Australia.

One could hardly find a greater contrast in two individuals in terms of character and style, but the combination of their skills and influence quickly gelled to shape one of the great football teams, and produced a style of play that was to have a lasting influence on Australian Rules football.

As always, when tracing the fortunes of individuals and clubs in the sporting world, it could have been so different. There are large elements of luck and fate in the way these things pan out, but in the case of East Perth in the 1950s there were also some good administrators and hard-nosed operators who did much to lay the groundwork, and attract fortune their way.

The man at the head was Fred Book, a tall, thin fellow with hooded eyes and the mournful look of an undertaker. He had held a variety of official capacities at East Perth from 1928 through to 1948, when he resigned as president. In 1940, when the club had been barred from using its traditional home at Perth Oval by the landlord, Perth City Council, East Perth's support ensured Book's election to the council, where he quickly engineered a resolution to the ground dispute. During 1955 he had been instrumental in securing council backing for a complete redevelopment of the oval involving a realignment of the oval to a north-south direction, and the erection of a new grandstand and clubrooms as modern as any club facilities in the country. At the East Perth annual general meeting in December 1955, Book was the only candidate for the club presidency for the 1956 season. The same meeting appointed a new honorary secretary, Eric Sweet, as the key administrator. Sweet had previously been the club treasurer, and had a sound background in the financial and insurance industry.

This election was extraordinary in that three of the candidates for election to the committee circulated a campaign leaflet. While football club elections could prompt fierce competition and lobbying, a manifesto of this type was unheard of. The main plank of the three candidates, Roy Hull, Merv Stirling and Laurie Reynolds, was a commitment to introduce payments to the players at the rate of "not less than £5.10 for each winning game and not less than £3.10 for each losing game."[1]

It was the first time in Western Australia that universal payments to players had been proposed. The pamphlet claimed that: "This monetary reward should stimulate football and create a keenness and enthusiasm that has been lacking for years ... We welcome and appeal to every player and every member, both past and present, to put all your support behind the East Perth Football Club and help lift it to the top of the football world."[2]

The three were all elected, and in implementing their promises, ushered in a new era of professionalism in football. The key man among them was Roy Hull, who ran a delicatessen in the heart of East Fremantle territory, and also owned and leased out a number of other delis around Perth. More than anything else though, he was a professional gambler, and a successful one. He had a shrewd and calculating mind—at the Tattersalls club he showed this as a champion whist player, unbeatable to the extent that for many years no one would challenge him—and a businesslike manner. Hull was the perfect backroom man. He shunned publicity, but craved success and pursued it with vigour, and had the resources and the ability to stitch together the necessary deals.

Hull and his friends, along with Book and Sweet, put together a five-year plan to establish East Perth as a football power. This involved a financial overhaul and administrative reform as well as building up the player strength. The planning had begun well before the December elections, with the approval for the Perth Oval redevelopment as the first major step.

When Mick Cronin announced his retirement as coach as the end of the 1955 season approached, the club was determined to find a playing coach to replace him. At the end of year ball, with Collingwood as their guests, and Farmer's apparent defection to Richmond the talk of the night, they made their first move.

The target was Bob Rose, "probably the greatest rover of his era, and as tough as he was skilful ... one of the greatest players never to win a Brownlow Medal."[3] Press reports claimed that East Perth had offered Rose £1000 to come over as playing coach for the 1956 season, and guaranteed to set him up in a delicatessen business on arrival—with a bit of help from Roy Hull no doubt. But the deal fell through. Injuries had taken their toll on Rose, and he retired at the end of 1955 and went coaching in rural Victoria.

Hull then turned his attention to Sheedy. By the end of 1955 Sheedy had played 210 games for East Fremantle since starting with them as a 16-year-old in 1942 in the underage wartime competition. While in the services he played eight games with South Melbourne in 1944, but he had never been tempted to stay in Melbourne. He was an inspirational rover, known as a master of the use of handball.

He had natural leadership qualities, and in his time with East Fremantle had been captain-coach in the 1949 and 1952 seasons, for fourth- and fifth-place finishes, and captain in 1950. But he was also a fiery, turbulent, at times unpredictable character. He is said to have 'played up' during his stint in charge in 1952, and the fifth place that year was only the second time in the club's history East Fremantle had missed a place in the four. He was demoted back to the ranks, until he regained the captaincy in 1955.

What Sheedy had above all other qualities was presence on the field. He was the type of player who could be quiet for most of a game, but when the moment required would produce a burst of play that had the touch of genius needed to turn the tide and lift his team. If it was not his use of the football, it would be his physical efforts. Despite his rover's stature, he was the most feared player in the League. His left jab is reputed to have been the best punch in the west, in or out of the boxing ring; delivered with no wind up, and a six-inch swing, it was lethal. And he was not averse to using it, if riled, or if he felt a bit of judicious violence was needed to change the course of a game. A number of his teammates and opponents have commented that Sheedy was worth five goals to his side, just by being on the ground.

Nineteen fifty-five had been a good year for Sheedy at East Fremantle, with his return to the captaincy, and a third best and fairest award for his trophy cabinet. Towards the end of the season, in particular, he had shown his prowess and his leadership qualities. In the final home and away game against Perth, with second place and a second semi-final berth at stake, the game was tied in the last minute when "his faultless acting and a great football display ... won the game ... Jack dived for a mark. He missed but managed to grubber the ball forward. Then he staggered forward, arms wide apart, every ounce, every muscle screaming 'Push In The Back'. Laurence Olivier or Marlon Brando couldn't have done it better." There was a free kick down the field, and an East Fremantle point won the game by the narrowest possible margin. "Perth supporters crowded close to jeer umpire Green. They shouted abuse at Sheedy. But Jack was laughing as he forced his way through jubilant East Fremantle supporters to the dressing room."[4]

Four weeks later in the Grand Final Perth had the last laugh, but not before Sheedy had flattened three Perth players in the first quarter, and kicked two brilliant goals early in the last quarter that appeared to have stolen the game for Old Easts until Big Merv McIntosh began his heroics.

Once East Perth had decided Sheedy was their man, they would not be denied. The way Sheedy tells the story: "They approached me to coach.

Roy Hull was the main bloke behind it all. I knocked them back about three times, but they kept upping the ante. I think my fee for '56 was £400, and another £50 if we got in the four, and £50 if we won the Grand Final." This was on top of the promised match payments to all players.

It was half the amount reportedly offered to Bob Rose, but he could command Victorian rates. Hull would have known that Sheedy was ready, and keen to have another crack at coaching. He was not one to waste money unnecessarily, and would have had a good idea of what he was bargaining against. As Sheedy says:

> At East Fremantle in 1955, as captain of the side, if we'd have won the Grand Final, one feller was going to paint my car, and another bloke gave me £25. That was two individual blokes; nothing else ... East Fremantle were renowned for not paying a great deal of money for coaches or anything like that. I didn't see that there was a future there. For the life of me, I didn't want to go to East Perth, but these guys on the committee came down ... It was money.

With the new administration and committee, the promise of being the first players in West Australian history to receive regular payments, the sight of the new stand and clubrooms growing before their eyes, and with Sheedy as the new coach, there is no doubt that there was an air of excitement about East Perth. It was also the club's golden jubilee year—the 50th anniversary of its entry into the League in 1906—and appropriate celebrations were being planned. Everyone felt that things were about to start happening, and there was an expectation that this would translate to on-field results. The five-year plan never envisaged a premiership in year one, but a finals berth was certainly on the cards for 1956.

All this momentum was building when young Farmer returned from his stay with Des Rowe in Richmond late in 1955, and must have been much on his mind as he wrestled with the biggest decision of his 20 years. At the time he had no special confidante or adviser in whom he could trust, and all his friends and acquaintances were firmly in the East Perth camp. As he had made clear in his comments reported from Richmond, the lure of the VFL was strong. Nothing could bring greater personal satisfaction than proving himself at the highest level.

But there was one ambition yet to be fulfilled in Perth. A premiership in the WANFL had been part of the dream since boyhood, and there was a sniff of better things to come at East Perth. On the other side of the coin, Richmond was a struggler in the VFL, then at the midpoint of a long slump that saw no finals appearances between 1947 and 1967. Team success was just as much a part of the dream for the Victorian phase of his career as individual achievement, and a VFL premiership would be the absolute pinnacle.

Looming greater than all of these considerations though was the unavoidable fact that if he took the plunge and left Perth, he would have to stand out of football for at least a year. The WANFL president, Pat Rodriguez, was an implacable opponent of the Victorians and their constant raids on the west; there was no likelihood of backdoor deals or private understandings that might see a clearance granted. In the end Farmer just could not bear the thought of being out of the game around which his whole life revolved.

Contrary to the popular myth that has grown up, there was no special deal offered to Farmer to make it worth his while to stay with the club. He agreed to stay on at East Perth for 1956 on the same basis as the rest of the team. Beyond the 1956 season there were no commitments. It was a decision that no one except Richmond would regret.

With his immediate football future decided, Farmer had other matters to attend to. Like East Perth, he was going through changes and branching out in new directions. With his apprenticeship completed, he found his first, and as it turned out his only, job as a qualified tradesman. It was at the government-run Plant Engineering Works in Jewell Street, East Perth. "It was neither good nor bad—there was no pressure on you—it was just a job."

He also moved out of his home of three years with the Lockyers. He stayed in Scarborough though, moving into a flat with Jack Hunt, a new recruit to East Perth, but an old friend of Farmer's. Jack was a Sister Kate's boy who had followed the path approved by Miss Lefroy, and gone to work on a farm out Mukinbudin way. A year or two older than Farmer and Kilmurray, he was a strong, hard ruckman-defender. East Perth had signed him up after seeing him win the best and fairest award at the 1955 country week football carnival at Northam.

Soon they were joined in the flat by Kilmurray, and then by Brian Williams, another old boy from Sister Kate's. Williams was just out of the army, doing a wool-classing course, and had no income, so was appointed cook in lieu of paying rent.

Farmer was by now well and truly an independent young man. He had turned 21 in March, just eight days before the first full training session with Sheedy. Not only did it mean the attainment of his majority, it formally marked the end of Ruth Lefroy's position as his guardian— though effectively she had ceased to fill the role when he left Sister Kate's. The development years were behind him. There was no longer a need for mentors or backstops. He knew his value to East Perth, and he knew that the Victorian option was wide open should he wish to take it up. He was ready to make his mark.

It was soon clear that Sheedy meant business. He was nearly 30 now, with the years and experience to command respect, and he thrived on the challenge posed by the new environment and the task of making Cronin's young team into a real football force.

Farmer and others talk of Sheedy as the 'icing on the cake' for the team Cronin had created. Certainly the bulk of the 1956 team had come up through the ranks under Cronin, but there was also a substantial infusion of fresh blood. Farmer and Sheedy were not the only wins for East Perth in the player trading that year.

Jim Washbourne was lured back to the club after a two-year break, and Charlie Walker returned from Manjimup after missing the 1955 season. Reg Hall, a rover who had played three seasons with Richmond in the VFL, returned home and signed up with East Perth. Gus Kikiros had thrown off his injury problems; with Jack Hunt new to the club, and young Laurie Kennedy poised to make the move into senior ranks, the team's big man strength was significantly improved.

A Perth teacher who had gone to work in the Northern Territory put the club on to a young Aboriginal fellow playing with the St Mary's club in Darwin. Billy Roe was convinced to come down and give it a go in the big League, and became the first in a very distinguished line of Territory footballers to play in Western Australia.

With Sheedy himself, these returnees and recruits, and Cronin's youngsters another year older and stronger, it was a strong list. Sheedy worked them hard: "We played a number of scratch matches at Inglewood Oval. I had to get to know all the players and see what they were like—put them together and sort them out. Then you could see the likes of Farmer and Kilmurray and Watts and these blokes. They were good footballers." Veteran winger Frank Allen recalls that: "We trained a lot harder. In earlier days, if you got a sweat up it was time to come off the ground. Whereas when Sheedy came, he seemed to have eyes in the back of his head. He watched every player. If he felt you were having a bit of a bludge he got on to you. He was a hard taskmaster." Allen had been planning to retire at the end of 1955, but stayed on, and played well enough in the early part of year to make the state team for the carnival. He attributes his improved performance and renewed enthusiasm to Sheedy's training.

When the interclub practice matches began the side repeated its 1955 effort of three straight wins, including, once again, a victory over the previous year's premiers. But this year, the club was confident there would not also be a repeat of the five straight losses once the season proper started.

Nineteen fifty-six was carnival year in Perth. There was to be a full round of seven club games, then a two-week break in June, when Western Australia would come up against Tasmania, South Australia and teams from both the VFL and the much weaker Victorian Football Association. A place in the carnival team was a powerful incentive for the leading players to start the season off on the right foot.

East Perth began the home and away games still without a home ground, as the builders raced to meet the schedule for a planned opening in the third round game against Perth. In the opening game against Subiaco, Easts were jumped in the first quarter and trailed seven goals to one, but "with many hard bumps exchanged" and a "vigorous" last quarter, "Jack Sheedy held the team together sufficiently to run out winners by 13 points" [5]

One aspect of the Sheedy influence was apparent already. He instilled a toughness in the team, and a level of fear in the opposition, that had not really been present in the Cronin era. John Watts, who is always inclined to express things in the most colourful way possible, put it this way:

> Sheedy gave us the strength out on the ground—because he'd dong people. We weren't used to people in our team doing that, we were always getting donged. When you're a kid you're very impressionable, you're a bit worried. It does go through your mind. You're not a squib—you'll have a go—but these bastards are built like brick shithouses. And they're just going to dong you, they're not going to let you play football. When Sheedy came into the side he gave us that strength. He'd start donging blokes … We all started to get a bit bigger. We [realised that] you hit somebody and they do lay down. You become a bit of a bully. You go to play sides and you use that to advantage.

Sheedy was reported in his first game with East Perth by field umpire Ray Montgomery for disputing decisions and using abusive and insulting language. At the tribunal hearing Sheedy created a sensation by producing a bible, and swearing on it that he did not use abusive language on a football field. The tribunal rejected his evidence, and he was suspended for four weeks. In retrospect it seems rather foolish of Sheedy to have taken such an action, for no one believed that he was any kind of an angel on the field, but perhaps he was desperate not to miss any football so early in his career with East Perth.

The incident entered football folklore, with Sheedy acquiring the new nicknames of 'Bible Jack' and 'Reverend Jack' that were to stay with him. It also marked the beginning of a feud between Sheedy and Montgomery that would not see its final episode until 1963.

Kilmurray was also reported in that first game, and got a one-week suspension. Kilmurray, it should be stressed, was not one of the hard men of the side, he was always a ball player, but he had finally reacted to a particularly bad dose of racial abuse. "You can only take so much, then you've got to tell them to either be quiet, or do something about it." The first flare-up of the day between Sheedy and Montgomery had been sparked by the incident between Kilmurray and his opponent.

The Royals backed up with another win over Swan Districts, to lead the ladder after two rounds. Fortunately, as it turned out, Perth Oval was not ready as planned, and the Perth game was switched to the WACA ground. It was no day for ceremonies or celebrations, with atrocious weather. At "Lake WACA", as the papers reported it, the game was played with most of the ground literally under water. Kevin McGill scored East Perth's only goal of the game five minutes from the end. Kikiros aggravated his leg injury, and never played again.

Hunt and Kennedy both made their debuts the following week. After six games East Perth were sitting second on the ladder with a four-two record. By this time another three East Perth players had been reported. Two cases were dismissed, and the other resulted in a reprimand, so there were no player losses involved. But the Royals were establishing their name as a hard and aggressive team.

June the ninth was a big day for East Perth. In the seventh match of the season it played its first home game, and the very first on the new oval. It was a gala occasion, with the official golden jubilee celebrations combined with the opening ceremonies. The city council had put £108,000 into the development, so Lord Mayor Howard was given the honour of tossing the specially engraved gold sovereign to start the match.

They were playing South Fremantle, which at that stage was sitting on top of the ladder undefeated. It was a hard-fought game right through. Kilmurray had put East Perth five points up at half-time with a long goal kicked after the siren following a mark on the bell. He was then treated at the half-time break for what turned out to be a double fracture of the jaw.

Farmer was quiet, struggling against South's usual double-teaming tactics. At three-quarter time Easts were three goals down. In the last passage of play "Kilmurray battled through to the ball on the half-forward flank. He wouldn't kick. He seemed determined to run. There were two or three rugged South defenders but he broke clear. His long punt spiralled slowly, it seemed to drift but it was there."[6]

The goal put East Perth a point ahead, and then the final siren blew. Kilmurray's heroics won him a place in club history. It was one of those victories that meant much more than just another four points, and not just because it came on a day full of both history and portent for the club. The way it was achieved, and the fact that it came against the competition leaders, made it "the turning point", according to Farmer. "Winning that game made the players realise that we were a force. [The team started to think] it might be a force, a contender."

The game was a fateful one for young John Todd. It was on this day that he snapped the cruciate ligament in his left knee. He was never able to play again at the same magical level that had made him such a sensation in his debut year. Many believe that he would have challenged, perhaps even surpassed, Farmer as Western Australia's greatest footballer if not for this tragedy.

It was also the last domestic game that Farmer would play with the status of an average star player. Within two weeks he would be elevated once and for all to the level of superstar. Up to this point in the season Farmer's form had been perfectly respectable, but he had not yet put in one of those totally dominating performances of which he was capable. In the media and public discussion of East Perth's improved performance, the attention focussed naturally on the new captain-coach, the inimitable Jack Sheedy. But now the local competition took a back seat, as all thoughts turned to the carnival.

The carnival, or Australian National Football Championship to give the proper title, was played as a round robin. All games were at Subiaco Oval, with two games on each of the five playing days. It was a punishing schedule for the players, with games on the first Thursday and Saturday, and Tuesday, Thursday and Saturday of the second week, each team getting one day off. Western Australia probably got the best of the draw, with its break coming on the middle Tuesday.

Their squad was considered a good one. Reigning premiers Perth supplied the coach and captain in Ern Henfry and Keith Harper. Farmer led a strong ruck division that included Jack Clarke and Keith Slater. Kilmurray and Everett were the other East Perth players in the original squad. Kilmurray's selection caused some murmurs after his poor showing in Victoria the previous year, but he and Todd were forced to withdraw after the South Fremantle game. Sheedy and Frank Allen made it in as last minute replacements.

The VFL side were of course the favourites, but with the advantage of playing at home, the Sandgropers were considered to have a real chance of being the first team to wrest the championship from the Victorians since 1921.

Western Australia won its first game against Tasmania comfortably, easing up in the last quarter for a 14.19 (103) to 11.14 (80) scoreline. The commentators gave South Fremantle's Cliff Hillier the votes for best on ground ahead of Farmer, who was clearly the outstanding ruckman in the game. Two days later, against South Australia, the West came from behind in the last quarter to get up by 11 points in a thriller, 11.9 (75) to 9.11 (65). Farmer put in his best game of the year to date. "Rucking strongly, marking brilliantly and finishing with a mighty burst he polled in front of teammate Jack Clarke and SA's mighty defender John Abley [to win] the Simpson Medal for the best player of the game."[7]

Clarke had been injured in the South Australian game and took no further part in the carnival, increasing the workload and responsibility on Farmer. As expected, the next Thursday's game against the VFA was an easy one, with the West recording an 83-point win. Farmer made the West Australian best player list again, but the commentators noted that he took things relatively easily, especially in the second half.

Clearly he was saving himself for the final game against the VFL. The Victorians had also won their first three games, and the scene was set for the finale on Saturday. The winners would take out the championship. The Victorians had been in awesome form, with a total of 405 points to their combined opposition's 173 in the three games.

As a decider, the game was a decided let-down, with the Victorians cruising to victory, 20.17 (137) to 9.19 (73) to take out the championship. Individually though, Farmer put in another great performance. The *Sunday Times* wrote that: "opposed to the best ruckmen in the game ... 'Polly' Farmer toppled the best of them each time he went into the ruck. Not very well supported by his rovers, he had to consistently battle his way through with the ball and his lone ruck effort stamped him as the greatest of the WA players."[8] The Victorian umpire, Harry Beitzel, watching the game, reported afterwards in the same paper: "His value to Western Australia yesterday was incalculable. If he had rovers or teammates as good as himself there could have been a different ending to the championship." [9]

The Victorian players were mightily impressed by his performance. Peter Pianto was carrying the roving for Victoria, with his co-rovers, Hutchison and Spencer, both injured. "He was far too good for our ruckmen. I can remember at one stage I started to rove to him. I thought there was only one way to get a kick—get a few off Polly. And it worked out all right, I played to him."

After the game Len Owens of the *Daily News* spoke to Roy Wright, from Richmond, a dual Brownlow medallist, regarded as the best ruckman in the country, at least up to that point:

> [Wright] said: "That bastard Farmer's a good footballer." I said: "You seemed to handle him all right today." He said: "I wouldn't want to play him next week. We did everything we could, and every time we did it he came back in a different way. We had no more tricks left. That bugger would have beaten us next week."

That evening it was no surprise when Farmer was one of five West Australians named in the All-Australian team. Then the voting for the Tassie Medal, awarded to the best player of the carnival, was announced. Farmer was a clear winner with six votes, two ahead of Peter Pianto and Ron Barassi. Over a two-week period that saw the absolute cream of Australian Rules footballers pitted against each other, he had clearly been the outstanding player.

With the carnival over the Victorian squad was heading home. Pianto was surprised when Farmer turned up at the airport to farewell them.

> He was the only player from the West Australian contingent that came out to the airport that night. I was talking to him there, and I got the impression then that Polly was wishing he was coming back to Victoria to play ... Only 21 he was, only a kid, [but] I was really thrilled to meet him. When I got in the plane I thought that was nice, I felt it was an honour.

Pianto's impression was spot on. Farmer recalls:

I liked the Victorians. I liked them and wanted to know about them ...
I was friendly with them, none of them put me down or anything like that ...
[I was] really just going to see them off, and wished I was going with them.

Perhaps it was strange that he should be wistful, even a tinge disappointed in the aftermath of such a great personal triumph, but the carnival had given him the opportunity to measure himself against the best, and he now knew as never before that he belonged with the best.

In the second round of WANFL games Farmer did little to distinguish himself:

After a big performance you can, through no fault of your own, not put the same amount of commitment into succeeding [at a] slightly lower level. I was like a lot of people who just didn't handle coming back from playing state football to club football, and performed poorly.

The competition was evenly balanced, with the *Football Budget* suggesting that six of the eight teams were capable of taking out the premiership that year. In round 12 East Perth had a comfortable win over East Fremantle that saw them displace that team at the top of the ladder, a position they did not relinquish from then on.

Against Subiaco, with the finals looming, Farmer received a heavy knock that caused him to "nearly collapse" in the rooms after the game.[10] For a time he was in doubt for the next Saturday, but it seemed that the knock served to bring him back to earth. With four home and away games left, it was as if Farmer suddenly switched back on. He came back with a vengeance, heading the East Perth best players list in each game.

The home and away round finished with East Perth a game clear of South Fremantle, two ahead of East Fremantle, and three games up on Perth. There was a two-week break until they met South in the second semi-final. They had beaten South in their two meetings, following up the thrilling one-pointer before the carnival with a rare 22-point win at Fremantle Oval. Despite this, South entered the final round as premiership favourites; they had finished the season well, and had a wealth of star players and a record of finals success, whereas East Perth's relative youth and inexperience was seen as a potential problem. South also had a better record than most clubs in curbing Farmer.

The East Perth brains trust may have been more concerned about the prospect of meeting Perth, for the Demons had proved their bogey team so far that year, winning at all three meetings by more than 50 points. But Perth bowed out for the year when they were comfortably beaten by East Fremantle in the first semi-final.

As usual, the first semi was preceded by the Sandover Medal count to determine the League's best and fairest player. Farmer had failed to repeat his 1955 successes in the lucrative media awards, finishing high on all the lists, but on top of none. He was given a chance in Sandover, but there was no clear favourite.

Back in the 1950s the marketing men had not come up with the idea of black-tie dinners with all the leading fancies present; Farmer was having a quiet night and missed the drama of the count. It was the closest tussle anyone could remember, with a dozen players in with a real chance as the end approached. Tom Everett, Charlie Walker and Kevin McGill from East Perth were all polling well. With the last envelope to be opened, Farmer was on 12, two behind Everett and Reg Zeuner of Perth, and with Cliff Hillier and Frank Walker one ahead of him.

> A hush settled over the delegates as Mr Rodriguez said: "This will decide
> the winner." There was general approval as Farmer's name was called
> first, taking his total from 12 to 15. "It is a fitting result," Mr Rodriguez said.
> "Farmer is a great footballer."[11]

Farmer got the news when he called into the deli run by his former teammate Vic Aitkenhead. He is scornful of the official best and fairest awards like the Sandover and the Brownlow, claiming that umpires are in no position to judge the best players, and says now that he had not expected to win that year:

> I didn't think I'd played well enough … I wasn't sitting listening to the count
> because really from my point of view I don't think I deserved to win it …
> I wasn't consistent enough, and didn't think I'd played enough good games
> to warrant winning.

Nevertheless, it capped an amazing year in terms of official recognition of his prowess. For a West Australian player the three most prestigious awards available are the Sandover, the Simpson and, at carnival time, the Tassie. Farmer had scooped them all in one year at the tender age of twenty-one. Merv McIntosh had achieved the same feat three years earlier, and at the time it was thought his performance would never be equalled. Certainly no one has done it again since.

The second semi-final was the first finals game for the entire East Perth team except for Sheedy and a couple of veterans of the 1952 side that lost in the first semi-final. There was an unusual touch before the game from John Todd, who was a surprise starter for South Fremantle in his first game since June:

> While the players of both teams moved around the field to loosen up, young Todd waited for Polly Farmer to move abreast of him. He then shook hands with Polly ... the congratulations of one Sandover medallist to another. Todd's gesture ... will long be remembered by all those who witnessed it."[12]

Sheedy won the toss and elected to kick against a stiff breeze. This enabled South to get ahead, and in a tight, low-scoring game, they kept a lead that varied from a couple of points to three goals until midway through the last quarter, when East Perth put their nose in front, and then sealed a seven-point win with a brilliant goal snapped by Billy Roe. They were in the Grand Final, thanks in large part to countering South Fremantle's usual anti-Farmer tactics: "East Perth won due to a winning ruck, with Hunt, Kennedy and Powell using their weight as a buffer to protect Farmer when he was flying for hit outs."[13]

South Fremantle had a clear win over their port rival in the preliminary final, and the two sides backed up for their fourth clash of the year on Grand Final day. Todd missed the game after hurting his knee again in the first quarter of the preliminary final. Kilmurray and Everett were in doubt up to the eve of the game from leg injuries suffered in the previous game, but East Perth went into the game with rover Reg Hall the only forced omission.

Sheedy lost the toss this time, but for the same result, East Perth had to go against the wind. They trailed by nine points at quarter-time, but from then on, the game was never in doubt. "Our centreline ... held complete control, Paul Seal doing everything right. Our ruck, led by Graham Farmer, was on top, and it was due to these two attributes that we were able to win so comfortably."[14] In the last quarter South cut the deficit from 33 points back to a final margin of only 13, but they never looked like bridging the gap.

The celebrations back at Perth Oval on Saturday night and Sunday were almost riotous. Sheedy was glowing—split ear, bruised nose and all—hailed by Fred Book as the conquering hero. At least two big bets of £2000 and £1500 had been landed by club supporters on the books run on the quiet by a couple of the town's leading bookmakers, and more than £1000 found its way into a bonus pool for the players.

It was the swansong for South Fremantle's golden era, and the beginning of East Perth's. The side had performed beyond all expectations, bringing home the ultimate prize in year one of the five-year plan. There was an almost unreal quality to the way it had all fallen into place: the anniversary; the new premises; three club veterans and favourites, Frank Allen, Jim Washbourne, and Ray Perry, who had been played for one game especially, all bringing up their 150 games to qualify for life membership of the WANFL; all capped by a premiership no one had really contemplated as recently as May.

And woven through all this were the incredible achievements of Farmer. With the premiership win he capped a phenomenal year, going one better than McIntosh in 1953. When he won the club best and fairest award as expected, well clear of Everett and Walker, he had pulled off everything that was possible in terms of individual and team achievement in one season, except the impossible dream of beating the Victorians in the carnival. And he had now, at the close of his fourth season, realised and exceeded the first part of the secret ambitions of his schooldays, when "I wanted to play for East Perth, I wanted to play in a premiership side, I wanted to play for the state." The next steps on the ladder, even in those days of dreaming, were "... and I wanted to play in Victoria, and I wanted to play in a premiership side in Victoria."

In the aftermath of the Grand Final East Perth went down by 11 points in a low-scoring game against the VFL premiers, Melbourne. They pushed Melbourne, making the Demons work harder than they had perhaps anticipated they would have to. Their coach, Norm Smith, heaped praise on the Royals afterwards, saying they would rank highly in the VFL competition. Once again Farmer put in an outstanding performance, a clear and unanimous choice for best on ground, capped by a couple of truly spectacular marks high over the top of packs.

At some point during Melbourne's time in Perth, Norm Smith met with Farmer to sound him out about joining Melbourne. He made a comment though that suggested his diplomatic skills did not match his renowned coaching abilities. He told Farmer that if he played for Melbourne, Barassi was a certainty to win a Brownlow Medal. By now Farmer had enough self-confidence to be uninterested in playing second fiddle to anyone. "My thoughts were that if I went to Melbourne, maybe I could win a Brownlow Medal."

On the Monday after the game against Melbourne, East Perth held its annual ball at the Canterbury Court Ballroom. It was a triumphant night for all the club's players, staff and supporters, and could hardly have been more of a contrast to the previous year's affair. Fred Book took formal delivery of the premiership cup and during the evening Farmer was also officially presented with the Tassie and Sandover Medals. On this note a golden year for East Perth and for Farmer drew to a close as far as football was concerned.

For Farmer, his football achievements alone were enough to induce satisfaction, but he had extra reason for pride and joy that night, for on his arm was his first regular girlfriend, a young Tasmanian by the name of Marlene Gray. Marlene had come to Perth in June on a working holiday, after being talked out of Queensland by some Perth yachtsmen she met at home earlier in the year. She first laid eyes on Farmer when she went with her friend to watch the Tasmanians play Western Australia in the carnival, and can still remember seeing him poised on a Tasmanian's shoulders taking a mark, just as she entered. A week later she had attended the formal end-of-carnival ball as a guest of one of the Tasmanian players.

She and Farmer met at one of the regular Canterbury Court dance nights not long afterwards. They enjoyed each other's company, becoming regular companions on and off the dance floor, and the romance blossomed.

In every way 1956 was a magical year for Farmer. He had no reason to regret his decision at the beginning of the year to stay in Perth. The perfect seal came on Christmas Eve, when he and Marlene announced their engagement.

6

THE ROYALS RAMPANT

Once the euphoria of the Grand Final victory had settled a little, the East Perth committee turned its thoughts once more to the future. They were determined to secure their new position as a football power. The central objective in achieving this was to hold on to Farmer. The players, the staff and the committee all recognised that Farmer was the key to the team, the man who got them first use of the ball, and got the side not just moving, but flowing.

This time around the negotiations and manoeuvring went on behind closed doors, with no leaks or press announcements. Club officials sounded Farmer out about his intentions. The two figures involved at first were secretary Eric Sweet, who was close to Farmer, and senior vice-president Jack Gabbedy. "He made his point, too," recalls Sweet. "He gave us the feeling that the club had to do something for him."

In those days it was felt that the club could not officially pay one player at a higher rate than the others. So other means had to be found. Gabbedy was the finance man at the club who kept a close eye on the budgets, and a strict control over expenditure. He was also a commissioner of the state-owned Rural and Industries Bank. He hinted at the possibility of assistance with securing a loan if Farmer wanted to settle down and build a home in Perth.

Then Roy Hull, the 'Mr Fixit' of East Perth, swung into action. He led the negotiations which resulted in a five-way contract being drawn up. The parties were Farmer and the East Perth Football Club, plus Hull himself and fellow committee members Merv Stirling and Laurie Reynolds.

The specifics of the deal are lost in the mists of time, but as far as can be ascertained, for the five-year period East Perth guaranteed to pay its standard players fee of £4 a winning game and two pounds a losing game, and the three committee men individually guaranteed Farmer an additional payment of four pounds each a game. Farmer was on £14 or £16 a week, when he played. No payments were to be made for games missed through injury or other reasons.

There is every chance that if Farmer had still been on his own he would have resisted the East Perth offer and tried his luck in Melbourne, but by now he had more to consider than just football. The deal he was offered had many attractions: good money—the best to date for a West Australian footballer, a relatively easy path into the great Australian dream of a house of his own, a secure beginning to married life, and stability. The trade-off was that he was asked to sign on for five years. It would commit him until the end of the 1961 season, when he would be twenty-six. With the vagaries of form and the risk of injury it could well mean that he would never get the chance to play in Victoria. On the other hand, Farmer was still tied to Richmond until the end of 1957 if he did go to Victoria, and they did not look capable of being a successful team, even with his influence, whereas East Perth was poised for further success.

Farmer was either not inclined, or more likely, not experienced and guileful enough to think of bargaining for a lesser term. "I had a great ambition to play VFL football," he says. "But I was thinking more in terms of settling down. I didn't quite give up hope that I would ever play in Victoria, but I sort of resigned myself for five years."

Farmer bought a block of land in Scarborough, and later, on the strength of the contract secured a second loan and mortgage to build a home on it. The payments from the committeemen were used to pay off the loans. Farmer never received a penny in cash. He remains proud of the fact that in the years to come he honoured the deal explicitly, never seeking to renegotiate it or seek additional terms. He had made his bed, and would lie in it, not without some regrets and second thoughts, but never stinting in his side of the bargain of performing for the team. Hull and his friends never had reason to regret the bargain they made.

East Perth looked to be in good shape as they lined up for 1957. The only serious loss to their player list was Billy Roe, whose leg was badly broken in a pre-season car accident. Spencer and Perry retired. Frank Allen tried to keep going, but broke down on the training track. The only one of the veterans to keep going was Jim Washbourne, who took over from Everett as vice-captain.

While they were settled and confident, there were changes afoot at East Fremantle; the club that was to emerge as their great rival over the next few years. Old Easts, as they were known, were the most successful club in the competition in terms of premierships and consistent appearances in the final series, but in the four years to 1956 they had suffered the anguish of losing two Grand Finals and two preliminary finals. This recent record added to the frustration caused by Sheedy's defection and immediate success with East Perth.

If there is a club in Western Australia that parallels Collingwood in terms of a record of success, a fierce pride in its traditions, and its reputation for ruthlessness, it is East Fremantle. They had a name for playing the game harder than any other team in the competition. Tradition is one thing, but success, which at a football club is even more important, requires a degree of pragmatism. In 1957, East Fremantle broke with the tradition of recruiting coaches from within their own ranks, and of expecting their coaches to do the job for a pittance. They appointed South Fremantle rover Steve Marsh as their captain-coach, at an annual fee of £300.

There were many parallels between the appointments of Marsh and Sheedy. Marsh was also a champion rover approaching the end of an illustrious career. Like Sheedy in 1955 at East Fremantle, Marsh had just won the best and fairest award at South Fremantle in 1956 and been captain of the losing Grand Finalists. He had wanted to coach, but South Fremantle had decided to reappoint Clive Lewington. Both Sheedy and Marsh were fiery individualists, and hard, canny footballers. But whereas Sheedy's fire came and went, and passed as good old Aussie larrikinism, Marsh could be a moody, temperamental character at times.

But there was no doubt about Marsh's coaching ability. East Fremantle quickly emerged as the main challenger to East Perth's apparent supremacy, and their fourth round clash was billed as the match of the season to that early stage. Farmer's early season form was good. The previous week he had been the dominant player in a Royals team that recorded a crushing six-goal win over their 1956 Grand Final rival, South Fremantle. But at East Fremantle Oval they found themselves four goals down at half-time until Farmer and his rover Kevin McGill "came into the game with a vengeance"[1] as the chief movers in a fight back that saw the Royals run out winners by nine points. In the *Football Budget* reports, not for the last time in a clash between the two Easts, the opposing ruckmen, Farmer and Clarke, were listed as the best players for their sides.

The East Perth fans left no doubt as to their sentiments, or their hero, when they carried Farmer from the ground on their shoulders. At the same time an East Fremantle fan vented his ire on the perceived traitor, Sheedy, and there was almost an ugly incident as Sheedy squared up to the man, until he was hustled away by an East Perth trainer. One way and another, the East Perth and East Fremantle clashes were beginning to take on larger-than-life dimensions. The Sheedy-Marsh confrontation was important at a tactical and personality level, but within the ongoing war between the clubs, the largest, most important battle was the Farmer-Clarke duel. There were many factors that contributed to the fierceness of the battle. Not least was the wider context of the importance to the teams of bettering their chief rivals, but the ruckmen were also waging personal campaigns.

Whereas Clarke had looked up to Merv McIntosh, he was always reluctant to concede the mantle of premier ruckman to the younger and less experienced Farmer. With his bluff country manner, and his retreat to the farm between games, Clarke was also removed from the circle of football cognoscenti, whom he felt had got on the Farmer bandwagon. Clarke was a player who needed the challenge of a top opponent, or a tight game. He claims he always played his best games against Farmer and the other top ruckmen, or when East Fremantle were losing. He is happy to admit that for him, the biggest challenge each season were the games against East Perth, and he set himself for these.

But underlying all these factors, and fuelling the clash between the two, was Clarke's abuse of Farmer. Clarke shared the racism common in Western Australia's farming districts, and it was from him more than anyone else that Farmer copped the racial taunts and abuse. East Fremantle generally were the worst team that Farmer and Kilmurray had to cope with in this regard, but Farmer was Clarke's particular target. Nowadays Clarke is "not real proud of some of the things I said", but claims it was all said "on the spur of the moment. You get crooked because the umpire's not doing the right thing, and I used to take it out on Polly. You'd say the first thing that came into your head. But it wasn't good tactics, it probably made him play better."

In later years the pair have buried the hatchet. In fact Farmer is on record as saying Clarke "would have been the best footballer of all if he had have made football his career, but he was a farmer who came down and played on a Saturday afternoon. If Jack had put the amount of time into football as I did, or John Nicholls or John Schultz, he would have been by far the best ruckman in history."[2] But friends and teammates of the time have no hesitation in saying that back then "they hated each other". Clarke sees it more as rivalry, explaining that "rivalry is hatred when you're on the ground, isn't it? But I always made a point if I could, after a game, if we won or lost, we'd shake hands. I'd seek him out and we'd have a shake of the hand." But the victim of racism is always more likely to take it personally than the perpetrator; Clarke's comments and attitude made a deep impression on Farmer, and as the years went by he was to use them as a motivating tool.

Though Clarke now concedes the error of his ways, his rationalisation is the one that was dominant in football for decades—what is said on the field in the heat of the moment stays on the field, and is somehow less serious than a similar comment made in everyday life.

At the midpoint of the season when there was a week's break for two games against the visiting Victorians at Subiaco, East Perth was sitting on top of the ladder ahead of East Fremantle. Eight East Perth players were selected in the state team, including Sheedy as captain and Washbourne and vice-captain. Clarke and Farmer led the West Australian ruck once again as teammates. As usual, the Perth media had convinced themselves that this State team was a particularly good one, and that they were in with a show. The Victorians won both games comfortably, with Clarke named as the West's best player in both games, and Farmer relatively quiet.

It was an article of faith among the commentators and the state selectors of the period that it was necessary to pack the team with big men to combat Victoria's traditional ruck strength, and for years this combination of Clarke and Farmer was the state's first ruck. Clarke has observed that "I always think that the coaching of WA wasn't good, in as much as they always put Pol and I on the ball together. We're both knock ruckmen [and] it's pretty hard to share the ruck knocks." Their difficulty in sharing was no doubt accentuated by their mutual antipathy, and just who would have taken the position of first ruck and the task of calling the other in for relief would not have been easily agreed.

The following Saturday they were rivals again, as the two Easts clashed at East Fremantle Oval for the second time in a row. Sheedy and Washbourne were both out with injuries from the state games, and perhaps the other East Perth state players were suffering from let-down, or the effects of the two games in four days against the Victorians. In another great struggle, the Royals surrendered a 21-point lead early in the last quarter to go down by seven points. Clarke and Farmer had broken even in the first half, but Clarke finished the game the stronger. The result brought East Fremantle level on points, but still behind on percentage on the ladder. East Perth won its next six games comfortably, while East Fremantle went through a slump. By the time of its third clash of the season, the Royals were firmly entrenched on top of the ladder.

East Fremantle broke the Royals' winning run, beating them by five goals this time around. Marsh won the tactical battle with Sheedy by pulling a number of positional changes, and crowding Farmer in the ruck. All reports of the game have him battling two and three players throughout, including Clarke. Both ruckmen were prominent again, but with "so many [East Perth] players out of touch the heroics of Farmer meant little."[3]

The two teams were expected to meet again in the second semi-final, but to the surprise of all, a 109-point win to Perth in the last home and away game boosted its percentage by a remarkable 9 per cent, and it slipped ahead of East Fremantle by the barest of margins.

The media awards were decided that week. In the *Daily News* prize, Farmer was pipped by a single vote by West Perth ruckman Brian Foley. But the result was reversed in the *Sunday Times* award. Accepting the £100 prize Farmer said it would go towards the house he and Marlene were building at Scarborough. Marlene was back in Tasmania. She would turn 21 on the day of the second semi-final. After the Grand Final, Farmer was heading to Hobart for his wedding.

Farmer felt that he had played a good season, and a more consistent one than in the previous year of triumphs. He expected to do well in the Sandover Medal count that week, and he was the clear favourite among the pundits. He was prominent throughout the count, with Foley hardly polling a vote, and the other fancy, Claremont's Kevin Clune, also well back. With one envelope to be opened Farmer was on 19 votes, two clear of East Fremantle's young centreman Ray Sorrell, and Jack Clarke. Clarke received two votes, which put the pair on level terms. But under the count back system that prevailed at the time Clarke had four first votes to Farmer's three, and was awarded the medal.

In retrospect, it is no doubt fitting that Clarke has a Sandover in his trophy cabinet, given his contribution to the game, but at the time there were those, including Farmer, who felt that he had been somewhat fortunate. In the East Fremantle best and fairest voting four weeks later Clarke finished fourth behind Sorrell. If the WANFL had followed a subsequent AFL initiative to award retrospective Brownlow Medals to those who had tied on votes, but lost on count backs, Farmer would have joined Haydn Bunton snr, Merv McIntosh, Barry Cable and Billy Walker as a three-time medallist.

Farmer had played the last three games of the home and away round with a shoulder injury, but the week's rest before the second semi-final saw him fighting fit. His performance on the day had even his most ardent admirers looking for new superlatives. Monday's *West Australian* was lavish in its praise: "The master of the situation and mainspring of the East Perth machine was Graham Farmer, who rose to remarkable heights of brilliance. Whether he was soaring high above the packs to direct the ball unerringly to a teammate or handballing deftly to a colleague in clear space, Farmer reigned supreme."[4]

After trailing by two points at half-time, East Perth raced away to an 86-point win. Farmer's statistics were nine marks, 24 kicks, 19 effective handballs, 39 ruck knocks, and three of East Perth's 20 goals.

East Fremantle won through to the Grand Final in remarkable circumstances. In the preliminary final it came from nowhere with a 10-goals-to-one last quarter to lead Perth by four points when the game stopped. Spectators flooded the ground before it was realised that it was a fake siren that had sounded. After long delays the game restarted, but in the 40 seconds left there were no further scores.

On Grand Final eve the *Daily News* reported that Farmer had starred at Thursday night's training and looked superbly fit. But by the time this story was on the streets, a full-blown crisis had overtaken the East Perth camp. Eric Sweet had been summoned to the flat in Scarborough where he found Farmer "lying in bed, like death warmed up. Overnight on the Thursday he had been struck down with a particularly virulent dose of the Asian flu that was going around town."

Kilmurray and Hunt were evacuated, and billeted at Sheedy's Savoy Hotel. Doctors and club diehards watched over him anxiously, but it appeared to be a hopeless cause. Had it been anyone else but Farmer, there would have been no question at all, they would have been ruled out; but as the clock ticked down the club officials and selectors bit their nails and delayed the decision. The annual report gives the official version of events. With only three hours to go: "Dr Cawley pronounced Graham unfit at 11 o'clock on Saturday morning. Ray Rowles was to take his place in ruck. A dramatic turn of events occurred, however, when Graham walked into the change rooms looking somewhat worn out, but assuring the selectors he was fit and wanted to play. This proved to be one of the most difficult decisions the selectors had to make, particularly when I gave them the doctor's report.

They acted against the doctor's wishes, but it was most hard when Polly appeared to be most convincing."[5]

It says something about Farmer's importance to the side, as well as his commitment—whether it is called stubbornness or determination—that he was able to declare himself in this manner, and take the field in a Grand Final, when he was not even fit to be in the stands watching.

The game became a war of attrition. Farmer's plight was clear to those watching: "He rarely took a mark and his judgement was astray. He was very sick without doubt. At times he hurled himself above the packs for driving knocks, but it wasn't as often as usual. His legs just weren't strong enough to carry his heart around."[6]

Nevertheless, he outlasted Clarke, who was forced off the ground early in the third quarter with an injured ankle. East Fremantle had also lost its hard-working ruck-rover, Alan Preen, at half-time. At half-time East Perth was four goals up. The third quarter was marked by a vicious brawl, followed by an East Fremantle fight back that got it to an eight-point lead at three-quarter time. However, East Perth was coming home with a strong wind, and seemed set to triumph.

The last quarter of the 1957 Grand Final has gone down in football lore as a triumph for the canny Steve Marsh. Plonked in the forward pocket, he appeared to be a spent force, hardly moving. Ned Bull began to run off him in an attempt to get in the play. Twice the ball drifted out to Marsh, twice he goaled, and East Fremantle kicked away.

According to people within the East Fremantle camp, the story of Marsh conning East Perth is absolute baloney. In fact Marsh had given the game away at three-quarter time. It is quite remarkable to imagine that a first-year coach could do so, when leading in a Grand Final, but apparently he sat 15 metres away from the team huddle, and did not address his players, who were left to their own devices. With their first ruck of Clarke, Preen and Marsh effectively out of action, and this pall of gloom from their leader, it is a tribute to the East Fremantle side that it held on. It was East Perth that got rattled by the turn of events. "Only once, when Polly Farmer turned on his true class, did East Perth look likely to break through."[7] It got back within eight points again, but Farmer had to go off the ball, and East Perth went off the boil. East Fremantle ran out winners by 16 points.

At East Perth the post-mortems centred on the decision to let Farmer play. "Many people have said that Polly should not have been allowed to take the field, and if a fitter man was playing we would have won the Grand Final," wrote Eric Sweet in the annual report. But as he went on to say: "On the other hand, if he had not been allowed to play, and the result was still the same, who would have been blamed?"[8] As it was, he still made the list of East Perth's best six players in most reports of the match, and whether it was wise or not, in some ways, it should go down as one of his most heroic efforts.

He paid a heavy price though. The toll on his weakened body allowed the flu to take hold more severely than ever, and when he left for Tasmania he was still in a very poor state. The wedding went ahead at St David's Cathedral in Hobart on 2 November, three weeks after the Grand Final. Farmer was a proud and happy groom, but the "thrill" was qualified by the fact that for "almost the whole period I was down with a relapse of the flu. I really stuffed it up for myself ... I wasn't in a fit condition." After a honeymoon on Tasmania's southwest coast, he and Marlene returned to their brand-new house in Scarborough, looking forward to a quiet and happy summer.

The Farmers had been in their new home a matter of weeks. It was far from grand, but modern and comfortable, in brick and asbestos, on a corner five streets back from the beach. Polly had decided to save some money by painting the external woodwork himself. As he moved one of the steel scaffolds that held the board he was working on, it came into contact with a live wire. The electricity coursing through his body caused his hands to tighten their grip on the scaffold, and he was left hanging there, certain he was dying:

> ... the thing I remember is that every moment of my life was like a spinning wheel, and it spun. So what I'm assuming is it spun in the sense that my life was draining out of my body, because I relived every moment of my life through that time. I'm just assuming that it's part of the spirit that leaves your body when you lose your life.

But he still had his voice and his wits. His screams for help brought Marlene running from inside the house, and the neighbours racing across the swamp that separated the two houses. Marlene arrived first, and he yelled at her to move the board that held the scaffold in its deadly position. She grabbed the board, got a shock herself, and dropped it, but as it dropped the scaffold slid off the wire, and Farmer fell to the ground in a state of shock.

Farmer sees the incident as a turning point in his life. His practical response was to immediately take out life insurance, but philosophically, it had a profound effect on his attitude to life.

> That was the only time that I've come close to dying. It has really left a great impact on me. From that day my lifestyle has been on a basis of enjoying each day, and not worrying too much about what's going to happen tomorrow. I became a day bloke, just lived for the day ... I wasn't looking to the future ... I felt I was there on borrowed time. All I wanted to do was just have a good attitude to each day. I still tried to do the right thing by everyone but it wasn't so important to me ... Before that incident I was probably a little more ambitious. That incident made me into a casual person who didn't care as much any more ... just thinking how lucky I was to still be alive ... I wasn't looking to see that I was going to make it next year or the year after. My consciousness was to enjoy. Basically any money that we had we spent not on any grand scale, if we had the money we enjoyed ourselves at the time.

It was a terrible beginning to married life, and to what would turn out to be his worst year of football with East Perth.

East Perth began the season with a two-point loss to West Perth. At three-quarter time of the second game against Perth, Easts were 19 points down. Farmer was playing poorly in this game, and fell heavily in the third quarter. At the time he thought nothing of it, and lifted to lead the East Perth charge in the last quarter that carried them to victory. But when he cooled off after the game he discovered that he had damaged his shoulder in the fall. He missed the next game against Claremont, then came back in the fourth round against Subiaco, but could not complete the game, staying in the change rooms after half-time.

In the press the injury was being described as torn shoulder ligaments, but the East Perth camp was getting worried, because they could not pin it down and it would not respond to treatment. He was doing the rounds of doctors and physiotherapists with no results. In desperation, and in great secrecy, East Perth sent him to see a psychiatrist. "I was receptive to anything to try to overcome my problems. Now he did a great job, because I still had a crook shoulder, but I went out and played, and still played very well." By this time though he had missed a further two games, including a seven-point loss to East Fremantle.

Finally he found a physiotherapist who located the problem just below his shoulder at the join between the rib cage and the spine. When the joint was extended as he reached for the ball it would give way. Through a combination of manipulation and exercise from the physio the problem was cured, but by this time the season was almost half gone.

East Perth was travelling reasonably well despite Farmer's problems. The problem of the previous season in the key forward positions had turned into an embarrassment of riches. Billy Mose was on fire at full-forward after moving from defence. At centre half-forward they had Neil Hawke, who had been recruited from Port Adelaide. Hawke was an immensely gifted sportsman who was to play cricket as a fast bowler for Australia. As a footballer he is credited with introducing the drop punt to Western Australia, and is still said to have had the longest drop punt seen in Perth. Kilmurray was swung into a ruck-roving role, and found that he relished the freedom, striking the best form of his career.

On form alone, Farmer was lucky to be selected in the state squad for the coming carnival in Melbourne, though there was never any doubt that he would make the squad. In fact, with the captain of previous years, Keith Harper, no longer in contention, Farmer had some advocates in the press for taking over the job. As it turned out, he was appointed vice-captain, with Clarke getting the selectors' nod for the job. The big surprise was the omission of Kilmurray, who could not possibly have been overlooked on form. It seemed that ever since his lacklustre state debut in Melbourne in 1955, the state selectors had felt that he was unsuited to the rough and tumble of interstate football.

In the two games between the announcement of the squad and its departure for Melbourne, Kilmurray starred again, as if to make a point, and Farmer finally came good with two classy, though not dominant performances. It quickly became noticeable that Kilmurray added another option to Farmer's choices at the centre bounces, with the understanding they had built up over so many years paying off well.

The carnival was the first to be staged in Melbourne since 1927. It was billed as the centenary celebration of Australian Rules football, and given a much better promotion than the Victorians usually bestowed on interstate football. At home, with the sense of occasion, and the domestic VFL competition suspended for the duration, no one seriously expected anyone other than the Victorians to win.

The West Australians got off to a good start with a solid three-goal win over South Australia, but any remote chances they had of a carnival victory disappeared in a shock loss to Tasmania while the Victorians cantered to a percentage-boosting win over South Australia. Both of the West's games were played under lights before very poor crowds.

An 11-goal win over the VFA restored West Australian morale somewhat, but coming into the final match against the VFL they needed to win by about 17 goals to draw level on points and percentage—an unlikely scenario. The VFL raced to a six-goal lead at quarter-time, but the Westerners fought back to go down by less than three goals. They won praise as the better side on the day from a Victorian press that had been gaily predicting a massacre, and glowing reports from the Perth writers.

Clarke and Farmer both performed strongly throughout the carnival, sharing the Burley award decided by a media panel for the team's best player of the championship. Farmer won the official Simpson Medal as the state's best player for his four votes in the Tassie Medal, which went to Alan Aylett with seven, on a count back from Ted Whitten. Clarke got three, as did Bob Davis. In the All-Australian team selected at the end of the carnival Farmer was leading the first ruck, with Davis as his captain and ruck-rover, and Clarke as a backpocket ruckman. The remarkable feature of this team of 20 was that it contained four East Fremantle players; as well as Clarke there were Norm Rogers and Alan Preen on half-back and half-forward flanks, and Ray Sorrell as a reserve.

During the trip press reports had hinted that not all was well in the West Australian camp, with the players getting lectured by the officials that football must come first on the trip. In one room at least there was little chitchat and camaraderie as they bedded down for the night. Clarke and Farmer had followed the tradition of the captain and vice-captain rooming together. And in this room there was a distraction from the task at hand. The captain of the Victorian team was the inimitable Geelong Flyer, Bob Davis, then playing his last year with the club, who tells the story of how he first got to know Farmer during this carnival. "He was a bit of a loner [and] I was the only Geelong fellow in the [Victorian] team. We knocked around together after the games ... We're talking, and we're interested in the races, we're sort of bosom mates from the first time we said hello. I don't think he had any mates in the West Australian team, he was sort of the odd one out ... I told him: 'I'll coach Geelong one day, and when I am, I want you to come over and play.' He said: 'Give me a call...'"

Clarke went out a couple of times on these excursions with Davis and Farmer. It was clear to him that Davis was wooing Farmer. The gregarious Davis may have just asked Clarke along because he was there, or perhaps he had Clarke in mind as the second string of his long-term recruitment plans. They must have made an odd threesome, with the voluble Davis spinning yarns and visions, making more than enough noise to compensate for any silences from the two big men.

When recalling these times, Davis went on to attribute what he saw as Farmer's alienation from his teammates to racism among the West Australians, and claims to have been told that the reason Kilmurray was not selected was because it would have made two Aboriginal players in the team, and Kilmurray was seen as "too black". Interestingly, former football writer, Len Owens, tells a story of Farmer returning on the plane from another interstate tour:

Just before boarding he had pocketed some money for doing a media interview. Most of the state players were drinking, and one challenged him to buy a round: "Come on Polly, take your bloody hand out of your pocket." Polly ruffled his head and says: "You know you can't upset me by those tactics." And he sat down [next to someone else], and said: "The difference between me and those blokes is that when I retire from football, I'm just another boong."

In the remainder of the home and away round East Perth were displaced from top spot on the ladder thanks to its third loss of the season to East Fremantle. Coming into the finals, Farmer had missed six of the 21 games through injury and state duties. Of those he played he failed to complete two, and probably only approached true match fitness in six at the most. For the first time since 1954 he was not in contention for the Sandover Medal. For the Sister Kate's gang though, it was still a great night, for the winner was Kilmurray. Kilmurray was still living in the flat, where he had listened to the count on the radio with a friend. "Within half an hour the flat was full of people, but Pol was the first [to get there]."

The second semi-final was a sensational game, but not for the quality of the football. With East Perth fighting back desperately, the last quarter was one of "wild scrimmages, jabbing elbows and fisticuffs". The drama reached its climax when Steve Marsh took himself off with a few minutes remaining, and put his replacement, Trizzie Lawrence, on to Sheedy, apparently with instructions to stir Sheedy up. Lawrence had been on the ground barely a minute when Sheedy decked him. It was another minute and more before Lawrence was able to stagger to his feet. When the siren went East Fremantle was still 14 points ahead, but few were paying any attention to the scoreboard. Old Easts fans were screaming abuse at Sheedy, a brawl broke out among the spectators in front of the grandstand, and in the confusion Sheedy struck again, only to discover later that the man he hit was not one of his tormentors, but an East Perth member. As the police restrained him, and then escorted him to the dressing-rooms, Fred Book twice pulled a press photographer from a chair to stop him getting any shots of the scene.

It was East Perth's seventh straight loss against East Fremantle in two years. When Sheedy was suspended for four weeks for striking Lawrence, few believed that they would be able to break the sequence, even if they got past Perth in the preliminary final. They had an added problem in attack; defender-cum-forward Billy Mose had completely lost touch, and there was talk of dropping a man with 110 goals against his name for the season.

The preliminary final against Perth was a scrappy game played in foul weather, with both sides having only three goals on the board at three-quarter time. The Royals won through six goals to four, but did little to inspire confidence for the following Saturday. John Todd said: "East Perth can thank Graham Farmer for their win ... and their chance to contest the Grand Final next week."[9] Even better was his announcement after the game that it was the first time that season he had pulled up feeling 100 per cent fit.

Mose kept his place in the Grand Final side, but rover Kevin McGill was forced out with a leg injury. Tough young defender, Mal Atwell, came back in after missing games from a broken collarbone. Sheedy, marshalling his troops from the bench, won the early tactical battles. Steve Marsh was playing his last game, fully expecting to go out in a blaze of glory. Mal Atwell, who was big enough to play as a ruckman, and was normally a key position defender, lined up on him, with instructions to play close. He did that and more, to the extent that "Marsh must have felt much relieved when Atwell did not return"[10] after half-time, having played the last 15 minutes of the half with his collarbone rebroken.

Sheedy's masterstroke though was to play acting captain Tommy Everett at centre half-forward on Rogers. There had been much speculation on how Hawke would handle him, or rather vice versa. According to Merv Cowan, who was in the East Fremantle team: "Hawke and Kilmurray were shit scared of Rogers. They'd played centre half-forward during the year. They put Everett there. Tommy's not frightened of anybody. Tommy walked up and started talking trotters to Normie Rogers. Bloody Norm got sucked in—took all his fire out of him." When Rogers did get his mind back on the job he was obviously riled, and gave away a number of free kicks and 15-yard penalties, with Everett provoking him every step of the way.

With Farmer prominent, and Kilmurray brilliant, East Perth could have wrapped it up by quarter-time but for bad kicking. But East Fremantle hit back with the breeze in the second quarter to be a point in front at the bell. The second half was played at a frantic pace, with the defences well on top. Ned Bull atoned for the flak he had received for his last-quarter performance on Marsh the previous year with a Simpson Medal-winning display on his half-back flank. Again, East Perth could have won it with the breeze, but again the score was 3.7 (25). Coming into the last quarter it was anybody's game.

East Fremantle quickly got the first two goals of the last term, and there was less than a kick in it. From then on no more goals were scored. Well into time on Clarke made a desperate lunge to try to prevent an East Perth score, cannoned into the point post, and snapped it at the base. The ball was cleared up field from the jagged stump. Farmer got it on the wing, and was about to pump it back into attack, when the siren signalled a two-point win to the Royals. "He flung the ball high in the air. Then exhausted, he slumped into the arms of happy East Perth trainers."[11]

The game went down as one of the all-time classic Grand Finals in Western Australia. For Farmer, it marked a happy conclusion to what had otherwise been a decidedly ordinary year; though for most players All-Australian selection and a Simpson Medal at the carnival would have been a career highlight.

More than anything else the result was an evener upper for the previous year. Farmer and his teammates on the one hand, and Cowan and Clarke on the other, all agree that the 1957 and 1958 results should have been reversed. In each year the better side lost the Grand Final. In isolation, each year seems almost an injustice. Taken together they are a perfect match, with justice embellished by drama.

Nineteen fifty-nine was never going to be anything other than East Perth's year. It totally dominated the competition, going through the first 17 games without defeat, and finishing the home and away round with a percentage of 151, five games clear of second-placed East Fremantle.

The core of the team now was the young brigade of Mick Cronin, matured into strong, consistent, experienced players in their prime. With more of the veterans retiring and Everett leaving the club, Farmer and Kilmurray were now the senior players after Sheedy. Along with Mose, they had reached their century of games in 1958. Watts, Bull, McGill and Seal reached the ton in 1959. There were another half-dozen with 60 to 90 games under their belts, plus those like Reg Hall and Neil Hawke with interstate experience. It was a great team without any noticeable weaknesses, at the peak of its powers.

Farmer was appointed vice-captain on Everett's departure. He attaches little significance to the appointment. "It really wouldn't have worried me if I wasn't vice-captain. It wasn't important ... It was Jack's side." The task involved filling in if Sheedy was injured, and the formality of sitting on the three-man selection committee on Thursday nights with Sheedy and Jack Lalor.

Of those 17 straight wins, seven were by margins of 10 goals or more, and only two were by less than three goals. It is no surprise that the only real pressure game was down at East Fremantle in round five, when they scraped home by four points.

Old Easts had not started the season well. Marsh retired after the Grand Final loss, and Clarke also announced his retirement, while his ruck partner-cum-centre half-forward, Percy Johnson, moved to Swan Districts as captain-coach. Everett's defection from East Perth was to take up the appointment as captain-coach at East Fremantle. Everett was a gregarious, hugely talented and tough player in the Sheedy mould. His attractiveness and potential for the position were obvious. The irony of doing a Sheedy in reverse was capped only by the sensation of Old Easts pinching the captain of the team that had stolen the Grand Final that should have been theirs.

The only trouble was that despite five separate applications from Everett, the hard-nosed committee at East Perth would not grant a clearance, and he had to begin the season coaching from the bench. The saga ran from the end of one season until well into the next. Within the Royals camp there was dissension, with the inimitable Roy Hull announcing his resignation from the committee.

Gradually things sorted themselves out for Old Easts. Everett got his clearance on a Saturday morning, enabling him to play from the third game on. His persuasions overcame the pressure on Jack Clarke from his father and brother to pull his weight on the farm, and Jack recommenced his Saturday morning drives down with his mother as he pulled on the boots again.

Given the circumstances, the clash was something more than the first return match since the Grand Final, and the game lived up to its billing. Surprisingly perhaps, it did not erupt into violence. But it was a dour, tight affair, with a long-range goal from Hawke late in the last quarter securing a four-point win for the Royals. Farmer had a head start to the season over Clarke, and it showed as he took a points decision with a strong finish to the game. More than one report described the ruck clash as another "classic duel", but they all rated Farmer as best on ground.

Once again Clarke and Farmer were named captain and vice-captain of the state team, this time for a tour taking in games at Melbourne, Hobart and Adelaide. However, the rains came late to the Wheatbelt that year, and sowing of the crop was delayed. Clarke was forced to pull out of the tour to man a tractor on the farm. Farmer became the captain of Western Australia without ever having led a club side at any level before.

The media were again writing up hopes of a West Australian upset, with a preview in the *West Australian* saying their build-up had been perfect, and the Victorians were less confident than usual. It was a foul Melbourne winter's day, so cold that the rain verged on snow at times. Farmer led the West on to the MCG with the team all fired up, but time passed as they did their laps slipping around in the mud, getting colder and colder. It was quarter of an hour before the Victorians showed, then they lined up on the ground for a team photo as the Westerners shivered, and the fire died in their bellies. The game was a total debacle, with the Victorians kicking 31 goals to three. The Victorian press was withering in its scorn, and the Perth scribes wrung their hands and moaned about it setting back West Australian football by 10 years.

Farmer regards the game as one of his great disappointments. He was genuinely thrilled to be leading the state, and to suffer such a humiliating loss on his debut was a bitter pill. In the aftermath he found that he had injured his shoulder again, though not seriously, and not unsurprisingly in the circumstances, had developed a bad cold. He came up well enough to play a good game in a midweek victory over Tasmania, but was quiet in a two-point loss to South Australia on the final game of the tour.

When he got home he spent much of the week ill in bed, but he fronted for the game on Saturday against East Fremantle. The Royals won by three goals, but Farmer lowered his colours to Clarke, "who it was stated 'saved' himself for Farmer [and] played his best game for the season."[12] Farmer's form remained moderate in the next few weeks, then he put in two good but unspectacular performances for the state in victories over South Australia at Subiaco, playing once again as Clarke's vice-captain. The following week he strained ligaments in his buttock, and was forced to miss two games, which turned out to be East Perth's first two losses for the season, against West Perth and East Fremantle.

Subiaco, in the fourth year of a rebuilding program under former South Fremantle ruck-rover Charlie Tyson, made a late charge to grab fourth spot and play in the finals for the first time since 1946. The team justified its place with a record-breaking 129-point victory over Perth.

In the lead-up to the second semi-final most of the speculation focussed on the Farmer-Clarke clash. Clarke had finished the season in great form, whereas Farmer was clearly still feeling the effects of the buttock injury, and not moving as well as he could. In the first half they largely nullified each other, and East Fremantle went to the long break eight points up. Clarke played much of the second half in defence, as the Royals gradually gained the upper hand, with Farmer playing his best half of football in a couple of months. Norm Rogers closed Langdon down, but the most telling duel was between Sheedy and his protégé-turned-rival Everett in the centre, with Sheedy taking the honours. Old Easts were still a chance coming into the last quarter, but the Royals held firm to win by four goals.

Subiaco's hot streak continued with a comfortable six-goal win over Old Easts in the preliminary final, with Everett's defensive coaching tactics coming under criticism for the second week running. It was to be the Lions first Grand Final appearance in 24 years, and a victory would mean their first premiership since 1924. As always in such circumstances, they had the sympathy of the public, and the hype and expectation built around them.

Many gave them a real chance on the strength of their last two games, with the *Daily News* tipsters on the eve of the game split three each in their selections.

At half-time it was anybody's game, with East Perth leading by seven points. Subiaco could have led but for a bout of finals jitters that saw a number of easy shots on goal missed. East Perth kicked away with the breeze to a five-goal break at the last change, with Farmer and Langdon leading the way. The last quarter began with only two men on the East Perth forward line, but Subiaco looked to be mounting a charge when they got the first three goals to be well within reach. Suddenly Sheedy swung his players out of defence back to their normal positions, they pressed forward, and Paul Seal put a long drop kick through to increase the comfort margin.

Farmer rucked all day in a "remarkable display of stamina and determination."[13] He capped his performance with the mark of the day in the dying minutes, and his only goal of the match, which put the result beyond doubt. He was chaired off the ground by Royals fans, and his performance won him the Simpson Medal for the third time, but this was the first for a Grand Final, the other two having come for interstate performances. The judgement was endorsed by the press, with all reports naming him best on ground. For Farmer and East Perth it was the second premiership in a row, and the third in four years. By ordinary standards Farmer had a highly successful year. He captained the state team, finished equal fourth in the Sandover Medal and second in a major media award. He won a Simpson Medal, and the East Perth best and fairest award with 136 votes, a mile ahead of Langdon on 93. The fact that he was no longer judged by ordinary standards, or even those that are applied to other star players, is indicated by the words in the East Perth annual report written by new club secretary, Hec Strempel: "Graham experienced a very indifferent season through unfortunate injuries."[14]

In 1960 the highlight of Farmer's year came early. Six weeks before the start of the season his and Marlene's first child was born at Mount Lawley hospital. The next day sports writer Austin Robertson bumped into him in the newspaper offices filling out an advertising form for the birth notice, and reported him as "grinning ear to ear" and describing it as "the biggest day of my life ... a bigger thrill than any trophy I've ever won at football."[15] The newspapers carried photographs of parents and child, and in his first week of life, they were wondering whether Brett would become a League ruckman.

As the opening fixtures approached, Farmer had more than a baby son to admire and his own form and fitness to worry about. He had volunteered for the job of coaching the East Perth thirds, which was an under-18 team. They played on Sundays, and trained on Wednesdays and Fridays. This meant that once the season got underway he was committed four evenings a week, and both days of the weekend, plus sitting on the selection committee on Thursday nights.

When the season did begin he started in sensational form. In his first nine games the *Football Budget* reports list him as East Perth's best player eight times. At this stage of the season his main rival in the media's best player awards was Kilmurray, who had also started the season in scintillating style.

Despite the form of this pair though, East Perth was having problems. As in 1954, the Royals had started the season a week early with a game against South Fremantle, for they were going on tour again. They had to front up without Neil Hawke, who had returned to South Australia, and Charlie Walker who had gone back to Manjimup. A big recruiting drive had brought a crop of youngsters into the club, but none who were able to immediately establish themselves in the team, and half a dozen of their regulars started the year with injury problems. When they drew with South Fremantle in their fifth game, the write-up in Monday's paper claimed that a number of their players were below League standard.

East Fremantle, with Steve Marsh back as non-playing coach, was also having problems. In the same week it suffered one of its worst ever losses, on the wrong end of a 100-point hiding from West Perth, which was starting to click under new coach Arthur Olliver, who had been a 270-game player with Footscray.

It was a season of topsy-turvy form, as shown the following week when East Perth had an easy six-goal win over West Perth. The main reason for this was Farmer's total eclipse of Foley and the other West Perth followers, in what was described as "one of his greatest games."[16] Yet when they lost their next two, to be on three wins, four losses and a draw, the Royals found themselves in the unaccustomed position of fifth on the ladder. Three successive wins capped by a 99-point victory over Swan Districts got them back into fourth spot by the time the fortnight's break for the Eastern States tour came around.

Farmer stayed in Perth for the forthcoming game against the Victorians, along with Watts and Atwell, and Sheedy, who was the state's non-playing coach that year. Once again Kilmurray missed out despite his red-hot form. And once again the Victorians won comfortably. It was during this game that Clarke and Farmer, who were captain and vice-captain, had a run in on the field. Farmer was supposed to be changing with Keith Slater, but Slater was stuck in the forward pocket. Farmer played particularly well during the second half, but at some point Clarke must have told him to give Slater a run. Farmer refused, and there was a bitter exchange between the two.

The first game up after the interstate match was against West Perth. At the first bounce down Farmer turned his ankle, and he spent the rest of the game as a very immobile full-forward. He managed 3.4 (22), but this time West Perth turned the tables with a nine-goal win. He missed one game, and had to pass a Saturday morning fitness test before being allowed back in the following week against East Fremantle. The Friday paper had shown pictures of flooded farms and washed out roads at Jennacubine, as Perth and the hinterland went through one of the wettest weeks in years, but Clarke left the damage control to the other men of the family, and made the trip down to Perth Oval. It was only three weeks since their clash in the state game, and according to the *West Australian*, "It is doubtful that Jack Clarke had ever played with more determination at centre bounces than in this game."[17] East Fremantle won a low-scoring game relatively easily, and East Perth tumbled out of the four again.

The Royals won all of their last round of seven games except that against West Perth, which was a draw, making the two sides even-stevens in their three clashes. They secured second place on the ladder, and were once again looking good for the finals. The season had been a tipsters' nightmare. The top four all finished on 13 wins. West Perth took top place on the strength of its three draws. East Perth and South Fremantle both had two draws, but the Royals took second place on percentage, with East Fremantle fourth.

East Perth's biggest problem all year had been the lack of goal-scoring forwards, as in 1957, before Mose and then Hawke answered the call. As in 1957, rover McGill was their top goal-scorer with 52. It is notable that Farmer's goal tally of 35 this year was by far his highest with East Perth.

The old firm of Farmer and Kilmurray dominated the end-of-season awards. Farmer won the Sandover by 10 votes, equalling Foley's margin of the previous year. Kilmurray was the runner-up, making it their third quinella in the three major awards. Farmer had also beaten Kilmurray for the first prize of £300 from the *Sunday Times*, with the result reversed in the *Daily News*' £100 award.

East Perth went into the second semi-final as the slight favourite, but could not match West Perth. As had happened too often throughout the season, there were too many players either completely out of touch, or only flashing in and out of play. Farmer and Kilmurray were the only pair to put in four good quarters. They came from behind to get within two points with nine minutes to go, but died on their run to lose by four goals. This set up another final-round clash with East Fremantle, which had accounted for South comfortably in the first semi.

The morning preview in the *West Australian* ran under the headline 'Feud Between Ruckmen May Reach A Climax', and tipped East Fremantle to win. At quarter-time it seemed that the selection would be proved correct; East Fremantle had been totally dominant, kicking 5.11 (41) while holding the Royals scoreless. Clarke had been the star of the game to this point, with Farmer quiet. Farmer got on top of Clarke, and the East Perth machine started to roll. The second quarter was a complete turnaround, with Old Easts held scoreless while the Royals scored 7.11 (53), to be two goals up at half-time. The third quarter was the killer; against the wind East Perth kicked five goals to two, and East Fremantle's resistance crumbled. In the last quarter "Clarke tried to get moving from the ruck but he was a spent force and there just wasn't anybody else capable of taking the initiative from the East Perth pack."[18]

The Royals won by exactly 10 goals, with Sheedy complaining that they should have kicked 10 goals instead of four coming home with the wind.

The Farmer-Clarke duel had not quite lived up to its billing, with neither dominating, but Farmer got a unanimous points decision, and both were in the top three for their side in all lists. Mal Atwell's display at centre half-back took the honours as best on ground. The pundits had given up trying to follow the form, and the Grand Final was being described as the most open in years, with media selections split almost equally, though slightly in East Perth's favour. The Royals biggest handicap was the loss of Jack Sheedy, who had come off second best in a collision with Farmer in the preliminary final. In Sheedy's absence Farmer led the Royals onto the ground, and won the toss, choosing to kick with a strong breeze. They led by 14 points at quarter-time, but surrendered the lead early in the second. Farmer remembers the game as the only one of his Grand Finals with East Perth that they never really looked like winning, he acknowledges West Perth as the better team over the year and on the day. Under Olliver, with three ex-Victorians in the side, West Perth played tight, disciplined football. It was by no means a thrashing, but the margin hovered between three and six goals for most of the game, with the deficit at the end being 32 points.

Farmer was East Perth's best player, giving "an outstanding display in the ruck, particularly in the first half, but his closely checked teammates were unable to take advantage of most of his efforts."[19] Foley led West Perth's four-man ruck battery, and put in a particularly good last quarter. Although the *West Australian* only listed him fourth in West Perth's best, his strong game won him the Simpson Medal.

At East Perth there was almost a sense of equanimity about the loss. Certainly there was none of the recrimination, nor the sense of having been robbed that followed the 1957 loss to East Fremantle. The club's annual report looks back with pride on the successful completion of the five-year plan launched in 1956 that had resulted in five successive Grand Final appearances for three victories. At the club's award night Farmer won the best and fairest for the sixth time in the past seven years. His ascendancy in the team is shown by the margin. He won with 293 votes, from Paul Seal on 191, with Kilmurray third on 178.

With four years of his five-year contract now gone, Farmer had lived up to the standard he set in 1956.

7

NOT QUITE ONE
OF THE BOYS

Five Grand Finals in five years for three premierships. It is the kind of record rarely achieved by a football team at the elite level, and enough to stamp the East Perth combination of the period as one of the great sides of West Australian football. Its only persistent problem was in the key forward positions. If there had been a Naylor, a Gerovich or a Robertson in the side—or even a full-forward who scored a regular 80 goals a year—it would have been near to perfect.

Sheedy had moulded a side that had three distinctive features: a toughness that bred self-confidence in the team and fear in the opposition; a mean yet talented defence; and most important of all, a squad of mobile, flexible on-ball players. He got this side playing a brand of football that can be seen in retrospect as a precursor of the modern game.

The emphasis was on movement of the ball and speed. The Royals would begin a passage of play with handball deep in defence at a time when it was still a dragging offence for a player to do this. They would run with the ball in numbers. They looked to feed the ball to a man in the open and on the run. Sheedy would not hesitate to ring the positional changes in the manner of Kevin Sheedy at Essendon 30 years later.

If there was one hallmark of the East Perth team it was the handball. The players used it more, and more effectively than any other team in Australia. "My philosophy was to try to keep the ball moving—quickly," recalls Sheedy. "Now that meant if you got a mark or a free kick, you handballed—there had to be somebody running past … You gained some ground every time, whereas if you go back for your kick over the mark you lost some ground. So everybody was imbued to use more handball." It might sound commonplace now, but in the 1950s this was a radical strategy. "A lot of the older coaches were still about then, and they frowned on handball. Handball was all right to your advantage—just a quick handpass to give to a guy … for a nice easy kick. But to use a chain of handpasses, one, two and three, that was unheard of."

Sheedy had been a handballer since his earliest days in League football. He had played a handful of games as an 18-year-old with South Melbourne in 1944, and seen how effective it could be when used well by the South Australian rover Jack Oatey, who also played a few games for the Swans while in Melbourne for war service. At East Fremantle, Sheedy and his fellow rovers became known for their snappy use of handball, especially at close quarters, in the style of Len Smith's Fitzroy teams of the late 1950s and early 1960s. He recalls leaving the field after one game with East Fremantle to be told by the coach's wife: "If you had boots on your hands, you'd be a good player."

Yet for all the team's strengths and Sheedy's innovative strategies, East Perth had one outstanding attribute: its number one ruckman, the incomparable Graham 'Polly' Farmer. 'Stop Farmer and you'll stop East Perth' was the catchphrase among the opposition and the pundits, and endless hours were spent in the clubrooms of the other seven teams of the competition devising schemes and strategies to this end. Within the Royals camp there was a similar acknowledgement.

The testimonials of his teammates convey the fact that his role in the team was far greater than just his dominance of the ruck duels. His presence and his style of play were the very core of the East Perth side and its success, and when through injury or any other reason he did not perform, the team was crippled:

Sheedy moulded the team round Polly's skills ... He got us going. He was the whole basis of the side, it revolved around his game ... He was getting the vital possessions—centre bounces and the ball coming back from the opposition forward line ... If he got the ball the team responded immediately. He'd done his work by winning that first hard ball, and so set the team in motion.

Frank Allen.

Everything revolved around Pol. If he had a bad day, the side would. Not that he had too many mind you ... You opened the paper on a Sunday, and 'East Perth best—Farmer'. You sort of expected that.

Ted Kilmurray.

[Sheedy] finished up with a very, very good side. The hub of the whole lot really was Polly, there's no two ways about that.

Tom Everett.

Pol was the key to the whole thing.

Laurie Kennedy.

Sheedy was indeed fortunate to arrive at East Perth and find a ruckman who was in every way the perfect focal point for the brand of football he wanted his side to play. Clarke was a champion ruckman, and Foley at West Perth and Slater at Swan Districts were great ruckmen; Clarke perhaps matched Farmer in terms of ability, but none of them had the football philosophy and instincts to fit the role that Farmer played, nor the mastery of handball to fill the role with such deadly effect.

Frank Allen's phrase is perhaps the key: "If he got the ball, the team responded immediately." Farmer's vice-captain, at Geelong in later years put it even more pointedly. John Devine was a half-back flanker in the mould of West Coast Eagles captain John Worsfold—mild-mannered, almost demure off the field, but fearsome on it. Thirty years on, sitting in the lounge of his Geelong hotel, Devine's eyes still lit up as he remembered: "Whenever Pol looked like getting hold of the ball, there were 10 of us running up the ground looking for it, trying to get an easy kick."

His teammates knew that more likely than not Farmer would win the ball in a contest, and they knew that he would then use the ball to maximum effect. So they were all moving to get in on the play instead of waiting to see the play unfold and then react. The side was anticipating, moving, co-ordinating, attacking, flowing. Farmer was able to get a team playing in the style that a coach dreams of, because his teammates believed in his ability to initiate the play.

By 1960 Farmer had perfected a style of play that maximised the use and benefit of his many skills to his team. He would contest the bounce downs and throw-ins, utilising either his pinpoint palming or the grab and handball. Between times he would mainly drift between the half-forward and half-back lines, showing a rare ability to read the play and position himself to either play the link man in an attacking move, or cut off an opposition thrust and initiate his own attack. This ability was partly a natural skill, but also an outcome of close study of all the opposition players and teams and their patterns of play that enabled him to judge which way a player would turn, who were the long-kickers, who were the twisters and turners who would kick under pressure and drop the ball short, what the next two and three plays and movements of the ball were likely to be.

When the ball did get past him he would drop deep into defence or attack if necessary, but more often than not, he would be in the vicinity of the ball as it came through. And as John Watts said: "If the ball was in a radius of 20 metres from him he basically believed that it was his ball ... He had the confidence to say: 'I can get that'." He would mark over a pack from the back, coming in from the side, or—as very few have the skill and courage to do—running back into the front of a descending pack. He would also win the ground balls and the loose balls.

And once he had it there was that immaculate, lightning-fast disposal with either hand or the left foot. Watts again:

> He would evaluate the best player ... to give it to. He never got rid of the ball to get himself out of trouble ... He always managed to get the ball away to an advantage to the team ... He played the game correctly ... Even when he fell to the ground he was still thinking, he'd still have possession of it, and [be] thinking where he was going to place it.

His disposal was aided not only by his skills, but by peripheral vision and an ability to know where his teammates were that they still recall with wonder. There are endless stories of the blind handpass, the backward flick, the pass threaded through a maze of bodies to pinpoint the right player on the run.

The other attribute he developed and honed as the years went by was consistency. Among the true champions of the game—the elite players who recognise each other in silent appreciation as a cut above the rest—this is the quality most admired, the ability to perform week in week out, whatever the quality of the opposition, whatever handicaps of injury, ground condition, or unusual circumstances might be thrown up.

To Farmer the key to consistency was his mental preparation. He sets more store by that than any other facet of his game, and keeps returning to it when discussing his football career. In the early years of his career he had devised exercise and practice regimens for himself long before the sports scientists arrived on the scene. By now he was developing motivational techniques years in advance of the sports psychologists.

For Farmer it was a personal journey of discovering what worked best, and it was a private matter. He expected other players to undergo their own preparation, but wanted to place himself in a position where he could perform to his utmost irrespective of the build-up for the rest of the team. The technique he used was images of desperation and hate. From the wider world he would conjure up images of:

> ...Indians when they had a war dance to get themselves into a frenzy before they went out and fought for their lives; ... weightlifters, how they got into their soul before they made that extremely big lift; boxers, how they eyeballed each other; ... the best example of all is fighting for your life, imagine what you would do if you were fighting for your life. One of my greatest inspirations is a little boy getting belted by the bully; he just keeps coming, gets up again, gets knocked out again. He gets up, the bully runs out of punches and he gets on top of him and overpowers him. In an artificial way I was trying to emulate that.

But as well as the general, he drew very much on the personal: "My memory bank ... every rotten experience of my life. I used to think about all the things and people that I hated, including Jack Clarke, including the dentist, anyone, anyone that was going to inflict pain on me."

He would begin the build-up in quiet moments on his own during the week, but the real work was done in the half-hour before the game, when he would go into a private world as he prepared himself for the game. But he insists the objective, and the outcome of this exercise was not to focus his hatred on the day's opponent. He wished to "transform myself into a person who's got the body of a man fighting for his life, but has got an intelligent capacity to handle it."

And the focus of all this intense energy was the football:

My only desire out on the field is to get the ball, or to get the person who's got the ball and take it off him ... But no other thing ... No matter what the player does to me he doesn't put me off, he doesn't break my concentration to get the ball ... You were never in the situation where you got the fumbles or anything like that, because of your possessed state and your commitment and your confidence. Your eyes would always be on the ball. You would always be watching the ball no matter what the effect of, say, a collision, or someone putting his boot into the ball as you're picking it up ... This commitment is only to give you the desire to go out and get the ball ... and suffer whatever the sacrifices are to get it. That was the whole idea of the preparation.

Though focussing and motivational techniques of this kind are relatively common in modern sport, in the 1950s they were virtually unheard of. There are still relatively few competitors who are willing and able to do it for themselves without recourse to coaches or professional motivators. For Farmer:

... the effect on my football performance [was that] it made me a person who was very difficult to stop ... It meant that almost every week I was going to play a competitive game. Some days were going to be better than others, but what I was looking for was to be consistent. If you use a scale of 10 being a perfect game, on a good day where I was an outstanding player I was going to be an eight or nine, and on a bad day I was still going to be a six or seven. So the difference between my best and worst was just a couple of digits, whereas other guys can have a nine out of 10, but on a bad day they're zero out of 10.

This capacity to perform at a consistently outstanding level is what Farmer prides himself on. It is difficult to extract from him, but when pushed to say which ruckmen could outplay him, or what style of player he found most difficult to combat, he says that the only ones that took the honours were those who encountered him on an off day, when injuries or other factors prevented him playing to capacity.

A player of Farmer's skills and techniques playing in this possessed state was incredibly difficult for an opposing coach to counter, no matter what tactics he used. At one level it seems that he developed these motivational techniques as his career developed as a counter to the increasing pressure opponents placed on him. At a personal level it made him a doubly fearsome opponent for other ruckmen, for it was almost impossible to throw him off his game with the tried and tested techniques of niggling and physical harassment.

Farmer insists he never set out to confront his opponents personally, or to counter the treatment dished out to him by the opposition:

> Because you're in that possessed state and you want the ball, you'll be prepared to put up with what the opposition players were prepared to do to you. Your only concentration was on getting the ball, it wasn't on retaliating, or thumping them, all it was was putting up with whatever came in your desire to get hold of the ball … If by chance a guy has knocked me over I do not take time off to seek revenge. I haven't got time, I only want the ball. But I know that during a game there'll be plenty of times when I'll get an opportunity to, in a fair way, even the score.

In another discussion he admitted that:

> In a discreet way you could say that I was a dirty footballer—in a discreet way. I used my leaps well and I didn't have to seek revenge because I could do it every time I went in the ruck. I'd get my legs up and you know, you line their body right up and they're going to get it in the chest and stomach and balls and so on. It happened with my legs and elbows. So I didn't seek revenge because I knew it would happen sooner or later.

Farmer was well able to protect himself, but there were also those in the East Perth team who played a large part in providing additional protection. This was not so much in the sense of physical protection as in protecting his territory. This was in the days before the centre square, when a team could throw as many players as it wanted in to congest the bounce downs. Farmer's assets were his leap and his agility and bodywork in the air, but to get airborne, he needed at least two or three paces to generate the spring. A primary tactic of the opposition was to try to get in front of him and block this run.

The blocking role usually fell to the opposition's second follower or ruck-rover. And in turn, Farmer's offsider's prime duty was to prevent this. Jack Hunt and Laurie Kennedy were the two the task fell to most often, changing as ruck-rovers out of the backline. Both were robust players, and Hunt in particular had the resilience of a steel post, borne of his years as a farm labourer. The opposition would just bounce off him.

Through the years Farmer's quieter days were often attributed to this screen not working, and when it did fall down, he would be quick to let his ruck-rovers know. His instructions to Kennedy were to "get these blokes out of my way ... He was adamant—we'd get a few whacks behind the ear to make sure ... As long as he could get those one or two steps up he'd go."

And once his protectors made sure he was up, there was the rest of the mobile brigade—Sheedy himself, McGill, Hall, Kilmurray, with the winger Seal and the flankers, all offering options to confuse the opposition and increase Farmer's range of choices. If he was having one of his eight or nine out of 10 days, dominating possession, and providing the spark to the East Perth machine, it took an extraordinary round-the-ground effort from the opposition to stay in touch; if he was down to six or seven they were in with a show.

Since the sports psychologist has become a part of the game some effort has been put into the question of trying to understand what makes footballers tick, and especially into what makes some tick better than others. As part of this elusive quest, a Melbourne psychologist once:

...used a test devised by Hans Eysenck to investigate [the personality pattern of the Australian footballer]. The qualities he was looking for were the introverted or the extroverted, the stable or the neurotic ... He found that footballers came out heavily on the side of extroversion and neuroticism— that is, to oversimplify, that they tended to seek the approval of others and were anxious about it, rather than being satisfied with achieving internal goals.[1]

If this profile was correct, Farmer can only be described as the exception that proves the rule. He was not a player who needed inspiration or praise from coach and teammates, he did not get involved in the on-field backslapping and encouragement that players use to spur each other on. On or off the field, he never lost that inward focus with which he emerged from Sister Kate's; a strength and steel in the soul that enabled him to set the internal goals and drive himself to achieve them.

And because he measured himself by these private standards, he neither needed nor particularly welcomed the backslapping and adulation that came with the achievements. But with his stature as a footballer continuing to soar during these years, Farmer became more and more of a public figure, and had to develop his own ways and means of dealing with all the advantages and disadvantages of that status.

In 1957, he moved out of the mechanic's workshop once and for all and traded the life of the tradesman to become a salesman. His first job of this type was with the auto parts company Repco, and after almost two years there he took a job selling cars. He acquired the jobs through football contacts, but not, as has been commonly supposed, as part of his deal with East Perth. His technical knowledge as a mechanic combined with his public profile made him perfectly suited for the positions.

It is commonly supposed, in Farmer's case as with other 'celebrity salesmen'—and especially sportsmen—that he was not actually required to do a job of work, that he was carried, and provided with a salary for the public relations benefit to the companies concerned. Farmer denies emphatically that this was the case: "In almost every sales job I had it was on the basis of a retainer, which was a commitment to get to work, and then any other penny you made after that was commission that you earned by the actual sale. So there were no free lunches."

He set about learning the art of salesmanship by observing and asking questions as was his habit, but also by spending good money—£300 on one occasion—on training courses and programs. He took his work very seriously, but "I wasn't a hot-shot salesman because I didn't put the time in. So I never got magical figures, but I got enough to enable me to have a job every week."

He did not put the time in because the sales work never took priority over football. With this form of employment, and the support of his employers, he was free to knock off in time for official training, for his coaching when he took on the East Perth thirds, or for additional private training or fitness work if he felt the need.

He also made good use of the slack times when there were no customers to be dealt with. A football was always handy, and he began the pastime which became part of the Farmer lore—like Bradman with his stick and golf ball—handpassing the ball through the open car window time after time, gradually closing the window to make the target smaller and smaller.

The sales work was a congenial and suitable job for Farmer, and the move out of the blue-collar workforce a tangible benefit of his football prowess. He was able to top up his less-than-spectacular sales income through the money from football—both the contracted payments from East Perth and the three committeemen, and the fringe benefits.

The fringe benefits came in many forms, and there were endorsements for products from barley sugar to football boots. He was in regular demand as a guest on the media—both radio and the football previews and inquests that were a feature of Perth television from its earliest days in the late 1950s—and it was a standard arrangement for Farmer and the other player guests to receive a few pounds in the pocket for such appearances. In his last years with East Perth his byline would appear above a column in the *Sunday Times* at finals time, analysing the games.

He did the media work willingly, as a welcome source of pocket-money, and because it was expected of a star footballer. He observed the sportsman's public code of modesty, emphasis on the team not himself, praise and respect for the opposition—he would never bag an opposition team or individual. But he was not a natural media performer, lacking the jocular, bantering, self-deprecating manner the Australian public expects of its sporting heroes. Somehow his reserve came through, his lack of the footballer's extrovert nature.

Footballers did not have agents in those days to manage these matters or to maximise the returns from them. Farmer and Marlene sorted it all out themselves. There were always requests to appear at functions and promotions, some paid and some not. Stories developed about his refusal to appear at functions without payment, and some still circulate—people will tell of when he refused to speak at their junior football club trophy night some 55 years ago. The truth is that he did many such functions for nothing, but if he had accepted every invitation there would never have been an hour to spend on his own, or with his family. But in the absence of an agent or manager to pass the bad news, people sometimes remember his straightforward manner as rudeness or greed. When he did attend functions he preferred to do what was required of him and then go home, rather than hang around for the endless chat sessions that people hoped for and expected.

If he had been an acquisitive man, or one driven towards business success, he would have been perfectly placed to enter the world of private enterprise either on his own or as the public face of a business partnership. But Farmer's ambitions were largely confined to football and family life.

There is no doubt that his near-death experience hanging from the scaffolding at his new home contributed to this attitude. With those things that he undertook to do, he gave his utmost, but the trappings and trimmings and the expectations of others were no concern of his, and he was not interested in building castles in the clouds for the future. His interests and energies outside the demands of work and football were channelled into more immediate pleasures: good times with a small but close circle of friends, and an increasing passion for the breeding and racing of horses.

There is a long-standing relationship between the football and racing fraternities. Many of the movers and shakers of the football world, like Roy Hull, were heavily involved in racing. There is a long roll of football personalities who have owned and raced gallopers, trotters and greyhounds, and gone into racing in a big way on their retirement from football. Jockeys and trainers were often avid footy fans, and frequent attendees at club functions and, when business permitted, at matches.

Thus it was through football that Farmer became involved in the horses. His first transport, a secondhand motorbike, had been purchased with the proceeds of a winning bet. And as the years went by his interest increased. As with the speculation that surrounds public figures, the kernel of truth has been exaggerated over the years, and any number of people will tell you that he is a gambling addict. He readily concedes that like nearly all gamblers, he has come out behind over the years, with some good wins outweighed by the losses. But while the horses are a passion that consumed much of the pocketmoney he picked up along the way, there is nothing to suggest the excesses of addiction.

Part of the attraction, as with many punters, was the discipline of studying the form and the challenge of applying his intelligence to the terrible task of interpreting and predicting what this meant on a given day. Gambling can be an intellectual exercise that provides an immediate and acid test of one's skill. It was also an outlet, a visit to the races with some mates was something removed from football, and he could talk horses and form at the track or elsewhere on the same level as everyone else—he did not have to play the role of champion footballer. He also developed a love of the horses as creatures, and a fascination with the science of breeding.

Farmer may have been the single most important factor in East Perth's run of success, but although he was treated with great respect he never became a favourite son of the club in the way that Kilmurray did, or Derek Chadwick in later years. The reasons for this are many. It is a subject that most people refer to obliquely, but the common way of approaching it has become another part of the Farmer lore: "Pol would never buy you a drink," they say. He was seen to be deficient in that great symbol of Australian mateship and fraternity and all it represents: returning the other bloke's shout.

Jack Sheedy is one of the great purveyors of this story. It was the first anecdote he told when interviewed:

Polly was always pretty careful with a quid. His philosophy was that if he went up into the clubrooms for a drink after a game and a fellow said: "Would you like a drink Pol?" He'd say: "Yes." That would be a squash. Well if the bloke said: "Would you like another drink," you would normally think under the old procedure that he buys the first and you buy the second. But that wasn't Polly's thought. If he wanted to buy Polly a drink that was okay; if he wanted to buy another one it was better still, and he kept buying—not Pol, the other customer.

He told a similar yarn as the opening part of a speech at a function at Subiaco Oval in Farmer's honour. Told in the right tone, with a smile on the face, it is seen as all part of the fun, and Farmer has learned to take it in good grace. But depending on the teller and the circumstances, there are hidden messages of the man being a miser, a loner, somehow aloof.

The fact that he was a teetotaller who disliked sitting at a bar with a bunch of drinkers at the best of times was of no account. Nor the fact that if he did hang around at the bar he would be the favourite target of all the tired and emotional supporters wanting to chew his ear with their expert opinions and criticisms of the day's performance. It was regarded by many as part of a player's duty to the club to fraternise with the supporters in this way—the club even provided the players with bar vouchers for the purpose—and the good ockers of the footy world could not quite understand why anybody would not want to let their hair down after the game anyway.

Farmer believed that his duty to the club was performed on the field. He also took seriously, and valued greatly, the off-field bonds and mutual support between teammates. But he could never see any value in the boozy mateship of the bar, and despite Sheedy's analysis, when he did front he found the succession of squashes bought by supporters a burden not a pleasure. All he ever wanted to do after a game of footy, even in the bachelor days of the flat shared with Kilmurray and Hunt, was soak the inevitable aches and pains away in a hot bath.

His friend and rover, Kevin McGill, had a similar attitude, and is angered by the stories that have grown over the years: "I think it started off as a joke, and some people latched on to the joke who've got no right to. It needs kicking in the guts."

McGill remembers sitting in the bar, "being a non-drinker among some of the best drinkers around the town", nursing a soft drink as the others quaffed beers at speed, and then wanted to keep on partying long after the bar vouchers had run out:

> Sometimes after you've played a game of football you're totally drained. I was a rover and I had to run a lot, and Pol was a ruckman and he had to work a lot, too. After we came off the football field I reckon it would have been different for us than for a position player; [they] go hard, but after an hour they're right for a few drinks. For a couple of days after a game [we] were really drained ... After a game was finished it would be go home with your family, have your tea, and sit down.

Farmer's friends also insist that though he was careful with his money, he was generous in his private way, whether it be shouting celebrations when a big prize came his way, or slipping poor Constable Watts a couple of pounds under the table so that the two men and their wives could go out to a meal without embarrassment.

But the bar stories are only an example and a symptom of his relationship to and status within the club. Farmer was an individual, on and off the field. His early mentor at Maddington, Steve Jarvis, always felt that with his reflexes and agility Farmer would have made a great boxer. It is likely that Farmer's character traits and internal drive would have made him a great in any individual sport that suited his physical talents. Australian Rules, though, is the very antithesis of an individual sport. At 18 men, the on-field team is one of the largest in any sporting contest. And the unstructured, free-flowing nature of the game that so confounds the uninitiated spectator demands that all 18 combine with and react to each other almost instinctively. Yet Farmer, the reserved individualist was the ultimate team player.

Off the field, a sportsman in an individual event can withdraw to his own company, or that of a core group of friends and supporters. In a team and a sporting club there is a different expectation. Farmer followed his own mind and his own inclinations, which did not always coincide with the model people expected. And because he was so important to the team, and such a public figure, these things were noticed and talked about.

There was also no doubt an element of straightforward jealousy, a wish in some quarters that the team was not so reliant on Farmer. His pre-eminence is demonstrated by the fact that except for his injury-plagued season of 1958, he won the best and fairest award every year from 1954 until 1961. And in this context it is interesting to note that the year he left, the prize for the 1962 best and fairest was boosted from 10 guineas to 150.

There were still those in the club who felt East Perth had made Farmer, and he still owed them and the club for all he had achieved. In a subterranean, unspoken way this was tied up with his background, his childhood at Sister Kate's and his Aboriginal blood. In the hefty clippings file on Farmer in the library of West Australian Newspapers the words Aboriginal or native do not appear in connection with him until a piece written in 1987. Even the references to Sister Kate's talk only of an orphanage, not an institution for Aboriginal children. Yet it is clear from talking to his contemporaries that it was a talking point among the public and the football community of the time. Most often it comes out as an expression along the lines of "with his background no one begrudged him his success," and "no one resented the money he was making, it was good to see an Aborigine doing so well for himself."

But this slightly double-edged, paternal attitude perhaps also masked an amazement, even a resentment that he had outgrown them; East Perth and West Australian football needed Farmer more than he needed them. This was at a time when Aboriginal affairs policy and attitudes in the state were still geared towards control more than assimilation, when the *Sunday Times* ran features on the colour bar in Gnowangerup, a Wheatbelt town that had been called 'Australia's Little Rock' in a parliamentary inquiry—a town where Farmer would not have been served at the hotel or cafe if he were not a champion footballer.

Farmer himself never made an issue of the matter. It was not what he had been taught at Sister Kate's, and it was not his style, or the style of the times. His reported comment on a plane trip with the State team about being 'just another boong' but for football shows an awareness of the irony of his situation; but his attitude was that through the education and opportunities provided by Sister Kate's in the first instance, and then through his own initiative and ability, he had made a life for himself much better than it otherwise might have been—and that was the only responsibility he had, to care for himself and his family.

Sheedy says that when members of the Aboriginal community did try to make contact with Farmer, Kilmurray and Hunt, there was an arrangement between East Perth and the Department of Native Welfare to shield them. "Some were unsavoury types ... the president or the committee at the time did have a few people from the Aboriginal Welfare out at the ground keeping an eye on anyone that was there that they could handle or talk to."

Being of Aboriginal descent was an issue in Farmer's life, and in his football—both on and off the field. But apart from the on-field taunts thrown at him in anger or in vain attempts to upset him, it was always something beneath the surface that meant different things to different people.

8

FAREWELL TO THE WEST

A t East Perth the peak of Farmer's involvement came in 1960, when he was vice-captain, a member of the selection committee, and coach of the thirds team. But by the end of the year he had only one year of his contract to run. There was a sense that his time was almost up. The off-field people he had been closest to had left or were soon to leave. He never had the same relationship with Hec Strempel as with his predecessor Eric Sweet. Jack Lalor was about to be posted to Geraldton by the railways.

In 1961, Farmer began the process of disengaging himself. Kilmurray took over the vice-captain's role, and Farmer also resigned as coach of the thirds. Before the 1961 season began he sounded out the committee as to what their attitude would be to a clearance application at the end of the year. He was preparing for the big move to Victoria, but he did not lose sight of the main game, the football season that lay ahead.

The year began with West Perth expected to continue on from its success of 1960. Their line-up had been strengthened further by the arrival at Leederville Oval of big Ray Gabelich. Since leaving the west in 1954, Gabelich had grown huge, and carved a matching reputation as a ruckman at Collingwood. With he and Foley teaming in the ruck it was felt that Farmer might be up against too great a challenge.

There was a big turnover among the League coaches, with Victorians Peter Pianto and Dan Murray taking over at Claremont and Subiaco, and Haydn Bunton jnr coming from Tasmania to take charge of the wooden spooners, Swan Districts.

The opening round of fixtures saw a Grand Final replay between the Royals and the Cardinals, with the Cardinals as hot favourites and interest focussed on the Farmer-Gabelich duel. It was soon clear that Gabelich was overweight and out of condition, and Farmer "let it be known right from the start that he was not prepared to hand over the number one ruckman crown to either Gabelich or Foley."[1] He was best on ground in a three-goal win that got the Royals off to the start they wanted.

The season continued in the same vein for both Farmer and East Perth. The only hiccup came in the fifth round, with a four-goal loss to East Fremantle, which saw them lose top position on the ladder for the only time in the home and away round. Farmer outpointed Clarke in this game, and put in another top performance in the return match against West Perth.

The following week all attention was on Jack Sheedy. He was due to break the All-Australian record of Essendon's Dick Reynolds of 320 League games. The previous year it would have been a walkover, but the Swans were showing promise under Bunton, and were jostling with East Fremantle and Subiaco for the three positions behind East Perth on the ladder. The *Football Budget* actually selected Swans to win at Bassendean, and in a "fierce, slugging game"[2] they almost did—the Royals were seven points down with five minutes to go, but Sheedy rose to the occasion in typical style with a couple of crucial marks and a goal to save his day.

Farmer's good form continued. He played a "superlative third quarter"[3] against Perth, but when he injured his shoulder and came off in the final quarter, Perth mounted a charge that saw it go down by only five points. Two weeks later against East Fremantle he was best on ground as the Royals doubled Old Easts' score. The Royals had an 11-win, one-loss record and had left the others floundering in their wake. Farmer was leading Ray Sorrell in progressive voting for the major media awards.

Nineteen sixty-one was carnival year once again, with the ANFC taking the adventurous step of invading rugby country by holding the championships in Brisbane. The state squad was announced the night of the East Fremantle game, and was greeted with howls of derision in the press: too many out-of-form players, no wingmen, not enough specialist and key position players, obvious choices left out. Although the official selectors took the flak, Sheedy had played a decisive role in selection of the squad. He insisted on the inclusion of Gabelich, and another out-of-form Victorian at West Perth, Don Williams.

Interestingly, neither Farmer nor Clarke were offered leadership positions this time around. In Clarke's case it might have been his indifferent form. In Farmer's, the explanation probably lies in the differences of opinion he had been having with League officials, both publicly and privately, in the lead-up to the naming of the squad.

In May, the *Daily News* had run a story in which Farmer confirmed his intention to move to Victoria in 1962. The WANFL still required its state representatives to sign the two-year non-clearance contract that had become an issue when he signed with Richmond in 1955. When pressed on this occasion he said he would not be prepared to sign such a contract this time around. When asked if this meant he would be prepared to miss the carnival he replied that he preferred to cross his bridges when he came to them. The story simmered away while there were some behind-the-scenes negotiations, until shortly before the announcement of the squad he said that he would probably sign the contract, as it had never been enforced before.

Farmer was not the only one unhappy about the contract. Gabelich was having a terrible season and a terrible time in Perth; a real estate venture had gone bad on him. Jack O'Dea—who so nearly got Farmer to play for Perth, and was now the general manager there—had been appointed manager of the State team. He recalls that:

> About a day or so before we left some of the players hadn't signed their contracts. The one I'm thinking of is Ray Gabelich. He went to Frank Excell, who was the assistant manager and had the job of getting these contracts signed, and said that he didn't want to sign it and wouldn't sign it.

Excell asked him why, and he said: "I want to go to Collingwood next year." Frank came flying back to us and to Frank Fuhrmann, who was the chairman of selectors, and told us the story. We got our heads together, and we went to Gabelich and Fuhrmann said: "I'll stick my head on the line. If you agree to sign this form, and play to the best of your ability in the carnival side, I will guarantee that the League will give you a clearance next year." Gabelich said: "Okay, that's on." So he signed it.

John Colgan of South Fremantle had been made captain of the state team, but had to withdraw with an injury on the eve of departure. He was replaced by Haydn Bunton, only halfway through his first season of West Australian football. All in all, it was one of the less auspicious build-ups for a West Australian carnival side. When they arrived they did not get any happier. Their first training run at the Gabba ground had them gasping for breath from the dust they raised and from the humidity. Keith Slater hurt his ankle when he kicked the ground, and all agreed that they had never had to play football on such a rock-hard surface.

The Brisbane carnival was a straight four-team round-robin competition, with the Victorian Football Association not present. All games were played at the Gabba Oval, a round cricket ground, with a greyhound track around the perimeter. The dimensions were most unsuitable for football. The goals were only just over a kick from the centre, and the wings were extremely wide. The Queensland public did not exactly warm to the Aussie Rules invasion, and the small crowds failed to generate any atmosphere.

Western Australia easily defeated Tasmania, but went down to South Australia, while Victoria, as usual, was undefeated coming into the last game. It was a familiar scenario; as in 1956 and 1958, Western Australia had to beat the Victorians to win. Thanks to their percentage booster against Tasmania though, it was not a 20-goal margin needed this time. Nevertheless, the odds on offer were five to one—as good as a write-off in a two-horse race.

There was a four-day break until the decider on Sunday. The squad took a day off to hit the beach at Surfers Paradise. It was sorely needed, with many of them suffering shin soreness from the hard ground. Of them all, Farmer was the worst, with an infected cut on his left knee to make it worse. He was reported as saying that if it was a Saturday game he would not be able to come up. As it was, he only made it into the final game thanks to treatment with a mysterious white ointment provided by the Victorian team's trainer.

The Victorians, too, had their troubles. It was not regarded as an especially strong squad, and a number of their stars went into the carnival carrying injuries. Between this start, the hard grounds, and some softening up from South Australian strong man Neil Kerley, they only just mustered a side for the final game and had a number of men playing out of their natural positions.

The match began with Bunton pulling the old captain's trick of pointing to the end he wanted before the coin had come to rest, and the Victorian captain, Barassi, either fell for it, or was unconcerned enough to let him get away with it. Kicking with the wind, the West led by a goal at quarter-time, but in the second quarter the Victorians got away to a five-goal lead, and it seemed the old story would be repeated.

Farmer was struggling with injuries, and with the South Australian umpire who continually penalised him "for using the back of blonde follower John Schultz as a staircase when going for the knocks."[4] To quote Keith Slater, who spent most of the game on the bench: "He didn't play a really significant part, but Victoria played three men on him, which gave a few other guys a chance."

In the third quarter the game came alight. Sheedy swung Gabelich from centre half-back into the ruck to support Farmer and Clarke, who were changing from the forward pocket. Gabelich inspired his teammates in a performance that has become as legendary in the west as his solo run for Collingwood in the 1964 Grand Final in Victoria.

"Using his weight unsparingly [he] crashed through the opposing forwards, spreading them all over the field."[5] He "took the Victorians on single-handedly," according to John Todd, "and gave the inspiration to us guys that they were beatable." Mal Atwell sent Ron Barassi to the ground a few times. John Peck of Hawthorn left the field with a cut to the head. The West lost vice-captain John Todd with a bruised chest. Denis Marshall, the young tyro from Claremont, took over from Gabelich at centre half-back, and with Mal Atwell, led a desperate defence. Clarke had an eyelid almost torn off, but played on. With passions and tempo rising the West clawed back to within three points at the last break, but Victoria had the breeze in the last quarter, and still seemed to be the winners. Early in the last quarter Sorrell, who had played a big part in the third-quarter comeback, went down with what was thought to be a broken leg. Don Williams, playing with a broken nose, was swung into the centre, and played brilliantly. The West hit the front. Clarke had the pleasure of listening to the Victorians "squabbling among themselves. We only ever knew Victorians when they were winning [and] everything was good. But they squealed and abused each other the same as we did when we got beat."

Nicholls had to go off for Victoria, then their wingman, Bluey Adams, turned an ankle, and when he limped off Victoria were down to seventeen men. The lead changed hands a couple of times, and the scribes were furiously working out percentages. With two minutes to go, Joe Fanchi, the West Perth rover who had been a controversial selection, and had come on as a reserve to replace Todd, kicked a goal that put the West nine points up. Williams took a screamer in the centre of the ground as the siren went, and jubilation broke out among the West Australians. They had done the impossible.

The Brisbane carnival remains a high point in West Australian football history, and in the careers of the players involved, including Farmer. Beating Victoria was the holy grail—a cherished dream that they never quite expected to achieve. If ever Farmer was tempted to break his teetotal habits it might have been in the riotous celebrations that evening.

Gabelich was the acknowledged hero of the hour. None minded the irony that his performance had been sparked by the desire to secure a smooth return to Victoria. He won the Simpson Medal as the West's best player of the carnival, and was named at centre half-back in the All-Australian side, which also included Clarke in the first ruck, Todd, Sorrell as a reserve again, and Farmer in a forward pocket.

The team was mobbed by an unprecedented crowd of 6000 people when it arrived at Perth airport on the Monday night, and there was a parade through the streets and a civic reception. As a sporting triumph for the citizens of the west, it remained unsurpassed until the America's Cup win of 1983. In football terms it remained the peak until the West Coast Eagles took out the 1992 AFL premiership.

There was a price to pay for the sweetness of the Brisbane victory. Peter Pianto, who worked at the same car dealership as Farmer, writing in his column in the *Sunday Times*, reported Farmer as describing the game as a bloodbath, "as he limped painfully around on badly lacerated and poisoned knees, and carefully guarded other bruises."[6] He did miss some training, going up to Geraldton for a few days, but he played on each Saturday, and put in some very quiet performances.

He showed some form in his fourth game back against Subiaco, where East Perth's 12-game winning streak came to an end. The next game was the third and last for the season against East Fremantle, and there was some speculation that the Royals might be in for a repeat of their 1959 end-of-season slump. Such fears were quickly put to rest by a 29-point win, with Farmer and Clarke each named as their side's best player in the *Football Budget*. Farmer finished the season strongly with best-on-ground games against Claremont and South Fremantle. East Perth finished with a 19-win, two-loss record, six games clear of Swan Districts, which snuck into second place on the last day.

The *Sunday Times* and *Daily News* awards both had the same finishing order for the top three places, Farmer winning ahead of Haydn Bunton and Ray Sorrell. These wins brought Farmer prizes totalling £600 plus bonuses, and he also won a trip for two to Surfers Paradise in a radio station award. It was thought that the same three would fight out the Sandover, with Farmer the clear favourite, though Perth centre half-back, Neville Beard, also had his fanciers.

On the night Farmer polled 16 votes to finish fourth, six behind Beard who beat Sorrell on a count back, and three behind Bunton. He had actually expected to win it that year, which would have put him on a par with Haydn Bunton senior and Merv McIntosh, and remembers the disappointment. No doubt he felt it would be an appropriate note on which to depart.

Subiaco recorded an impressive five-goal win over East Fremantle in the first semi-final. The second semi was a disappointment as a spectacle, with East Perth recording a 14-goals-to-seven win over a seemingly disorganised, lacklustre Swans. The old team of Farmer and Kilmurray got the nod from most writers as the Royals' best players.

The same writers had the premiership flag safely in East Perth's hands already, with Subiaco warm favourites to oust Swans from the race in the preliminary final. The first leg of this prediction appeared likely to be vindicated when Subiaco got out to a big lead, but an eight-goal final quarter, including four from a young Bill Walker in his debut season as second rover to Bunton, saw the Swans into the Grand Final.

Swan Districts, the last of the eight teams to enter the competition in 1934, had been perennial battlers. This was their first Grand Final, and public sentiment swung behind them in a huge way, making the sympathy of 1959 for Subiaco look pale by comparison. Out in the heartland of their support base excitement was almost hysterical. The Grand Final week press was describing it as the most exciting season in the west, with the carnival victory, the West Perth flop and Swans' surge from last year's wooden spoon, and sensational mid-season resignations of coaches Marsh of East Fremantle and Dick Miller of Perth. All that was needed to cap it off was a Swans premiership. But it was impossible to find anyone willing to actually predict that it would happen.

On the Tuesday before the game the coverage took a new twist when the *West Australian* carried a piece headed "East Perth Will Not Give Away Its Ruck Champion". The article intimated that East Perth, contrary to the public impression, had indicated that it was not under any obligation to release Farmer to play in Victoria at the end of the 1961 season. Clearly the writer had been talking to people within the East Perth hierarchy. The sting in the tail came in a paragraph that revealed the attitude of his detractors within the club:

> Some supporters of East Perth say they would like to see their team try to win the match without Farmer—"just to prove that we have a great all-round side that does not depend on one man to show the way." [7]

On a Friday about six weeks before the Grand Final Haydn Bunton had been having a drink at the City Hotel with Len Owens. Owens was no longer writing football, but retained his interest, and was known as a passionate East Perth supporter. According to Owens, Bunton told him, "You blokes will beat us in the second semi, but we'll beat you in the Grand Final."

'How do you work that out?" asked Owens.

'Well you can do things in Grand Finals you can't do in other games."

Bunton was born with football in his veins. His father was the most decorated footballer the game has known, with three Brownlow and three Sandover Medals. Bunton jnr overcame polio to become both a brilliant rover and a natural football leader. He became captain-coach of South Australian club Norwood in 1957 at the age of 20. In 1959 in Tasmania, where he had gone to coach, he suffered injuries in a car accident that had doctors saying he might not walk again. At 24 he came to Perth to take over the wooden spooners, and before the Grand Final had already covered himself in glory by lifting them to second place, by his outstanding play, and by captaining the triumphant carnival side.

As a coach, Bunton was a strategist who was ambitious enough in his debut year in the west to target one game in the year—the Grand Final. His side had a good following division, with himself and Walker as rovers, and a class ruckman in Keith Slater supported by the rugged and competent pair of Cyril Litterick and Fred Castledine. He had brought Max Kelleher, a tough centre-man, over from Tasmania with him, and had a very talented young centre half-back in Ken Bagley who was turning 21 on Grand Final day. Beyond this group though, it is fair to say that the rest of the team were somewhere between fair and average players; good, honest footballers whom Bunton moulded into a team that would have a real go.

Bunton and his lieutenants knew that they could not match the class of East Perth, and knew that if East Perth played to its capacity they would win. The way both Bunton and Slater have put it is that they knew that they did not have two wins against East Perth in them. So they had to do two things; lull the Royals into a false sense of security, and save any special tactics they had devised for the last shot.

FAREWELL TO THE WEST

On the day, East Perth won the reserves premiership as an appetiser. When the teams appeared for the main game, Sheedy won the toss and elected to kick into the breeze—the previous year all four final-round games had been won by the side that lost the toss and kicked into the wind.

Swans tore into the football from the beginning, and into East Perth, which seemed to be unsettled—not quite on song. It was four goals to one at quarter-time, and could have been more, but it was expected that East Perth would hit back with the breeze. Instead Swans got the first two of the second quarter to go to a five-goal break. East Perth clawed back to within seven points late in the quarter, but went to the half-time break trailing by 13. They were playing without system and without rhythm—because Farmer was just not firing. Gus Glendinning had replaced Jack Lalor as chairman of selectors and Sheedy's off-field lieutenant. He recalls:

> At half-time Sheedy was ropeable. He said: "What are we going to do with the big bastard?" I said: "Look Jack, leave him there mate, and don't get on his back. Leave him. There's no way he'll play like this in the second half."

Those who had wanted to prove that East Perth could win without Farmer were getting their chance, and were discovering it to be not very palatable.

The two rival coaches, Sheedy and Bunton, sat down together 30 years later and discussed what had happened that day. "I thought Slater beat Farmer pointless," said Sheedy. "... Did you have a plan that day to beat Farmer?"

"Yeah," replied Bunton. "Fred [Castledine] had to come in and get hold—get his left arm out of the way. Once he had that arm [up in the air], that was it. Keith Slater was coming in on his right, and Castledine was getting in the way of that arm before he could get it up. The umpire didn't pick it up. I don't know whether it was interference, because he didn't actually hold on to it—just sort of got in the way and hooked it. We had rehearsed this."

There was another element to the strategy as well, that Slater worked out with Castledine and Litterick. Slater had been battling Farmer since his debut game in 1955, when Farmer had him in tears at half-time and he responded by coming out and knocking Farmer down. These clashes were the benchmark of his season. "I became very determined against Polly.

I wasn't in Polly's class, but he was the challenge ... I don't think anyone ever beat Polly Farmer, what you hoped to do against Polly was make a good contest."

On this day they decided to try a new tactic:

> Polly always liked to know where his opposite number was ... at the last moment he would look to see where you were, so he could jump into you and take the ball. We didn't allow him to do that in the '61 Grand Final. We got behind him, and as the umpire was bouncing the ball we came in fast past him ... My job was to get behind Polly, where he couldn't see me. If he wanted to see me he had to look behind. And when he looked behind, which he always did, you ran past him and then propped, and then you went again. And it worked. But we never tried that in the second semi. That was all saved up for one game.

He also added the comment that: "I got away with a few illegal things in the Grand Final of '61. That's the luck of the draw."

So Farmer had Slater behind, and running round his right side, while Castledine and Litterick did all in their power to interfere with his left arm that he used to grab or knock the ball. He was used to encountering—and usually countering—such sophisticated tactics, but on this day he could not.

Swans kicked away again at the start of the third quarter, and from then on the margin hovered between three and five goals. Until near the end, there was always the sense that the Royals would start to fire. The game never seemed quite out of their reach, but the spark would not come.

Swans won by four goals. Bunton was chaired from the ground with blood streaming from a cut below his eye, and fists clenched in a triumphant salute. For Slater, it was his greatest moment in a distinguished sporting career. He won the Simpson Medal for his performance, and even greater plaudits when it was revealed that he had played the whole game with a cracked rib.

It is interesting to note in hindsight that if things had gone the way Keith Slater had hoped, he would not have been playing for Swans in 1961. A press report after the Grand Final claimed that "earlier this year [he] wasn't at all sure he wanted to go back to [Swan Districts]."[8] His very first preference though would have been to be in England with Richie Benaud's cricket team contesting the Ashes. Slater opened the bowling for Western Australia in the Sheffield Shield, and had played test cricket for Australia. He had been thought a real chance for the Ashes tour, which did not conclude until mid-September, but missed selection

For Farmer it was a bitter end to his time with East Perth, and a day that he still ruminates over. He is quick to praise Slater, and readily concedes that he was clearly beaten on the day, but insists that he did not actually play a bad game, as some claim. The statistics bear him out. Many lesser players would describe four marks, 11 kicks and eight handballs as a reasonable performance, and some of his teammates did considerably worse than this. But on the Farmer scale of ten it was perhaps a five, not the nine he and others would expect in a Grand Final. He knows that he should have done better, that he was capable of overcoming the tactics employed against him. He can only say that on the day he did not prepare himself properly, for some reason, he did not get himself into that possessed state in which he played his best football.

To most of his fans and most of the football world his performance was inexplicable. Some rumours flew around that he had been bribed to lie down, but anyone who has had anything to do with him over the years is contemptuous of the story. Peter Pianto both raises and refutes this matter:

> A lot of people thought Polly played dead, but no way. I wouldn't believe that ever of Polly. But there were people that did think that way—I spoke to quite a lot after [the game]. I said, "OK, you should have been here [at Youngs where they both worked] on the Monday morning, and you'd know whether he played dead or not." He was bloody upset, and he was bloody wild. Same as he was after [Geelong] lost the Grand Final in 1967.

Farmer blames no one but himself for his own lack of preparation, but he also says that the team as a whole was not prepared. In the only criticism that he makes of Sheedy, he says:

> Apart from the fact that all the players have got to accept responsibility for losing, the coach has got to as well. [He has] to make them ask and think what happens when you get beaten, but that never happened ... At no stage did

anyone say there's a chance that this team we're playing can beat us. That was all that we needed, just the fear of defeat ... The players went out onto the field expecting to win, but not taking it on themselves to lead the way.

It was a terrible note on which to finish the first major phase of Farmer's career, although in a perverse way, by showing in the most dramatic possible way the consequences of a rare failure, it underlined the extent of his greatness. Only in the hearts of the bitter or the small-minded could it detract from the phenomenal contribution he had made to the East Perth Football Club, and the Western Australian National Football League and its competition.

Immediately after the Grand Final, Farmer gave his full attention to the matter of the move to Victoria. This had been the plan from the time he decided during the previous summer that 1961 would be his last year in the west. He had told everyone—East Perth, League officials, the ever-curious and endlessly persistent media, and the VFL clubs who courted him—to wait until the West Australian season was over.

When his intentions had first been publicly confirmed in May, during the build-up to the Brisbane carnival, there was an immediate rush of interest from the VFL, with letters coming from Richmond and a number of other clubs trying to arrange meetings with him before, during or after the carnival.

Richmond went so far as to send Des Rowe and committee member Ron Garraway over to Perth to see Farmer before other clubs could get to him in Brisbane. "We took a stack of money with us, Ron and I," says Rowe, but Farmer remained non-committal. By carnival time the message had got through, and he was left to play football and nurse his sore shins.

While he was playing his cards very close to his chest, Farmer was thinking hard about his options. He developed a very particular set of criteria. He did not want to walk into one of the powerhouse clubs. He wanted to be, and to be seen as, a key ingredient in building the premiership team:

I wanted to get with a club that had struggled and were looking to achieve some sort of success, and I wanted really to be a part of the success story.

To me, with a team that's already successful, I don't feel I'm contributing, all I'm doing is sustaining ... I had a lot of confidence in my own ability. All the clubs that I've been to were struggling when I went to them ... I suppose it was just pride, wanting to be part of a battling side that had a chance and offering them something.

He was also keeping his eyes open and his ears to the ground. He had always followed the ups and downs of the Victorian competition, like all in the football world, but throughout 1961 he paid specially close attention, avidly reading the back pages of the Melbourne *Sun*. Hawthorn had beaten Footscray in the VFL Grand Final on the day of East Perth's second semi victory over Swans, and for this reason, if no other, had been ruled out under Farmer's criteria. Richmond did not qualify "because I wanted to help a team to succeed, but there had to be some sort of signs that they had the nucleus of a good side, and I don't think Richmond had that nucleus."

As the season drew to a close two clubs began to loom large in his thoughts. St Kilda were in their first year under Allan Jeans, who at 27 was believed to be the youngest non-playing coach in the history of the VFL. He took them to fourth place, and their first finals appearance since 1939. As he had predicted to Farmer, back in 1958, Bob Davis was now coaching Geelong. In two years he had improved the Cats position on the ladder from 10th to ninth in 1960, and then to sixth in 1961, with only a loss to Footscray in the last game robbing them of a berth in the first semi-final. According to Davis they were a better team than the premiers, Hawthorn, except for their lack of a class ruckman.

These were the two clubs that Farmer decided had the potential and the attitude that he desired. He was one of the few footballers over the years fortunate enough or good enough to be in a situation to exercise such a level of choice on their entry to the premier competition.

St Kilda was one of the clubs that had made mid-season approaches, and had gone so far as to send him a detailed offer. Farmer had discussed this offer with Peter Pianto, a Geelong man, who extolled the virtues of his old club, and the small-town, country atmosphere of Geelong. Pianto suggested that he write to Geelong club secretary, Leo O'Brien, giving details of the

St Kilda offer, and Farmer quietly agreed. As Pianto subsequently realised, it was a shrewd way for Farmer to let Geelong know what was going on, and what they were competing against.

It would seem that O'Brien had this information well before Geelong first approached Farmer. When they did make contact, it was during the middle of the West Australian finals round. Nine days before the Grand Final a story appeared in the *West Australian* reporting that Geelong was chasing Farmer and Denis Marshall. Bob Davis was quoted as saying that Marshall was on his way to Melbourne for talks, and Farmer had agreed to be a guest of the club on its end-of-season trip to Surfers Paradise. This story had in turn prompted the Grand Final week report about East Perth fighting to hang on to him.

Two days after the Grand Final, with the bitter taste of the defeat still strong in him, as Pianto recalls, Farmer flew out of Perth for Surfers Paradise. There was no hard sell, both sides treated it as an informal, getting-to-know-you exercise. Farmer was able to unwind from the long months of football with days on the beach, swimming, lazing, playing touch rugby, and a couple of trips to the races, and simultaneously make his own quiet assessments of the players and officials of the club.

Davis did sound him out about his intentions on the eve of their departure, and he left Surfers Paradise convinced he had the deal sewn up. But Davis, in his usual style, had been very vague as to the specifics, and Farmer had not committed himself. Within five days of getting home, he was on the plane again, this time with Marlene, going to Melbourne as a guest of St Kilda. The picture of them being met at Essendon airport by St Kilda president, Graham Huggins, sent waves of panic through the Geelong camp. St Kilda was more professional in its approach. Their offer was on the table, and they took Farmer to see one of the city's major Holden dealers about a sales job.

In an episode that has entered Geelong folklore in a dozen different variations of the great ambush story, the Davis-O'Brien connection was at work, trying to lure him out of the clutches of the Saints. O'Brien had staked out the George Hotel in the main street of St Kilda, where the Farmers were staying. According to Farmer:

He tried to get in there, but the hotel staff weren't giving anything away. So Leo was sort of hidden in his car outside the front door, waiting for the opportunity to get hold of me ... He caught us, Marl and I, and arranged for us to go down to Geelong while we there at the expense of St Kilda, which I didn't think was very fair, but nevertheless we went.

O'Brien drove them halfway, through Melbourne's industrial western suburbs to Laverton, where they met Davis. To add a touch of farce, Farmer had to push Davis' car to get it started. But they had a day in Davis' company inspecting Geelong and the football club, before making it back to the George by nightfall.

All these comings and goings, apart from the secret day trip to Geelong, took place in the full glare of media coverage and speculation. The Farmers returned to Perth in the last week of October promising St Kilda that they would announce their decision within a week.

A t the time Farmer was planning the move to Victoria new horizons and models were beginning to open up for professional sportsmen in Australia. If there is a scale in such things that moves from true-blue amateurism, through 'shamateur' status in all its shades, to semi-professional and professional, different sports were at different stages, but the trend in all major sports was progressing along the scale. Probably no sports within Australia were fully professional in the sense that an athlete could make a living from competition alone, but among elite athletes there was a growing expectation of reasonable recompense for their skills and efforts. With his five-year contract at East Perth, Farmer had been a trendsetter in Western Australia, but more and more, throughout the sporting world, under-the-table deals were being either replaced or supplemented by upfront deals.

What was Farmer worth? It was a question that exercised many minds. The VFL's Coulter Law that governed player payments and transfers appeared to impose a limit of £15 per match, plus additional payments from provident funds on retirement. Ross Elliott of the *Daily News*, writing in the nationally distributed *Sport Magazine* in September, ignored such technicalities in a piece headed 'Farmer Wants Lettuce!' He provided a glowing resume of Farmer's skills and achievements, and speculated that Melbourne clubs were prepared to offer up to £100 a week. For Farmer, wrote Elliott, football was business pure and simple, and he would not hesitate to sell himself to the highest bidder.

But Elliott was wrong. Certainly, Farmer was not going to sell his services cheaply, but his football ambitions and sense of what he wanted to achieve were a greater priority. He had narrowed his choice down to two clubs on this basis, before even considering financial factors. And when it came down to money, Farmer says: "If it came to be just a business transaction, I'm sure we should have gone to St Kilda, because in terms of the package being offered it was overall substantially greater." This is confirmed by Pianto, who saw the St Kilda offer, and later became familiar with the terms Farmer got from Geelong.

In the end it was primarily a lifestyle decision, and in this regard Geelong probably owes much to Marlene and Brett, who was still at that stage the Farmers' only child. "St Kilda in those days [seemed to be] a den of iniquity. I'm not saying that it was, but it appeared to be ... It really was a question of making up in our minds whether we wanted to live in Melbourne or Geelong [and] the thought of going to a country town appealed to me more."

On 30 October, Farmer rang Geelong and St Kilda to inform them of his decision, and then met with the East Perth committee to formally advise them that he would be seeking a clearance to Geelong. It was headline news on the back pages of the next morning's papers in both Perth and Melbourne.

The next day Davis and O'Brien arrived in Perth. Their first step was to secure Farmer's signature on the official VFL Form Four, which would tie him to Geelong. But this was not as straightforward as they had hoped. Farmer had called in his old friend, the former East Perth secretary, Eric Sweet, to assist him in the negotiations. They met in Sweet's office, and Davis and O'Brien laid out the terms of their offer. "They said: 'We'll rig up a contract'," recalls Sweet. "I said: 'No, you won't rig up a contract at all. If anybody's going to rig a contract up it will be a solicitor. And it will be my solicitor that will do it.'"

Sweet was firm in his advice to Farmer that the contract be finalised before he committed himself. Sweet went to his solicitors, and the urgent request for assistance caused some consternation in the legal offices, where they had no experience in such contracts. Senior partners were consulted, and some precedents found from the world of English soccer. East Perth vice-president, Jack Gabbedy, was consulted on some of the financial detail, and eventually a draft was finalised. The Geelong pair agreed to the terms, and undertook to get it signed by their club authorities.

In essence, the terms of the contract provided for a base rate of £1000 a year, plus payment of the rental on his accommodation, plus a guarantee of a job with a certain level of income. It was certainly a substantial contract in terms of the football market, but it was way under some of the wilder speculation that had circulated, and a good deal less than he could have attracted if he had encouraged the Melbourne clubs into a bidding war.

With the contract drawn up, and agreed to in principle, Farmer signed the Form Four. He was now tied to Geelong, but the saga had only just begun.

That night Davis and O'Brien met with the East Perth committee to formally request a clearance. They presented their case, then, according to Davis:

> Fred Book stood up. I'll never forget it. He said: "We're quite happy to clear Graham Farmer." I looked at Leo, and I said: "We've done it again, what a beauty." Then Fred Book said: "We're quite happy to clear him for £2000." We'd never heard of such a thing. We'd never paid for anyone. I jumped up and said: "You're wasting our time." This little fellow, [Jim] del Piano said: "And you're wasting our bloody time too." And that was it.

Geelong's president, Jack Jennings, summoned his coach and secretary back to Victoria via the sports pages of the Melbourne papers, and they returned without having a second scheduled meeting with the East Perth committee.

On the surface things seemed bleak. VFL clubs were not allowed to pay transfer fees, under the provisions of the Coulter Law. East Perth were adamant that there would be no clearance without payment, and the WANFL would not even consider a waiver of their two-year contract with Farmer without East Perth's endorsement. But one important point had become clear—as far as East Perth was concerned a clearance was a possibility, at a price. With this as a starting point, all things became possible.

Farmer had waited for Davis and O'Brien back at their rooms at the Palace Hotel the night they met with the East Perth committee. He says they were "completely white faced and horrified" when they returned to give him the news. While acknowledging that the club "were entitled to negotiate fairly for themselves ... I was disappointed because I thought I'd given them good service, but all it did was make me more determined to go." He was angry as well as disappointed, and swore that he would never play for East Perth again.

He made his intentions clear publicly, announcing that he was putting his house on the market, and that he was moving to Geelong at the end of the year. As far as he was concerned he would play in the VFL in 1962, it was up to the clubs and the authorities to sort out their differences. For the third time in a month he flew out of Perth, this time returning to Surfers Paradise with Marlene and Brett, taking up the radio prize he had won. On the way home they spent four days in Geelong, laying the groundwork for the move over. Farmer did the first of many interviews with the Geelong *Advertiser*, and had talks with a car dealer in the town about a sales job.

As the summer months rolled by there was a constant stream of public reports and comments, allegations and speculations flowing back and forth across the Nullarbor, while behind the scenes negotiations and manoeuvring continued. Consideration of Farmer's first application in late November for a release from his two-year contract with the WANFL was deferred, with President Pat Rodriguez saying there was no need to hurry things. This did not stop the Farmers making the move east in the first week of the new year. The timing of the move was dictated by the need to fulfil a 13-week residential requirement before he would be eligible to play with Geelong.

In the lead-up to the next WANFL meeting in January, Perth secretary, Jack O'Dea, indicated that he would move for Farmer to be released from the contract. This was an indication of the chickens set loose before the Brisbane carnival coming home to roost. For Farmer's situation was being linked to that of Ray Gabelich, who was by now also living back in Victoria, preparing for a season with Collingwood. While West Perth was willing to let Gabelich go, O'Dea and others had to ensure the WANFL would waive the contract, to keep the promise they had made to him.

At the meeting Merv Cowan of East Fremantle made the move foreshadowed by O'Dea, for all state representatives to be released from the contract. Once again a decision was deferred. But Rodriguez had no hesitation in launching an attack on Farmer in the press:

> Farmer came to me early last year and asked for advice whether or not he should sign the contract because he planned to go to Victoria. I would not advise him but said ... "If you don't sign you won't go to Brisbane and the decision is up to you". I emphasised that no player could hope for any special treatment if he signed the contract and later wanted to be released from it. After a while Farmer said he would sign. Later he said I had misled him.[9]

Whatever had passed between the two men, Rodriguez's claim to the high moral ground was seriously undermined by the deal that had been done in the Gabelich case. At this stage East Perth was avoiding fire by saying it could not deal with Farmer's case until the League made a decision, while League officials were hinting that it would be easier for them if East Perth took a clear stance one way or the other. East Perth's tune changed when the League met again late in February. The numbers were in favour of the Cowan resolution, and if it went through, there was the possibility that Farmer could escape their clutches without them getting any return. They moved a successful amendment against a universal waiver of the contract, gaining instead agreement that a waiver could be considered in particular cases, and only when sponsored by the players club. Under these arrangements West Perth quickly processed a clearance for Gabelich, and though East Perth could no longer shelter behind the League, they now held the whip hand.

By now the 1962 season was rapidly approaching, but still the uncertainty continued. East Perth was waiting for its money. The messages were becoming blunter, with Fred Book reported in Melbourne as saying that it would be Geelong's fault if he did not play, and that "Geelong knows what is required, and unless it plays ball, Farmer will not appear in Victoria."[10]

Davis and O'Brien were out hustling. Davis was telling anyone who would listen that with Farmer in the side they would win the premiership. And in the early practice matches at Kardinia Oval Farmer's sensational form gave every indication that this could be true. Eventually a dairy farmer friend of club official Tom Morrow agreed to put up some cash, so that East Perth might be satisfied without Geelong getting its hands dirty. Negotiations with East Perth began in earnest.

Emissaries were sent to Perth and offers made. An East Perth committee meeting on a Wednesday night continued into the small hours of the morning, but secretary Strempel would only tell the press that the matter was still under consideration. According to subsequent press reports, coded telegrams were sent back to Geelong, producing a flurry of activity. A private loan of £500 was arranged and a bank-draft sent to Perth. Three days later, meeting after East Perth's final practice game, the committee accepted a cash offer of £1500. At 9 o'clock on a Saturday night on the last day of March an operator telephoned Farmer with the text of a telegram: "Meeting tonight recommended your clearance to Victoria. Good Luck. H. Strempel."

Farmer's confidence had been vindicated. Four days later the formality of a clearance from the WANFL came through. He was a Geelong player.

9

GREAT EXPECTATIONS

For six or seven months of the year a mad contagion runs through the Press,
TV, radio and everyday life. Melbourne has no summer—only a period
of hibernation between football seasons.[1]

If football is king in the Perth winters, in Melbourne it is God. The
city is famed for its sporting passions, with a record of turning out for
high-class sport—be it cricket, tennis, golf or horseracing—in numbers
unparalleled anywhere in the world on a per capita basis. But footy occupies
a special place in the hearts and minds of the populace. Melbourne's own
game, it is entwined in the life of the city and the state at every level from
the street corner and factory floor to the boardroom and the Bourse.

Academics could both analyse the sport—and be taken seriously—
and lose themselves in the passion of a Saturday afternoon at the game.
Major artists, from Arthur Streeton on through to Noel Counihan, found
inspiration in football, along with playwrights, and poets like Bruce Dawe
in his poem *Life Cycle:*[2]

When children are born in Victoria
they are wrapped in the club-colours, laid in beribboned cots,

having already commenced a lifetime's barracking.

...

the tides of life will be the tides of the team's fortunes

— the reckless proposal after the one point win,

the wedding and the honeymoon after the Grand Final.

In the early 1960s, this grip of football on life in Victoria was as strong as ever. Some had predicted that the introduction of television in the late 1950s would weaken its grip, but live broadcasts of the final quarters, then Saturday night replays on all stations, and a feast of pre- and post-match panel shows only proved that you could not have too much of a good thing, and attendances remained as high as ever.

The 1961 Grand Final was fought out between Hawthorn and Footscray, two of the League's unfashionable and least successful teams, with 'Kennedy's Commandos' recording Hawthorn's first premiership win. This was in marked contrast to the previous year when the two traditional titans, Melbourne and Collingwood, had clashed in Melbourne's seventh straight Grand Final for five premierships. Collingwood had been the victim on three occasions, but had broken through against the odds in 1958 to interrupt the sequence of Demon triumphs.

Victorian football had always been physically tougher than in the west or anywhere else. This could be seen in everything from the periodic flare-ups of crowd violence that marked football history in Melbourne, through the on-field brawls and the antics of the enforcers who were included in most teams, and the preparedness to shirt-front or run through the opposition, to the way players were prepared to attack the ball. One history of the game titles the chapter covering the period from 1946 to 1960 "Knucklemen and Bond Slaves"[3], and though others dispute his assessment, Jack Dyer has described the early 1960s as "the years of the bash", when "the tough enforcer-type player thrived. Each week players would go down clutching their heads. The stretcher was a very common sight during these rugged years. It was an aftermath of the great Melbourne reign ... most of the clubs thought that these roughhouse tactics were the only means of success."[4]

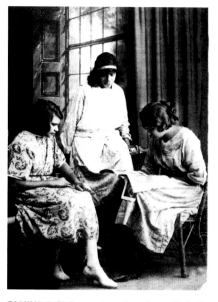

CHEEKY: A young Farmer in Greenbush days.
(FAMILY COLLECTION)

FAMILY: (L-R) Farmer's mother, Eva, with Dolly Wheeler and Emily Keen in the 1920s.
(THE SOUTH WEST ABORIGINAL STUDIES COLLECTION, DEPT OF ABORIGINAL PROGRAMS, EDITH COWAN UNIVERSITY)

PREMIERS: Farmer (top) with Ted Kilmurray, another "graduate" of Sister Kate's, in the Maddington 1952 premiership team photo.
(FAMILY COLLECTION)

→ **EARLY SUCCESS:** The apprentice mechanic in his final year at Winterbottom's. This photo was published in June 1955 with a story speculating accurately that he would be chosen to make his debut with the state side. (FAMILY COLLECTION)

FLYING HIGH: Early days at East Perth. The skills that would become familiar were clearly on show in this classic mark in a match against Claremont. (FAMILY COLLECTION)

PROUD: Farmer posing in his WA guernsey before his first representative game for the Sandgropers.
(FAMILY COLLECTION)

WINNER: Farmer in the West Australian dressing room at Subiaco Oval during the 1956 carnival, en route to the Tassie Medal. As was the custom at the time, he had swapped guernseys with his Victorian opponent. Behind him is full-forward John Gerovich, who was selected with Farmer in the All-Australian team. At 21, Farmer still looks too lean and youthful to be able to compete as he did against the hardened Victorian ruck brigade. (FAMILY COLLECTION)

WORKING HARD: A determined man. Farmer works out in February 1963, preparing to come back from the knee injury. For the rest of his career it was a daily routine, designed to strengthen the leg muscles that supported the knee, and to add strength and bulk to his body. (FAMILY COLLECTION)

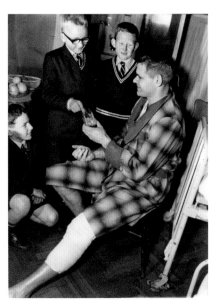

FAN FAVOURITE: Throughout his career, Farmer was always a fan favourite and always available to sign autographs, even during hospital time! (FAMILY COLLECTION)

TECHNIQUE: Farmer was a tremendous kick of the football with a classic style, as this photograph, taken during training with the Victorian team, clearly shows. (FAMILY COLLECTION)

CELEBRATION TIME: The moment that climaxed celebrations in Geelong the night of the 1963 premiership. Farmer holds the cup high on the balcony of the Geelong Town Hall. On his right is full-back Roy West.
(PHOTO BY NEWS LTD / NEWSPIX)

↑ **CHAMPS ALL:** "He would get between his opponents and the ball … and give us an easy ride … and we would look like the stars," recalls John Newman. L-R: Newman, Farmer, John Nicholls, April 1965. (PHOTO BY NEWS LTD / NEWSPIX)

HANDBALL WIZARD: Classic posed photo from Farmer's heyday in Victoria. His handball skills were legendary, so why not set up a shot for him to shoot the ball through a half-closed car window! (FAMILY COLLECTION)

PANIC: Farmer is carried from the field after hurting his bad knee against North Melbourne in 1966. With the finals only two weeks away, the sight caused panic in the Geelong camp, (FAMILY COLLECTION)

GAVE HIS ALL: The exhaustion shows as Farmer leaves the ground after a game. He would lose up to six pounds (2.7kg) in weight during the course of a game. (FAMILY COLLECTION)

The superstar of the competition was Melbourne captain, Ron Barassi. It has often been said that Barassi had relatively little natural ability—some go so far as to say, with tongue slightly in cheek, that he could not run, could not kick and could not handpass. But under the guidance of his coach and personal mentor, Norm Smith, he virtually created and perfected the role of ruck-rover, and through sheer force of personality, absolute dedication, and an intimidating presence, he established himself as a pre-eminent player and leader. He epitomised the qualities the football fans most loved and admired. Barassi was not one of the 'enforcer types'. To use a phrase that has come into vogue since then, he was a player who was hard at the ball. The characteristic of his play most commented on was his ability to break open packs.

Dyer names Hawthorn under John Kennedy as the main exponent of the brand of football he describes. Kennedy and his players would no doubt take exception to the comment, but they did pride themselves on being tough. The 'Kennedy's Commandos' tag was bestowed when they underwent pre-season training at the Puckapunyal army base. Another commentator wrote of the 1961 season:

> Kennedy was convinced that most sides were just not fit enough, so his plan was simply to make Hawthorn super-fit and then, by keeping the ball moving all the time throughout their games, wear the opposition to a standstill ... The Hawk's desire to win the ball bordered on the fanatical—opponents certainly knew they had been in a football game after meeting Hawthorn.[5]

The Barassi style, which he was to develop later as a coach, together with the Kennedy theories of super fitness, an unrelenting attack on the ball and harassment of the opposition, marked the beginning of the process of turning the physicality and violence which had always been part of football into the applied science of controlled aggression that is such an important facet of the modern game.

Geelong had been the glamour team of the competition in the early 1950s before Melbourne's rise to power. During the Second World War they had been the only team forced to drop out of the VFL—for the 1942 and 1943 seasons, when it could not muster enough players for a competitive team. From there it had been a hard slog for coach Reg Hickey to put a team back together, but by 1950 he got them to fourth position and the preliminary final.

The Cats then won successive premierships in 1951 and 1952, with the 1952 team in particular totally dominating the competition. They were acknowledged as the fastest team to have played to that time, and combined this speed with precise teamwork to produce a brilliant, attacking style of play. A half-back line led by John Hyde was one of the first to develop rebound football, running the ball out of defence. In a team full of stars, the flashest and most flamboyant was the big yet fast half-forward flanker they called the 'Geelong Flier', Bob Davis.

Halfway through the 1953 season, Geelong established a record, which still stands, of 23 successive wins (before going down to the Magpies, who also conquered Geelong in the Grand Final, in round 14). The Cats made the finals for the next three years, but then slumped dramatically to take consecutive wooden spoons. When Davis took over as coach after a year out of the game, they were among the competition's easy beats.

Geelong stood apart to some extent from the other 11 clubs in its nature as well as its geographical location. It had always been known for producing skilful players, but was not regarded as one of the tough teams of the competition. It had a reputation, in good times and bad, among the public and their opposition as 'the handbag' team, or more colloquially, 'a bunch of poofters'. The club also had a reputation for infighting, backbiting and intrigue—though it was not alone in this regard.

Population patterns in Melbourne had changed as the city grew rapidly in the post-war years, fuelled by the baby boom and large-scale immigration. Numbers fell in the inner suburbs where most of the Melbourne-based clubs were housed, and a large proportion of the remaining residents were now new immigrants with more interest in soccer than Aussie Rules. The tribal loyalty of Melbourne footy fans remained, but the tribes were now scattered through the ever-expanding suburbs. But Geelong remained a one-team town.

The Ford motor car factory had brought heavy industry to the town, but it retained something of a country feel, and took pride in its role as a port and service centre for the rich wool and wheat farms of Victoria's western half. The huge woolstores on the Barwon River, just down the road from football club headquarters at Kardinia Park, were a prominent feature of the town.

The status of the football team in the town, and the attention lavished on it, had more in common with the Eagles in Perth and the Crows in Adelaide in the 1990s than with the Melbourne-based clubs, where the tribes were many and the attentions of the media and the public divided. The football club was the most public and in many eyes the most important institution in the town. Positions of prominence in the club, and especially on the committee, were highly prized. The team's successes and failures were equally keenly felt, discussed and dissected. The heat that such talk and dearly held opinions could generate was magnified by the smallness of the town.

The negotiations to secure Farmer, during which club president, Jack Jennings, had summoned coach, Bob Davis, and secretary, Leo O'Brien, back from Perth, were carried out against the background of a particularly bitter and dirty election in December 1961 for positions on the 1962 committee. A reform group supported by O'Brien and many of the players was running for office. Players were out doorknocking members, drawing strong rebukes from Jennings, who was one of the targets.

As the votes came in, some envelopes were being diverted and steamed open, and many votes for the incumbents disappeared into a fireplace. Knowing this, the reformers were sure of success, and could only explain their defeat by their belief that the incumbent faction had printed and filled in extra ballot papers. After being returned, Jennings publicly attacked his opponents as ruthless and bitter.

Jack Jennings had become president when there were no other takers in 1945—with the club at its nadir after two years out of the competition then two wooden spoons—and was to remain in office until 1970. He was an unusual man for a football club president, being neither a former footballer nor a high-flier from the business world. Normally at least one of these was a necessary qualification for the position, but Jennings was a car salesman. He represented the club well in the cut and thrust of VFL headquarters at Harrison House, and was an affable and able public figurehead, but he was not a president with a vision or plan to create a great football team, and was not known for his rapport with the players.

By 1959, the club's favourite son, Reg Hickey, had filled the coach's job forever, it seemed. He had actually been the coach since 1949, but before that, had held the position for a year in 1932, and then from 1937 to 1940. He had also played well over 200 games from 1926 to 1940. He had seen the ups and downs of the club, with two premierships as a player, and three as a coach, and the wooden spoons thrown in. But as the team slumped in the late '50s, Hickey was ageing and tiring, and he and the club knew that he was not the man to oversee another rebuilding period. Davis was the heir apparent, and stepped into the job as if by right in 1960, with an open brief to mould a new team.

Davis was a man with boundless confidence, a talker and hustler:

> It's very hard to say [but] from the moment I landed in Geelong as a kid, I was a personality. I could play, I was a showman, and I got on very well with the media—they loved me. I would say things and do things. I wasn't as good as Ablett, but I'd play like Ablett—carry the ball and turn somersaults. So I've always been very big in Geelong. Then when they wanted a coach, I got the job. I knew I was going to get it.

He had retired prematurely after the 1958 season in which he was Geelong, Victorian and All-Australian captain:

> I had done everything else except win the [Brownlow] Medal, and I was favourite to win in '58, and I got five votes or something. The television had just started, [and] the phone rang one day and Channel Seven offered me big money ...

As a coach, Davis was not a deep-thinking strategist. He says himself: "I probably wasn't the greatest coach of all time, I know I wasn't." His approach was straightforward:

> I used to get 'em fit, keep 'em happy, put 'em in the right position, and send 'em out on the field and say: "We're going to do to them exactly what they think they're going to do to us, we're going to fix 'em right up." And that was it ... I taught 'em to love to play football, that there was a thrill in playing

in the League, that it was a game and you played it as well as you possibly could play. We put 'em in their best positions, and they all knew what they were expected to do.

His great gift in the situation in which he found himself, was an ability to pick a young footballer with potential. Working closely with Leo O'Brien and Tom Morrow, a teammate from the 1951 side he brought in as chairman of selectors, he scoured the countryside for young talent:

The team had been nowhere, so we cleaned the whole team out and got a new fresh team ... I had 115 kids at the ground the first time. We just kept sifting through 'em, sifting through 'em, until I got about 35 that I knew could play.

With this young side Geelong improved steadily through 1960 and 1961, to the point where it challenged for a place in the 1961 final round. But to date, Davis had not been able to find a ruckman of class. "If you've got a weakness, then you go out and get the best, plug up the hole with the best." And so he launched his bid to secure Farmer.

Farmer arrived in Victoria amid greater hype and with higher expectations on his shoulders than any newcomer to the VFL before him. The ongoing drama surrounding his official clearance did nothing to diminish this, nor did the motor mouth of Davis, who was telling anyone who would listen that Farmer would turn Geelong into a premiership team.

There was also "a touch of mystery about Polly" according to John Devine:

His reputation was such that we treated him with awe—the great man's arrived. From an outsider's point of view the touch of mystery about him was the fact that he was one of the Aborigines, who I'd never associated with. It was something that was different about him: "How are we going to cope with him, is he any different to the rest of us?"

There were doubters within and without the Geelong camp as to whether he would measure up to his reputation. And among the Geelong hierarchy some questioned whether anyone could be worth the money they were paying. Other clubs would happily have paid more, but Geelong was not one of the big money clubs of the League. Geelong itself had not paid a transfer fee, but they did have a contract with Farmer. He was on £1000 a year—the same as coach Davis—free rental on his accommodation, plus the standard match payments.

Davis often tells a story of how he secured Farmer for a straight £1000 a year, but when he arrived "he woke up that he'd sold himself too cheaply" and began asking for extras, such as the free rental and match payments. Farmer lets this go by in public, but the record suggests that these provisions were in the contract that Sweet helped him negotiate back in Perth, and he insists that, as at East Perth, he honoured the deal explicitly once it had been made, never asking for more. He points out, in fact, that after a year he purchased a house in Geelong and paid it off himself, thus saving Geelong from shelling out rent money.

It seems more likely that Farmer was trying to get Geelong to honour the full terms of the contract. More than one of his teammates has spoken of the gap between promises made at the time of recruitment, and the reality on arrival at the club. But such matters were of minor concern when the Farmer family arrived in town at the beginning of 1962.

He and Marlene quickly got to know many of the players and their families. Any sense of mystery was quickly dispelled, and friendships that have lasted ever since were established. Davis took them down to Barwon Heads where Terry Callan had a speedboat. Farmer's determination quickly impressed winger John Brown when he tackled the task of learning to waterski. "He almost pulled the boat out of the water because he wouldn't let go of the rope when he went down ... but he got there. There are few challenges he doesn't master." The family settled in to the house provided, and Farmer started a job at the same dealership as Jack Jennings, selling Holdens.

He was happy in Geelong and the world of the VFL. For a man as committed to football as Farmer, Victoria was a natural home. The passion for the game, and its place not only in the mainstream, but the very heart and soul of the people's lives, formed part of the lure for footballers from interstate, almost as much as the need to test themselves against the best. Their arts and skills could only ever be truly appreciated here in the spiritual home of the game.

There were other appealing aspects too. Though there was some initial curiosity, his race was always less of an issue in Victoria than it had been in Perth. And the change of clubs was, if anything, overdue. He left behind a club where there were still those who felt that in some sense they owned him, and that he owed them. He came to Geelong as an established champion, bestowing his favours by choosing them. He came on his own terms, and he came as his own man, not as the boy from Sister Kate's.

Despite all this, or because of all this, he was very much under pressure to produce the goods. For Bob Davis, too, a lot rode on his performance. Davis had staked a large chunk of his credibility on his efforts to secure Farmer and persuade the committee to meet the necessary terms, and had enemies within the club who would not hesitate to point the finger if things went wrong.

The squad settled into a heavy pre-season training schedule. Davis and the club medical officer, Dr Kevin Threlfall, had taken note of the headline-gathering training methods of athletics coach Percy Cerrutty and his star pupil, Herb Elliott, who churned out the miles on the back beaches and dunes of Portsea, at the other extremity of Port Phillip Bay. They took a leaf out of the Cerrutty book, and did much of their fitness work on the dunes out of Geelong, mixing the gruelling running work with ocean swims.

Farmer always maintained his fitness levels, and perhaps needed the work less than the others. But he revelled in it, often leading the charge to the top of a steep dune. It was second nature to him after his years on the Perth beaches. And it helped put endurance and strength in the legs of many of his teammates.

Then the practice matches began. In Victoria these were all intra-club games. Farmer had created such interest that unprecedented crowds turned up. Folklore has it that there were 10,000 at the first Geelong scratch match of the season, and that, with the club charging admission, it recouped all the money outlaid on Farmer on this first day.

He did not disappoint. His form in the practice games was sensational. Marking, palming, round the ground, he dominated. Comment was soon passed on the way he was combining with rover Bill Goggin, who was already emerging as a star in his own right. And best of all, there was that phenomenon until then unknown to the Geelong fans, the marvellous grab and lightning handpass from the ruck duels. One of the spectators recalls:

> The ball was bounced and the first thing Polly did was to reach the giant paw
> up and let the ball roll down the arm and shoot out a 20-metre handpass to
> a teammate who didn't know what to expect. The crowd was quite amazed
> to think that he wasn't attempting to tap the ball out ... People were oohing
> and aahing, and just generally being quite amazed by his skill and his quick
> thinking.

The scribes were raving:

> Former Westralian star Graham 'Polly' Farmer made football look easy in
> Geelong's main practice game today ... Rovers Billy Goggin and 'Sago' Rice
> had an armchair ride roving to Farmer who completely dominated the game.
> The large crowd cheered Farmer every time he handled the ball realising
> that in the West Australian champion they had got the man who can take
> them into the finals.[6]

Another writer noted that: "He combined brilliantly with rover Bill
Goggin, and it is obvious the pair will develop into one of the most feared
combinations in the League."[7]

Farmer's performance in these games ensured his acceptance among the
Geelong players. Davis says:

> We'd never brought a high-priced player in. He was the first one ... and
> bringing him in was a bit of a gamble ... But I kept telling all [the players] that
> if we get this feller, we'll do anything. So after [the first practice match]—he
> handballed it to everybody on the ground—I said: "How'd you get on with
> Pol?" "Oh what a beauty," "He gave me three handballs," "He gave me this,"
> or "He gave me that." And he was set. No one ever queried what he was
> getting, they didn't even care.

The doubting Thomases of Geelong pretended that they had known all
along. There was a buzz around Kardinia Park, and around the town,
thanks to Farmer. The pictures and the features in the *Advertiser*'s sports
pages were largely devoted to him, and the Melbourne papers were not far
behind in the number of column inches written.

Such an impact did he make, that there was serious speculation of a totally unprecedented move to make a first-year player the club captain. It would have been astounding, but there was some rationale given his experience relative to the rest of the team. The 1961 captain, John Yeates, was set to become his junior partner in the ruck, and was entering only his fourth season of football. Farmer had nine years, state captaincy and 176 games under his belt. Of the rest of the team, only winger John O'Neill had passed the ton, with 116 games. Farmer was clearly the senior player, in all except VFL experience.

Yeates retained the captaincy. But as the opening day of the season approached, with Geelong down to play Carlton at Princes Park, all attention was focussed on the debut of the gun ruckman from the west.

There was a definite sense of occasion as the day dawned. Melbourne's favourite football writer, Lou 'The Lip' Richards, said in the Saturday morning *Sun* that "the Carlton-Geelong game promises to be the social event of the year—it marks the coming out of the state's top debutante 'Polly' Farmer."[8]

On the morning of the game Farmer received a pile of telegrams from friends and colleagues in the west, urging him on and wishing him luck. Now that he was in Melbourne even those who had sought to keep him at home wanted to see him uphold the pride of Perth football. Farmer was expectant and confident: "There wasn't room to be nervous."

It looked like being a testing debut. Carlton had finished below Geelong in 1961, but was tipped as an improver for 1962, and it had a strong ruck battery, led by two state representatives in captain Graham Donaldson and John Nicholls. Nicholls was still at a relatively early stage of his career, but already had the status of a champion. However, he was ruled out of the game at the last minute with an ankle injury. Instead, Donaldson was partnered by Maurice Sankey, another tough campaigner. Before the game Davis had counselled Farmer to be careful out on the ground, warning him that he would be targeted by the opposition.

It was a sell-out crowd estimated at 37,000 at Princes Park. The first bounce of the first game of a new season is a sacred moment in the football world: the release from the long, barren months of empty Saturdays; all the hopes and anticipations for the winter ahead are suddenly on the line.

At any game it takes the crowd a minute or two to settle into the rhythm of the game after the opening roar of cheers and abuse. It is even more so on the opening day, when the vocal chords are still rusty and the scarves and beanies are fresh from the mothballs.

As they settled at Princes Park, Carlton moved into attack from the opening bounce—Farmer failed to prevail at his very first VFL contest—then there was a scrambling passage of play as Geelong forced the ball back upfield, and eventually over the boundary line between its half-forward flank and forward pocket to produce the first break in the play.

As the boundary umpire's throw-in arced through the air, Farmer took front position, rather than his usual boundary tactic of coming from behind or running alongside his opponent. There was a tangle of bodies that crashed to the ground, with Farmer beneath Donaldson and Sankey. Somehow Donaldson emerged with the free kick, but the trainers raced out on to the field to attend both Farmer and Sankey.

Sankey shook them off, and was quickly back in the play. But "Farmer was in the hands of the trainers for some minutes. Recovering, he went to the forward pocket, and was not seen much during the next 10 minutes. The crowd, many of which probably attended to see Farmer in action, was stunned when it appeared he might be seriously hurt."[9] Not only the crowd were affected. "When he went down," says Callan, "I felt sick. And the crowd had gone quiet. To hear [37,000] people go so quiet—it was awful."

Davis recalls the day well:

> He's limping up in a forward pocket and he hasn't really done anything. In those days there used to be a little coach's box right against the fence. They were hammering on the fence: "Where's the famous Polly Farmer? Where is he? Where's the mongrel?" [In the second quarter] a ball went up to the forward line, and he made a run at it, and he jumped up right over the top and just grabbed it. I jumped out of the box, and I said: "Do you see him there? Number five! Just watch that. That's what he's going to do to you all day for the rest of the day. So just leave me alone." He went back, kicked the goal, was the best player on the ground after half-time.

Carlton had jumped Geelong six goals to three in the first quarter, but as

Farmer came into the game, kicking four goals, creating many others, and rucking strongly, Geelong fought back and then pulled away to a 39-point win. The press reports all rated Farmer Geelong's best player. "Faster, fitter and Farmer, those three Fs were the key to Geelong's victory over Carlton on Saturday," was the opening sentence of the *Sun*'s match report.[10] Yet he had played all except the opening minutes of the game with a damaged anterior cartilage in his left knee.

The injury happened because Farmer had decided to ease into the VFL game, testing the waters, so to speak. "I blame my cautious start for getting me into trouble." The caution was not due to the warning from Davis, prophetic as it turned out to be:

At the time there was a fair amount of unfair publicity against me because of my rucking style, because I was a bit of a jumper and I was getting the ride. They said I was interfering. Well in the first game against Carlton I decided that I'd just take it easy. I didn't run and jump and kick off them. It was more or less a straight jump at the ball, instead of using them as a springboard. Because of that I was taking up front position and as three of us flew for the ball I got knocked over and lost my balance, and as I came down my legs were tangled with Maurie Sankey and Graham Donaldson. They landed on top of me, and bang went my leg.... [I was] in terrible pain. My feelings were all gone, all gone before I started. But I continued to play, because you sort of don't want to let people down. We ended up winning the game, but it was probably the worst thing in the world. If I could have gone off the field I probably wouldn't have ended up with a bad knee that year.

The saga of Polly Farmer's knee became just about the biggest football story of 1962. In this era before modern advances in diagnosis and treatment, and before the advent of the arthroscope, a 'dicky knee' meant the end of a footballer's career more often than not. During 1962, five VFL players played their last games when cartilage operations were unsuccessful.

Farmer believes that the disasters that followed could have been avoided. He was used to carrying injuries, and believed that to do so and to bear the pain was part of a footballer's duty. He had always hated to miss a game of football in any circumstances, and how much more so now, when he was so desperate to prove himself and to play a part in a Geelong surge up the ladder. He knew in himself that the injury was serious, but not what the consequences of playing on it were:

> See, I didn't understand the make-up of my knee, the design of my knee and what was happening, and no one was telling me ... In different circumstances, if we had someone who knew really what was wrong with my knee [they could have said]: "If you rest your knee for four weeks you'll be right, because all the pain will disappear, you can build your muscles up, and you should be all right."

He says he is "inclined to blame Bob [Davis] a little bit, for wanting me to continue to play." Davis' story is somewhat different. After the first game:

> Threlfall came in and said ... "He's gone." I said: "What're you talking about, he's gone." He said: "He's finished, his cartilage is gone, it'll have to be operated on". I said to Pol: "Listen mate, you're in desperate trouble, you've got to be operated on." He said: "It'll be all right. I tell you, it'll be all right, don't you worry about it."

From others the general impression is one of ongoing uncertainty and confusion over the specifics of the injury, and a continuing state of drama. It seems more likely that the definitive diagnosis recalled by Davis came somewhat later in the piece than immediately after the first game. John Hyde was back in Geelong by now, having been replaced by Pianto at Claremont, and was on the committee, which appeared to be better informed than Farmer himself of the state of affairs:

> When he hurt that knee, it was one of the biggest sensations of all time. We went to committee meetings, and Dr Threlfall, he introduced this knee joint, and all this was explained to us, what happened, and how it was improving. I've never forgotten it—at that stage it was one of the biggest things in his medical career.

In the aftermath of the Carlton game Geelong played down its concerns in public, and Farmer fronted up for the second round game against Melbourne. On a wet day Geelong went down by seven points in a low-scoring affair, though only three late goals made it seem like a close game.

Rex Pullen in the *Sun* gave Barassi the best-on-ground vote, but named Farmer as Geelong's best, and opened his report with glowing praise:

> If only Geelong could have kept champion ruckman 'Polly' Farmer on the ball all day against Melbourne on Saturday, that would have made the difference between defeat and a win. As it was Farmer did the work of four men but he had to rest sometimes and Geelong went down.[11]

The third game was against reigning premiers, Hawthorn, at Kardinia Park. After the disappointing performance against Melbourne, Geelong hit its straps with a vengeance to record a six-goal win. The *Advertiser* placed Farmer second behind Alistair Lord on their best player list this time, but once again, their praise was effusive:

> Graham Farmer's ability to pull new tricks each week and to work out new moves ... was a constant source of delight to the big crowd, as well as contributing materially to the team's success. Hawthorn had no counter for him without infringing the rules ... [After the game Farmer required stitches to a head gash] ... The [second] quarter saw some of the best football produced for a long time ... Farmer arrived at the scene of a ball-up in front of Geelong goal in time to grab the ball and slam it through. The next two goals saw football at its best. From a throw-in, Farmer palmed the ball in front of a pack where Bill Goggin raced round the pack and headed for an open goal. Again Farmer put Goggin in possession. He sent to the goalmouth where Yeates tipped it through ...[12]

With only three games under his belt, Farmer had confirmed the highest hopes of his fans, and turned around the sceptics. A new force had arrived in the VFL, and Davis' confident predictions of Geelong's chances with their champion ruckman in the driving seat were sounding ominous to the opposition.

But the 'unfair publicity' about his ruck style was reaching new heights. In the Melbourne game he had argued briefly but fiercely with umpire Schwab when a free kick was awarded against him. He had gone up above Len Mann and palmed the ball away cleanly, but Schwab penalised him for having a hand on Mann's shoulder. He was free kicked on other occasions that day by Schwab. But despite this, Melbourne officials claimed he had got away with murder, and their coach, Norm Smith, while praising Farmer's football, insisted that he did infringe almost every time he contested in the ruck. Controversy raged in the papers, with everyone having an opinion, and the umpire's adviser being asked for official interpretations of the rules.

Farmer's style was new to the Victorians. He did, in one sense, play the man by seeking to use his opponents as a 'springboard', but always with the ball as his objective. Nor could he have avoided the clashes, for the opposition were deliberately crashing into him and running across him in a bid to keep him away from the ball. He may have been a rookie, but already he was the chief target of the opposition strategists and tough men. There is no doubt that in the cut-throat world of the VFL the other clubs were playing the controversy for all it was worth, hoping to unsettle him, and influence the umpires.

The *Truth* leapt to his defence:

> There is a smear campaign against Polly Farmer. It should be nipped in the bud. Great players are always the target for abuse and Polly is great. I would hate to see his greatness curtailed by the storm of controversy over last Saturday's game between Melbourne and Geelong.[13]

Another aspect of the pressure he was under was highlighted in a letter to the editor signed 'Carlton Supporter', recalling the weekly attention received by Essendon's champion full-forward, John Coleman, a decade earlier:

> It is distressing to see the harm that the VFL teams are doing to the sport. I refer to the obvious intention of Geelong's opponents to injure, maim or just break the spirit of ... Farmer. He is an acquisition to the game, a delight to see in action no matter which team one follows. He could be the number one drawcard but the opposing coaches, backed by biased and unsporting committees, will put him out of our game unless checked ... Don't let them do a Coleman on Farmer.[14]

Just as he had entered the competition in an 'unprecedented blaze of publicity', Farmer remained the centre of attention as the football season got into stride. But the Hawthorn game was the last one he was able to complete for the year. He almost did not take the field the following week against Richmond. A player was taken out of the reserves team as a standby. "However, a midday conference between the match committee and Farmer established that [he] was fit to play."[15]

In the third quarter of the game he went down, and did not come up again, being stretchered off. First reports suggested he had taken a knock to the head, but the real problem was the knee giving up the ghost. Perhaps he got knocked out, and because of this landed badly, for in one report he said that he could not remember how it happened, only going for the ball, and then being flat out on the ground. But if he was unsure how it had happened, he could certainly feel the consequences.

"I thought my left knee had split in two. The pain was almost unbearable and I had visions of watching from the sidelines for the rest of the season," he told the *West Australian*'s Geoff Christian, who rang from Perth. "... Since then I have been told by experts that there is no ligament or cartilage damage, but that there is severe bruising and swelling."[16] He talked hopefully to Christian of missing only the one game.

The knee failed to respond as he hoped though, despite an intensive exercise program to strengthen the surrounding muscles. He had missed four games when Threlfall made yet another examination, and gave a gloomy report to the committee. The Tuesday headline was 'Bad News For Cats On Farmer'; he was definitely not going to play against Essendon on Saturday as he had hoped, might be out for the season, and there would be a decision about an operation after a consultation with a specialist in Melbourne.

But the next day he went straight from the specialist's appointment to a fitness test at Kardinia Park, with an all clear to try the knee out. He took the field at Windy Hill against Essendon, but was in trouble early in the first quarter when he tripped over an Essendon player, and rose limping. Then halfway through the second quarter he was chasing his opposite number, Don McKenzie, on the outer wing, when he tried to turn, but went down clutching the knee. "There was sympathetic applause from the Essendon members' stand when he left the field. Essendon supporters remembered the breakdown of their own star forward John Coleman," who had been put out of the game by a knee injury in 1954. [17]

Monday's paper had pictures of him commiserating with St Kilda full-forward Bill Stephenson, who had also unsuccessfully tried to come back from a knee injury on the Saturday. Both were announced to be out for the season, with Farmer apparently conceding the fact himself, saying he hoped that it did not mean the end of his career, and that he would be ready for the start of the 1963 season.

He must have had second thoughts though, and on the recommendation of a former Geelong player went to see a trainer in Colac who was reported to work wonders. This fellow claimed to have put the knee right, and that Farmer would be all right within a couple of weeks.

After missing six games, he came back and played for the reserves against Collingwood, in the third last game of the home and away round. It was his first game for a reserves team since his debut year of 1953. He was chosen for the seniors the next week against North Melbourne, in what was billed as a do-or-die attempt to prove himself fit for the finals—Geelong's form had been somewhat patchy, but it had by now secured a spot in the final four.

For a player on one leg, with less than two quarters of League football in the previous 12 weeks, it was a remarkable performance:

> There is no doubt that for two quarters and 18 minutes there was a 'King' of Kardinia Park—Polly Farmer. Every one of the spectators, and every other player on the ground wanted to see Polly succeed in his comeback bid. He had only to get near the ball to be cheered. And he got near the ball often enough and effectively enough to give the fans a real run for their money.[18]

But the inevitable happened midway through the third quarter. He contested a hit out with North Melbourne ruckman Noel Teasdale, and came down off balance, landing with his full weight on the bad leg, and found himself once again limping around the boundary line supported by a pair of trainers.

This time there was no avoiding the inevitable, and on the Wednesday he was under the surgeon's knife in a Melbourne hospital. He had to listen to the last game of the round from his hospital bed, as his teammates defeated Fitzroy to secure second spot and a second semi-final berth.

It was the three games against Melbourne, Hawthorn and Richmond that had done the damage. The initial incident against Carlton had bruised the cartilage, and a period of rest and rehabilitation at that stage could have healed the damage. But by playing on, the stress continued, and the excruciating pain he experienced when he went down against Richmond was the cartilage giving way altogether.

Threlfall's gloomy diagnosis appears to have been the correct one. A combination of unwise advice from the specialist and the Colac trainer, and his own stubbornness and determination, saw him attempt the comebacks against Essendon and North Melbourne that really confirmed rather than aggravated the injury. Once the cartilage was torn, when pressure went on the knee, "the torn part moves and your knee gives way. I was lucky that in the process of continuing to play I didn't cause more damage to my ligaments."

Without Farmer Geelong failed to make any impression in the finals, though they were far from disgraced. In the first half of the second semi, despite missing full-forward Doug Wade as well, the Cats kept up with Essendon to lead by a point at half-time. But they faded to go down by 46 points. In the preliminary final against Carlton, they led by two goals entering the final time on period, but the Blues fought back dramatically to tie the game. Another thriller in the replay saw Carlton scrape home by two points, after a controversial umpiring decision seconds before the final siren saw a Doug Wade mark disallowed just 30 metres from the Geelong goal.

It was a devastating end to the season for the Cats, to be 'robbed' of a Grand Final berth in this fashion. It could be argued that the team's performance in these games, and throughout the season with such a limited input from Farmer, showed that they were a top team without him. Yet when asked if they might have won the premiership with Farmer in the side, Davis exclaims: "Won it! We'd have won it by 100 yards!" When it is pointed out that Geelong were beaten by more than 40 points in the finals by Essendon, which went on to beat Carlton easily, he responds: "I don't think that's a worry. Farmer was worth more than 40 points ... As far as a team goes, he was probably worth two or three players."

With the season over, there was only one question on everyone's lips in Geelong. Would Farmer recover from the operation sufficiently to play in 1963?

The joke that did the rounds of Geelong was that he was exercising the knee even before he came out of the anaesthetic. The knee would always remain 'loose'. The cartilage was removed, not repaired—no one had heard of a 'knee reconstruction' in 1962—and he had to live with it.

Farmer would never play another game of football without soreness and swelling. He would never play again with unrestricted movement. He would never be able to launch himself with abandon into a ruck contest, or a spectacular leap for a high mark over a pack; always as he took off he would have to be considering how to ensure that he could land on his good right leg, instead of relying as of old on his cat-like reflexes.

But unlike some, he never doubted that he would come back. The secret was to protect the knee as much as possible by strengthening the thigh muscles that supported it. And to this end he undertook a rigorous program of bicycling and weights. He did not test the knee under match conditions until the practice games of the next March. But by then his legs had become massively muscled and hugely strong.

The gym work also served to increase his all-round bulk and strength, something that he had realised he would need, partly because of the buffeting and attention he received in the games he did play, and partly because he knew he would be less mobile from now on, and hence less able to use his agility to avoid the knocks.

He was joined in this gym work by a mate from East Perth, the irrepressible John K Watts. Watts came to Geelong as Farmer's man. He and Farmer had corresponded throughout the year. Farmer suggested that he come and try out with Geelong. The Cats were not exactly in need of key defenders—in full-back Roy West and centre half-back Peter Walker they had two of the best in the business. They were certainly not chasing Watts of their own accord. It is a measure of Farmer's clout with Davis and O'Brien that they agreed to take Watts purely on Farmer's recommendation.

The disappointments of 1962, and some of the snide gossip about the 'expensive crock' that surfaced, made Farmer more determined than ever to succeed. He drove himself, and Watts as well, telling Watts that he would have to work to succeed at Geelong. Farmer says that it was during this lay up and recuperation period that he focussed and honed the art of the mental preparation for a game that he had first developed at East Perth. He entered 1963 knowing in himself that he would never be less than 100 per cent ready for a game, in his mind at least. Never again would he be cautious, or caught off guard as in that first game. Never again would he play a game other than on his own uncompromising terms.

IO

THE ULTIMATE GOAL

By the time summer gave way to autumn in 1963, it had become the
accepted wisdom in Geelong that Farmer's absence had cost them
last year's premiership. As the new season approached his knee
maintained its status as the major football story. There were progress reports
of his recuperation and the special strengthening and fitness program he
was going through, and each new milestone was marked with a story and
picture: the first kick of a football; the first real practice session when he put
the knee to the test in marking and rucking contests with John Watts. And
as each hurdle was jumped, hopes grew down on Corio Bay.

At the first practice match a record crowd gave an early £800 boost to
club coffers, and almost a thousand membership tickets were sold. Club
membership actually doubled between 1961 and 1963 as the Cats' fortunes
rose, and Farmer acted as a magnet for the fans. His practice match form was
a repeat of the previous year. In the press previews and predictions leading
up to the opening round of matches he was being freely tipped as a likely
Brownlow medallist, and on the strength of his sound condition, Geelong
was vying with 1962 premiers, Essendon, as favourite for the 1963 flag.

Brian Hansen in the *Truth* went one step further:

Geelong will win the 1963 VFL premiership. I am sure of that even this far from home. They have all the answers to the brilliant Essendon combination. I predict Polly Farmer will stand up to every test and will prove the most devastating ruckman in the League.[1]

Geelong's first game of the year was at home against last year's wooden spooners, South Melbourne. The expectations of the Geelong faithful are indicated by the fact that despite the lowly opposition, the game attracted Geelong's second-best home crowd of the season. It proved to be a disappointing spectacle as a contest, with Geelong six goals up at quarter time, and 59 points clear at the end. Farmer made the Geelong best player list without being spectacular, and did enough to reassure the faithful.

True to Geelong tradition, the big win was followed by a shocking loss. The second game was their first real test, against Essendon. The Cats journeyed to Windy Hill without Bill Goggin, who had strained his knee, and then Doug Wade was knocked out in the first quarter. Farmer was criticised in the press for handballing recklessly, with Essendon players sharking them more often than not. After being only 10 points down at half-time, the Cats lost by exactly the same margin as they had won by the previous week, to find themselves seventh on the ladder with a percentage of exactly 100. It was to be the only week they were outside the four for the season.

Over the next three weeks, Farmer came up against some of the League's top ruckmen: 1960 Brownlow Medallist John Schultz of Footscray, North Melbourne's ungainly but tough and effective Noel Teasdale, and the St Kilda pair of Allan Morrow and the debutante Carl Ditterich, the latter of whom was creating a huge impression with his reckless, athletic leaping, and his long blonde hair. Farmer dealt with them all in turn, as he began to stamp his authority on the competition, and Geelong recorded three solid wins.

Now in third place on the ladder, Geelong was beginning to look impressive. A notable feature that was starting to emerge was that they had learned the need to provide Farmer with protection. Farmer's reason for wanting Watts as a teammate became clear. Watts was changing out of a back pocket with Geoff Rosenow, who had developed since his debut the previous year, and the pair were filling the Jack Hunt, Laurie Kennedy role of East Perth days. "Watts never attempts to interfere with Farmer's work in the ruck, but nevertheless does a power of work in the packs where his strength counts."[2]

The defence, and especially the half-back line of John Devine, Peter Walker and Stewart Lord, was winning many plaudits, but they were having problems in attack. Wade came back in the St Kilda game with five goals after missing two weeks with concussion. But the rovers Goggin and Rice were not getting any goals, and the lack of system was reflecting in a team tally after five games of 49 goals and 96 behinds.

The next game would see Farmer return to Princes Park, the scene of the previous year's dramatic debut. Carlton and Geelong had clashed four times in 1962, including the drawn preliminary final and replay. But in the first game John Nicholls had been out of the Carlton side, and Farmer had missed the last three. This game would see football's most talked about personal battle since the '30s. It was spoken of in terms of Farmer's superior skills against Nicholls' enormous strength.

According to the *Sporting Globe*:

> The clash ... got away to a thrilling start with the Blues' skipper taking the early points. The two met solidly at the opening bounce. Nicholls recovered quickly, swept the ball out of a Geelong player's hands and drove it into attack. He then effortlessly outmanoeuvred the former West Australian at the first throw-in and earned a free kick at Farmer's expense at the next. However, Farmer cleverly won the next bounce to get Geelong moving for the first time. The pair broke even on the day after a vigorous, but fair and entertaining tussle.[4]

Other press reports had the pair breaking even in the ruck contests, but Farmer's around the ground work putting him ahead overall. Like the clashes with Jack Clarke that had been the talking point of the WANFL competition for many years, from now on every meeting between Farmer and Nicholls would be eagerly awaited, and then minutely dissected as on this occasion. And both were such great players, and such intense competitors that a complete whitewash of one by the other would be a rare event. Much more common would be a fierce clash in which the partisans for each could find grounds for the claim that their man was the better.

The match itself was almost a sideline to the battle of the ruckmen, Geelong held on for a six-point win that took them to second place. It would have been more comfortable, but once again the forwards could not find their range, kicking 7.22 (64).

In four weeks against probably the four best ruck combinations in the League (though Gabelich and Weideman at Collingwood, and Paterson and Crowe at Richmond would challenge Teasdale), Farmer had scored two knockouts and two points wins. Hansen's prediction was ringing true. He missed the next game against Hawthorn with a bruised hip. The Hawks were showing signs of their 1961 form again, after slumping to a ninth position finish in 1962. The Hawks jumped the Cats, who fought back to earn a draw. John Watts put in a best-on-ground performance, starting off for the first time in his career as a lead ruckman, then moving to the more familiar full-back position where he curbed the League's leading goalkicker, John Peck.

The following week Farmer was quiet in his return game, as Geelong put in its second shocker of the season, managing only four goals against Melbourne. But his form before this had been such as to make him an almost automatic selection for the Victorian side to play at the MCG against South Australia the following weekend.

It is worth remembering at this point the 'secret ambitions' of the youngster at Sister Kate's playing for Kenwick in the suburban B grade competition:

> I wanted to play for East Perth, I wanted to play in a premiership side,
> I wanted to play for the state, and I wanted to play in Victoria. And I wanted
> to play in a premiership side in Victoria, and also for the state.

Being chosen to wear 'the Big V' meant that all but one of the dreams had come true. He was playing as part of the most awesome array of talent that Australian Rules football could muster, alongside the like of Whitten, Barassi, Baldock, Nicholls and Skilton.

As it turned out though, the team did not perform to its capability. The South Australians had taken the unprecedented step of choosing a squad at the beginning of the season, and training together for over two months.

Their concerted campaign paid off when they pulled off an upset 9-point victory. Farmer acquitted himself well, being the Victorians' best ruckman, but emerged from the game once again nursing injuries—this time a bruised shoulder and "a slight thigh muscle strain".

After the South Australian game the Victorians selected a touring squad to play two games in Perth and a return match in Adelaide. The expected return of Farmer to Perth was causing great excitement in the west, and speculation of a record crowd for an interstate game at Subiaco. As it always has, Western Australia was basking in the reflected glory of its sporting exports, with regular reportage of Farmer's triumphs in the VFL.

There was consternation in Perth, and some anger in Melbourne, when his name was not in the squad when it was announced. 'Omitting Polly Is Sheer Folly', was one Melbourne headline. And writing from Perth for the *Sporting Globe* on the day of the first match, Austin Robertson claimed that: "Although Victorian officials will not admit it officially it is generally agreed that a big 'blue' was made not including Graham Farmer in today's line-up. It definitely would have added much more interest to the game and increased the gate. Coach Bob Davis reluctantly admitted that Farmer should have been in the team."[5]

Farmer comments drily: "The side is decided by people who have their own opinions. Why I missed out, God only knows. I know if I was picking [the team] I wouldn't have missed out." The injuries suffered in the South Australian game may have been a consideration, though. Farmer had three fairly quiet matches for Geelong while the Victorians won their three games on tour. The most notable of the Geelong games was against Fitzroy.

Both coaches were absent on the day, as Fitzroy's captain-coach, Kevin Murray, was in the Victorian side. Fitzroy had not won a game all year, but in the upset of the season, on a mud heap at Brunswick Oval, Geelong managed only 3.13 (31), and went down by six goals. For the first time in the season, Farmer clearly lowered his colours to the unknown and unglamorous Brian Clements.

Reports from the game suggest that Fitzroy used tactics remarkably similar to those of Swan Districts in the 1961 Grand Final. There was a Bunton connection to Fitzroy; perhaps word had travelled along this route, or some other circuitous branch of the football grapevine. What is surprising is that one does not come across more reports of the tactic being used. Perhaps it was tried at other times when Farmer was on the boil, without success, and then discarded.

The Fitzroy loss was followed by a two-goal win over Collingwood. This saw a full round of 11 games complete, with Geelong third on the ladder with seven to go. But it was not a secure position with a log jam at the top, and Cats fans were worried by their team's inconsistency—it would be ordinary for long stretches of a game, then produce a brilliant burst to secure victory. And some weeks the burst failed to materialise at all, resulting in the insipid losses to Essendon, Melbourne and Fitzroy.

Within the Geelong camp there was an enormous build-up for the return game against Essendon. "Players, officials, all members of the staff, and supporters rallied to create a Grand Final atmosphere."[6] The attendance at Kardinia Park was 7000 more than the next best for the year in the opener against South Melbourne, with people arriving from dawn onwards, and almost 41,000 squeezing through the turnstiles.

Geelong had not beaten Essendon since 1958, and the last two meetings had been thrashings. This was the motivation, but the objective was to prove itself as a serious contender for the premiership, as a team capable of rising to the occasion.

Fred Wooller lost the toss, and Geelong had to kick against a strong wind. The half-back line lived up to its reputation, and held firm against a series of Essendon attacks, and Geelong actually turned with a three-point lead. They built on this to go in four goals up at half-time, and managed two goals to Essendon's three in the third quarter. They were looking good, but when the Bombers got the first of the last-quarter to cut the Geelong lead to 11 points, there was a flutter of nervousness around the ground, as Essendon had won their last two games with overwhelming last quarter finishes. But then "Farmer grabbed the ball from a pack and an accurate kick went home."[7] Essendon was gone, and Geelong coasted home to a six-goal win, to the jubilation of supporters, who chaired many of the players from the ground.

The Geelong camp was upbeat, and was particularly encouraged by the performance of their rovers, Goggin and Rice, who got a bag of goals, with five between them, and dominated round the packs. But the star of the day was Farmer:

> Behind most of [Goggin and Rice's] play was the cool, calculating work of Graham Farmer who scarcely made a mistake in the match. He dominated the packs, his hand and foot passes went unerringly to their destinations, and he thrilled the huge crowd with towering marks such as we have seldom seen from him this season, and his kicks with the wind covered long distances.[8]

Two more virtuoso performances followed against Footscray and North Melbourne. He was gathering votes and either leading or threatening the leaders in the plethora of media awards in Melbourne, with their rich variety of prizes. In the *Herald*'s £200 award he was level with Darrel Baldock, the Tasmanian sensation who, like Farmer, was performing brilliantly after injury problems in his debut the previous year.

St Kilda and Geelong were due to clash, with much at stake for both teams. The Saints had just taken hold of fourth place ahead of Essendon on percentage. They could not afford a loss, and played accordingly, pulling away against a slight breeze in the last quarter. Geelong ruined its chances with another atrocious display in front of goal, kicking 8.21 (69).

The result created an intriguing puzzle for the finals. With two weeks to go, Hawthorn was safe on top, a game ahead of Geelong, which was only half a game ahead of the next three contenders. Melbourne led on percentage from the Bombers, whose thrashing of Fitzroy had leapfrogged them back ahead of St Kilda. Geelong had to win its last two games— against Carlton at home and Hawthorn away—to be sure of a finals berth. Depending on the outcomes, they could finish anywhere from first to fifth.

The Cats played against Carlton in the manner required, starting well and increasing their lead in each quarter in their most consistent game of the season to date in a 10-goal win. Wade's four goals were his best bag since round seven, in what had been a disappointing year. His tally was matched by 'the Tooleybuc Kid', young John Sharrock, who was showing signs of real class in his first season. To some, the most pleasing feature was that the team had been able to perform so well on a day when Farmer had his colours lowered. He was "outpointed by burly John Nicholls particularly after he had received a sickening kick in the groin in the first quarter and later when he stopped a hit between the eyes." Despite this punishment, he was "never really out of the play, but was just not the Farmer Geelong supporters know so well."[9]

The other four teams in the finals race also won, and the ladder positions remained unchanged from the previous week. With Melbourne, Essendon and St Kilda all playing lower-ranked teams, the acid was on the Cats. They had to beat Hawthorn to be sure of maintaining their position—even a draw would not do as their percentage was inferior to the three sides below them, thanks largely to their terrible inaccuracy in front of goals.

In effect Geelong had to treat the game as an elimination final, but the Hawks' Glenferrie Oval was no MCG. It was the smallest and narrowest ground in the League, with the boundary line tight up against the fences. Its cramped spaces suited Hawthorn's harassing, physical, non-stop style of game—there was nowhere to hide, and no flanks to create space for the loose man. A number of the Geelong players, including Farmer, had never been to the ground before. The club brains trust went so far as to get in an aerial photograph of Glenferrie in order to brief the team before the game.

Terry Callan, who had been in superb form all year in the back pocket, twisted his knee against Carlton. It put an end to his season, and exposed new boy Ian Scott to a baptism of fire. John Watts was missing for the fifth game in a row, after breaking his thumb, though he did come into the reserves team.

Hawthorn had worse problems though, after a tribunal hearing on the Tuesday night that was described as the most important since John Coleman was suspended on the eve of the 1951 finals series. Lead billing for the hearing at Harrison House went to Ron Barassi, who was suspended for four weeks for striking Roger Dean of Richmond, putting him out until the next season. But the Hawks' lead ruckman, 'Delicate' Des Dickson, suffered the same fate when found guilty of striking North Melbourne's Noel Teasdale at a boundary throw-in; and star full-forward John Peck—

who was leading the League goalkicking—received his second two-game suspension of the season for using abusive language to central umpire, Ron Brophy, in the same game.

Fred Wooller's capacity to lose the toss in the important games was becoming legendary at Geelong, and this Saturday he lived up to his record, ceding first use of the wind to Hawthorn. The game started at a furious pace. Hawthorn spent most of the first quarter in attack, but failed to capitalise, leading by only eight points at the first break. It clearly missed the strength and scoring ability of Peck, and lacked system. The second quarter gave heart to the thousands who had trekked down from Geelong to pack the terraces of the Glenferrie outer. Hawthorn were held goalless against the wind, and Geelong got out to a 15-point lead at half-time. And at the final break they were clinging still to a five-point lead, and coming home with the wind.

All of the Geelong 20 were desperate, but there was one in particular with the aura of a man on a mission; he had come too far to fall at this crucial hurdle. "There was no doubt at all that Graham Farmer was determined that Geelong would play in the finals. There was strength and purpose in his every move. His leaps for the ball were amazing, even to those who have seen him in all his games."[10] The uniqueness of Farmer's genius was demonstrated yet again though, for his contribution in this situation was not to try to win the game off his own boot. "Above all was the creativeness of all his work, whereby his quick thinking brought so many colleagues so often into the play. Here is the complete footballer if ever there was one."[11]

The members' stand fell "strangely silent" at the beginning of the last quarter, when Geelong produced one of those magical spells of football that made them the most exciting team in the competition by a country mile. Suddenly finding space that should not have existed in the cramped confines, they poured on four goals in nine minutes, to leave Hawthorn needing five goals to get back. The Hawks steadied, then rallied, but West took a couple of screamers on the goal line, and they were unable to notch a reply. Late in the quarter, Wade notched his sixth—his best tally of the season—to put the seal on a very convincing 38-point win. The victory put them equal on points with Hawthorn, but behind them on percentage. The scene was set for a second semi-final rematch in a fortnight's time.

The jubilant Geelong fans made merry out on the oval, but inside the rooms the triumph was tinged with worry. As Bob Davis puts it: "They tried us right out ... they were putting [our players] into the fence and everything ... They had a brick fence just near the goals. If you weren't careful they ran you straight into a brick fence ... They were ratty—they'd round arm you, and do anything. And most of 'em couldn't play."

Kevin Threlfall did the rounds of the weary and battered players on the dressing-room benches, and reported to Davis that there were "five or six" who might be doubtful for the rematch. Just as Threlfall gave him this news:

> One of those round the ground reporters put a microphone underneath my nose, and said: "You've beaten Hawthorn, what do you think of them?" I said: "They're the roughest, dirtiest side that I've ever seen. And I don't care about them. Any time they want to play football, we'll give them a hiding." It never worried me. I mean I like John Kennedy, he's a very good feller, and we get on very well together. But at that time it wouldn't have worried me what I said to him.

For a coach to publicly call the opposition 'dirty' was beyond the pale in terms of the unwritten code that governed relationships between clubs. Davis and Kennedy both tell of a writ or injunction of some kind being taken out by Hawthorn to prevent Davis from making further accusations against the club. However, the press of the time makes no reference to any legal action, and it is unimaginable that in Melbourne in September it would have passed unreported. Presumably there must have been a privately conveyed threat to take action if Davis made any further comments.

Kennedy laughs the affair off now, but does not entirely forgive and forget: "I am mates with Bob, but we both know that we both still know about it." He draws the line at allegations of dirty play, and especially at the suggestion of premeditated intent to take out opposition players:

> I would expect every player to test every other player on the field, but no, you wouldn't go out to—probably press people wouldn't believe me on this, but I would be very surprised if any coach ever said to a player: "You go out

and fix him up." I mean, that bloke would have every right to say: "No John, you go out and fix him up. Don't you tell me to do that" ... I would always say: "Look, you know what you are up against. It's no use coming in and squealing about it. Just get on and run straight at the ball and if anything gets in the way, split it in halves." That, I think, is fair ... I guess that football being what it is, and things happening on the ground—we have all done things of which we are not proud later on the spur of the moment. That's in a different category ... You are not really proud of that, but you have got to live with it.

Whatever the different perspectives of the two coaches, then and now, there was even more 'needle' in the atmosphere than is usual for the main rivals for a premiership preparing for a showdown.

For Farmer there now came a familiar September routine. There was a week's break for the first semi-final, and a spell at the centre of attention as the best player awards were distributed. The media awards were a three-way split between him and Darrel Baldock, and South Melbourne's Bob Skilton. Between them they took off all the major prizes. Farmer had his nose in front in the richest awards though, eventually winning two new cars and cash prizes worth £200.

He already had a mortgage on a prize of a third car, in an award restricted to Geelong players carried in the Geelong *Advertiser* and sponsored by one of the rivals of his employers at Winter and Taylors. But this would not be formally decided until after Geelong's last game of the season. There was much comment on the problems he would face with the Taxation Department, as they were strict on the ruling that tax was to be paid on the full value of any prizes received. The Farmers finished up selling all three cars: one paid for the tax, and the others were converted into a deposit on the house they bought in Geelong.

On Brownlow night the judgement of the umpires reflected that of the media experts. In that era all the best-on-ground votes—worth three each—were counted first, followed by the twos, then the ones. At the conclusion of the three-vote round Farmer had scored five times, to lead Skilton and

Baldock, who had each got four. He only scored a single two, but on 17 still led the other pair, who had both moved to 16. But he stayed marooned on 17, joined by Baldock, and passed by Skilton who picked up four singles.

As seemed to happen throughout his career in the Sandover and Brownlow voting, he rarely picked up second and third votes, having to rely on his dominant games for the major votes. It seems strange for a player who was a major contributor in virtually all his games.

St Kilda had eliminated defending champions, Essendon, from the finals by virtue of a huge win over North Melbourne that boosted its percentage above that of the Bombers. But as in 1961, the Saints failed narrowly in the first semi-final when a last quarter comeback left them seven points short of Melbourne. It was Melbourne's 10th straight year in the finals, but despite the win it did not look convincing; even when Barassi was playing it was not the same powerhouse team of the late '50s and 1960.

On the basis of their win at Glenferrie, Geelong entered the second semi-final as favourites. It was thought that the finals experience of 1962 would stand them in good stead, and to quote Lou Richards, "the Cats have three Ps that Hawthorn can't come close to matching—pace, polish and Polly."[12] The one question in most minds was whether their undoubted polish would dull under the anticipated barrage from Hawthorn.

As expected the opening of the game was fast and furious, but it was Geelong that held sway, scoring three goals in the first 10 minutes through Goggin, Wade, and youngster Gordon Hynes, each coming from well co-ordinated attacks. John Yeates, playing as a forward pocket ruckman, added a fourth before Hawthorn hit back with two. Early in the second quarter Stewart Lord went to ground, and for a moment it seemed that a brawl would break out as players converged. It did not eventuate, but a couple of minutes later Lord was taken off on a stretcher.

With Lord off, and Peter Walker filling in for brother Alistair in the centre, Devine was the only member of the key half-back line still playing there. Geelong appeared rattled as Hawthorn came back strongly and moved to an 11-point lead. Farmer had been relatively quiet until this point, but all the match reports show him exerting his influence at the critical juncture. "[He] started the move which proved one of the most important in Saturday's semi-final. Late in the tense second quarter Farmer rose high in the air from the centre bounce. He got his hand to the ball and shot it 40 yards to captain Fred Wooller. Wooller kicked accurately and Geelong's seventh goal came up."[13] "In the dying stages of the quarter he kept cleaning the ball from a centre area that looked like people's day at the Show."[14] He was involved in two more goal-scoring attacks before the bell that enabled Geelong to go to half-time eight points up.

Hawthorn got the first goal of the third quarter to close to within a point, but from then on Geelong pulled away to record a convincing, but certainly not an easy victory. Hawthorn never stopped coming at them, with West, Wade and Scott all coming in for some punishment during the second half. Davis was moved to comment once again after the game, when asked for his thoughts, "That's all that's going to happen to them all the time. They'll never beat us, as long as football's being played, they'll never beat us."

For Geelong, the most pleasing aspect of these last two encounters was its ability not only to withstand the physical pressure, but to bounce back full of run and still play good football. Strong last quarters in finals football require strength, and reserves of physical and mental stamina. Hawthorn was supposed to be the fittest team in the League. But Billy Goggin has noted that this was the time when those pre-season miles in the sand dunes over the previous two years really paid off. He believes that as much as anything else, Geelong ran the Hawks off their legs with superior fitness.

G eelong was in the Grand Final. One more match to get through, to win. It was the hot favourite by now, and in the one-team town expectations and hype mounted. Hawthorn met Melbourne in the preliminary final. It just was not meant to be Melbourne's year. Already struck by the loss of Barassi, their acting captain and star wingman, Brian Dixon, had to pull out on the morning of the game, and ruckman John Lord was injured early. In another rugged game, the Hawks led most of the day to record a nine-point win. It meant that Geelong would play its third straight game against the Hawks.

The Grand Final in Melbourne was traditionally held on the last Saturday of September, but due to the washout of a complete round of

CAPTAIN: Farmer leads the team out for the 1967 Grand Final against Richmond at the MCG. He would rue the loss as the one that got away. (FAMILY COLLECTION)

CLASSIC POSE:
A perfect example of Farmer delivering the long-range handpass—poise and power, with the right hand speeding the ball on its way while the left fist strikes.
(HARRY BEITZEL)

RECORD BREAKER: Cheer squads and players form a guard of honour for Farmer as he runs on to Leederville Oval for his 339th League game in May 1971, breaking Jack Sheedy's All-Australian record.
(FAMILY COLLECTION)

↑ **DON'T MESS WITH ME:** Captioned in the *West Australian* as "Master makes a point", this shot was taken after Ron Alexander of East Perth had downed Farmer at a centre bounce during the 1971 second semi-final. Note that Farmer has not lost possession of the ball. Looking on are field umpire Lindsay Johnston and East Perth's Derek Chadwick. (FAMILY COLLECTION)

← **CRUNCH TIME!:** Farmer is king of the castle in this pack of big men in the 1968 WAFL second semi-final, including (L-R) Bill Dempsey (West Perth), Brian Sampson (West Perth) with the grimace, Paddy Anonte (Perth) and Graham Edwards (Perth). (FAMILY COLLECTION)

SPOILS OF VICTORY: Farmer unfurls the flag after West Perth's premiership of 1969. He led the club as captain-coach to flags in 1969 and 1971. (FAMILY COLLECTION)

WINNERS: The prize is his. Farmer holds aloft the premiership trophy after West Perth's 1969 Grand Final triumph—his first as either captain or coach. (WAN)

FAREWELL: All good things must end. Farmer looks back as he is chaired from the ground by his players after West Perth's 1971 WAFL Grand Final win, his last game of senior football.
(FAMILY COLLECTION)

↑ **RESPECT:** During 2013, Geelong Board member Gareth Andrews brought Farmer to meet the modern-day players, who were in Perth for an encounter with West Coast. Pictured with Farmer are (clockwise from Farmer's right) Steve Johnson, Tom Lonergan, James Podsiadly, James Kelly, Travis Varcoe, Joel Selwood and Mathew Stokes. (GARETH ANDREWS)

games in July the season had been set back a week. The Grand Final was played on 5 October, a warm spring day with the temperature rising to 73 on the Fahrenheit scale (23°C). In this energy-sapping heat there was no doubt that the week's rest for Geelong while Hawthorn slugged it out in the preliminary final was an even greater benefit than usual.

In that era, the attendance at the Grand Final would fall just either side of the 100,000 mark, and in 1963 the official figure was 101,452. The VFL Grand Final crowd in three huge tiers ringing the vast MCG stadium is without doubt the most awesome sight in Australian sport. There is a sense of atmosphere and occasion that other sporting codes can only envy. To appear and perform before this great assemblage is a footballer's dream and an honour in itself, but it is also a daunting prospect.

Even the ice-cool Farmer was prepared to concede after the game that the sense of occasion affected him: "It gave me a tremendous thrill to play before a hundred thousand people, but it also was a great strain. I was worried all the week before the match."[15] But he handled it better than some of his colleagues. Davis admitted to pacing the streets of Geelong from the crack of dawn. While Captain Wooller—not the first or the last to suffer in this manner—was physically ill with nerves after a sleepless night, vomiting in the early hours of the morning, and again in the dressing-rooms when he got to the ground.

The game opened with the traditional scuffling, pushing and shoving before umpire Crouch had even bounced the ball. Hawthorn got the first two scores, but both were behinds. During the first Geelong attack McPherson flattened Colin Rice "with a strong but fair shoulder bump." Rice showed that the Cats were determined to meet fire with fire when "he bounced to his feet in a second and gave McPherson as good as he had handed out."[16] Geelong scored the first goal after a brilliant high mark by Yeates. Shortly afterwards, Stewart Lord went to ground in a similar manner to the previous game, and Crouch spoke severely to Kevin Coverdale, but this time Lord played on. Woodley goaled for Hawthorn from a hotly disputed free kick. The rest of the quarter was a nip-and-tuck affair, with plenty of physical clashes, and Crouch working his whistle vigorously. Devine and Watts were playing strong games in defence, winning much of the ball, repelling Hawthorn attacks, and providing a physical counter-attack. At the first break Hawthorn led by 3.6 (24) to 3.3 (21).

Geelong dominated possession and play in the second quarter, but failed to press home the advantage. Sharrock was dumped twice, after which "Gary Young had a price on his head as the Cats tried to track him down."[17] Hawthorn's only two decisive attacks for the quarter resulted in goals, while Geelong squandered opportunities, kicking 4.7 (31). Farmer was in the thick of play. He created scoring opportunities with a handball to Hynes and a tap to Goggin but both shots went astray. Then he missed a set shot himself from a mark. The highlight of the quarter came when he flew high over a pack, grabbed a mark on the way down, and before he hit the ground, shot a 30-metre handpass to Alistair Lord who kicked the Cats' final goal for the quarter. It was the perfect piece of Farmer signature football— a move that no one else would contemplate, let alone accomplish.

At the long break Geelong appeared to have Hawthorn's measure, but the Hawks could be relied on to keep plugging away, it was far too soon for celebrations. Sure enough, the Hawthorn counter-attack came. The Hawks poured players into the centre and around the field bounce downs, congesting the play, and closing down Geelong. Vinar was off the ground, replaced by Goodland, and West at centre half-back was limping, allowing Coverdale too much freedom. Hawthorn full-back, Phil Hay, had been on the end of drubbings from Doug Wade in the last two encounters, but had kept him goalless so far in this game, forcing Davis to swap Wade and Wooller around.

After 20 minutes Hawthorn had scored 2.2 (14) to nothing, to come within two points. "Farmer was trying desperately to open up the game for Geelong with 20-yard [handpasses] into the open but more often than not a Geelong man was not there to get it."[18] Then he managed to get a long kick downfield to Wooller in the goalsquare, for a mark and a goal, and a little breathing space. Peck's third goal shortly afterwards brought the margin back to a point. Geelong appeared to have lost its rhythm; two desperate attacks registered behinds, but as the quarter entered time on the momentum was definitely with the Hawks, and they were pressing hard. Then "just on the siren, Farmer, from a ball-up hit out superbly to Rice who kicked a goal to give Geelong a 10-point lead."[19] Ron Barassi's analysis of the game in the *Sun* identified this as the critical moment of the game:

> Not only did Rice's goal stop Hawthorn's run, it must have broken the Hawk's hearts. They had given everything they had to catch Geelong, only to see their efforts smashed by a typical piece of Farmer football magic. This goal sent the Cats into the last quarter with all the trump cards. [20]

On the hot October day the two teams went into their three-quarter time huddles relatively close to each other, both seeking the shade thrown by the members' stand. Davis sensed that his moment of triumph was at hand; never the cautious strategist, but always the showman, he wanted to savour it to the full. His three-quarter time address must rank among the more unusual in Grand Final history:

> It was evident that we were going to beat 'em. They were getting tired, and we were fresh as a daisy. I said to [the players]: "What I want you to do in this quarter is to show 'em up for what they are. I don't want to see 'em touch the ball. You can do what you like. You can lair up, bounce it away from 'em, just put it in their face. Do whatever you want to do and just show 'em up for what they are."
>
> Well it was the best quarter of football seen in years. We took the ball from one end to the other and never let 'em touch it, and just laired right up 'em. It was incredible.

In a repeat of the final quarter four weeks earlier at Glenferrie, four goals in the first nine minutes put the issue beyond doubt. The last of these four goals is the one they still talk about at Geelong:

> Geelong sealed the 1963 premiership with a chain of passes that was a joy to watch. First move was a Polly Farmer handpass to Bill Goggin. Goggin ran, drew a Hawthorn defender out of position, kicked to John Sharrock, ran on for another handpass, kicked to John Yeates and Yeates kicked to Fred Wooller, unguarded in the goalmouth. Wooller executed a little dance of joy even before the ball reached him and he turned to tap through the Cat's 13th goal.[21]

Hawthorn was playing now with heart, but without hope. The Hawks fans began to stream out of the MCG, their hopes consigned now to the next season. The rest of the game was little but a formality. Hawthorn managed only three behinds for the quarter, while Geelong added two more goals. When the siren came it was a relief to all.

There was not a single writer or broadcaster in all the commentary that appeared after the game who did not give his votes for best-on-ground to Farmer. He was the undisputed hero of the hour. The Norm Smith Medal for the best on field in a Grand Final was not in existence in 1963. If it had been, there is absolutely no doubt that it would have adorned Farmer's trophy cabinet.

For Graham Farmer this was the sublime, defining moment of a football career. How many of us are lucky enough, or strong enough, or good enough, to have a dream as a school child, and make that dream come true? Step by step, he had done it. For a footballer there can be no greater feeling, and no greater distinction among one's peers, than to be the best on ground, the match winner, in the Grand Final—the only match that counts.

Footballers are as individual and as egotistical as most sportsmen. There is a public code of self-deprecation that often rings false. But when the Bob Skiltons and Greg Williams of football say they would gladly trade their Brownlow Medals for a premiership medallion, they do not lie. Each year, from the beginning of the pre-season grind to the last game, is a quest for that holy grail in which the self does become bound up in the whole of the team, and the glory of success is a sweetness each player can both savour on his own, and celebrate with his fellows.

Farmer had known this sweetness before, but this surpassed the flags won with East Perth. For a start, this was the VFL, the pinnacle of football. But it was also the culmination, the moment of fulfilment of the last in that series of secret ambitions he had carried within him since the days of kick-to-kick with Square Kilmurray, Jack Hunt, Bruce Ashwin and others in the paddocks of Kenwick. And it was the completion of the mission he had set himself at the outset of 1961—a mission few would be audacious enough to contemplate—to personally take a VFL team and lift it to a premiership.

Some look back nostalgically on the Geelong team of 1963 and call it one of the great sides. The fact is that they did not dominate the 1963 competition until the finals came around, and they did not do enough either side of 1963 to justify the tag—the reputation actually rests to a large extent on that magical quarter of football that is recalled with such nostalgia. The goal-to-goal line of Roy West, Peter Walker, Alistair Lord, Fred Wooller and Doug Wade was top class. Goggin was a top-notch rover. John Sharrock on a half-forward flank—though his best was still to come—and John Devine on a back flank were very good players, and Stewart Lord could hold his head up in any company. The rest of the team could play good football, but would never make it to the halls of fame. The team was capable of brilliance, but too inconsistent to rank among the greats.

One man made the team special, one man provided the spark and the creativity that lifted them above the rest. Baldock at St Kilda was magic. Skilton at South Melbourne was consistently brilliant. Barassi at Melbourne was inspirational as always. But 1963 was the year of Farmer. Skilton may have won the Brownlow, and no one begrudged him it, but Farmer was acknowledged by his fellow players, and by the experts of the media and the terraces as the dominant player of the League.

The other man with a sense of mission accomplished was coach Davis. He had set himself for this moment many years ago, while still thrilling the crowds of Kardinia Park with his famous dashes down the flanks. With his boundless confidence and exuberance, he had not been shy about telling the world that he would coach his Cats to the flag. And he knew—and was more than willing to admit—that Farmer was the key to it all. He loves Farmer for this as much as for his inordinate football talent. Farmer made his dream come true, and made good his boast.

It was in the aftermath of the Grand Final, talking to a reporter from Perth while "exhausted after many hectic hours of celebration," that Davis first made the statement he has repeated countless times since: "Graham Farmer is the greatest player who has pulled on a pair of boots." [22]

But beyond Farmer and Davis and the rest of the Geelong team there were all the thousands upon thousands who shared the dream in a less direct but only marginally less intense fashion. It provided an exhilaration, a fulfilment, and a set of memories that would sustain the Geelong fans through the long years until their next premiership success. This is surely the magic of a great sportsman, that he can reach out and bless in a mysterious manner the lives of so many. And it is why Farmer occupies such a special, almost mystical niche in the Geelong pantheon. The 1963 premiership perhaps did not belong to Farmer, but it was identified with Farmer as an individual in a way that no other premiership can be tied into a single player among the successful 20.

Keith Dunstan—a features writer and columnist with the *Sun* who was later to become known as the founder and chief propagandist of the AntiFootball League—was assigned to cover the post-match celebrations in Geelong. He took the train down with the joyous Geelong fans. "We were like Caesar's legions returning to Rome for our well-earned triumph." He joined the throng he estimated at five to six thousand fans at the Town Hall to await the return of the team, and described the festivities, speeches and shenanigans. As civic dignitaries and club officials made speeches there were chants from the crowd of 'We want Polly, we want Polly'. "The climax of the night came when he did emerge and 'held high the big cup and put it to his lips. Geelong was his.'"[23]

It is worth recording at some length just two of the tributes that were written at the time to a man at the peak of his powers and achievements. Lou Richards, as ever, provided the hyperbole:

> You can call him the Big Cat, Mr Perfection from Perth, or the G that starts and ends Geelong. For my money he's Farmer the Charmer, the priceless pedigree pussy who carried the Cats to the 1963 flag on Saturday.
>
> How much did you pay for Farmer last year, Geelong? Well, take it from me, you got a bargain—he's a million dollar baby without a single flaw. On Saturday's virtuoso performance, Farmer's left leg should be insured for $100,000, his golden palming paw for $200,000, and another $200,000 for the fastest and most accurate handpass that's been seen round this town.[24]

And the Geelong *Advertiser's* correspondent, known only as 'Play-On', provided the adoring tribute:

> Without any question, Graham Farmer was not only the keynote of Geelong's Grand Final success, but he was just as certainly the best player afield and one whose display thrilled many thousands of spectators.
>
> His personal success on Saturday ... was a magnificent tribute to that

discipline and dedication by which he rose above the adversities and disappointments of last year to be so generally acknowledged the great force in 1963 League football ... Graham Farmer's sights are set so far above ordinary levels that he does not conform to standards usually applied to sportsmen. A perfectionist in all he undertakes, Farmer has been at pains to condition himself thoroughly to achieve his goal. No personal sacrifice has been great enough and no self-discipline sufficiently severe, to cause him to deviate a hair's breadth from the path he set out to follow and the goal which he pursued.

In my time, and in the sports which I have followed, only Sir Donald Bradman stands out as a similar example. He maintained his position at the top of the world of cricket for longer perhaps than the stresses of football night allow Farmer to do, but he did so with equal dedication.

Nowhere has Farmer shown better that perfect conditioning, mentally and physically than at the MCG on Saturday when against probably the toughest opposition Victorian football can offer, he was playing on as strongly at the end as at the start ... By the fourth quarter, his strong, rugged opponents who had offered such vigorous opposition earlier could make no more than token resistance.

Farmer has won many rewards from football, but who can say they have not fallen to one worthy in every way to receive them. It was forecast in this column on Saturday that 'here was the man, the hour and the occasion', and countless thousands will rejoice that they were privileged to see Farmer at his best in a VFL Grand Final.[25]

II

FALLING SHORT

The man of the hour was characteristically subdued, even at the high point in his career marked by this premiership win. Farmer was a man dedicated to the journey. Arrival at the desired destination was satisfaction enough in itself, and did not require celebration. Few could be as deadpan as Farmer when pressed to describe his emotions at the time.

> Once the game is over it's a letdown. I like to build myself up for the game and when the game is finished I would be happy to recover in my own home ... but my wife wanted to participate in the enjoyment of it. From my point of view, once the game is over that's when my recovery takes place. I'm basically quite happy to get home and just take it easy and probably go to bed ...
>
> The VFL premiership was part of my ambitions achieved, my personal goals, and I don't think I felt any better than I did with every other personal goal that I achieved, but I just think that the feeling of being a winner is always the same no matter what the circumstances are. There's not a grade for winning, as there's not a grade for losing. If you lose it's demoralising.

After the celebrations of the weekend there were a few days to relax and recover, but then he was off to Perth as a guest of the Channel Seven television station. The VFL finals always got some coverage in the Perth press, but this year, with Farmer and Watts involved, there had been far more interest.

Their performances—Watts had also been among Geelong's best with some spectacular marking in defence—had been cause for another surge of parochial pride, typified by the *Daily News*' back-page columnist Kirwan Ward's tongue-in-cheek observations:

> While Swan Districts were getting deeper into that premiership winning rut last Saturday, East Perth, thinly disguised as Geelong, were busy taking out the Victorian championship on the MCG. The subterfuge of wearing those dark blue hoops on their guernseys may have tricked most of the 101,452 characters present but it didn't fool us. The moment we saw Polly Farmer and John Watts we knew.[1]

The west's inferiority complex was something like the national cringe of the '50s and '60s that required Australians to 'make it' in England to confirm their status; from the Indian Ocean perspective, the big time was Sydney, or in football terms especially, Melbourne. Farmer's enhanced status was emphasised by the scenes on his Friday night arrival. Amid a crowd of "several hundred people ... it took the football star more than 10 minutes to make his way to a private room at the airport."[2]

It was in all ways a flying trip. After the appearances for Channel Seven he flew to Bunbury on the Sunday, where he donned an East Perth jumper for the first time since the 1961 Grand Final to play for the Royals in a charity game against a combined local side. Even in this social atmosphere he drew rave reviews for his game from the local press. Then it was straight back to Melbourne to join a huge party of Geelong players, officials and supporters on an end-of-season trip with a difference.

Under the chairmanship of Kevin Threlfall a committee had been raising funds all year to finance a trip to America, with an itinerary that included Honolulu, San Francisco, Sacramento, a detour to the casinos of Nevada, and Los Angeles. It was Farmer's first journey outside Australia.

The idea for the trip had been prompted by a former Geelong resident who was living in San Francisco, and had taken on semi-official tones through a formal invitation from the San Francisco mayor to his counterpart in Geelong. It had been heavily publicised in Geelong, and promoted on the theme of the first Australian football team to visit American shores.

Somewhere along the line the Melbourne club had become involved. The two clubs were traditionally on friendly terms, with an annual out-of-season picnic with social tennis and foot races between the players held at Bacchus Marsh. It was arranged that matches between the sides would be played at Honolulu and San Francisco. The trip is described by the participants in much the same terms as most such club jaunts—a mixture of civic receptions, sightseeing, and allusions to all sorts of escapades that no one is prepared to detail—just in more exotic locations than usual.

During the premiership celebrations a number of Geelong players had confidently predicted the 1963 success would be repeated in 1964. Farmer was slightly more circumspect, but also indicated that he felt that the team was capable of more. Most of the press was of a similar opinion; in pieces written after the Grand Final and in the lead-up to 1964 there was much talk of a new era to compare to the Geelong of the early '50s, or the more recent reign of Melbourne.

There was a sound basis for such an argument. The side was still relatively young, but with a core of experienced third, fourth and fifth year players. It had more than its share of brilliant players, and was acknowledged as the most skilful and the paciest team in the League. Only one player from the premiership side, second rover Colin Rice, did not front for 1964. Seven of a panel of 10 press commentators making their predictions for the season chose Geelong as likely premiers, with the other three placing them second.

Geelong had also pulled off the recruiting coup of the year when they signed Denis Marshall from Claremont. Marshall was a tremendously gifted footballer who had been earmarked for stardom from the time of a brilliant debut as a teenager. He was a solidly built six-footer with speed, all the skills, and a beautiful raking drop kick. He had played most of his football on the half-back line, but was immensely versatile, and his style seemed more suited to the role of centre man, which he preferred, or the half-forward line. By the close of the 1963 season, while still short of his 23rd birthday, he had played in the winning carnival side of 1961, been runner-up to Haydn Bunton in the 1962 Sandover Medal, and won three best and fairest awards at Claremont.

But it was a while before Marshall was able to show his wares. Clearance wrangles and an official investigation into possible breaches of the Coulter Law delayed his debut until the eighth game of the season.

Farmer would have had grounds for arguing with Geelong that whatever Marshall was getting, he was entitled to at least as much, and probably more. But he was happy to keep going on the terms of his original contract, and in fact by this time had bought the house in Geelong, and relieved the club of the need to keep paying his rent. Marshall recalls that Farmer talked to him early on in the piece to quietly let him know that whatever he had negotiated with Geelong—and he was not interested in the details—was great, he should take whatever he could get and enjoy it. Marshall was never bashful or uncertain of himself, but this reassurance and sign of approval from the great man of the club meant a lot to the new arrival.

Of course, while the Marshall saga dragged on the real football action began. Geelong's first-up game was back at the MCG against Melbourne, before a crowd of 70,000. In a contest described by the Sun as a "Grand Final at the wrong end of the year," with its "heart-thumping tension [and] fierce tackling," Geelong played in bursts to record a come-from-behind 13-point victory.[3]

From that solid start Geelong rolled on impressively. Apart from one uninspired performance against Essendon, it recorded wins against all teams to head the ladder with a 10-win, one-loss record after a complete round of matches. Farmer was consistently among Geelong's best, but did not put in a really big game until round six, when lowly Richmond threatened to upset the Cats until he took over the game. This match was notable as the first full game for a young ruckman fresh from Geelong Grammar named John Newman.

Newman and another youngster, Bill Ryan, who had played a handful of games in the middle of 1963, were challenging the other big men of the side, Vinar, Watts, Yeates and Lowe, for the right to play a supporting role to Farmer. The Geelong Advertiser noticed the influence of Farmer on the pair, who had both adopted the early leap, and Newman in particular already showed the capacity for the grab and handpass that was the Farmer trademark.

The Cat's 10th win came up in a canter against Carlton at Princes Park, on a day when Nicholls was the only player to stand out for the Blues, taking a points decision in a titanic battle with Farmer.

In June Farmer played in both of Victoria's interstate matches for the season, against South Australia in Adelaide, and Western Australia at the MCG, with both resulting in wins for the Victorians.

Geelong had now been on top of the ladder since the start of the season without ever looking entirely convincing. There had been no real four quarter performances, and it had struggled against the lowly sides. Its three largest wins had come against Melbourne, Hawthorn and Collingwood, placed second, third and fifth, with two of these coming in the first two games. Rather than consolidating in the run home though, it almost appeared that the wheels were falling off, with the last seven games producing three wins, three losses and a tie. The first of the three wins came against Collingwood at Victoria Park, after Farmer had been up almost the whole of the Friday night prior for the birth of his second son, Dean. He still managed to be one of Geelong's best on the day.

Coming into the last home and away match of the season, against St Kilda, Geelong were a game clear in second place. St Kilda had disappointed some of the pundits who had tipped it as the big improver, and after an inconsistent year was entrenched in sixth place. But it was the Saints' last game at the St Kilda Oval, as they were to move to Moorabbin in 1965, and as is often the case in such situations, they rode on the crest of an emotional wave to lead the Cats all day and get home by two goals. The stumble left Collingwood, Essendon and Geelong each on 13 wins, four losses and a draw, and they finished in that order on percentage, forcing the Cats into a cut-throat first semi-final against the Bombers, whom they had not been able to conquer in two encounters.

Melbourne had never relinquished top position after taking it from Geelong, but could easily have finished in fifth position. A freak goal from Hassa Mann late in the game had secured a four-point victory over

Hawthorn in the second last home and away game. If that result had been reversed, Hawthorn would have been on 56 points, two clear of the other three teams.

These two consecutive years of traffic jams at the top of the ladder show just how close the competition was in that era. The results over a two-year period indicate that there was virtually nothing between Geelong and five other sides—Melbourne, Hawthorn, Essendon, Collingwood and St Kilda. Its greatness lay in its potential, and the irregular bursts of brilliance, not in its results.

Jack Dyer has written that Farmer played better football in the 1964 season than the previous year:

> It was then that he developed into a complete League ruckman. I've seen all the greats of the past but in '64 Polly convinced me that he was as good as any of them. He was unbeatable and often made his opponents look like schoolboys. He had unlimited stamina, fantastic body manipulation to get into the best position to get the ball and uncanny accuracy in getting the ball to his rover …
>
> And it was in '64 that he directly influenced the brand of football being played in the VFL. Other ruckmen copied and learned that to be tough and strong was one thing but to be skilful was another. Polly had the strength to get himself into position and protect the smaller player, but he was also the most skilful ruckman that ever lived.[4]

The week-by-week reports and the best player awards do not tend to support Dyer's opinion. He shows up as playing consistently good and creative football, with some bursts of brilliance and inspiration when the moment required. In the awards Farmer generally finished a few votes and half a dozen places behind the winners. But the judgement within the club is perhaps reflected by the fact that he won the best and fairest award with more votes, and by a higher margin than in 1963.

The match reports also indicate that the double and triple teaming against him, and the buffeting and general level of harassment was even greater, if anything, than in the previous year. The other noticeable feature was that the opposition were beginning to develop more sophisticated methods to deal with his distribution of the ball. This is one of the reasons Goggin was copping so much attention—including concussion in three consecutive games. Unable to stop Farmer, opponents would simply charge at Goggin, aiming to pick him off before or as he received from Farmer. But Goggin was as tough as they come, and just kept bouncing back, to play a particularly good season of football.

Geelong's last seven weeks of football had certainly brought out the critics. Nobody doubted the side's ability to take out the premiership, but many doubted that it was playing well enough, or with sufficient cohesion to string together the three wins it would need to take the flag from fourth position, with some thinking the Cats would fall at the first hurdle against an Essendon combination that seemed to have the wood on them.

The team's problems seemed to be due to a combination of injury and form problems preventing them from getting a balanced side. The Cats' defensive six were the same as the previous year, and were still one of the great strengths of the team. For the second year in a row they were the meanest in the League in terms of points conceded. The centreline had been a worry though, with a constantly changing line-up, and Wade was having injury problems, and was not getting big bags of goals.

The performance against Essendon was probably the side's best for the year to that point. On a day of patchy rain and a muddy ground, in front of a record first semi-final crowd of over 92,000, Geelong started quietly to trail at quarter-time, but dominated the rest of the game to record a very solid 19-point win. It was an even team performance, with Devine, Alistair Lord, Marshall, Farmer, Goggin and Closter all prominent.

Bob Davis was on top of the world after the game, predicting a premiership win, and commenting that "the recent criticism that has been levelled at the team brought out the necessary will to win. We wanted to show our team at its very best, and all the players responded."[5]

In the second semi-final Melbourne showed that it would be a formidable opponent. After Collingwood got the first two goals, Melbourne got 19 to four to treble the Magpies' score, in one of the easiest passages of all time to the Grand Final. Collingwood had snuck into the four late in the season at Hawthorn's expense, and their second-position finish was seen as somewhat fortunate, with both Geelong and Essendon, and even the Hawks, being ranked as better teams by most judges. With this feeling reinforced by performances in the two semi-finals, the Cats entered the preliminary final as clear favourites.

Heavy rain that set in at the outset of the second quarter turned the ground into a quagmire and reduced the advantage of the Cats' superior pace. Nevertheless, throughout the first half Geelong dominated the ball without being able to convert in front of goal. They led by six points at the long break. The Magpie defence closed Geelong down in the third quarter, and Collingwood was eight points clear at the last break.

Farmer had been the dominant player on the ground to this point, but the moves he created were not being finished off. But in the last quarter, as Geelong pressed constantly forward, his "exhibition was fantastic as he tried to pull the game out of the fire. Once, near the centre, he was tackled by three Magpies but, with sheer strength, he brushed all aside then handballed perfectly to Billy Goggin only to see the move break down when Kenny Turner cleared."[6]

Farmer lifted Geelong when it flagged and with the help of Goggin almost carried Geelong to victory. "Some of his marks elicited spontaneous applause from every spectator, and it is indeed a rare moment when Collingwood supporters acclaim opponents."[7] This last comment could hardly be overemphasised given the context of a dour, tense elimination final.

With Farmer and Goggin driving the ball constantly forward, it appeared inevitable that the Cats would overcome. They were looking for Wade, and four times he took strong marks. Four times he could have put Geelong in front, but the result was two behinds and two that fell short. A Wooller goal got his team within one point, but Collingwood forced the ball forward in a series of scrimmages, and Waters snapped a goal. Wade got one of his points from a shot right in front, a long shot from Farmer was touched through, and Routley missed from 25 yards to make the difference just four points. On their last sally forward, Wade flew for yet another mark, well within scoring distance, but just before his hands wrapped around the ball, the siren sounded, and he had no chance to redeem himself. The day belonged to Collingwood.

Farmer remembers this performance as one of his best individual games, and there are others who agreed. Jack Dyer described it as "one of the most brilliant rucking performances I have ever seen."[8] And the *Geelong Advertiser* summary of the game recorded that: "Although Geelong lost Saturday's VFL preliminary final, the match will be remembered best for the football played by Graham Farmer. In modern sport description, where battered superlatives lose their value and flavour, perhaps it is sufficient to say that Farmer's display will be stored as a treasure in the memories of Australian Rules followers."[9]

But such superlatives are little consolation for a final-round loss that should have been a victory. Commentators, Geelong players and officials all said at the time, and on many occasions since, that Geelong lost the game more than Collingwood won it. They had the lion's share of possession, the two best players on the ground in Farmer and Goggin, six more scoring shots than the opposition—everything except the score on the board.

In the Geelong camp it has always been seen as a premiership that got away from them. They firmly believe that they were the best team in the competition in 1964, and that if they had been in the Grand Final they would have won it. Instead, Melbourne and Collingwood battled it out. Melbourne were hot favourites, but Collingwood clung to them like leeches, and actually hit the front approaching time on after Gabelich's famous 70-yard, four-bounce dash down the flank. Then a goal from nowhere by back pocket player Neil Crompton stole the game back, for Melbourne's 12th premiership.

The day after the preliminary final loss Farmer had made clear his displeasure at the team's performance in an interview on the *World of Sport* program, commenting that when the pressure came on, some of his teammates decided "to live and fight another day."[10] As the 1965 season drew near, there was mixed opinion as to whether the experience would provide a salutary lesson, or prove the start of a decline.

The side now had a lot less of the 1963 look about it. Captain Fred

Wooller had gone to Tasmania as captain-coach of Penguin. Stewart Lord, John Brown and Hugh Routley all went to coach and play in country leagues. Terry Callan finally succumbed to his bad knee. Roy West's back injury was to keep him out for the whole year. And at the start of the season Alistair Lord was in dispute with the club; he also wanted to play and coach in Tasmania, but Geelong was refusing to clear him. There were no star recruits to fill the gaps. Of the new players that came into the club, only young Gareth Andrews from Geelong College would make a substantial impact, with no other first-year players racking up more than seven games.

This decline in player strength was the biggest concern in assessing Geelong's chances, according to Alf Brown in a preview in the *Herald*. The biggest boost he saw for them was the prospect of a "more inspiring leadership."[11] In his third year with the club Farmer was appointed captain. John Devine was reappointed vice-captain for the fourth year in a row, under his third different captain. Although there were some hints that Devine might have felt hard done by, Farmer's appointment was generally acclaimed as right and proper.

Brown thought that: "This year, with Farmer urging them on, Geelong may fight harder each Saturday. Obviously Farmer and ... Devine are trying to put more backbone into Geelong's game. In a recent practice match these two loomed up from opposite directions. Both kept going and the crash was shattering as both must have realised it would be, but both went on with it."[12]

Opening day for Geelong was on the Monday of a split round, but conditions more like those of mid-July than mid-April made it difficult to gauge the team's performance. They slogged to a two point win over Footscray after a first quarter in which they failed to score while Footscray got one behind.

Top of the ladder after the first round was Carlton, following a good win over Hawthorn. A sign of things to come, hoped the Blues fans. For a club as proud as Carlton it had been a long time between drinks, with its last success coming in 1947. But this year it was hoped that things might be different. In possibly the biggest sensation in VFL history, Ron Barassi had become Carlton's captain-coach. Until the bombshell was dropped, Barassi was Melbourne, and Melbourne was Barassi. The ties between he and the club, and especially between he and his coach, mentor and father-figure, Norm Smith, were so strong that no one even imagined they might be broken.

But Barassi wanted to coach; it could be said that he was born to coach. Despite their success in 1964, he knew that the Demons were on the decline. Nor did the thought cross his mind of usurping Smith. So, to the despair of the thousands of boys who wore No. 31 on their backs, and to the outrage of the traditionalists, he sought new pastures.

For an early season clash there was much at stake for both teams on that Anzac Day weekend at Princes Park, and the game was played accordingly. In a ferocious first quarter, Marshall went to ground three times, at the hands of Nicholls, then Barassi, then back flanker John Gill. Nicholls was reported for the first time in his career for striking John Fox, and Farmer and Barassi clashed twice. The first time "Farmer flattened Barassi with a beautiful bump,"[13] then "Farmer and Barassi brought a gasp from the crowd as they spreadeagled each other."[14] Amid all this action, eight goals were scored—five to Geelong and three to Carlton. Three of Geelong's goals were scored by Farmer. In his 45 games before this one Farmer had spent the vast bulk of each on the ball. But in this game he spent long periods in the forward pocket alongside Gareth Andrews who was filling in at full-forward for an injured Doug Wade. Barassi still rues the fact that he did not send Nicholls down to cover Farmer.

Geelong lost its lead early in the final quarter, but with Farmer prominent, a series of counter-attacks produced a goal and a clutch of behinds that took them to a six-point victory. The fighting win left the Geelong camp in high spirits. The experiment of using Farmer up forward had produced five goals—his best tally for Geelong, exceeding the four in his debut game, also at Princes Park. And Newman had come of age by holding his own in extended jousts with Nicholls. The *Sporting Globe's* votes all went to ruckmen—three to Farmer, two to Nicholls, and one to Newman. The *Geelong Advertiser* concurred, invoking the words of Banjo Patterson:

> "He was the daddy, the master, was Pardon the son of Reprieve" … the same words describe Graham Farmer's exhibition against Carlton … Farmer has let few football honours elude him, but one unwon is the Brownlow Medal. He

only has to turn in another six or seven games like Saturday's to be well on the way. His handball, marking and kicking seldom could be faulted, and it was a true captain's game.[15]

Subsequent wins against North Melbourne and Collingwood had Geelong off to a good start of four straight, but then it was back to the old pattern of inexplicable lapses and form reversals. The Cats outscored the Demons by seven goals to three in the second half, but still went down by 14 points. Victories against Fitzroy, Hawthorn and St Kilda left them with eight wins and one loss, and in second place on the ladder. Alistair Lord had come into the side as a shock last-minute inclusion against Fitzroy after burying the hatchet with the club. But he was unable to wrest the centre position back from Marshall, and was playing mostly off the half-forward flank.

Following the St Kilda victory Geelong went into a topsy-turvy period of alternating defeats and wins that saw it going up and down the top half of a congested ladder. Bob Davis was shifting players all over the place in an attempt to set the team to rights. Sharrock played across the centreline, and even put in a game at full-back, as well as sharing the centre half-forward position with Andrews. Devine appeared on a half-forward flank for a few weeks

Farmer's best game in this period came in the return clash with Carlton:

Farmer, although shaded in the ruck by Nicholls, played inspiring football around the ground for four quarters. Farmer had nineteen kicks for the match spread evenly through each quarter, took four marks and used handball with his usual efficiency. Much of his work went unnoticed because it was apart from his ruck duels with Nicholls, but for a ruckman to have 19 kicks is an amazing effort![16]

His performance did not count on the day though, with some players accused of "putting in the short step to avoid collisions".[17] A four-and-a-half goal loss saw the Cats drop out of the four on percentage, being one of five teams placed second to sixth all on nine wins. They got back to fourth place with a win over North Melbourne, but with three rounds to go their future was up in the air. Injuries to Scott against Carlton and Wade against North put each out for the remainder of the season, to add to the club's woes.

Interspersed with the home and away round during this middle part of the season was the year's interstate football. The first was at the MCG against the South Australians. With open selection for this game John Devine joined Farmer and Goggin as Geelong representatives in the Victorian team. South Australia started at a great pace, and had the Victorians fumbling and disorganised in the opening minutes. After the opening barrage the Victorians pulled away to a very comfortable 10-goal win, with Farmer among their best and scoring three goals.

One of the great photographs of Farmer came out of this match, when he got high off the ground for a classical two-handed mark in front of goals. It is the personalities as much as the action that makes the photo. Farmer has planted his knee in the back of his own full-forward Ted Whitten to get the ride, with South Australia's Neil Kerley flying from behind, but hopelessly out of position. Captured in the one shot are perhaps the favourite football sons of each of the three major states.

The caption to the picture says that Whitten staggered away from the incident holding his back. Whitten, who had the photo in his office, recalled it vividly when interviewed in 1992, and claimed that his back was still hurting:

> I have got the ball in my sights—the next minute, this knee in the middle of my back, and I went down. I said to him: "What'd you do that for Polly, I'm the full-forward, you're the forward pocket." He said: "I thought I was in a better position Ted, so I just went for it."

Farmer smiled at the photograph, and at the memory. "It really is a good mark isn't it? There's no doubt about it, it's a great feeling to be in a position to do that."

A couple of weeks later a Victorian touring party set off for two games in Perth, and a return match against the South Australians in Adelaide. Farmer was accorded the significant honour of the Victorian vice-captaincy under Bob Skilton. Interestingly, he was one of three former East Perth players in the Victorian team, the others being young Graeme John and Ralph Rogerson, in their second seasons with South Melbourne and Fitzroy respectively. It was not to be a happy tour for Farmer though.

In the first game at Subiaco Oval the Victorians suffered their first loss at the venue since 1948. They had led by 13 points at three-quarter time, but succumbed to a five-goal last quarter from the Sandgropers. Farmer got two of the Vic's eight goals, but was part of a ruck division beaten by a West Australian squad led by his old sparring partners Keith Slater and Brian Foley. He also emerged from the game with a strained knee and a split eye, which caused him to miss the second game on the Tuesday, in which the Victorians reversed the outcome.

In Adelaide, Victoria suffered its worst ever defeat. After leading 2.1 (13) to 1.5 (11) at quarter-time, they scored a solitary goal for the rest of the game to go down by 62 points. To add to the misery, Farmer received a broken nose, but with Barrot and Parkin already off the field by half-time, he played the game out. The nose job came courtesy of a Neil Kerley forearm, raised when Farmer tried to lay a tackle on him.

At that point Geelong's roller-coaster ride had only just begun, and they were still relatively secure in the four. The break to his nose was quite severe, and the advice was that a further blow could cause serious problems. When asked why he did not rest for a week, he seemed bemused at the thought. "Purely and simply pride—a desire to be part of the team. I really didn't want to miss a game." So with some help from the medical staff he fashioned from fibreglass and strapping a fearsome and uncomfortable-looking noseguard for the game against Footscray. He says that "the worst part about it was that everyone wanted to go for it." Perhaps it was lucky that he was playing against gentleman John Schultz—his ruck partner on the interstate tour, and the man acknowledged as the cleanest ruckman of the era—but he survived the game well enough without being too prominent, and fronted the following week for the Carlton game.

The crunch in terms of Geelong's finals ambitions came in the third last home and away game against Melbourne. The two teams were sitting fourth and fifth on the ladder, equal on points, both having come off losses to Collingwood and South Melbourne respectively. The loser would drop a game behind in the race for a finals berth with only two rounds to make up the deficit. Melbourne took the honours in the first quarter, but Geelong dominated the rest of the game to record one of their best wins of the season.

The following week Farmer was brilliant—16 kicks, 20 handballs, and the crucial last quarter goal that sealed the game—but the rest of the team was lacklustre in a win over Fitzroy that secured its position in the four. The Cats then finished the home and away round with a resounding victory at Glenferrie Oval against Hawthorn. They finished in third place on the ladder when Essendon dropped its last game against Carlton.

Once again Farmer finished behind the leaders, but ahead of the main bunch in the media awards. On Brownlow night though, the men who should have known picked him as a likely winner. The leading umpires were gathered in a place many supporters would have liked to consign them to permanently; they had been persuaded by prison chaplain, Father Brosnan, to give a talk at Pentridge.

"We all met over there," says Jeff Crouch, "and we decided, let's all have a think about the Brownlow. Ken Fraser's name came up and Polly Farmer's came up more than others ... So we decided that it would be out of Ken Fraser and Polly Farmer that year. No one mentioned Ian Stewart ... but each one of us must have given him a three vote, and he won the Brownlow."

Others were as surprised as the umpires at the result—the first of Stewart's three medals. He won on a count back from Noel Teasdale, followed by Baldock, then Fraser. Farmer finished back in equal ninth position with fellow ruckmen Morrow and Schultz.

The side Geelong fielded for the first semi-final was notable for its youth. Wade, Sharrock and Scott were all out injured. Alistair Lord was named in the side, but tonsillitis forced him to withdraw at the last minute. The 18 that took the field included five teenagers—including the whole full-forward line of Newman, Andrews and second rover David Brown and three 20-year-olds.

Despite the inexperience and holes caused by retirement and injury, no one doubted that the Cats had the capacity to win the premiership if they performed to their best. The big problem was that they would have to produce this in three consecutive games—something that they had failed to do all season.

In the first minutes of the game Essendon coach Coleman had half of his players lined up out of position, and then switched them all over the field before settling them back to their usual positions in mid-term. The ruse appeared to work as Geelong floundered. It was also lacking the usual drive from Farmer. Big Brian Sampson took up position in front of him to block his ground, with Don McKenzie and the other support ruckmen flying over the top, and throughout the first half he struggled.

Davis rang the moves without success. Marshall popped up all over the ground, but not in the centre where he had played his best football for the year, and where young Newland was getting a bath from 200-game veteran Jack Clarke. Farmer came into the game in the second half, but by then it was too late, as Essendon coasted to a stunningly easy 103- to 51-point victory.

It was a truly disappointing effort for a final-round game, with no fire shown, and many Geelong players hardly sighted. "Polly tried his damdest. He, Billy Goggin, John Devine, Tony Polinelli and Gareth Andrews were the only ones who appeared to put effort into their work."[18] The only consolation to be found was that Essendon went on to prove that it was indeed the superior team of the season. In two more devastating performances the Bombers doubled Collingwood's score in the preliminary final and beat St Kilda by almost six goals in the Grand Final, to complete perhaps the best sequence of final-round performances in VFL history.

12

"HE HAD SOME MAGIC ABOUT HIM"

He was the player that caused more concern to all players and coaches than any player I have known. And that includes the Colemans and the Wades and the Hudsons and the Locketts and the Dunstalls. Farmer created more concern for coaches and opposition players than anybody I have ever known. They couldn't set themselves a way of retarding his brilliance.

These are the words of Ted Whitten, who had good reason to know, as the captain-coach of Footscray during the time Farmer was at Geelong. Farmer had done at Geelong the same as at East Perth. Using the creed of his own, the philosophy that defined his own role as "to get the ball and give it," he played a brand of football that was all his own, but simultaneously could make a whole team hum.

He was impossible to stop because he had such a wide range of attributes as a player, they could not all be countered. He was so feared not only because of his unstoppability, but because his style of play was so productive.

In the one sentence his disciple John 'Sam' Newman, describes Farmer as both "the consummate team player" and a "selfish player." Selfish because "he worried about one thing only and that was how he played and how he handled the person who played against him." But "all the rest followed ... because of the way he played football, he brought people naturally into the game."

Father Brosnan, the knockabout priest who boasts of being dropped from the Cudgee State School football team that only had 12 kids in it, perhaps comes closer than any to defining the way Farmer worked. Though he was actually talking at the time of Farmer off the field, it applies equally well to his football. Reaching back to his seminary training in the philosophy of causality he cites the proposition that: "The formal cause has its effect by its mere presence."

This is obviously not to suggest that Farmer was a passive force on a football field, but rather that he was a natural force in his own right whose presence and play inevitably created its own effect. The great forwards whom Whitten names were feared less than Farmer because they relied on others up the field to create for them. Farmer created in his own right. He was almost always the originator of the play.

This comes back in part to his position as a ruckman, at the bounce or throw-in that starts the play. But it has more to do with his particular creed of 'get it and give it.' Farmer was not a receiver, he had that faith that Watts describes that once the ball came anywhere near him it was his. He could scrabble in the packs with the best of the rovers and shoot the ball out.

Much modern coaching is built around a theory expounded by the great Allan Jeans of St Kilda and Hawthorn. Some credit the theory to him, though others trace it back to Len Smith. Jeans says: "In football, from the time you bounce the ball until the end of the game the ball can only be in one of three phases. It's either in dispute, we have it, or they have it. It can't be in any other area." From this analysis the coach then lays down 'fundamentals' as to how players should move and respond in any given phase and its many variations.

The most critical phase is the one where the ball is in dispute. Herein lay half of Farmer's genius. He was among the best there have been at winning this ball. Throughout a game he consistently shifted the game from the 'in dispute' phase, to the 'we have it' phase. The possession that does this—

wins the neutral ball, or creates the turnover—is the critical one whose worth never shows up in mere statistics. When this is combined with the other half of his genius—his acknowledged status as the best user and disposer of the ball in the game—his value to a team can begin to be appreciated.

This ball-getting ability was even more critical in the hard-slogging, relatively low-scoring Victorian Football League than it had been in Western Australia, where a more free-flowing, open style of football prevailed; the ball was in dispute more often, and tended to be disputed more fiercely.

Newman scoffs at those who deny there were deliberate attempts to nobble Farmer:

> Absolute bullshit. They are not going to say that for their own credibility ...
> It is sheer folly to suggest—whether they would be fair or not in using tactics—[that] they didn't spend hours trying to work out how to combat Farmer. Some stepped out of the bounds of what was asked of them, and others wouldn't. Those who didn't step over the bounds would have no flat chance. Those who did step over the bounds, you would find that they spent a lot of time in the medical room after the game, nursing injuries that no one ever saw them get. He was a professional.

Rod Olsson succeeded Farmer as the coach of Geelong in later years, but also played against him as a Hawthorn ruck-rover. One of the best-known incidents of Olsson's playing career came when he was knocked cold by Ted Whitten, receiving severe concussion. When asked in his Geelong days whether Whitten was the toughest footballer he had played against, he apparently replied that there were two tougher, Darrel Baldock and Graham Farmer, while noting that between the pair they were only ever reported once. Whitten himself tells a story:

> One day I fixed up Denis Marshall down at Geelong, and Polly leapt over and said: "You shouldn't have done that EJ." "It was an accident," I said. "No it wasn't," he said, "you shouldn't have done that." Before the game [finished] I was in a pack. Geez, he gave me a beauty ... quite legitimately though. He was pretty strong. And nobody saw it. But you accept those things ...

just things we all do during the course of a game. You don't bitch about it because, I mean, they're only receipts.

Farmer passed the acid test of the VFL tough men with flying colours. And the opposition could find few other ways to frustrate his effect on a game. Whitten again: "We were very jealous because he had created something within himself that he could control and we couldn't." Newman commented that:

Farmer worked on the basis that if you have had your opponent change his game to try to combat you, the thing that they had to concentrate on—the football—was out of their mind. A lot of ruckmen used to look at the ball and look at Farmer. They used to be preoccupied with what he was doing, where he was. That is what he worked on, the fact that you play your opponents on their weaknesses, not on their strengths.

Even his arch-rival Nicholls was forced to play on Farmer's terms during their meetings:

I probably didn't jump as early as [Farmer], but when I played him I did ... With Polly, I never gave him any advantage because I'd do the same things as he did ... We would both jump early for position—particularly at centre bounces—and quite often the ball would come down and neither of us would get it.

Nicholls feels that the two of them tended to nullify each other, and for all the hype their confrontations created, in many Carlton-Geelong games, neither would have a great influence:

Probably I used to regard him as a better player than I was, and probably more skilled than I was, so I really had to dish it up to him all the time in ruckwork. At the centre bounces and boundary throw-ins I had to be aggressive to him every time. If I didn't attack him on an aggressive basis every time, he would beat me.

We used to play it very hard, and because we both used to jump early and use our arms and things, we quite often had blood noses and things. But we've always been good mates ... I've always said that Teddy Whitten was the best all-round player I've ever seen, but certainly Farmer was the best ruckman without a doubt. A lot of others have been very good and come close, but there was only one Polly Farmer and he was the best.

Farmer came to Geelong virtually as a finished product as a footballer, merely adding the touches he felt he needed of additional strength and a greater mental and physical toughness. He played the same game that he had at East Perth of feeding the ball out to the running players. Through his first couple of years one reads in some of the match reports that his handball was astray, and being sharked by the opposition.

Farmer takes umbrage at this. As far as he was concerned his handballs always went exactly where they were intended. What he was trying to do was educate his teammates to his style of play, to be moving towards goal as they received the ball from him. Even now watching an old video he gets annoyed at a commentator saying that a handpass missed its target. "The ball was in the right place, Alistair Lord just didn't move to meet it."

Newman comments that it took about a season and a half for this to sink in with the whole team. "Farmer never sat down and said that he was going to do this. He would just do it, and many times Farmer would hit guys who didn't realise what he was doing." Some, like Goggin, adapted very quickly, but after a time they all "learned that when he got the ball they had to be on the move".

Goggin's understanding of Farmer's way of playing football had been instinctive, as if the pair were made for each other. Goggin's mate, and long-time Geelong trainer, George Clark conjures up a Schwarzenegger and De Vito-like image:

> They were almost like twins—this sense between them. And it came out of nowhere. And they were magnificent to watch. Billy would say: "I knew what he was doing before he did it, and he knew where I was going to be." Billy would just run, and he'd just hit him on the chest. "I knew it was coming. I'd look over my shoulder, and here it comes."

Farmer revolutionised the game of football. This is a statement one hears and reads over and over. It is a claim made about no other player. It is by no means universally accepted as a statement of fact, but the fact that it is heard so often says something about his impact on the game. It is usually taken to mean that he was the pioneer of the art of attacking handball that has become such a central feature of the game, or that he was the progenitor of play-on football.

Some argue that this had begun with the Len Smith mosquito fleet at Fitzroy, where flick-passing and quick movement of the ball at close quarters had taken a team of ordinary players to the finals in 1960. Footscray under Ted Whitten played this same style in reaching the 1961 Grand Final against Hawthorn.

Others say that Farmer was unique unto himself, and though some tried to emulate his style, handball did not come of age as an integral part of football until the historic 1970 Grand Final when Carlton came back from the dead to steal the premiership from Collingwood, thanks to a half-time instruction from a desperate Ron Barassi to handball at all costs.

What all the insiders agree on is that Farmer opened their eyes to the possibilities of handball, and what it could do when used so well. No one had utilised it in the same way, and to the same effect before Farmer arrived. In this sense, even if he was not a revolutionary, he was a central figure in the evolution of the modern game.

The effect that his handball had on the patterns of play and the way the ball was moved down the field was just as important as the use of handball as a technique. Essentially football had been a straight-ahead game. The flick-passing game could get the ball out of packs or manoeuvre it to advantage, but essentially it shared the ball between players running down the same line.

The long handball that Farmer introduced had the capacity to completely change the direction of play, to cut right across the field. This would provide increased options for the receiver, by throwing defenders out of kilter, and opening up new lines of attack. At its most perfect it created football that was beautiful to watch. It became one of the classic football passages— Farmer to Goggin out wide, streaming downfield, delivering perfectly to Wade, mark, goal.

Farmer's insistence on putting the ball in front of the receiver, forcing him to move forwards as he took the ball, created a new pattern that gradually became more and more important: lateral movement to create the space for a forward thrust. Barassi's triumph in 1970, initiated to overcome Collingwood's superior aerial strength by going around their big men, gave coaches and players the courage to use the same pattern of play out of defence.

As the game has evolved further, so the understanding and usage of the tactics have developed. Barassi makes the point that:

> ... there has to be someone to give it to. The guy running past was the key; not so much the handballer, but the handballee, so to speak. When Barry Davis went from North Melbourne back to Essendon [in 1979] to be a coach, he began to take stats on who were the receivers of a handball, indicating that he wanted to know who the hell was running past.

But it was Farmer 15 years earlier, when Barry Davis was just beginning his football career, who had, if not created, at least opened the eyes of the football world to the real value of the handballee, the man running past.

It has come to the point where good sides will chip the ball backwards and forwards across the field by hand and foot until the right opening is created for the movement forward. But now, as then, it still works best when giver and receiver have the speed, the vision and the understanding to create the movement quickly and unexpectedly, catching the opposition off guard.

Farmer made the moves more quickly, more unexpectedly, and more tellingly than anyone. 'He hated to waste a possession' is another of the recurring statements made about him. Yet he needed no time to make the assessment of the best option. With uncanny peripheral vision and knowledge of where his teammates were, and lightning hands, the ball would be on its way almost before he had it in his hands.

Ted Whitten describes the process in almost mystical terms:

> He had some magic about him whereby he had full control of the football ... You could sort of tell that he would bring it down with him. He had the amazing sense of being able, when he was in the air, to know where his men were situated around him, because the moment he hit the ground it was either a kick or a handball directly to his team men. He got up in the air and he would think about it coming down: "What will I do with this one!" And he had that unique sense, he would mesmerise players. You would really think

they were stopping to see, just to watch him, just for a split second—and bang—and then they would start again.

On top of all these attributes was his phenomenal consistency. "He did the job *every* Saturday," says Bob Davis. "He never had a bad day when people could have said that he was trashed or didn't contribute," says Newman. "When he was having a bad day he would always be competitive, his effectiveness would never drop below 75 per cent. He was the consummate competitor."

Farmer was a crowd-pleaser, too. In his Geelong days, though he took many a strong mark in the packs, his loose knee meant that he rarely took the high-flying screamers of his youth. He did not run with the ball as some of the crowd favourites do. He did not dodge and weave. (In fact he has little time for the players who do this. He believes it the sign either of a fumbler, or worse, the player who is intent only on breaking clear himself, instead of the more important task of releasing the ball into the clear.) The crowds got their thrill from Farmer from those special touches of magic that seemed unique to him. The ball that seemed to roll down his outstretched arm in a ruck duel. The twist in mid-air as he came down with a mark and shot the ball out before his feet hit the ground. The 40-metre handpass that released a player to charge down the flank. These were the moves that would bring gasps and then rushes of applause—even from the Collingwood fans. And along with the success of the team, they were responsible in large part for the Geelong membership and the attendances at Kardinia Park soaring to record levels in the mid-1960s.

In Geelong, Farmer became an absolute idol, a cult figure whose status has only ever been rivalled by the Cats' other great No. 5, Gary Ablett. The round of public appearances, in the media, at schools, at functions and openings and country socials around the western districts, was enormous. He also did much unpublicised work in the community. He often went with Father Brosnan out to Pentridge, where he was a great favourite. He was known as generous with his time for children.

Thus far the move to Victoria had panned out almost perfectly, apart from the team's failure to fulfil its potential in 1964. On and off field his football prowess had earned accolades, and he had reaped the rewards. He was close to being a fully professional sportsman, with the direct earnings, together with the endorsements and advertisements.

He continued his daytime work selling Holdens until 1966, when he began work with an insurance company. He earned his commissions, but it was not too demanding. Bill Goggin tells of Farmer calling in from time to time at the Corio Meatworks where he was employed. Goggin would get a message that Polly wanted him, they had to do something for the club, and they would disappear for the day—off for a round of golf, a game of tennis, or a day at the races.

The two of them were fierce competitors. They usually played tennis at the home of their mutual friend, Mick O'Bierne. They cheated each other terribly on the line calls, and O'Bierne tells the story of the two of them sitting at either end of the court for 20 minutes, each refusing to budge over a disputed call. But Goggin believes that the time spent together off the field helped them to develop their on-field rapport. Everyone at Geelong seems to have been into the horses, and the midweek race meetings in the district were a diversion for many of the players and others around the club, including Farmer.

He had formed a number of good friendships, with teammates and others around the club and town, such as his exercise partner, Kelvin Darcy. Some of them were mates, for the racing and sporting pursuits, and the card nights at Leo O'Brien's. Others also became family friends, who shared summer days at one another's places. Marlene enjoyed Geelong, and also took advantage of the proximity to Tasmania to see more of her family.

A football star in Victoria is a star like few others, the public interest is so pervasive, so intense and passionate. Farmer was a star in spades. Yet in the early years at Geelong there appears to have been very little of the down side of jealousy and pettiness within the club that so often accompanies the star status. He always got on well with Bob Davis—there was none of the subtle tension or rivalry that had existed with Jack Sheedy. And among the players he was well liked.

Many of the team and those who were close to them recall the 1963 side specifically as being a particularly close bunch—like brothers, says Father

Brosnan. Watts was the clown of the side, at the centre of unofficial team activities, practical jokes and good times, often with Farmer at his side urging him on:

> He loves a laugh, especially if I'm jamming it up somebody else. "Go on John, get Devine, get Devine with a Catholic gag" ... There's not one I wouldn't call a mate, a real good mate. Four of us were freemasons, me and Pol and the Lords, and all the rest were micks. We used to jam it up 'em—friendly rivalry ... From top to bottom, the whole of the Geelong club, there wasn't a snag in the side.

These sort of sentiments are echoed by all of the team, and emphasised by Devine. "There's always something special about a premiership side. People don't really understand the closeness that becomes developed."

Much of the aura that still surrounds Farmer and the side in the hearts and minds of the Geelong diehards derives from the fact that they remained the Cats' last premiership team until a 44-year drought was finally broken in 2007. But they did have something special, and for all that he was one of the lads at Geelong, it had a lot to do with Farmer. As Davis says:

> I think they joined together more because Farmer came, because he made them winners. I mean we did things that no one ever heard of. We got in a plane and went to America. It wasn't his personality, it was his playing ability that got them all. I'm quite happy to say that Farmer took the club to America.

It could be said that for a footballer life begins to end at 30. For even the greatest and the hardiest the new decade signals that the end is within sight. The public and the pundits assume that it can only be a downhill run, as the legs lose their zip, the years of wear and tear begin to take their toll. Farmer had turned 30 at the beginning of the 1965 season, and in many ways the year can be seen as a turning point.

In the club best and fairest award at Geelong, counted after the disappointing first semi-final performance, Farmer finished fourth behind Peter Walker, John Devine and Sam Newman. It was the first time he had played a full season of senior football and not taken out the club award.

Until this point in his career Farmer had collected official and media awards at a rate perhaps surpassed only by Haydn Bunton senior. In the next two years he finished runner-up at Geelong to Denis Marshall then Bill Goggin. His votes in the Brownlow declined from 11 in 1965 to eight and three in the subsequent seasons. He never repeated his success of 1963 in any of the media awards.

Geelong's elimination in the first week of the finals was a disaster by Farmer's standards, following as it did six consecutive Grand Finals with East Perth and a premiership and an unfortunate preliminary final loss with Geelong.

Was the Farmer magic wearing off? No. Was his brilliance beginning to dim somewhat? Perhaps a little. There is no doubt that as each year went by his knee felt the pressure more and more, and his agility decreased. He had never been flamboyant, but his play perhaps showed fewer flashes of the crowd-thrilling brilliance. He used all his experience and guile to cultivate a beautiful economy of style. Newman recalls:

> He would patrol that imaginary square that wasn't on the ground in those days. It was like the old bull and the young bull. If the ball would go over the boundary line, the [other] ruckman would rush down to where the umpire was going to throw the ball in while the ball was still in the crowd, while Farmer would walk in. He would just watch the ball as it came down from the crowd and be thrown to the umpire. As the umpire was about to throw it, he would be there. He would be in front of the other guys. It was uncanny. Everything was done to the economy of movement, and getting through 100 minutes of football.

Whilst Newman and the others who played with Farmer through his time with Geelong insist that he was just as good, just as great a contributor at the end as the beginning, they do acknowledge that he changed with the years. Newman comments:

> I noticed a perceptible change in his modus operandi, if that's the word. In the early years he still had the athleticism. In the latter years, with age and the debilitating injuries, he became more wily, more cunning and just used his body and the art, the subtle art, of just jumping early and positioning ...

He started to think that maybe the younger guys were more valuable and more competent in getting a hit-out. He would look at the ball. He would get between his opponent and the ball, but he would give the impression that he was going for it. He would give us a chance and give us an easy ride. We would get the stats and we would look like the stars.

There were other ways, too, in which 1965 marked a watershed. It was really the final disintegration of the 1963 combination. With Ken Goodland, Ian Scott and John Yeates all retiring, and John Watts departing to run a pub and coach in Hobart, half the premiership team that took the field against Hawthorn had departed by the end of the year. Two other 50-game players in John Fox and Gary Hamer also left, along with occasional forward Brian Brushfield. No recruits of any note came into the team.

Farmer and others are critical of the club for letting too many players go too quickly, without enough effort to persuade them to stay. He blames this more than anything else for the club's failure to go on after 1963.

But there was a more significant departure than the players. The creator and architect of the team left the helm, too, as in 1959, Bob Davis quit the club and went to work as a television commentator and writer.

His departure was a messy 'did he jump or was he pushed' type of affair. Technically the coaching position at Geelong had always been an annual appointment at the discretion of the committee, with an annual salary but no security. Despite this, through the Hickey and Davis eras there had been a record of long service.

Davis had challenged the system, and effectively challenged the committee's power, in the aftermath of the 1963 premiership win. Davis claims that he was actually appointed coach of Claremont for the 1964 season to replace his former teammate Peter Pianto, after the West Australian club made him a "huge" offer. He says that he felt he had done what he could do at Geelong, and wanted to get out while he was "right on top, but the club wouldn't clear me".

The alternative version that appeared as a snippet in the Melbourne press, was that, "after taking the Cats to the premiership last season, coach Bob Davis asked for a salary rise and a three year contract, but received neither!"[1]

Given that there was no clearance requirement for coaches, it seems more likely that Davis was considering the Claremont option, and used it as an unsuccessful bargaining chip in negotiations with the committee.

Whatever the precise details of that earlier episode, it is clear that the rivalries and tensions within the club had not disappeared in the wake of the premiership. It was still very much divided into the O'Brien-Davis camp and the Jennings camp.

Though it is difficult to pinpoint from this distance, there are indications that as early as 1964 the unique spirit of the 1963 team was starting to dissipate. The 1964 annual report provides a hint in its opening paragraphs:

> The performance of the team in the opening match was first class and provided good reason for the expectation of another good year. Several incidents during the season, however, had a marked influence on the players and affected the teamwork which was missing for most of the year.[2]

When questioned about this Farmer has no recollection of specific troubles, but does comment:

> I don't know of anything intentional, but obviously we weren't all on the same wavelength as far as our performance was concerned. So it's more that each individual is probably starring in his own right for himself, not necessarily for the team. I think it was that as much as anything—the keenness of the individual player to star.

Certainly the comments of the press writers during and after the 1964 season supposed this view. This dissension and drift within the Geelong of 1964 makes a stark contrast to the purposeful approach of the East Perth club in 1957 that ensured it maintained its supremacy within the West Australian League. Geelong could certainly have done with a Roy Hull or two.

In retrospect one can mount a case that it may have been better for all concerned if Davis had taken the Claremont option. There was no doubt he had shown the capacity to build a team, but he was not a strategist like Jeans or a disciplinarian like Kennedy with the temperament for the long haul. He was a players' coach, rather than a coach of players. He had a genuine love of the lads he had brought in from the farms and country towns. He praised them, celebrated with them, went punting with them, was really one of them. He probably did not have enough distance either to see some of the problems that emerged, or to impose the required discipline. "I think perhaps he should have kicked some of them in the backside," says Devine. "He'd give them the benefit of the doubt."

But this is very much a retrospective analysis, picking up loose threads and snippets with the benefit of hindsight. At the time Geelong was a power in the competition, with four successive finals appearances. The team's greatest problem was inconsistency, but it undoubtedly had the capacity to match any other side in the competition.

At the end of the 1965 season, rather than automatically reappointing Davis, the committee decided to advertise the coaching position. From all reports, this had little if anything to do with a strategic analysis of the club's position and problems. Davis was actually invited to apply, and was expected to retain the job. It appears to have been a matter of the committee exercising its authority, making the point about who was boss. Davis took offence, and decided not to reapply for his job.

If the Davis departure had been more orderly and less bitter, there is every chance that Farmer would have succeeded him, and become the Geelong captain-coach. Playing coaches were still very much a part of football in the 1960s. During the 1965 season there were four: Barassi at Carlton, Whitten at Footscray, Arthur at Hawthorn and Skilton at South Melbourne.

As early as the start of 1964 Farmer had been tipped for the role at Geelong at some point. The report then of Davis's unsuccessful bid for a three-year contract was actually buried within a piece lecturing Farmer for arguing with umpires, and suggesting that because of the differences with Davis, "there are rumours that [Farmer will) be coach next year ... the boys who put the biscuits in the tin to enable Farmer to be cleared from East Perth are now shouting 'Polly for Coach'."[3]

Farmer was renowned as a deep thinker of the game, a man with ideas on how the game should be played, and the ability to put these into effect. He was a natural leader in the team. He was absolutely dedicated to the game in all its aspects, from training and preparation through to execution on the field. In many ways he was tailor-made for the role.

Although he was very much a supporter of Bob Davis, and would not have considered applying for the position on his own initiative, he may well have considered an approach if one was made by the committee. Certainly no such approach was made, whether the idea was given any consideration within the committee rooms is not known. But given the animosities that were unleashed within the club by the Davis episode it is unlikely.

Peter Pianto was the man given the job. After returning from his stint with Claremont, he had spent the previous two seasons coaching in Colac, where he owned a sports store. But his appointment did not end the turmoil within the club. Virtually on the eve of the first game of the 1966 season Leo O'Brien's tenure as club secretary came to a very sudden end.

O'Brien was a forceful and colourful character: "bombastic" according to Jennings; "a rather contentious sort of person who knew what he wanted," according to his friend Father Brosnan. The specifics of O'Brien's departure are no longer remembered, but the clear impression is left that his position was made untenable by the committee. His feud with Jennings had been long-standing, but must have been brought to a head over the Davis affair. With his sudden and untimely departure there was no one at the administrative helm of the club for the first weeks of the season, until a golf club manager from Sydney was recruited.

Farmer is still angered by the treatment of two men he regarded as friends:

> The committee was very unfair ... it was terribly wrong what they first did to Bob, and then to Leo. There was no justification whatsoever [for advertising the coaching job] ... they came up with some fairly crazy reasons. It appeared to be a power play. They probably resented the fact that almost all the talked about success of Geelong Football Club was basically round the fact Davis was the coach and O'Brien was the general manager, and they did it. There were a lot of jealous people on the committee. It was the truth. It was the truth, but there were a lot of people who resented this.

He felt strongly enough at the time to organise a farewell function for O'Brien, "at some risk to himself," according to Father Brosnan. "We held it at the Belmont Hotel, and Pol was the master of ceremonies ... there was a lot of feeling, and he maintained that the committee had spies there to see who was there, to count heads and so forth."

Farmer himself says: "I made no secret of the fact that they were very unfair to Leo O'Brien." And he suggests that relationships had deteriorated to the extent that Jennings implied he might not be around that much longer himself. "When Leo and Bob went, the president actually said to me: 'Ah well, your contract will be finished.' And I said: 'You can jump in the lake and I'll go when I'm ready'."

13

ALMOST A GRAND FINALE

Peter Pianto and Bob Davis had played together for seven years at Geelong in the 1950s, including the back-to-back premierships, but they could hardly have been more different in temperament and attitudes. Pianto would never dream of telling a team to 'lair up'. He was a believer in hard work, discipline, and 'the fundamentals'—shepherding, backing up, and tackling. Although he does not say it in so many words, he obviously believes that a combination of the troubles within the club and the laid back regime of Davis had caused the side to lose its edge.

One thing he did share with Davis though was an unbounded respect and admiration for Farmer. He was astounded at the first pre-season meeting of the match committee to hear one of the club's movers and shakers, who was not even an official member of the committee, raise the question of the captaincy and propose John Devine for the job. With no disrespect to Devine—a natural leader forced by circumstances to take the role of deputy—one can only wonder at the small-mindedness that had come to dominate the club. Dumping Farmer would have done more than cause a sensation in the football world, it would have sent the worst possible message to Farmer himself and to the Geelong loyalists who idolised him.

But those who wished to bring him down a peg or two did not find an ally in Pianto:

> I said, "Hold on a minute, I've only been here one bloody night. I'm not going to make a decision on who should be captain until I've seen them perform" ... Of course, then the whole thing went quiet, and they didn't pursue it any more. Polly was reappointed.

Pianto's prime objective as he saw it was to turn the side back into a team. He needed not only to communicate his ideas, but to show his authority if he was to bring them round to his way of thinking and playing. The biggest hurdle in his own mind initially was getting Farmer to accept this, as his own inclination was to defer to the great ruckman. He was worried that Farmer was used to doing his own thing, and may not accept Pianto's methods. He need not have worried. "Polly never did anything that would resemble trying to be a rebel or 'I'm going to do it my way'. He was a perfect player to coach."

Farmer's grudges were against others, and did not extend to Pianto. In fact, the new coach's philosophies were probably closer to Farmer's own than those of Davis:

> Bob probably expected more of the players—what they could do for themselves, whereas Peter was going to do more to help them do well for themselves. Bob's assumption was, I think, if you're a League footballer, you should be able to do everything for yourself, and I think Peter was more of a professional from the point of view that he believed that he could probably help a player more.

While coach and captain established a good relationship from the beginning, Pianto did have his troubles with other players. There was a confrontation with Devine at a weekend camp on Kevin Threlfall's property. It is said that Pianto and Bill Ryan hardly spoke to each other during Pianto's five years as coach. Coming to Geelong also meant renewing his acquaintance with Denis Marshall, whom he had coached at Claremont, and the two had never hit it off. It was a case of a personality clash, and different beliefs on how the game should be played. Marshall's continuing litany of injuries, gashes and stitches bore testimony to the fact that he was never shy of being in the midst of the action; there were other players in the side though whom Pianto believed were a bit shy when it came to the physical stuff, which he could not abide.

The draw for the 1966 season saw the Cats with the toughest of challenges in the opening round. They had to journey to Windy Hill to take on the reigning premiers, after first enduring the ceremony of the unfurling of the premiership pennant. They were unable to overcome the Bombers, but put up a spirited display, leading at half-time, and only going down by two goals. Wins against South Melbourne and Footscray were followed by losses to St Kilda and Richmond, and a victory over North Melbourne, to leave Geelong three and three, in seventh place on the ladder after the first third of the season. The side was still settling down, with many positional moves reported, but none more so than Marshall. He was playing well, with a couple of starring performances, but already had played in half a dozen positions—sometimes three or four in the one day as Pianto swung him all over the field.

Farmer had started the year in great form. The statistics are incomplete, but reports show 15 handballs in the opener against Essendon, all effective; 33 disposals against South Melbourne, again all to teammates; and then in his best game in the early period, 17 kicks, 18 handballs, eight marks and two goals against Footscray, without counting his ruck knocks.

> For two and a half quarters Farmer had a sinew cracking tussle with Footscray's champion ruckman John Schultz. He could have left the field then and rested content. Instead, Farmer took control of the game for Geelong with marking, kicking and handball which no textbook could describe ... [He] kicked a torpedo punt from 60 yards out on the flank to put Geelong in front, repeating the effort from the other flank a few minutes later![1]

1966 was a carnival year, the first since the West Australian triumph in Brisbane in 1961. When the Victorian squad was announced after the sixth round, the lead story in press comment was the omission of Farmer. Ditterich, Schultz and Barassi all missed out as well, thanks to the 'two players from each club' policy. Geelong's representatives were Marshall, and defender Peter Walker, who had done little to draw attention to himself at that stage of the season. Ruckmen selected ahead of Farmer and Schultz included Crowe of Richmond, Beck of Hawthorn and Waters of Collingwood. It was certainly not the strongest team the VFL competition could have fielded, and it almost came undone. In the final game, with the Victorians and Western Australia both undefeated, Victoria trailed until halfway through the final quarter, and fell over the line to take the championship.

There was one round of games between the selection of the state squad and the carnival, and it saw Carlton coming down to Kardinia Park. Carlton was a game ahead of Geelong on the ladder, and a loss for the Cats would have made a final four berth a very dim prospect. The flow of the game reflected the fortunes of the personal battle between Farmer and Nicholls, which "saw some merry exchanges. Farmer gained three free kicks early from Nicholls' jostling play, then the Carlton followers roared as Nicholls took his first free. Farmer stole the honours for the first quarter," and Geelong were three goals up.[2] "Then Nicholls gained the upper hand during the second and third quarters, and much of Carlton's drive emanated from him," as they kicked seven goals to one, and turned for home with a three-goal advantage.[3]

"But [Farmer] was so constructive with looping handpasses in the final term that Nicholls could only stand and stare ... The ball was forced around the flank for a throw-in. Farmer crashed to the turf and the ball landed beside him, he seized it and from a sitting position handballed 12 yards to Goggin who spurted into the forward pocket and goaled ... Farmer, again prone, wafted another handpass to Ken Newland," who got it to Ryan for another goal.[4] Hynes soccered a goal that levelled the scores. Then, in time on, Carlton's back flanker, John Gill, threw his boot in desperation at the ball as Hynes was about to swoop again, and the footy slewed through for a Geelong behind that clinched the game.

No wonder Pianto loved him. Against Footscray and Carlton, Farmer had engineered victories with team-lifting play at crucial stages. A four-three record was much more comfortable for a new coach than two-five. Farmer followed up with best-on-ground games against Collingwood and Fitzroy while the carnival was on, as if to prove a point. Against Collingwood he played on young Len Thompson, who had debuted in the 1965 preliminary final and was earmarked as a rising star after a sensational start to 1966. He was a good four inches taller than Farmer and the other leading ruckmen, but fast and agile too, unlike most of the giants of the competition. He had already shown a liking for the Farmer-style grab and handpass, and had shown all the skills.

Farmer was a benchmark for these rising young turks looking for another notch on their belts. But he "emerged from [the] encounter with his football image untarnished ... [he] was giving away height and reach, but after 10 minutes of 'sizing him up', adapted his play to take control of the bounces and throw-ins. Thompson lacked the balance of The Master, and Farmer manoeuvred cleverly to keep him off balance for the rest of the game."[5]

The Fitzroy game was the halfway point of the season. Geelong was on five wins and four losses in sixth place, a game and percentage behind Essendon and Carlton, with Richmond, St Kilda and Collingwood further ahead. They would have to show more consistency in the run home, said the pundits. Any more than one loss out of the nine games, and they would struggle to make the finals. Carlton dropped away with a couple of losses, and it became a five-way race, as Geelong went from strength to strength, but not without some drama for Farmer.

In the 10th round against Hawthorn, Farmer was reported for the one and only time in his career, for "striking D. Dickson with a clenched fist in the first quarter." 'Delicate Des', as always, made life as hard as possible for Farmer, "jumping at him, giving him a rough time," says Terry Callan, who was calling the game for Geelong radio. Callan had a bird's-eye view of the incident, which happened at a boundary throw-in right in front of his broadcasting box, but his defence of Farmer is not entirely convincing. "There was absolutely nothing in it. He didn't hit him, he didn't really connect with him. It was frustration on Polly's part, I've never seen him do it before."

The sequence of pictures taken from television film that took up most of the front page of Monday's *Sun* did not look good. Farmer's left arm is thrown out behind him, and Dickson's head is jerked back, then he is in a heap on the ground—though interestingly he has fallen towards Farmer, in the opposite direction to the thrust of any contact, and Farmer's hand is open, not clenched. It has the appearance of a vigorous backhanded brush off more than a blow. Dickson certainly made the most of it. He was not the type to crumple under a backhander. He admitted many years later to Father Brosnan at a country sportsmen's night that he had taken a dive. Farmer says:

> It was just a matter of a lack of self-control ... after all these years, I'm still embarrassed about it, because for me, the whole basis of my game [was that] my concentration couldn't be broken ... I'd made position to go for the ball in the ruck, and Des got there too late and he hit me on the head. I didn't know who it was. I didn't look back. I just put my arm back, I hit who was behind me.

Farmer pleaded not guilty, with the defence that he had thrown his arms backwards in trying to keep his balance, after being cannoned into from behind, and that it was not a blow, as he did not even know whether it was a Hawthorn or a Geelong player who had run into him.

There was a long tradition at Tribunal hearings of the stricken player giving quite outrageous evidence to support his charged opponent. At times in the previous couple of years the Tribunal chairman had issued warnings to players over such evidence that stretched the credibility of proceedings. Dickson did not take this option, even though the nature of the incident was not blatant, and he could have assisted Farmer without going too far.

"Dickson said he fell to the ground when hit 'more out of shock than anything else. I was off balance.' When the Tribunal chairman asked if it was Farmer who had hit him, Dickson replied: 'Yes, on the forehead.'"[6]

There was an anxious quarter-hour wait for Farmer and club officials, reporters and photographers, and the 50-odd supporters gathered outside, as the Tribunal retired to consider its decision. He was found guilty, but escaped with a severe reprimand on the basis of his previous unblemished record. His first reaction on emerging was to ring Marlene with the good news. She had gone to Tasmania to introduce their daughter, Kim, the third and last of their children who had been born earlier in the year, to her family.

On the Saturday, Farmer and Marshall were Geelong's best pair for the third time out of the nine games in which both had appeared, as the Cats strung together their first sequence of three wins for the season, on the first Saturday of a split round. The following weekend Geelong journeyed to Horsham to play a combined Wimmera side. This was Doug Wade country, and for once Farmer had a rival in the popularity stakes among the young autograph hunters.

The visit home seemed to reinvigorate Wade. In the first nine games his best tally had been three goals, and then he spent two weeks in the reserves. But he came back into the team, marked everything on a wet day, and kicked eight to be the leading light in a 10-goal thrashing of Essendon. It was vintage Geelong, with Alistair Lord, Farmer and Goggin the best of the rest, and the win lifted them into the four for the first time in the season.

'Geelong Sets Sail For The Finals' was the hometown headline. The subeditor on the *Advertiser* must have been a moody fellow though. Despite two more wins against South Melbourne and Footscray, in a fortnight he came up with 'Dons Win May Scupper Geelong Hopes'; with four games left they still held fourth place over Essendon on percentage, but were thought to have a harder run home. Then a week later, it was 'Geelong Lays Siege To A Premiership', after they came from behind to defeat St Kilda, with Wade getting another eight.

When they backed up by thrashing Richmond at the MCG there was a real tinge of excitement in the air. It was their eighth win in a row. In five weeks they had beaten three of their four rivals in the finals race. The second loss in a row for Richmond had tumbled them from first to fifth place, boosted Geelong to third, and St Kilda to second. Once again, Marshall and Farmer were the leading players.

Pianto was riding high, and Geelong had become 'the team to defeat for the VFL premiership' according to the *Advertiser*. But the cooler heads pointed out that Richmond was only half a game behind the Cats—a loss in the last two games could still tumble them out of the four. Nor could they bridge the percentage gap between themselves and the Magpies and Saints, so unless one of this pair stumbled, and blew the double chance, Geelong would still have to win five games in a row to take out the premiership.

A week later though, despite another victory against North Melbourne, the balloon of euphoria was pricked. 'Farmer's Knee—Only Time Can Tell' was this week's headline. It was 1962 revisited; round 17 against North Melbourne, with the finals a fortnight away, and he was carried off Kardinia Park.

Farmer had played solidly in leading Geelong to a six-goal lead at three-quarter time, when seven minutes into the final quarter he flew for a centre bounce against Barry Allan:

> There was a tangle of legs and as the pack dispersed Farmer lay writhing on the ground. Trainers—all six of them—sped from all parts of the boundary, as Farmer, clutching his left knee, sat up. A stretcher was signalled for and was raced across the ground while the crowd remained shocked and silent. Geelong players were watching Farmer and not the ball as play went on, and North's Ken Dean goaled, and many spectators, watching the drama in the centre, did not know.[7]

The rest of the game was academic. North banged on another three goals before the Cats got their minds back on the game and steadied, while "Geelong supporters conferred in worried groups and radio broadcasters scurried for information from the Geelong trainers, as gradual realisation of the significance of Farmer's injury sank in."[8]

Farmer himself feared the worst at first. "He said that the sudden wrench when his knee twisted under him was similar to when he tore a cartilage in 1962, and he did not move because he felt it unwise to take risks."[9] But as Saturday turned to Sunday and the medicos and specialists and quacks all took a look, and the ice took the swelling down, it became apparent that the damage was not serious. Nevertheless the soreness persisted. With the final home and away game being against the Nicholls-Barassi combination at Princes Park, and a finals berth riding on the outcome, there was intense speculation early in the week as to whether he would come up. But by midweek it became apparent that the Cats would have to take their chances without the skipper; at least one, and perhaps two weeks out was the consensus.

Carlton had faded after a strong start to the season, but at home, against a Farmerless Geelong, no one thought the game would be a walkover. That's what it turned out to be though. Geelong put in a devastating performance to record a 70-point win. The Cats' camp was on top of the world. It made ten wins in a row, and a perfect entree to the finals.

Collingwood finished on top, a game clear of St Kilda, which headed Geelong and Essendon on percentage. The first semi-final would be a replay of the previous year.

When Farmer turned out on the training track on the Tuesday night for the first time since his injury, all eyes were on him. He tested the knee with some full-strength kicking, and convinced all that he was right to play. But he was far from 100 per cent when he fronted up at the MCG on the Saturday, and was able to exert little influence on the game.

At half-time it appeared that it would be a repeat of the previous year's whitewash, with a lacklustre Geelong trailing by seven goals. In the third quarter the Cats pulled one goal back, but were still 33 points down at the last change, and seemingly a lost cause. Two minutes into the final term, though the gap had narrowed to just 15 points, after goals to Wade, Ryan and Newland. The record crowd of 93,000 was roaring when Newland got another at the seven-minute mark to bring Geelong within two kicks. The Cats were dominating possession, but frittered their chances with five successive behinds. They got within four points as the time on period started, but could not bridge the gap, with Essendon getting home by 10 points.

Geelong was out in the first week of the finals for the second year in a row, but in contrast to the previous year's humiliation, there was some consolation in being described as "the best finals loser in years."[10] Who knows whether the Cats might have been able to go on to win two more games against St Kilda and Collingwood if a couple of those frantic last-quarter snaps had found the mark? With Farmer's knee improving by the week, they would have been in with a chance.

The Bombers could not repeat their amazing feats of 1965. They bowed out in the preliminary final to St Kilda, their Grand Final victim a year earlier. In one of the classic Grand Finals, the Saints went on to record their first premiership in a one-point victory over Collingwood. One is left to wonder if St Kilda might have achieved the ultimate dream a little earlier—

perhaps during its finals appearances of 1963 and 1965—if Farmer had chosen them above Geelong back in 1961.

The last clipping in Farmer's files for 1966 is a photograph from the *Geelong Advertiser* that shows a clutch of Geelong players and officials on the steps of Parliament House in Canberra. As an end-of-season trip, it was a much more modest affair than in seasons past, but there is an irony in the photo. In the centre of the picture a beaming Jack Jennings stands between Farmer and their local member, Hubert Opperman—the former cycling champion who had become a Minister in the Menzies and Holt governments—as the two shake hands. With an election looming it was a great piece of publicity in the local paper for Opperman.

At the back of the group, watching the handshake closely, is Neil 'Nipper' Trezise. Trezise had made his name as the other half of a great roving pair, with Peter Pianto, in the Geelong sides of the 1950s. By now he was not only the Geelong vice-president and a match committee member, but also a Labor Party member of the state parliament. At the urging of Jim Cairns, he had approached Farmer to stand for the ALP in the seat of Corio against Opperman at the 1966 federal election.

Farmer was a Labor man in a quiet way, and he and Trezise were friends. Trezise had fallen over the line by 32 votes in his first election win, thanks largely, he believes, to a few favours done for him by Farmer at the time. Trezise told Farmer he could still play footy—one or two days a week in Canberra would be enough, until he hung his boots up. There was a precedent at the state level: Melbourne captain, Brian Dixon, combined his football career with his duties as the Member for St Kilda in the Victorian Parliament. Trezise suggested that Farmer could gradually ease his way into political life, and be the Member for Corio for as long as he liked.

Three years earlier, a young trade unionist by the name of Bob Hawke had come down from Melbourne to contest the seat. As an out-of-towner he surprised some with a strong showing, a swing that had the seat in doubt for the early part of the count on election night. He returned to Melbourne and his job with the Australian Council of Trade Unions after this unsuccessful tilt, and would take a few detours en route to Parliament. But during that short stint in Geelong, in the aftermath of the 1963 premiership triumph, his four-year-old son had caught Farmer fever, and become a Geelong fan.

To put it mildly, Farmer had a greater recognition factor around Geelong than Hawke. The ALP was confident that it would walk in in Corio if Farmer would stand. But he resisted all of Trezise's persuasions.

As the 1967 season approached, there were mixed feelings about Geelong's prospects. On field the big loss was John Devine, who left to coach North Hobart in the Tasmanian Football League. His loss meant another gap in the feared backline of a few seasons earlier. Without Stewart Lord and Devine flanking Walker, the half-back line was seen as a problem rather than a strength. But he was also one of the few in the line-up who lent a real touch of meanness to the team. These factors, plus his leadership, and his qualities as a clubman meant that he would be sorely missed.

This loss was covered to some extent by the emergence of rookie Geoff Ainsworth as a permanent back pocket player, giving Pianto the options of Ron Hosking, the emerging Terry Farman, and Marshall for the flanks. Paul Vinar also retired after years of solid service everywhere from the ruck to the wing. But another rookie, ruckman Chris Mitchell, boosted the squad of big men supporting Farmer. With Newman, Rosenow and Ryan, this area was not a worry. Alistair Lord, forced off the centre line by Polinelli, Marshall and Closter, was still on the training list at the start of the season, but never played a game, unhappy with either his spare parts player status, or Pianto, or both. There were also concerns over John Sharrock's wonky knee, with no one certain when he would be able to take his place in the team.

As for Farmer, there was more and more speculation about his legs, his knee in particular, his ability to keep going and keep being a power in the competition, and his age. There had always been stories floating around Melbourne that Farmer was older than he said, that he had put his age down on arrival at Geelong, that there was some kind of mystery perhaps associated with his orphaned background. When asked Farmer gave his age correctly—32 by now—but people continued to whisper that he was really 35 or 36, and surely he could not last much longer.

After Nicholls' runner-up finish in the 1966 Brownlow, many were of the opinion that he had usurped Farmer as the League's premier ruckman.

Certainly his legs were five years younger, and had not yet begun to suffer badly from the ankle troubles that plagued him in later years; he was reaching the peak of his powers, whereas some thought Farmer had started on the downhill path.

Some of the pundits were tipping that Geelong would miss the finals for the first time since 1961, but six weeks into the season such talk had disappeared, with the Cats sitting in second position on the ladder, undefeated. They had begun with a stirring one-point victory over Grand Finalists Collingwood. The lead changed 12 times, with Geelong only winning from a Ryan goal after the siren—after his first kick had gone into the man on the mark. The other highlight was Geelong's first win at Windy Hill in 13 years in the fifth game, though it should be pointed out that the Bombers had had a horror start to the season, without a single win to this point.

Wade was showing the best form of his career, with bags of nine against Fitzroy and six against Collingwood and South Melbourne, to leave Hawthorn's hot new property, Peter Hudson, in his shade on the goalkicking list. Newman had begun the season in sensational style, taking best-on-ground honours in the two opening games, and continuing to be prominent, and young Mitchell was also doing well. Marshall was also playing brilliant football, usurping Newman's place as Geelong's best for three weeks in a row. But in a manner that seemed to be par for the course by now, Marshall continued to take batterings week in and week out: two knees in the kidneys against Collingwood; "absorbing punishment like a sponge" against Hawthorn;[11] then against South Melbourne a truly torrid game in which he was repeatedly put to ground, and received "a bruise for almost every kick he won—and he won many."[12] This last effort had the *Geelong Advertiser* bemoaning the fact that "no player has stepped forward to take Devine's place as 'protector'."[13]

In contrast to the previous year, Farmer had a very quiet start to the season. It was noticeable that he was leaving much more of the ruckwork to Newman and Mitchell, though as Newman has pointed out, he still made his presence very much felt in a quieter way with some heavy bodywork to ease their way. After the second game against Melbourne, the *Sporting*

Globe reported that: "There was general talk at the MCG on Saturday that Farmer had reached the end of the road." But the writer begged to differ:

> A spent force? Don't fall for that one. He's the most cunning player in the business. The way John Newman is playing, Polly can rest and save himself for when the going gets really tough. Did you notice the way he came into the game in the third quarter when the Demons started to apply the pressure? ... But there's one difference in Farmer's game this season which could have the fans a little puzzled. He no longer does all the bullocking and won't knock himself out chasing the ball from end to end. He's a rear-guard man playing a kick behind the play. To the opposition he must look like a brick wall when he bounces the ball back at them just when they look like breaking clear.[14]

Farmer squeezed in a midweek trip to Perth after the sixth game. The occasion was a testimonial night at Perth Oval for his oldest friend, Square Kilmurray. Kilmurray had racked up 257 games for the Royals, playing his last in 1966. The last couple of years were marked by battles with a bad knee. He had tried to come up again for 1967, but a couple of games in the reserves had convinced him that the battle was finally over. By this time his nickname had been adapted to 'The Old Grey Square.' The gang from the glory years were gathered to see him receive a £2000 cheque from the club provident fund, and relive the good days. Farmer told the ever-curious Perth media that he hoped to play on in Victoria for as long as possible, and at least until the end of 1968.

Back in Victoria, the next game was at the MCG against Richmond, tumbled out of the four by Geelong last year, but now shadowing Geelong in third position. The first half was a terrific battle, with Geelong up by a point at quarter-time, and the ledger square at the long break. Wade, with four goals from four kicks, was strong and steady for the Cats. At the other end, Royce Hart, the Tasmanian recruit who was outshining even Hawthorn's Peter Hudson, was pulling in screamers, but not kicking to match. In the thick of the battle Farmer was playing his best game of the year to date. Fifteen minutes into the third term though, Richmond had raced to a six-goal lead, and by the break had scored eight goals to one.

It was scintillating football, described by *The Age*'s Greg Hobbs as "the best quarter of football I have seen."[15] Geelong outscored the Tigers in the final quarter, but the game was all over.

The Tigers' brilliant display—15 minutes of football that wrapped up a game—was reminiscent of the Geelong of 1963, and confirmed them as a real threat in the competition. Already there was a clear break between the first four of Carlton, Richmond, Geelong and Collingwood and the rest. Barring upsets or dramatic form slumps, they appeared set to fight out the finals.

Greg Hobbs was at Geelong's next match, too, Carlton at Carlton:

> Actually there were two matches at Princes Park. The second was between Australia's best known ruckmen—Polly Farmer and John Nicholls. And a few times these 'gentle giants' did not exactly see eye to eye, and umpire Ray Sleeth had to keep a sharp look-out to see that trouble did not develop. Farmer was a better player than Nicholls, although neither of them had a great influence on the result.[16]

His summary is remarkably similar to the assessment that Nicholls makes of their clashes in general.

In the last six games of the home and away round Farmer was never out of the Geelong best player list, topping it on three occasions, including the next two games against Melbourne and Hawthorn.

The Cats lost the game against Hawthorn, to send a slight shiver of nervousness through the club. It left them fourth on percentage behind Collingwood. But more worrying, on the same day St Kilda recorded its sixth straight win in a late run that had put it clear of the rest of the pack, only a game behind and with a superior percentage. But wins against Fitzroy, South Melbourne and Essendon secured Geelong's place. Coming into the last game, at home against Richmond, a second semi-final berth was still a remote possibility, but only if a victory was complemented by an upset win over Carlton by lowly South Melbourne.

Such hopes disappeared though in the first quarter, in another brilliant burst of power football from the Tigers. Kicking with a fresh breeze they turned the throttle to full, and raced to a nine-goals-to-two lead. From that point Geelong was playing catch-up football, which they did with a steady purpose, failing by only two goals in the end. They had to settle for third place, and their fourth successive appearance in the first week of the final round.

After the game the mood in the Geelong camp was upbeat despite the loss. They claimed that they had outplayed the Tigers for three of the four quarters. *The Age* agreed, reporting that: "If anything, Geelong appeared slightly more pleased with its loss than Richmond with its win ... [and] ... Farmer's performance, up to the standard of his great years, was probably the most encouraging feature of the match for Geelong, and the most ominous for other premiership contenders."[17]

Looking back, those within the Geelong camp claim that it was the best team of 1967. On the record of the home and away round it is a case that is hard to sustain. A 13-five record is hardly overwhelming, and the Cats failed to beat the two teams who finished above them, going down to Carlton once and Richmond twice. Perhaps what they are remembering is that there was a real premiership attitude within the club for the first time in four years, a feeling that they could do it and should do it, as opposed to the over confidence of 1964 and the hopefulness of 1965 and 1966.

They had started the season on a fighting note, and kept the solid core of the team throughout the year. The only major injury problem had been in the case of Ron Hosking—snapped knee ligaments mid-season had put him out. Ten of the side had not missed a game, and another five had only missed one each. Their prime movers were all in good shape. And their trump card and on-field general, Farmer, had come good at the right end of the season. Farmer realised that this was his best, and perhaps his last chance to add a second VFL premiership to his illustrious record, and was quietly determined and confident.

On the other hand, the Collingwood side they opposed in the first hurdle on the road was at a low ebb. After a strong start they had lost four of their last seven. The Cats entered the game warm favourites to notch up their third win for the season over the Magpies.

Unlike the last two years, this first semi-final was what the public expected as the two sides fought to establish supremacy. Geelong always looked the better side, but a desperate Collingwood traded goals and the Cats couldn't break away. Geelong had bad injury problems. Gareth Andrews had come on when Newman was forced off the field in the first quarter after a Collingwood player landed in his back, though at the time it was not clear what was wrong with him. In the second, Marshall had cannoned head first into the fence and got up groggy, and had to retreat to a forward pocket to recover. And Roy West had got a kick on the knee that left him on one leg in the closing stages.

At three-quarter time Collingwood had got within a point of the Cats. In Newman's absence, Farmer was carrying more of the load in the ruck than he had been used to all year, going head-to-head with Len Thompson:

> Farmer's relentless application of physical strength and his willingness to compete strongly for the ball eventually took full toll on the only good follower the Magpies had all day—Len Thompson. In the end Thompson was forced to leave the ruck for a well-earned breather and when this happened Collingwood's ruck resistance caved in.[18]

Ten minutes into the last quarter, while the young tyro took his rest, the old master who was supposed to be gone kept rolling along, and the floodgates opened. Wade got four for the quarter and eight for the game, as the Cats pulled away to a five-goal win. Farmer was almost a unanimous choice in the press as best on ground. He had 13 kicks and 11 handballs, 11 marks—the most of any player, and a large but unrecorded number of ruck knocks that unerringly found Goggin, who shared the next best honours with Wade.

It had been a good win, but not a great one. Many felt that they had taken too long to shake off an undermanned and outclassed Collingwood side. And they soon found that victory had its price. It was discovered that Newman had suffered severe internal injuries. He was in hospital throughout the rest of the finals round, after having a part of a kidney removed. He had become an important cog in the side in this his fourth season, and was not easily replaced.

In the second semi Richmond vindicated its top position finish with an impressive victory over Carlton. The Tigers led by two or three goals for most of the day, then pulled away in the last quarter to win by six. The bad news, though, came when their lead ruckman Neville Crowe received a four-week suspension for striking Nicholls, putting him out of the Grand Final.

The result set up a preliminary final between Geelong and Carlton, a repeat of 1962. But this time the Cats would be led into the game by Farmer, playing his 100th game of VFL football. Geelong did not boost its ruck strength to replace Newman; Andrews came into the starting 18 as a forward, releasing Bill Ryan into a supporting ruckman role, and fourth gamer, John Scarlett, took his place on the bench.

The preliminary final turned out to be a game in two halves. Barassi switched his men all over the place, and Carlton got away early with a five-goals-to-one first quarter. Geelong clawed one back, but it was still 10 to six at half-time, with the Blues looking good. Farmer, to the surprise of all, had spent most of the half on the backline as Mitchell and Ryan did the heavy work against Nicholls:

> It was the reverse of the system adopted by Geelong when it had to contend with Collingwood's match winner, Len Thompson … Farmer came in fresh after half-time. By the third quarter Nicholls' spring had diminished to the extent that Farmer was able to wrest control and help spark Geelong.[19]

Spark them he did, as there was a dramatic turnaround in the game. Goggin was picking up kicks left, right and centre. Sharrock cut loose on a flank with three goals, and Wade got two. Geelong got eight for the quarter to Carlton's one, and went to the final break with a 14-point lead. The Cats got a further four in the last term while holding Carlton goalless, and coasted home as 29-point winners.

Buoyed by their solid wins over the Magpies and the Blues, Geelong went into the Grand Final extremely confidently. To quote Farmer, the team was playing "Rolls Royce football". Pianto recalls that: "the atmosphere around the club was very, very good. In the 1967 series the further we went the better we got, and definitely the signs were there for a premiership."

But Richmond was a formidable opposition, and the firm favourite with the unofficial bookmakers and the press pundits. It had got to this stage through a long-term recruitment strategy to build a tall but fast and mobile team. Apart from the roving duo of Kevin Bartlett and Billy Brown, the elusive goal sneak, John Northey, on a forward flank, and the mercurial 'Bustling' Billy Barrot in the centre, there was hardly a man under six foot. Francis Bourke and Dick Clay were a new breed of wingmen. Hart had become a first-year sensation at full-forward, and at centre half-forward there was the big and tough veteran Paddy Guinane, the enforcer of the side.

According to Pianto though: "We knew that Richmond played very much on confidence. They were brilliant footballers, but they played strictly on confidence." His main concern was to prevent the Tigers getting a run on at any stage, as they had done to create their two victories in the home and away round. "So we got together the night before, and I said: 'We've got to get in front early, and we've got to stay in front and build a lead up'."

In summer temperatures approaching 80 degrees Fahrenheit (27°C), the two teams put on a performance that has been described as one of the greatest ever exhibitions of Australian Rules football; a fast-paced, attacking game of fluctuating fortunes, pulsating backwards and forwards with moments of high drama.

Geelong got the early break that Pianto had demanded, with goals to Sharrock and Wade before Richmond registered a major. But the Tigers hit back, aided by critical and hotly disputed free kicks on the forward line. "You never blame umpires, I know," says Pianto, "but they got two free kicks, and they were the most unreasonable free kicks I've ever seen ... and they kicked two goals. One was against Denis Marshall, and it definitely wasn't a free kick. They got back in the game."

Indeed they did, to the point that they led by 4.3 (27) to 3.3 (21) at quarter-time. During the second quarter the ball hurtled up and down the field, more often than not passing through the hands of Barrot, who was dominating the centre. Pianto switched Closter out to a wing and Marshall into the middle in an attempt to quell Barrot, and Newland to the unaccustomed position of back flank, where he showed great poise. General play was even, but Richmond converted better, to extend its lead to 16 points at the long break. It would have been more, but for a Goggin goal right on the half-time siren.

Farmer was good, but not dominant to this point, with Richmond's Paterson contesting strongly. Farmer claims that he was getting the rough end of the stick from the umpire, penalised too often, and not getting the whistle when Paterson jumped all over him.

The opening of the third quarter was make-or-break time for the Cats. They had to get back into the game quickly—and they more than answered the challenge. Before a minute had passed Goggin had another after swooping on a loose ball on the fringe of a pack. A wobbled punt from Andrews went through, then Sharrock was dumped on the half-forward flank and Wade goaled from the free kick downfield. Farmer palmed the ball across his body at a boundary throw-in, landing the ball at Goggin's feet; he was off, to Sharrock, and a little pass to a leading Wade, and almost before anyone had realised, the Cats were eight points up after seven minutes. Richmond managed a reply, when Hart marked one of Barrot's searing drop kicks, but another to Gordon Hynes, and Geelong looked almost unstoppable.

Richmond seemed to gather their breath, and there was 10 minutes of thrust and counterthrust until Farmer marked near centre half-back and produced one of his magic touches. He spotted Closter loose on the outer wing and shot one of his mammoth 40-metre handballs. It drew a gasp of wonder from the 110,000 people at the ground, and set Closter free for a passage that brought up Geelong's 13th goal from Sharrock. Billy Brown got necked in a desperate passage of play in the Richmond goalmouth and kicked truly, to bring the margin back to eight points. With time on approaching the game was finely balanced.

Then the unimaginable happened. Right in the centre of the ground a pack flew and then crashed to the ground, Farmer reached out of the pack after the ball, but as it spilled away and the play moved on, he remained on the ground. First thoughts were of his knee as the trainers raced out towards him. But it was cramp. This was Farmer's 277th game of senior football, and never before had he cramped. He could not believe what was happening to him. It seemed that the heat, the exertion of two and a half games of finals football, covering the loss of Sam Newman, doing more of the ruckwork than he had all season, had all caught up with him at the worst possible time.

It also seemed to put a damper on the head of steam the team had built up, as "Geelong players seemed to falter and Barrot, with an aggressive dash from the centre, scooped up the ball and goaled, and Richmond trailed by a point."[20] The Tigers dominated the remaining minutes of the quarter. They could not score a major, but three behinds gave them a two point break at the last change.

Farmer played on, but he could hardly run, and could not jump, "because in the effort of getting off the ground, you tighten your muscles up, and I was trying to alleviate that." Bartlett got an early goal in the last quarter to give Richmond some breathing space, but Geelong would not die. For quarter of an hour the defences dominated until Bill Ryan marked and goaled. Geelong pressed the attack, but could score only behinds. Colin Eales had three shots in a row for two points and a miss, but one of them levelled the score, and the other put Geelong ahead. Then Richmond rushed a point.

John Ronaldson, Richmond's big, ungainly third-string ruckman in as a replacement for Crowe—who had done nothing all day—marked, and shocked everyone by drop kicking a long goal from an acute angle. "Farmer, although he could barely leap off the ground, lifted Geelong into the picture with a 30-yard handpass to Tony Polinelli [who] found Sharrock who goaled with a rare right-foot snap." [21]

Six times in the last quarter the scores were level. There was a boundary throw-in on the Richmond half-forward line. Farmer was free-kicked, and Ronaldson turned himself into an unlikely hero. As he later admitted, he was only trying to land the ball in the goalsquare, but he connected perfectly, and the ball sailed 70 metres, just above the fingers of the outstretched pack for his second goal.

Geelong counter-attacked, and a couple more points made the difference less than a kick, but with time on ticking down, Bartlett swooped on a ball that had spilled free, ran into an open goal, and it seemed the Tigers were safe. Once again the Cats hit back. Yet another two points, making 2.8 (20) for the quarter, but they were still more than a goal behind. One last sally, and a Goggin kick sailed goalwards, splitting the middle. Geelong people swear that the saving mark of Richmond skipper, Fred Swift, was taken behind the line, but it did not matter. As his clearing kick sailed towards the half-back flank the siren sounded. Richmond were premiers for the first time since 1943, nine-point victors over the Cats.

Geelong was showered with praise in defeat, but the taste was no less bitter for that. Farmer shared the podium with Swift as the presentations were made. Like all defeated Grand Finalists, he was unable to hide the grim reality of defeat, with shoulders drooping, eyes downcast, and mouth turned down.

Farmer knew in his heart, though he did not say it then, and has not said it since, that if his leg muscles had not seized on him, he could have turned the result around. Take nothing away from the Tigers—they were a great side, and had played a heroic game—but Farmer had turned enough matches in the last quarter in his long career. He wanted this one so badly, and there is no doubt that he would have done it once more on this occasion if his body had answered the call.

14

A COLOSSUS DEPARTS

As has been noted earlier, Farmer is a man who stews over the losses more than he savours the victories. Of all the losses, and especially among the Grand Finals that escaped him, the one that still turns a knife in his guts when he thinks about it is that 1967 Grand Final against Richmond. He is absolutely convinced that Geelong should have won the game.

Bad luck, the run of the ball, poor umpiring decisions, a Sharrock lunge at the ball on the goal line early on that Geelong claimed as a goal, but was given as a point, the sequence of behinds that could have been goals in the last quarter, Newman's absence, the cramp that crippled him from late in the third quarter; if just one of these had been different, so would the result have been. Even the loss of Crowe for the Tigers was offset by the inclusion of Ronaldson, and the freakish part the battler played in the agonising final minutes.

"If you look at games, when a team completely dominates in the marking area, that indicates control of the game. We probably had 30 per cent more marks than they did, and we still didn't win it." The actual statistics were 79 marks to 58 in favour of Geelong, as well as 223 kicks to 207, and 55 handballs to 50:

On the day we had more of the play. I'd say probably two guys kept them in the game, or even one guy—Bill Barrot, because he was in sensational form. He was on a roll, he was playing like a man possessed, with his 70-metre drop kicks.

It gets worse every time you look at that match—the replay. You realise that you were robbed ... The variables in the free kicking; the things, for instance, that Mike Paterson did in the ruck where he wasn't free-kicked, and the things I did in the ruck where I was free-kicked. They weren't controversial incidents, but it's a matter of where the umpire was at the time. In the last quarter Ronaldson gets a free kick and he kicks [his second, unintentional] goal. Well it definitely wasn't a free kick, because I had the front position. I got in front, I ducked and I got in front and as I stood up I eased him out of the way—but he came into me and he bounced off me.

There are three different counts of the free kick tallies in the press, variously 38 to 31, 42 to 29, and 40 to 28 in favour of Richmond. In the first quarter, where Pianto claimed they brought Richmond back into the game, it was 13 to nine in favour of the Tigers, and amid the hectic heroics of the last quarter they were favoured nine to four. And Farmer reckons that seven or eight of Richmond's frees were within range of the goals:

A lot of us—I mean everyone at Geelong—we feel in our hearts that we were robbed. Probably we are no different from any other team that loses. Loss is a bitter thought, and just statistically looking at the game it's very difficult to realise that we were beaten. Because we did dominate the game and we dominated everything [except] in the free kick department and getting an even break with the decisions ... We can't change a thing, but you know when you're replaying and you're looking at incidents in the game, we got beaten by less than two goals; and there were some fairly glaring mistakes that took place, and the mistakes were made by umpires.

With this sort of feeling inside them, the generous applause from the crowd after the game and the praise of the press for their mightiness in defeat was little consolation.

Talking to members of the Geelong camp twenty-five years later, it was astounding to hear emerge from some quarters two separate sets of speculation—theories held strongly by those who advanced them—that there was something crooked about the game. There are suggestions that people connected with Richmond had been overheard saying that they were prepared to pay any cost to win a flag, and dark murmurings about the amount of money bet on football, and two theories on what might have taken place. One theory is totally unbelievable, and the other stretches the bounds of credibility to its limits. Both are unprovable, and hence unrepeatable. It seems more likely, that in the bitterness of defeat, and the need to somehow explain it, some minds have jumped a couple of steps too far. More than anything, these stories are an indication of just how hard the loss was taken.

The club's second venture overseas for its end-of-season trip—this time to Singapore, Malaysia and Thailand, with two days in Perth at the end—was a chance to let their hair down and try to shake off the blues, but ultimately it was small consolation. Farmer had plenty to stew over as spring slipped towards summer, and he took up his off-season routine of pressing weights at the gym each morning, and devoting more time to family and work.

The logic of the Cats' analysis of the year was that rightfully they were premiers, which should in turn have indicated that the players, coaching staff and administration were doing at least reasonably well. But that is not how many saw it.

Earlier in the season there had been a report in the *Truth* about moves for a mid-season coup at the club. After their great start, the Cats had slumped to three losses in four weeks. When they came up for their second game against Collingwood in the 12th round, it was a crucial game that many thought they would lose. As it turned out, they won. According to the *Truth*:

> Defeat at Collingwood and the strong possibility of missing the finals was to have been the trigger to a reform move at Geelong ... influential Geelong businessmen and supporters are keen to have former secretary Leo O'Brien back with the club ... Unless Geelong performs dismally in the finals, the reform group may not make a move. They do not want to act prematurely because they have their sights set on Tom Morrow, the president Jack

Jennings, and to a lesser extent, John Hyde. The reformers are prepared to hold back their move until the time is right to strike.[1]

The finals performance could hardly be described as dismal, but a challenge of sorts was mounted, with the election due on the second weekend in December. No one nominated against Jennings or Trezise for the presidency and vice-presidency—an irony given that Trezise had been a member of the unsuccessful challenge against Jennings in 1961, and had only got on to the committee in later years. Nor were Morrow and Hyde under threat, as it was a normal election, and they were halfway through two-year terms. But all four retiring members renominated, and found that they had four opponents, one of whom was Leo O'Brien. There was not a reform ticket as such. O'Brien said he was running as an independent without a how-to-vote card. It seems that perhaps the concerted reform push had fizzled out, but the 'dogmatic' O'Brien insisted on pursuing his course.

Then a week before the election was due, while the football community of Geelong was consumed by politicking and manoeuvring, Farmer dropped a bombshell. Word leaked out that he was negotiating with the West Perth Football Club over the possibility of taking over there as captain-coach.

[Farmer confirmed that] a group of West Perth supporters had offered him about $5000 a year plus fringe benefits to coach the team. This is believed to be one of the biggest offers in League football. And in Perth on Tuesday night the West Perth club is likely to decide to appoint him playing coach. "If it's offered to me I'll accept it," Farmer said. "I'll have the club send over papers immediately to sign."[2]

There is an unintended ironic touch to this story in the *Herald* that presages the end of the greatest phase of Farmer's career. He is pictured at home with his family, reading a bedtime story to Kim. On the reverse side of the clipping is another photo of a lithe young tennis player, perfectly poised as she plays a graceful backhand. It is "young Aboriginal Evonne Goolagong, 16, the brightest star on Australia's tennis horizon, treat[ing] Melbourne's tennis public to its first real taste of 'Goolagong magic'."[3] Goolagong had just won the Queensland and New South Wales junior championships, and was appearing at Kooyong in the Victorians, as she embarked on a career that would see her replace Farmer in many eyes as the greatest Aboriginal athlete the country has produced.

The week that followed was packed with drama. Farmer received the phone call from West Perth president Fred Ptolemy confirming the committee's decision to offer him the captain-coach's job. He accepted, and told the press that he would be leaving in the new year. When asked about a clearance he said pointedly: "I haven't talked to Geelong about leaving and none of the Geelong officials have said anything about it to me."[4]

The next day he appeared on the local Geelong radio station along with Leo O'Brien, and endorsed him as a good candidate in the club elections. This infuriated Jennings—who commented acidly and inaccurately that it was the first time players had entered into a club election—and one of the retiring committeemen, Vern Johnstone, who said: "I don't encourage players taking part in club politics or elections and I think Polly Farmer should have kept well out."[5]

Farmer defended his right to free speech, and dismissed the furore as a mountain out of a molehill. This was on the Thursday. On the Friday the picture and story plastered across the front page of the afternoon *Herald* was of Farmer at lunch in a Melbourne hotel with Lou Rocka. Like their mutual close friend Alex Popescu, Rocka was a Romanian-born post-war migrant who had made good in business in the Geelong district, and an important financial backer of the football club. He was a more public and flamboyant figure than Popescu, the timber and hardware merchant. Rocka wheeled and dealed on the international trade scene. On his own initiative Rocka launched a private bid to keep Farmer in Geelong. He had secured a deal to act as Australian import agent for the Romanian government, specialising particularly in tractors, and offered Farmer the position of part-time public relations man at the then staggering figure of $12,000 a year.

Technically, Farmer's options were still open. No papers had arrived from West Perth at this point, and no clearance applications had been lodged. He told Rocka and the press that he would think about the offer, but the hints and speculation indicated that he would stick with the West Perth decision. Farmer was a man who prided himself on his word being his bond, and he had certainly given the West Perth hierarchy a verbal commitment.

Nevertheless, the next morning in the *Truth* Jack Dyer was speculating: "They say Polly Farmer's future hinges on the result of the election this weekend. If voting for Leo O'Brien means Geelong will keep Farmer, then I'd vote for O'Brien."[6]

When the votes were counted, three of the four retiring candidates were returned, including Johnstone, and the new man to get up was not Leo O'Brien. If there had been any chance of Farmer renouncing his stated intention to move, it was gone now.

W hy did Farmer decide to leave Geelong when he did? There is no doubt that he was capable of playing on. He finished the 1967 season as runner-up in the Geelong best and fairest award for the second time, 33 votes behind Billy Goggin, but 24 clear of the third-placed Peter Walker—and Goggin himself believes that Farmer was robbed of votes:

> I don't believe they were giving him the votes they should have been. That's my opinion ... if he was playing now there would be more scrutiny of the people giving the votes ... Like, 'He has won two in a row, we're not going to give him any more,' ... The tall poppy syndrome—he had to put up with that, and I would say that's one of the reasons he might have left. I would think he felt [that] they don't appreciate you if you're there long enough.

Pianto and the players all knew that he was still the most important cog in the team by far, both for his ball-getting ability and his ability to marshal the side on the field. And he had proved to those of his critics who thought at the beginning of 1967 that he was 'gone' that he was far from it, with three quality performances in the ultimate football cauldron of a VFL finals series. In possession terms alone he had been remarkably consistent in averaging 13 kicks, eight marks and 14 handballs in the three games. And that does not take into account the balls palmed down from the ruck to initiate a Geelong attack, the numerous spoils and tackles, or the quality of the disposal.

Perhaps he had slipped to the extent that he would no longer be the automatic first choice in a coach's dream team, but among those in the know he would still have been in the first half-dozen selected.

Even from halfway through the 1963 season, there had never been any shortage of public and private speculation about his future with the Cats, with the option of returning to Perth always prominent on the list of possibilities. But although he was known to be interested in coaching, the indications, again both publicly and privately, had always been that he would prefer to see out his playing career in the VFL with Geelong.

There had definitely been approaches from Perth clubs during 1963 seeking him for the 1964 season. In 1964, when East Perth decided they needed to replace Jack Sheedy with a playing coach for 1965, they tried Farmer unsuccessfully before turning to Kevin Murray of Fitzroy. And each year since, the issue had come up as a football perennial, especially in the still Farmer-mad Perth sporting press.

During the 1967 season, despite the early speculation about his form, there was no report seriously suggesting that it might be his last season with the Cats, unlike the intense build-up there had been to his departure from East Perth. In the final round the sense of occasion came from his 100th game, not from any imminent sense of departure and loss. Farmer went into the Grand Final aware that it might be his best and last chance of another VFL premiership, but with no secret knowledge, or even any feeling that it might be his last VFL game.

The initial approach from Fred Ptolomey had come shortly after the Grand Final, and though Ptolomey probably did not know it, his timing was perfect, catching Farmer when "I was bitterly disappointed in the loss, and so I wasn't in a positive frame of mind". As he privately weighed the offer, the turmoil within the club mounted, and "I wasn't in love with the administration at the time, the committee". He loved Geelong the town, and the life and friends he had made there, but had grown weary of the club. "If Leo and Bob—well not so much Bob, because I was not unhappy with Peter [Pianto]—but if Leo O'Brien was still involved with the club, I probably would have stayed there and played my career out as a player."

Even after the election, there was still a chance for Geelong to keep him. Firstly because at a technical level it had to provide him with clearance papers before he could play in the west. Secondly because this opened up the opportunity for them to negotiate with him; work with Rocka or make an independent counter-offer, demonstrate that they did still want and value him, that they were prepared to try to heal the wounds that had been opened up.

On election day Jennings had made all the right noises about being reluctant to let such a valuable player and commodity go, and doing all in the club's power to hang on to him. But there are many at Geelong who recall with anger that there was no real effort made to persuade him to stay. Others go so far as to suggest that some within the club were glad to see him go. John Devine is blunt in his assessment of the period:

> People got jealous of him. He was taking all the glamour, and [they] weren't getting any of it. Polly never suffered fools readily. He could see all this was happening, so he was never really comfortable in the last couple of years. They were always trying to control him, saying: 'You can't do this, you can't do that, this is not on, that's not on.' I'm sure of that. He never, ever told me, but I'm convinced that's what happened. It became more political, it became better to get rid of him.

Farmer himself says:

> Geelong did not try one bit. There wasn't one effort made to keep me there. It really didn't make sense. I would have thought it should have showed a bit more interest, because there probably was a premiership there the following year—we were the best side in the competition at the time.

Farmer was an icon, and they let him go too easily, even happily in some quarters. It is this as much as his loss on the field that prompts Goggin to say: "I felt the heart went out of the club as a team because of his leaving ... it was just sort of a disintegration ... we just kept going downhill ... In the meantime Polly's over in Western Australia dominating."

With Farmer's departure, at one level he passed out of the consciousness of the parochially minded Victorians. Just as they had said while he was there—only half jokingly—"Perth, that's the place that Polly Farmer comes from"; many ask in puzzled tones now: "Where did he go when he left here?"—completely unaware that there was a third, equally distinguished part to his playing career. But he left a legacy, a reputation and memories in the hearts and minds of the Victorian football world that is in some ways unparalleled.

Most of the football legends created their story, and their place in the hearts and minds of fans, over long careers of a dozen and more seasons, and 200-plus, or even 300 games. Many of them also continued on as coaches over long periods, garnishing their reputations. Others have been almost permanent personas in the public mind from the day their on-field careers finished through their media work. Farmer came and saw and conquered, and then left again for the wilds of the west. Among the true legends only Coleman of Essendon is comparable, with his career cut short after just 98 games. Even he, though, stayed on to become a premiership coach, and for a time a writer and commentator before his early death in 1973.

In his six years and 101 games, Farmer had an impact that is often compared to Coleman's in the early 1950s. He was brilliant, he was unstoppable, he was feared. His peers regarded him with awe. When the experts and past players indulge in the exercise of ranking the all-time greats, he is usually second to Whitten, and sometimes at the top. Whitten underlines the regard in which he was held:

> After a game we would talk, and when he spoke everybody stopped. In a group of players, say six or eight or 10 players, everybody is talking at the same time. When Polly spoke, nobody spoke ... I've got a title here of 'Mr Football', but I felt it an honour to play against him. I felt it a tremendous honour to play with him in state football, and to be an opposing coach to him.

And then there is the claim, discussed and analysed in an earlier chapter, that he revolutionised the game, and set it on the modern path. His greatest fan, Bob Davis, perhaps distills it to the bottom line. He cites a list of the other greats of the game, and says: "Yes, they were all great, but they didn't do anything new, they just did the same old things better. Polly is the only player to have made an original contribution to the game. Until he came along, no one had thought of the idea of grabbing the ball from the ruck, and handpassing it out." John Schultz, the Footscray ruckman who played through the '60s in the shadow of Farmer and Nicholls says:

His game was revolutionary. It was totally different to anything that anyone I knew of knew about ... We definitely adapted our style—I think John Nicholls would agree with this—with the way that Polly played, and brought it over ... Farmer was just in front [of Nicholls]. Initially he would have been a long way in front, but Nicholls, because of the reaction to Farmer's style, became a much more damaging player. Farmer was the trendsetter.

Perhaps most importantly the football public loved him, and flocked to see him, from his first practice match in 1962 until the end. Jack Dyer noted that:

VFL chiefs expecting a big lift in attendance next season because of the extra two rounds could be in for a shock to the pocket. The loss of Polly Farmer to Victorian football will mean a loss of revenue equivalent to a complete round. The magic of his play attracts thousands of spectators each game.[7]

This pulling power was confirmed by Ron Hovey, who served on the committee at Geelong from when he stopped playing in the late 1950s through to 1998, including a stint as president. He cites the scientific head counters of the AFL who swear that Gary Ablett in his prime is worth 5000 to 6000 people through the gate, and states that Farmer was just as good, if not better, with Coleman and perhaps Jesaulenko as the only other two who held the same magnetism for the punters who clicked through the turnstiles.

If the public at large loved him, the public of Geelong absolutely adored him. In the mythology of the club he occupies a pedestal raised far above any other.

The only blemish on the record of his time as a player and captain with Geelong is the common acknowledgement that there should have been at least one, and probably two, more premierships. But no one would suggest that the failure to accomplish this is any fault of his. In the time he strode the stage of the Victorian Football League he was a true colossus, outshining even the best of the rest.

15

PLAYING COACH

In the six years that Farmer was in Victoria most of the faces in West Australian football had changed. Of the men who captained and coached the eight teams in his last year with East Perth, only two were still on the scene in 1968. John Todd had finally succumbed to his bad knee in 1964, then after a year coaching in the Sunday League, had returned as coach of South Fremantle in 1966. Haydn Bunton had left Swans after the 1964 season, but returned to Perth in 1968 as captain-coach of Subiaco. The big men whom Farmer had battled were gone: Clarke in 1962, Foley in 1965, and Slater played his last year with Swan Districts in 1967, after having spent three years with Subiaco as captain-coach. The only big men of real class who had emerged were John McIntosh at Claremont, and Bill Dempsey, who had built a solid reputation at West Perth.

If the 1950s was the decade of the class big men in Perth, the 1960s had seen the small fellows take over. Bunton had not only led Swan Districts to three successive premierships in 1961 to 1963, but had been best and fairest in each season, and won the Sandover Medal in 1962. As he left, Billy Walker stepped from his shadow, only to be challenged by the emerging brilliance of Barry Cable at Perth for the title of the state's number one rover. From 1964 to 1968 the pair shared the Sandover Medal between them. Walker won three, sharing one with Claremont rover John Parkinson, and Cable won the other two, while finishing as runner-up to Walker twice. Their clashes took on something of the status of the Farmer-Clarke duels of earlier years.

Another small man whose star shone brightly in these years was Sydney Jackson. Born at Wiluna, but raised at Roelands Mission in the southwest, the brilliant young Aboriginal player had been spotted and nurtured by Bunbury football identity Ern Manea, who pointed him in the East Perth direction. Playing in the centre, he had tied for the Sandover Medal in his debut year of 1963, but was ineligible due to suspension. For five seasons he played mercurial, often match-winning football. But by 1968 he was lost to the west, standing out of football for a year when the League refused him a clearance to Carlton.

In the premiership stakes in 1964, after the Swan Districts hat-trick, unfashionable Claremont—with East Fremantle stalwart Jim Conway at the helm in place of Pianto, and without Denis Marshall, who had left for Geelong—snuck into the four, and then upset the favoured opposition for three games in a row to take out an astonishing last-to-first premiership. In 1965, East Fremantle, under big Bob Johnson, took the flag from Swan Districts, after three successive losing Grand Finals.

In 1966, a new football force emerged. Sheedy protégé Mal Atwell quit the Royals—after a prolonged clearance wrangle—to become the captain-coach of Perth. In his first season he led his new club to victory over Kevin Murray's Royals in the Grand Final. East Perth must have wished it could have held him another year—not only to avoid this disaster—but because he would have made a natural successor when Kevin Murray left the club unexpectedly at the end of 1966. Instead they appointed Derek Chadwick. Atwell had two years experience on Chadwick, and was a tougher, more wily character. Chadwick was a brilliant and courageous footballer who led his team by example.

In 1967, Chadwick appeared to be carrying all before him, with East Perth finishing four games clear on top of the ladder. But Perth beat the Royals by five points in the second semi, and after a seven-goal performance from Syd Jackson in the preliminary final, Atwell and Cable engineered another Perth victory in the Grand Final to retain the title. For the second year in a row Cable took the Simpson Medal for his Grand Final game.

There was a move from within some quarters of the East Perth camp to replace Chadwick, initiated largely by Farmer's first League coach, Mick Cronin. And the man Cronin had in his sights as a replacement was Farmer. Farmer's own recollections are not specific. East Perth had approached him at various stages during his time at Geelong, and he saw Cronin regularly when the old fellow came over to visit relations in Ballarat. But he seems to think the idea never got very far, as Chadwick had a contract for the job.

Others are adamant that East Perth let a chance slip by. Frank Allen spoke to Cronin afterwards, and says: "Mick came back and laid the proposition on the table to East Perth, and the response to that was 'he was overpriced and he was over the hill', and he finished up going to West Perth." The possibility was considered by the East Perth committee. One member, Len Owens, recalls the discussion, and says he suggested that secretary Hec Strempel should find out whether Farmer was in fact available. But Strempel appears not to have pursued it with any vigour. He had never been close to Farmer, but he loved Chadwick, whom he had recruited from Busselton:

> We had a person like Derek Chadwick, who had played 200-plus games. [Actually 170 at the time.] He'd never put any demands on the club. He'd been a great player for the club. He gave everything every week, Chaddy. We appointed him coach and he had one year to run. Now there's no doubt that if it had been the year after, Farmer would have been our coach, no hesitation ... We had principles and ethics ... Polly would have been a great asset to the club. But Chadwick—the press would have killed you. Your own members would have killed you. Chaddy was up there—he was a pinnacle. I mean Polly was too, but Polly had gone. Chaddy was still with us.

Farmer makes the point that he has never applied for a coaching job in his life. He has always responded to approaches from clubs. Attempting to reconstruct the past, it seems that in that period of October-November 1967, East Perth could, if it had wanted and been prepared to pay a reasonable amount, have secured Farmer as their playing coach. They would pay for not doing so.

armer had not been a lay-down misere for the West Perth job either. Captain-coach of three years, Rick Spargo, had told the club early on that 1967 would be his last year, and quite a field had put in formal applications for the job to compete with Farmer's verbal negotiations with West Perth officials. One of the contenders was Brian France, a West Perth stalwart who had started in 1958, and built a formidable reputation as a key defender through the 1960s, finishing third in the Sandover in 1966 despite missing seven games, and fourth in 1967. There was also some concern over Farmer's soundness and his future as a player.

In the 1967 annual report, prepared after Farmer's appointment, secretary Kevin Bradley conceded:

> Graham Farmer's appointment at first raised some eyebrows in several quarters and frowns in other quarters that had leaned to, and hoped for, the appointment of a local man. However, generally speaking the appointment, the subsequent decision of Graham's to honour his verbal agreement with the club despite a mammoth offer to keep him in Geelong, and the favourable publicity, was received by everyone with much acclaim.[1]

Farmer quickly wrapped up his affairs in Geelong, and he and the family moved back to the west. Once again, he stayed close to the beaches he loved, buying a house in Trigg. He saved the club the usual bother of finding a job for players or coaches transported across the Nullabor by continuing his association with the same insurance company he had been working with in Victoria, and quickly settled down to the task at hand.

Since the 1960 premiership in Arthur Olliver's first year as coach, the Cardinals, as they were called then, had been a middle-of-the-road team, finishing between third and fifth for the next seven years. Olliver had stayed a further three years. Clive Lewington of South Fremantle fame had held the reins for a year. Then Ricky Spargo had been captain-coach for three years, finishing fourth, third and fourth, with two losses in first semi-finals, and reaching the preliminary final in 1966. The results seem to indicate a team not quite achieving its potential, but Spargo deserves—and receives from the players—some credit. He pursued a youth policy, and blooded an extraordinary number of new players, doing well to take them as far as he did.

In 1968, Farmer had a squad that contained "the nucleus of a good side." Brian France sought a clearance to East Perth, and when this was refused, stood out of the game. This left Mel Whinnen and Bill Dempsey, both approaching the 150-game mark, as the club veterans. Already, although less than halfway through their careers, this odd couple were favourites of the club. Both had started as 17-year-olds in the premiership year of 1960, though only Whinnen was in the premiership 20, as a reserve. Whinnen was a local lad who had come up through the ranks and developed into a polished centreman, a possession-winner, and a great team player. He had won the club best and fairest in 1962, 1964 and 1967. Dempsey had come down from Darwin in 1960, more as a companion than a prospective player. He had played in Darwin with the Buffaloes, where one of his teammates was a brilliant rover named Jim Anderson. Both had grown up at the Rhetta Dixon home for Aboriginal kids. Anderson had been spotted by ex-West Perth player Jack Larcombe and recommended to the club, but only lasted three weeks in Perth on his first visit down. West Perth attempted to persuade him to stay in Perth by bringing Dempsey back with him, but in the event Anderson returned to Darwin and Dempsey stayed. He never lost the rough knockabout edges of a Darwin boy, but everybody at West Perth loved him. He developed into a classy ruckman despite his relatively small size, with an uncanny ability to take the timely defensive mark over and over again.

West Perth were well equipped in the big-man department even without Farmer. As well as Dempsey, they had Brian Sampson, who had played in the Essendon premiership side of 1965, and joined the Cardinals in 1967, Ray Boyanich who had four years of experience, and Norm Knell who had completed two seasons by the time Farmer arrived. Dave Dyson was a solid key defender with a few seasons under his belt. Young John Wynne had established a reputation as a good and tough key position player in his two years of League football. Of the rest, there were a lot of young players of promise—rookie full-forward Dennis Cometti was seen as a star of the future, and Steven Smeath was a flanker with skills and with pace to burn—but they had yet to prove themselves.

Off the field West Perth was a well-run club, with a tight-knit committee with a blend of football experience and business know-how. The presidency passed from Fred Ptolomey to Len Roper in 1968. But Ptolomey's departure was voluntary and the accession of Roper, a former secretary of the club, was unanimous. There was only one other change on the committee, whose key members were another former secretary, Les Day, the hard-nosed Ed Cooley, who doubled as the team manager, and the astute Ron Bewick, a 100-game player who was also chairman of the selection committee.

With any new coach there is a testing period as he and the administrators and the players get to know each other. It must have been a relief to Farmer to find that there were no dramas with the club administration. All his requests and requirements were met in terms of facilities. Bewick and Cooley provided his lines of communication on football issues, and the three were able to work well together.

Among the players Farmer had the advantage of his status as a footballer, but according to Cometti there were some question marks at first: "Why is he doing this? Maybe he is not right in terms of fitness? There was almost that thought—he is too good to be coming back to West Perth from Geelong, why is he coming back?"

Also, in the West Australian context he was still regarded as an East Perth man, and there was a traditional rivalry between the two clubs. West Perth had suffered through the East Perth supremacy of earlier years, and had lost a series of off-field battles over player swaps and transfers. Mel Whinnen says:

I guess the committee—and there is always a gulf between the committee and the players—decided he was the sort of bloke we needed. The players weren't too sure of that though—getting one of these opposition blokes in to run the club. West Perth had never liked East Perth that much, there was no love lost. And all of a sudden we have an East Perth coach. Certainly for a while in 1968 all the players wondered—until Polly was able to generate the respect a coach must get, the players were not too rapt.

Whinnen stresses that it did not take long for the necessary respect to be generated. And Cometti, from the perspective of the younger players, says: "Once they saw him and saw that he could still play at top level, and was totally dedicated still—as a role model, he was just terrific if you aspired to be a successful League footballer. The majority of people down there were obviously very keen to play footy, took one look and fell in behind him."

It soon became clear that Farmer was not just another coach over from, or back from, Victoria with the latest fashions from the VFL stylebook to offer. He certainly brought that experience with him, but he added ideas borrowed from rugby and American gridiron, introduced concepts that were completely his own, and even went back to the Sheedy days at East Perth for some old ideas.

He says he "had never given coaching a lot of consideration" before he took the task on. The principles he developed were essentially based on his own attitude to the game:

> The whole basis of coaching from my point of view was the fitness of the player, the strength of the player, the skills of the player, and the attitude of the player … My basis of football was to develop a natural habit, where people automatically responded in the correct manner. The first commitment is always to get the ball; it's what you do with the ball after that that will decide how far you take it down the field. If there were five or six variables to make a play, they had to pick the right one … The basis of my training was always to give it to a footballer who was moving down the field. We were giving them the ball as they were sweeping down the field.

First came fitness and strength. The West Perth players found themselves running more miles than they ever had, and hitting the dunes at Trigg. One of Farmer's first steps was to upgrade the gym at the club, and to require of each player that he complete a set number of circuit training programs each week. This was still before weights and gym work had become a normal part of football training. The players were expected to do the circuits in their own time, not as part of the scheduled training. Players had to learn to use their bodies, and to harden their bodies. As Mel Whinnen explains:

> He would get us bumping. We would stand in two lines and one bloke would have to run from the end, and he would have to bump with the right and bump with the left, and have to go from one end to the other and bounce off the blokes on both sides. As well as this there were the 'bumping bags',

the big, body-sized punching bags used by rugby players for tackling practice. He had the bag hanging from the support and a bloke would have to hold the bag and you would run into it. Blokes like me—I mean, if I was holding it for Polly he would just bowl us over. It was not only a test for the bloke that was running at the bag to get used to bumping someone. It was for the bloke who had to stand there and brace himself.

According to Dempsey: "You could get a stick and hit someone, or someone hit you with it, and the bloody stick would break—that's how tough you got. That's what he bred into us."

Farmer was also demanding of his players in the skills department. "I guess the other coaches taught us how to handball and how to kick, but Polly would teach us to do it more precisely," is Whinnen's comment. "We would do drills over and over again." He introduced the 'marking machine' that had been used at East Perth in the 1950s. This was simply a football dangling on a pulley from a scaffold that could be adjusted higher and higher, forcing each player to learn how to jump those extra few inches that would get him above a pack or an opponent.

And he passed on some of his tricks of the trade, including one of the elements that gave his own handball such power and precision:

With the handball you are always taught to just hit off the hand, but Polly always taught us that you actually moved [the hand holding the ball] where you wanted to hit it. There was this relative movement between the two hands, that is all the umpire is looking for ... This is something that nobody thinks of, but it makes handballing so easy.

This technique can be seen in some photographs of Farmer that capture him after a handball is released. The striking hand has hit and followed through short and sharp, but the holding hand has actually followed through further, swinging the ball on its way.

At training, Farmer stressed that "the ideal was to go, go, go, all the time—train as you play." The drills were always competitive, because skills had to be honed under pressure. When the big men practised marking man-to-man, small men were placed in front and behind, and if the ball spilled from the marking contest, all were expected to follow-up hard and contest the ball when it hit the ground. "Jesus, we used to hate training," says Dempsey. "But I tell you what, it paid off. We were really physically and mentally strong." Even a notoriously lazy trainer like Dempsey conceded that "it made you feel good, because you knew you were bloody fit as anything."

But Farmer expected yet more. He wanted the perfect attitude and absolute dedication. Farmer never ceased to expect his players to emulate his own fierce desire for personal and team success at any cost. He put this in terms of a personal challenge. "The basis was for a person to discover for himself what he had to do to be successful."

Interviewed in the *Football Budget* before the main season began, he indicated the sort of standards he had in mind:

There's no secret [to success]. It's merely a matter of hard work and practice and more practice ... I believe it is up to the individual to plan his own successful life and each individual's plan is different. Coming to sport, of all the champions of the world I can think of there isn't one who doesn't train once on every day of the week. Most proven champions of long standing guard their position zealously and probably train twice a day. Of champion footballers who come into this category there are Haydn Bunton and Barry Cable. When one considers their stature, the long periods they put into their training has certainly made the difference between both being footballers and champion footballers. The day West Perth footballers start to take advantage of proven champions by making their own program [and] their own success plan it will certainly have a profound effect on lifting football at West Perth and in WA.[2]

Farmer increased the demands on the players hugely. Training was increased from three nights a week to four, and the Sunday sessions were upgraded. There was the circuit work to be done in their own time, and Farmer told the players that if they were serious about their football they would undertake their own training during the Friday off. An instructive incident that Whinnen recalls occurred early on:

Dave Dyson hadn't turned up for Sunday training or something, and Polly said to him: "Why didn't you come to training Dave?" Dave said: "Hang on, I had to work Pol." So Polly said: "Hang on, what's your top priority, working or playing footy?" For the first time, everybody spun around and thought, this is a changed scene ... Polly loved his footy and work took second place ... so he expected us all to do the same sort of thing. I think the main thing he was saying was: "Hang on, you've got to up your priorities, not just leaving footy to be the last on the list and everything else comes first." You had to start to whack it up the list a little bit. That was a good thing. They started to become more dedicated.

He expected super professional attitudes in a League that was hardly even semi-professional, because he believed that players should want this for themselves. Whinnen and Dempsey remain forever grateful to Farmer, because they discovered that they were better footballers than they had previously realised. They talk about Farmer renewing and extending their careers by taking them to new heights as individuals, quite apart from what he did for the team.

Farmer in turn is grateful to the pair for responding and setting an example. They were the undoubted leaders among the players, and if they had rebelled against the strict regime there could have been trouble:

Mel Whinnen and Bill Dempsey were veterans in the side. They'd been successful and they had a good outlook on life. When your leaders of your club are good guys it makes it very easy for other people to become good as well. You often have outstanding footballers who are not necessarily good characters.

In an unusual arrangement, Whinnen was appointed Farmer's assistant coach, while Dempsey became vice-captain. The club was anxious to look after them, and to make sure they did not feel slighted in anyway by Farmer's arrival. Neither actually had much to do in their official roles. Whinnen thinks: "those sorts of decisions were to give Demmo and I a couple of extra bob without us having to do too much." But it was a very satisfactory arrangement, with Farmer setting the tone, and Whinnen and Dempsey bringing the team along behind them.

Of course the patterns of training and play and, particularly, the mesh of personalities within the club all took some time to bed down. Nothing works until it is tested under fire, and only results and success will ultimately bring satisfaction within a football club. Both within and without West Perth, eyes were focussed on Farmer to see how he would perform not only as a coach, but as a player after six years away. The man who had left as a star and returned as a legend was returning to the Perth stage.

On the opening day of the season, West Perth came out on its home ground with all guns blazing to record an eight-goal win over East Fremantle. It held the form to be second on the ladder with a six-win, one-loss record after the first round of games, with the only blemish being a narrow loss to undefeated Perth. The Cardies fans knew they had a team with the goods. The players could see they were heading somewhere, and that the hard work had been and would be worthwhile.

The second game win against East Perth was probably the most important in terms of establishing their credentials. They went in as underdogs, playing away from home, but jumped to a first quarter lead, and increased it steadily all day to record a comfortable win, thanks largely to a dominant ruck led by Farmer and Sampson, and Farmer's move of Dempsey to centre half-back where he quietened East Perth's fiery star, Mal Brown. Brown was reported twice in the game by umpire Montgomery for elbowing first Wynne, and later Dempsey, and got a three-week suspension.

Farmer himself started relatively quietly, showing his hand when he had to. His first big game was against third placed Subiaco in round six, when West Perth racked up a 16-goal win over a side that had given Perth a big fright the week before:

> Farmer placed West Perth on the offensive from the start when he took complete charge ... [He] must have been pleased with his contribution as a player but it was his influence as a coach that produced the style of football that reduced Subiaco to impotence for nearly three quarters of the game. The master of the handpass used his left hand to punch the ball effectively 17 times during the match. One classic example came in the last quarter. Rover Craig Baker called for the ball when Farmer was lying surrounded on the ground. The call did not go unheeded. Farmer shot out a handpass straight to Baker 15 yards away who turned and coolly kicked a goal. West

Perth players have learned their handball lessons well. Farmer's example was copied all over the ground with telling effect.[3]

Farmer was sharing the ruckwork around with his fellow followers, and playing the role that had first been described early in the previous season at Geelong by a scribe defending him against those with temerity to suggest he was gone. It was the role he would develop to an art form in his four years at West Perth. When on the ball he generally played a kick behind the play, floating between the half-back and half-forward lines, marshalling his troops, directing the traffic, and above all, locking the ball in. His specialty was cutting off the opposition's defensive rebound, and with a quick handball or a well-directed kick, turning West Perth back into attack. And when there was a bounce or a throw-in to be contested, he would appear in the nick of time, as Sam Newman described, but always, it seemed, in the perfect position to contest.

It was a role that especially suited his new position as captain-coach. Not always in the thick of the play, he was able to read both the ebb and flow of play, and the performance of his players, and the little things they did or did not do. Sometimes he made his own moves in the course of play, but he also relied on his bench of Ron Bewick and runner Roy Porter. If they felt a change of some sort was needed, Porter would come out to Farmer with the suggestion, and he would either give his consent and send Porter on his way to the player with the message, or veto the move and send Porter back to the bench.

He also had plenty to say to his men in the general course of play. Whinnen saw it as "a big asset on the field. If you made a blue the shadow would loom up behind you and quietly whisper in your ear: 'Do that again and you're off,' or something like that, with a few little superlatives thrown in ... Polly would let you know, and that kept you on your toes. You didn't lose your concentration or get a bit slack." When asked about his methods Farmer replies simply: "You didn't have much time on the field, so you were very, very rude. You haven't got time to be nice. You've got to be impactive. The important thing was, it always stayed on the field."

More than anything else though he set the tone and the pattern of West

Perth's play. The tone was hard; once he was on the field he was ruthless, is the comment of more than one of his players. This aspect of his game was bewailed by some of the football purists who had loved him so in his East Perth days. The pattern was movement, movement, movement—players and ball always moving forward. The other players could see and know exactly what he wanted, because they saw him doing it over and over again, and he communicated it to them all the time in the course of the game.

As at East Perth and at Geelong, the team's play came to revolve around him. It was his presence as a player as much as a coach that lifted a team essentially the same as the year before from the middle of the field to the top of the competition. Says Dempsey: "His physical presence on the ground was great, because there's a lot of games I saw him play where he didn't take an active part, but he'd direct the traffic, you know, and we all used to play to a plan."

It had become a plan rather than just the Farmer cause and effect because he had the authority of a coach. But the testimony of the players is similar from club to club, as Whinnen shows:

> We revolved around his style of play because Polly brought a lot of players into the game. Particularly a guy like Steven Smeath. He was built like a matchstick but could run like the wind ... When Polly was down past the centreline and there was a bounce down he would just grab the ball somehow or other—he would either bump the bloke out of the road or just stand there and grab it, and Smeathy would be going down the side and out would come the ball ... In the pack Polly would grovel on the ground and get the ball and then he would get the handball out. There would always be the Smeaths and the Watlings and the runners all around the pack, waiting for the ball to come out.

West Perth went through the second round of seven games undefeated. It hit top spot when Perth went down to East Perth; beat East Perth itself the following week; and then gave the reigning premiers an eight-goal hiding. The Perth match was perhaps not a true test, with a number of players on both sides, including Farmer and Wynne of the Cardinals, and Atwell and Cable of Perth, absent on State duties.

West Perth extended its winning run as far as the 15th game, against East Fremantle. Farmer missed this and the next game against East Perth when he came down with the mumps. The East Fremantle game showed the first danger signs for the Cardinals, with the press suggesting that individualism had broken out at the expense of teamwork. The warnings were vindicated when the winning run came to an end against East Perth. This enabled Perth to draw level on points, and two weeks later when the two teams clashed, Perth got back to the top of the ladder.

Farmer was far from panicking at this minor slump of two losses in three weeks. There was no danger of missing the second semi-final, with a four game break by now between West Perth in second position, and East Perth and Subiaco in the next two places. But the Cardinals were unable to regain their top place despite three strong wins to end the home and away round, as Perth also won its last three.

West Perth's second last game was against Subiaco. Captain-coach of Subiaco, Haydn Bunton, remembers the game for a reason that shows another side of the supposedly ruthless Farmer:

> It was Neil Balme's first game, he was only a kid. And Neil did pretty well. I've got an idea Polly relaxed a bit, to help the kid along. I'm not kidding. I don't know whether he'd ever admit that, I know that day I was really surprised. I mean, he had a bit of go in him, Neil, but I don't think Polly put the whole effort into it.

Balme was only 17, and still at high school. It was his first full game after a couple of stints off the bench. For such a youngster it must have been a daunting prospect to face Farmer, supported by the biggest and strongest ruck combination in the League. Farmer does not recall the game specifically, but says Bunton is probably correct:

> He was just too young. His body would be too soft and he wouldn't handle it. You'd feel awful if you did [anything]. I wouldn't have used my legs on him. Probably I tried to beat him without hurting him.

He might have gone easy on Balme, but he was rated best on ground in a match that produced a crushing 10-goal victory for the Cardinals, and an amazing statistic by the standards of the 1960s:

> West Perth used effective handpasses at the rate of more than one a minute ... in a smooth display of team football ... [They] made 126 constructive handpasses to work the ball into an advantageous position and then used long kicks to achieve a neat blend between the use of hand and foot as a means of disposal.[4]

Despite finishing a game behind Perth, and having a one-win two-loss record to them, West Perth entered the finals confident that they would come up trumps in the crunch games. Their two losses to the leaders had been by eight and three points, whereas their victory had been by a crushing 52. They firmly believed that they were not only the best, but also the hardest and fittest side in the competition. It was a matter of playing to their potential. Two games later though, a sense of shock and bewilderment had overtaken the club. They were out of the action after losses to Perth in the second semi-final and East Perth in the preliminary final. The two games followed different patterns for equally disappointing results.

In the second semi West Perth trailed in the first half, kicked five goals to two in the third quarter to go into the last looking good with a 15-point break, and then stopped to a walk, kicking only three behinds for the quarter as the favourites swept past, and then left the Cardinals in their wake. Farmer himself had a quiet day, and his ruck division as a whole was beaten. West Perth was criticised for playing a negative game, with its best key position player, Wynne, at centre half-back not centre half-forward, and the ruckmen packing the backline and not pushing upfield.

Interviewed on television the next day, Farmer "criticised some of his teammates for failing to show initiative and for not fighting the issue out to the end," commenting that: "Several of our players have plenty of natural ability but little else to go with it."[5] No doubt there were equally harsh words behind closed doors at Leederville Oval, but expressed more bluntly. They did not have the desired effect though.

East Perth did not exactly come into the preliminary final on a hot streak, having just scrambled past Subiaco with a last-kick victory. The game reflected the lapse in form of both teams, with the first three quarters unanimously condemned as unattractive, scrappy football, unworthy of a finals game. Farmer gave "a wonderful all-round display of his football skill. His brilliant first-quarter performance should have been an inspiration to his teammates."[6] His fellow ruckmen were also good, to give the side plenty of the ball, but they lost rover Craig Baker to a leg injury in the first five minutes, and there was no system. In the second quarter they did virtually nothing with the wind, and by three-quarter time they had only 3.6 (24) to East Perth's 7.10 (52).

Farmer did his ankle and surprisingly placed himself in the back pocket for the final term as his side mounted a fightback. Six goals in the first 15 minutes took them to the lead. With 10 minutes to go, East Perth goaled to regain the lead, and then its old hands in Chadwick, Brown and Graham led a rearguard action to hold Farmer's troops off, and see their team out of the finals. For the third straight year Perth and East Perth played off in the Grand Final, and for the third straight year Perth won the premiership and Barry Cable took home the Simpson Medal.

No one looking back at it now can explain the dismal performance of West Perth. Says Dempsey:

> I've never been able to work it out. Probably a combination of being a bit cocky and because it was Polly's first year and a lot of guys still working him out. You think back on that season and we should have won it, but when you try to think why it's very hard to pinpoint because we had such a good season.

At the time though, the club president and the coach had some pointed observations to make. In his report published prior to the annual general meeting, president Roper wrote:

> Our League Team's performance in the Finals was a very disappointing conclusion to an otherwise quite successful season of football ... These two matches lead me to the conclusion that we had in our team, players who have not the dedication and determination—or THE ABILITY to lift

themselves and play football of the standard required for the pressures and tensions of final-round matches. I believe it is vital that we take stock of this state of affairs before the next season commences, for I am convinced—I'd have always maintained—that only those players who are prepared to give of their best ALL THE TIME and develop an almost fanatical devotion to their Club and the 'guernsey', should be permitted the honour of representing West Perth.[7]

Addressing the club members at the meeting in December that received this report, Farmer "made some extremely pertinent comments about commitment, desperation, desire and a physical approach. He suggested that measures would be taken to overcome the problem."[8]

16

THE ARCHITECT

The West Perth squad may have been waiting with some apprehension to see what their coach's remedial measures would be. No doubt many expected that the training regimen would become even harder, and the admonitions from the coach more fierce. But Mel Whinnen indicates that this was not the case:

> I think what really happened—Polly had some very strong ideas, and what he had to do was modify his ideas because we were down here with our standard, and he was up there with his ... Polly had to drop his standard a little bit and then lift us up a little bit further ... He found it hard because he knew what we had to do—he had done it by the time he came to us.

Dempsey recalls that: "over the summer we had a few golf days and social gatherings and the fellows all got to know one another a bit better." It cannot have hurt for the players to get to know their coach outside the confines of dressing-room, training track and playing field either. He had acquired respect quickly; as the second year unfolded there is clearly a sense of a more comfortable relationship developing to complement this. He did gradually step up the training requirements, to the point where the players remember 1969 as a harder year on the track than 1968, but as a happier one, too, where all knew what was expected and where they were heading.

A common standard was required in terms of effort from the squad, but he was able to drive those who would respond to being driven, give space to those who could be trusted to get on with it, and encourage where he felt it was worthwhile. Young Cometti was one of his problem players. He undoubtedly had potential, but admits: "I wasn't your dedicated footballer ... I was wanting to do other things, in broadcasting—I was a radio announcer at the time. The two things just weren't compatible."

He was exactly the sort of player Roper and Farmer had been referring to at the close of 1968, but Farmer's reaction was not to dismiss him out of hand:

> He would come around home and speak to my mother, and try to get me to go to training and all this sort of stuff ... Perhaps he was acting out of self-interest too, but it did give me an insight into the fact that he was prepared to do a fair bit of leg work to try to get people to do the right thing ... What impressed me about Pol was his resolve to try to make it work for me, given that I wasn't doing the right thing.

There were no big-name recruits to bolster the team in 1969. Cometti turned out to be a lost cause. He did not leave the club, but lost his spot at full-forward and became a fringe player. A number of other local juniors emerged as League players, including defender Tony Dragun, winger Alan Watling, and rover Bill Valli, and country recruit Keith Miller settled into a forward flank position. Two fringe VFL players, ruckman defender Neil Evans, and defender Brian Pleitner from Essendon and Hawthorn, were the only imports.

The first two games of the season were against teams with new coaches for 1969, but both were very familiar faces to Farmer. Denis Marshall left the VFL on the high note of a second-place finish in the 1968 Brownlow Medal to return to Claremont as captain-coach. At East Perth, Derek Chadwick had stepped down from the coaching position while continuing as captain. Moving in to take his place was none other than Jack Sheedy, back for the first time since 1964.

Farmer missed the opening game against Claremont with a leg injury. If Marshall was hoping that life might be a bit easier back home, he soon found otherwise when he had to leave the field in the second quarter. He was collected by John Wynne, and finished up with a bruised leg, and yet another head gash, this time requiring 13 stitches. His head was still clear enough to instigate a series of positional changes that sparked a third-quarter surge that took Claremont to the lead, and it managed to hang on for a draw. The showing was a false dawn for Claremont, with their first win not coming for another 10 games. One player who made his debut in the game was an 18-year-old ruckman, Graham Moss, who would emerge as the west's next ruckman of real quality.

When Sheedy brought his East Perth charges to Leederville Oval for the second game of the season, it was the first time Farmer had opposed him since 1955, when Farmer was with the Royals, and Sheedy with East Fremantle. Farmer was still far from fully fit, and it appears to be the only game in his career when he did not actually play as a ruckman, spending the game at full-forward. A loss left West Perth in sixth place on the ladder, but it was still waiting on clearances for Pleitner and Evans, had Farmer playing on one leg, and six others on the injury list.

In the third week, the Royals emerged as the season's trendsetters when they defeated Perth. They were the only undefeated side, and their scalps had been the other three finalists of 1968. They were getting great drive on the ball, with Keith Doncon lured back from a year's retirement roving to Mal Brown. Brown seemed to be relishing Sheedy's decision to play him as a ruckman, recording best-on-ground votes from the media in all three games.

West Perth got on the winning list with a mammoth 21-goal win over Swan Districts. Laurie Richards, who had been alternating with Cometti in the full-forward position, finally came good with 12 goals in the slaughter. He followed up with another seven in a win against Perth that took the Cardinals into third place ahead of the reigning premiers, but was coming under notice for his spectacular aerial skills as much as his goal scoring. Another victory over Subiaco continued its climb up the ladder to second place.

The following week against South Fremantle, Farmer played his 300th game of senior football. With the milestone he shrugged off the effects of the injury and began to show that there was life in the old legs yet. His form got better and better as West Perth continued to rack up wins leading up to the return meeting with East Perth.

This top-of-the-ladder clash for the 'Perth Derby' drew a record crowd of 26,760, that still stands as the best ever attendance at a WANFL qualifying game. They were treated to a high standard of football, with the game fluctuating through the first three quarters, until Farmer engineered a strong final term that saw the Cardinals kicking five goals to nil, for an impressive victory. This left them only half a game adrift of the Royals, with a thirty point advantage in percentage. This was the last round of domestic games before the 1969 interstate championships in Adelaide.

With his slow start to the season Farmer had not been named in the original squad for the carnival, but came in after a reshuffle caused by injuries, along with Derek Chadwick, who was named captain. It was Farmer's fourth appearance in the national championships. His first in 1956 had seen his emergence as a star player. Of the other players who had participated in that Perth carnival, only Ted Whitten and Haydn Bunton were still playing senior football, and neither was appearing in Adelaide. His longevity is emphasised by the fact that Mal Atwell, who had made his debut with East Perth five years after Farmer, was now his non-playing coach.

Atwell showed no deference to his seniors when he named Farmer as a reserve for the opening game against South Australia. In his 17th season of football, it was the first time he had started the game on the bench—and he was not impressed. He was brought onto the ground late in the third quarter, too late to have any impact on a game that the Sandgropers lost by two goals. Four days later he was in the starting line-up for a head-to-head clash with Nicholls. The West was never in the hunt, down two goals to nine after one quarter, and six to 15 at half-time. They recovered a little ground in the second half, but Victorian coach Ron Barassi claimed he had told his players to ease up in the last quarter and save themselves for the decider against the home state. The press had Nicholls as Victoria's best player, and Farmer as the West's second best after Bill Walker.

Farmer bruised his back against Victoria, and missed the final game against Tasmania, in which the West scored its only win of the carnival. When team officials cast their votes for the squad's best player, he did well enough from his one full game to score nine votes, the same as rovers Cable and Walker. He and Cable could not be separated on count back, and so shared the Simpson Medal, giving them four each.

W est Perth's performance through the second half of the season was patchy, largely due to injury problems. At the worst point, when the Cardinals went down to East Fremantle, they had 14 players on the injured list. It had started in the game after the championships, where they finished a game against Perth with only 16 men on the field. The only constant, as they staged a seesawing battle with Perth for second place and the double chance, was the form of their captain-coach. In the last 11 weeks he was not out of the best player lists, and at one point was listed by the *Football Budget* as West Perth's best player for five successive weeks.

One of these games produced a classic battle between the veteran and the angry young man of the League, in which both Farmer and Mal Brown showed their leadership qualities:

> Farmer lifted himself for the final drive for victory after three quarters of fiery ruck duels against East Perth's big, virile followers, Mal Brown and Bradley Smith. The clashes in the packs were fierce—Farmer received eight free-kicks and gave away as many ... [His] value to the team was increased by his steadying influence and his ability to channel play coolly in a desperate quarter when tempers flared under mounting pressure. Brown and Smith lack Farmer's knowledge and skill, but were of great value to East Perth in the general play where their strength and energy had a profound influence on the game. It was Brown's sheer power and competitive spirit that played a major role in keeping the scores locked together for the closing minutes of the game. His value to East Perth at this stage was comparable to Farmer's influence on the game earlier in the quarter.[1]

Brown was still only 22 years old at this stage, but already in his fifth season of senior football. He was certainly well past the Neil Balme stage of the soft body which Farmer would treat with caution, as the report quoted above shows. Whether Brown felt aggrieved by something Farmer had done, or whether it was just the impetuosity of the young bull eager to knock the old bull off his pedestal, he had overstepped the mark earlier in the game, as the same report notes, in qualifying the compliments: "It was disappointing to see Brown fell Farmer from behind in a third-quarter incident that was a throwback to Brown's immature days in League football."[2]

It was as a result of this tie that the Cardinals slipped behind Perth on the ladder. When poor kicking saw them lose to Perth by two points a fortnight later the gap widened to a game plus percentage. Then they succumbed to Subiaco, and only stayed in touch because Perth went down to fifth-placed East Fremantle on the same day. Nevertheless, with only two games to go to the finals, a second semi-final berth looked an unlikely prospect. Even more worrying was that in the space of four weeks they had faced the three other teams who would appear in the finals, and their best result was a draw.

West Perth did all that it could by winning the last two games against South and East Fremantle. The first of these was a crushing 19-goal win that lifted its percentage above Perth's but left it a game behind. Farmer must have felt the gods were smiling on him when Perth collapsed against bottom-placed Claremont in its last game. The Claremont win enabled Marshall to escape the indignity of the wooden spoon but, more importantly, allowed West Perth to slip into second place at the death-knock.

They finished two and a half games behind East Perth. It was seen as an open final round, with East Perth favoured, but at far from unbackable odds. The Royals' top-of-the-ladder finish had been due largely to the brilliant form of Brown throughout the season. This was reflected in his clean sweep of the media awards that netted him cash, holiday trips and a new car. Runner-up in all but one case was none other than Farmer, who had steadily worked his way up the lists as the season progressed. He also finished second behind Brown in the Sandover Medal count.

As the final round approached the events of 12 months earlier were uppermost in Farmer's mind, and he was absolutely determined to prevent a repetition of his team's inglorious performance. He was not unhappy with the situation as it stood. He believed that the qualifying round was played with the objective of reaching the second semi-final, and that had been achieved, if only just. The Cardinals played from here on level terms, with East Perth gaining no reward for its extra 10 points, and there was something to be said for being the underdogs and having the attention and flattery focussed on their rival.

The injury problems had cleared up, leaving him with a full list to choose from, and the side was more settled in many respects than in the previous year. The ruckmen were no longer having to plug key position gaps. The experienced Dyson was now performing well at full-back. Second year player, Greg Astbury, had taken over centre half-back. Whinnen as always was in the pivot. Wynne had laid claim to the title of top centre half-forward in the competition with an outstanding year of football, despite playing the second half of the year with a chipped bone in his right ankle. He had also acquired the reputation of the team's tough man. With Richards continuing to perform at full-forward, and Smeath and Miller on the flanks, the team had a potent and settled attack, as reflected in some of their high scores and big winning margins during the season. The following division was still the best in the League. Valli had been one of the boom recruits of the year, establishing himself as first rover. Dempsey was free to do what he did best, supporting Farmer in the ruck, and they had able supports in Evans and Knell.

Farmer believed he had the ammunition. It was a matter of performance, and especially of attitude. He drummed in the lesson of the year before, telling them that they had wanted victory, but not been prepared to make the sacrifices necessary to achieve it. In the press there was talk of their reputation as 'brittle' in final-round football, and of East Perth being the team to exploit this.

The match would turn out to be "one of the most memorable and talked about final-round games on record. This was because of the sheer ferocity of the first quarter."[3] "Hips, shoulders and bone-cracking bumps were traded freely in the first term, which was described by many critics as the hardest and best brand of football seen for years."[4] By the time the quarter ended, any question marks hovering over West Perth had well and truly disappeared.

Farmer sprung the tactical surprise by placing his tall defender, Brian Pleitner, on a wing for the first time. Pleitner was very quick off the mark, and strong overhead. The idea was to provide an extra avenue into attack away from the congested centre, but Pleitner was also able to provide additional strength at the centre bounces where most of the heavy action took place. West Perth sprung out of the blocks, having 2.1 (13), all scored by rover Valli, in the first five minutes. Then came the first of the talked about incidents. John Wynne shirt-fronted East Perth rover Hans Verstegen, and left him in the hands of a pair of trainers who propped him against the post in a forward pocket. His place on the ball was taken by Keith Doncon, who had hardly entered the fray when he was flattened by a bone-shattering bump from Farmer. Sheedy, watching from the sidelines, "thought he was dead", and indeed, it was some time before he too was able to stagger up to the forward line to recover. The Royals began chasing the man rather than the ball. Bradley Smith caught up with Pleitner, to make it three men down in the first 15 minutes. Wynne was reported for "unduly rough play" after remonstrating with Smith, but he was also dominant at centre half-forward.

West Perth had five goals on the board before the Royals got their first and started to get their minds back on the game, so when the first break came it was six goals to two. The crowd was so excited the roaring hardly abated as the players went to their huddles. It was the football as much as the violence that had them on their feet though. Valli had had 11 kicks already, including three goals, and three passes that had set up the others. Richards had scored two of these and dragged down a couple of his screamers. It had been an electrifying 30 minutes. The rest of the game never reached the same height of drama. It was as if West Perth had squeezed all the passion of a final into that torrid quarter of an hour. The Royals held their ground for the rest of the game without ever looking like they might bridge the gap. West Perth got through to the Grand Final with a very convincing 26-point victory.

All the analysis after the game naturally focussed on the sensational opening and its consequences. "Former umpire Fred Woods said that it was the most vicious opening quarter he had seen."[5] Whereas John Todd felt "the first half of the match was one of the best exhibitions of hard football I have seen for years."[6]

Farmer himself says: "It was a fierce and committed West Perth side whose eye was on the ball—that's what they wanted and they went in hard." This was the general assessment at the time, as Todd's comments show:

"West Perth's approach was fanatical, but the players did not at any stage play the man instead of the ball. However, East Perth, upset by the vigorous play, tended to retaliate and in the process lost concentration."[7]

The Verstegen and Doncon incidents have been remembered ever since, largely because in both cases it was rovers being taken out by big men. In particular the story of the Farmer–Doncon clash is recounted again and again—always prefaced by the comment that it was a fair bump—but often cited as an example of Farmer's ruthlessness and of how he had been changed by his time in Victoria. There is a photograph of the incident. It does not show the moment of impact, but in its own way it does emphasise more than anything the important element of the day—the fanaticism for the ball. Doncon is prone, face down. Farmer must have gone to ground too, he is captured also horizontal, lying across the top of Doncon, but oblivious to the man underneath him as he scrabbles after the ball at the right of the picture. When asked about it he responds:

> It was a good fair bump. But it was bad luck, because it probably put an end to Doncon's career. That was the tragedy of it ... It was rare for me to bump rovers, and that was probably the worst part about it, because Doncon was a lot smaller than I am. But there was no thought other than to bump him.

Given the message he had been drumming into his players, and with the ball at issue early in the game, in one sense Fanner had little choice but to set the example by continuing flat out as the clash loomed. However, there are two ways to bump a player: in one he can be bumped off the ball, in the other, nothing is held back.

One is left with the sense that it is the incident in his career that he regrets, when he refers to it in another conversation and says: "He was really too small to be bumped." When asked if he would have gone softer if he had his time over again, he replies:

> You'd probably have to think twice about whether you'd effect the bump ... The whole basis of people like me was to get the ball in the rough and tough and give it to the smaller player and let him run free so he didn't get hurt. To me, you weren't there to beat the small players, you were there to beat the people you were up against.

Dempsey talks of how one of the messages he drummed into his own big men over and over again was that they must always protect the small players of the side, by getting the ball for them, by positioning themselves properly and by delivering the ball to them correctly. The bump on Doncon was legitimate, perhaps in the context of the game it was even necessary. But it was against Farmer's personal code of how football should be played, by himself and others.

It was thought that in the preliminary final a shell-shocked East Perth would succumb to Perth, which had beaten the Royals six times in succession in final-round football. But Sheedy reshuffled the side and it came out fighting for a 46-point win, setting the scene for a return bout with the Cardinals.

Once again Farmer had his team training on the off weekend to keep them sharp, and he put on a barbecue for players and their families at his home. West Perth was doing everything it could think of to ensure that the season ended on the right note. The most inspired touch came from Les Day, who came up with the idea of flying Bill Dempsey's mother down from Darwin to watch him play. She had never been to Perth. Dempsey convinced her that there was not enough time to catch a bus, and that she would just have to overcome her fear of flying. She was adopted into the West Perth camp as the build-up came to a head. Also down from Darwin was Jack Larcombe, as the Cardinals' faithful gathered in expectation.

On the Thursday night there was a players' tea at the clubrooms. It was the final gathering of the team before they assembled at Subiaco on the Saturday. "The speech that he gave that night," recalls Dempsey, shaking his head:

> I'll never forget it. It was just so inspirational for me to listen to the bastard. He had a way with speaking to people, without raising his voice and thumping the table ... He just stood there and gave this speech, and you wished it was Saturday and you were running out on the ground. He just said all the right things.

There was more of the same in the rooms before the game, but the last words of his pre-match address were his own football philosophy distilled to a single statement: "I want you to want the ball more than anything else on this earth today."[8]

In its own way the first quarter of the game was almost as sensational as the second semi-final. West Perth had 18 scoring shots to East's four. But for the fact that this bombardment produced 6.12 (48) rather than the other way round, the game could have been all over. Richards took a series of sensational high marks, but wobbled three punts through for points. As he lined up for his fourth shot, Farmer glided up from behind and told him to try a drop kick. He switched his grip on the ball, and sent the ball spinning right through the middle. Farmer patrolled just forward of the centre, and each time Matson kicked out after a Cardinals behind, he seemed to intercept and pump the ball forward again. Whenever the Royals tried to go forward the man in the way was Dempsey, who pulled in mark after mark.

When the second quarter got underway, East Perth needed to hit back to stay in the game, but there was more of the same, except West Perth started to kick straight. Ten minutes in it had four more goals on the board, and a lead in excess of 50 points. East Perth was rattled, and once again playing the man instead of the ball—to no avail.

In the third quarter the game turned into a total rout. As a contest it was pathetic; as an exhibition of methodical, powerful, precise team football, it was ranked by one commentator as "football as it had never before been played."[9] Dempsey continued to reign supreme in the air in defence, surpassed only by the spectacular Richards at full-forward. Watling and Whinnen dominated the centreline, feeding Smeath and Miller on the flanks. These two were switching sides all the time, running rings around their marksmen. Smeath in particular was sensational, bagging six goals for the game. For the quarter, the score line was 8.5 (53) to a single behind, to give West Perth a 16-goal lead.

In the last quarter the Cardinals took their foot off the accelerator, allowing the Royals to score six goals to three. Even then the West Perth tally of 21.21 (147) was the highest Grand Final score ever, and the winning margin only five points short of the record. So comfortable was Farmer that he took himself off the ground 10 minutes from the end of the game to give Brian Sampson a run.

It was an astounding triumph. For the first time in his career he was the man who stood on the dais and received the premiership trophy, not only as the captain, but as the coach and the undisputed architect.

He was, as always, quiet and modest in victory. The pundits though were generous in their praise. The combination of the controlled power of the second semi-final, and the overwhelming football perfection of the Grand Final saw West Perth's display ranked as the best team performance seen in Western Australia, with some suggesting they would be a worthy rival for the Richmond team that took the VFL premiership on the same day.

Farmer visited the East Perth rooms to commiserate. The side still contained two players, in Chadwick and Graham, who had been teammates of his, and there were many familiar faces and old friends in the ranks of their officials and supporters. It was the Royals' fourth losing Grand Final in a row, all to sides led by former East Perth men. For his own players he was fulsome with his praise, and told them: "One day you will realise when you look back what a wonderful thing you have been part of."[10]

This statement has rung especially true over the years for Bill Dempsey, who had considered returning home to Darwin after the disappointment of the previous year. He was the unanimous choice as the recipient of the Simpson Medal, which his delighted mother insisted on calling the 'Simpson Desert Medal', despite his best attempts to correct her. With Farmer, he shared the limelight in the post-match celebrations, which in his case involved being "pissed for a week". Among the West Perth players who were lucky enough to play in more than one premiership, 1969 has always been the sweetest. For Dempsey the day has always remained the highlight of his career. The medal, and the presence of his mother, were personal touches, the fact that he had waited nine years for it meant that he savoured it, and "what made it even more beautiful was that we beat East Perth."

"After the game I was just sitting down, stuffed, having a beer, and I was just watching Pol. And you could see in him that he felt real bloody good ... He wasn't skiting or anything like that—he never got carried away with it. But you could tell, he was enormously proud." At the celebrations at Leederville the next day, Dempsey recalls through his haze: "All I can remember of him is just seeing his big tall head with a big smile on his face and shaking people's hands ... Oh, he was in his glory, too, you know."

17

"DO IT FOR POLLY!"

A t the end of 1969 Farmer was probably the hottest 34-year-old football property in the history of the game. Key playmaker and inspiration in the premiership side, winner of a Simpson Medal, comfortable winner of the club best and fairest award, and runner-up in the Sandover Medal; it is the resume of a footballer in his prime. As always through his career, there was speculation about his next move.

The wise men had been saying through the latter part of 1969 that he would return to Geelong in 1970, with the only question being whether he would be the playing or non-playing coach. Reports out of Melbourne were also suggesting that he was a chance to become the coach of Fitzroy.

He had come to West Perth on a two-year contract, with an option for a third if both parties were agreeable. At the start of 1969 West Perth had offered to extend the contract into the third year with a further option, and at some point Farmer gave a verbal agreement to this. On the Sunday, presumably during the celebrations at Leederville, president Len Roper announced that he would be continuing with the club. There were references to the club being eager to avoid a repeat of the 1961 slide out of the four after their 1960 premiership. Farmer sent a slight shiver through the camp when he said in the press that he had not yet signed the contract extension, and that there were matters still to be discussed with the club. His terms were met, and he signed on, ensuring that he would continue his football career into the 1970s.

When the 1970 season began Perth were thought of as the team that was under pressure and in danger of slipping down the ladder. Atwell had retired as a player, and Cable had left to play with North Melbourne. There was a question mark over East Perth, with the appointment of Mal Brown as captain-coach, the youngest in the League since John Todd's unsuccessful year at South Fremantle in 1959.

When West Perth annihilated South Australian glamour club Sturt in a practice match many thought it was a good sign. But after that performance the wheels fell off the team. Dempsey can only explain it as a "head job"— too many players still carried away with the success and exhilaration of the year before. Farmer attributes it primarily to no longer having the players he needed.

John Wynne left to play with Norwood in South Australia. He was certainly one of the success stories of 1969, and his presence on the field and around the club were worth more than his mere statistics showed. Valli went to try his luck with Collingwood after just one year, despite being frustrated in this ambition by West Perth refusing to grant a clearance. The departure of backup ruckmen Sampson and Evans left only Dempsey and Knell to support Farmer, and restricted his usual tactics in the deployment of his big men.

What was shown up was the lack of depth in the club. Its reserves were the chopping block of the competition. During the year the Cardinals were competitive when they had all players available, but struggled whenever injuries struck their player list. After the first round of seven games they were in fifth place on three wins and four losses. The start of the second round saw them beat ladder-leader Claremont, and sneak into fourth place ahead of Perth and East Perth on percentage. This opened up an opportunity, with a follow-up game against Subiaco, which had replaced Claremont on top. However, they went down by eight points, and lost their brief hold on a top four place. A week later, after a second loss to East Perth, West Perth was back in sixth place, two games out of touch with the four.

This is where it remained for the rest of the season, despite a strong five-win, two-loss finish in the final round of games.

As in 1969, Farmer had started the year slowly. There were no specific injuries, but his knee appeared to be giving him trouble, and there are a number of references in the football press about him not being 100 per cent fit in the first half of the year. Whinnen remembers him having "a heel problem more than people knew, and other problems—he found it very hard to keep going as a player, I think .... Polly often ran up and down the middle of a field, he didn't get out to the boundary lines because he wasn't as fit as he would have liked to have been."

He did not make the West Perth best player list in the *Football Budget* in the first five games of the season. However, in the 14 out of 16 he played after that, he was in the side's best three in 10 of them, and best player on four occasions, once again with a very strong finish to the season. For all the trouble he had coming up for the game each Saturday, he finished a close third in the club best and fairest with 41 votes, behind Whinnen on 46 and Smeath on 43. The fact remained though, that for the first time since 1955 his side did not finish in the finals, making it a bleak September. And as captain-coach, just as he was the acclaimed architect of the previous year's triumph, this year he had to carry the responsibility.

There was, however, a bright spot to the season, one which in West Australian eyes is very much part of the Farmer legend. It was another defeat, but acknowledged by all as a heroic one.

At the start of the year he had been named as coach of the state side. It was common for the job to go to the coach of the previous year's premiership team, who would then play a hand in selecting the squad, and bring it together for a couple of training sessions before departure on tour, or the games at Subiaco.

The interstate fixtures for 1970 included a tour at the mid-point of the season to play Victoria in Melbourne on a Saturday, and Tasmania in Hobart on a Monday, then five weeks later a match against the South Australians at Subiaco. The holy grail of West Australian football was the notion of beating the Victorians on their home turf, on the most famous of football grounds, the MCG. The closest they had ever come was seven points, in 1952. The 1958 side that Farmer played in got within 17, but there had also been some awful drubbings handed out to the Sandgropers. Their interstate stocks, after the previous year's carnival, were low.

Farmer set himself a mission to try to pull off the impossible. He must have thought back to his first game for Victoria in 1963, when South Australia had pulled off the same feat, thanks to the selection of a squad before the season even began, and a prolonged training campaign and build-up to bring the players together as a team. Presumably with some prompting from Farmer, the WANFL included a bye after the third week of games for a full-scale state trial game, as a prelude to selection of the squad.

The squad, when it was named, was not seen as an especially strong one. Cable was gone, leaving the inexperienced Bruce Duperouzel as Walker's roving partner. There was some speculation over whether Farmer would even play. Other ruckmen were Dempsey—thought to be too small to combat the Victorians—Subiaco's Burton, and East Perth's Brown and Smith, who were really key position players. First choice full-forward Austin Robertson withdrew with an injured shoulder. There was less than the usual sprinkling of players with the VFL experience that could prove crucial, especially in bad conditions; only Farmer, Marshall and Hassa Mann qualified on this score.

Farmer put the squad through an unprecedented four consecutive nights of training before departing the day before the Melbourne game. When they arrived in Melbourne he arranged for the legendary coach, Norm Smith, to address the players. He was doing all he could to weld them as a unit. "Farmer preached his gospel of teamwork and courage continually for six days leading up to the game, during which time the players trained five times under the control of a football superstar."[1]

The Melbourne weather was atrocious, and traditionally this factor went against the West Australians. "If it had been just slippery it would only have been bad for us, but it was such a mudheap it was bad for both sides. It was just a slog."

The crowd of 46,000-plus at the MCG was good for an interstate game, especially considering the conditions. Part of the reason was that it was billed as Farmer's farewell performance in Victoria. It was a formidable contract. At 35, in heavy conditions that would take their toll on his increasingly suspect legs, he had to marshall his own troops as on-field coach, while leading his suspect ruck division against a combination of John Nicholls, Len Thompson, Sam Newman and the up-and-coming Footscray champion Gary Dempsey.

The nature of this task was the other reason, apart from his natural class and form, that Bill Dempsey was in the West Australian side. Dempsey had usually been overlooked for state sides previously because of his small size for a ruckman. While Sam Newman would probably rate above Dempsey as the best out-and-out ruckman Farmer played with, the Dempsey-Farmer combination formed the best ruck partnership of his career. At six feet two inches, Dempsey was an inch smaller than Farmer. They nearly always played against bigger combinations, but they were rarely beaten.

Part of the reason for their chemistry was that they played as equals. Dempsey was one of the few not overawed by Farmer; the knockabout Darwin lad took a backward step for nobody. Their partnership was based on mutual respect, and the antagonistic banter that is the sign of friendship among Australian sportsmen. Says Dempsey:

> I was the complete opposite to him. I was a boozer and a smoker. He used to say to me: "I don't care how much you eat, drink or smoke, or keep late nights, but the minute you put in a bad game, then mate, you're gone." I said: "Well I'm not going to give you that satisfaction you bastard."

But when it came to the business side of ruck contests they harmonised beautifully:

> We had a little system which used to work out real good. He was a real cunning bastard Polly. At centre bounces he'd say: "If it goes straight up in the air I've got it, or leaning my way it's mine. If it goes your way, it's yours, right." But the thing was that when it was his I had to take out the bloke that was closest to him. I'd come in near him, run through him, whatever. I went in the pretense of going for the ball, and just took the other fellow out.

When the ball went Dempsey's way, Farmer would return the favour. The concept was not unique, but they did it so well together:

You'd go for boundary throw-ins, and there'd be about four of us going. Pol'd be off to the side, and I'd go in with these two other ruckmen, and those two blokes never got off the ground for some unknown reason—maybe because I was hanging on to them, or standing up and bending them over—and Polly'd go up, and whack, zoom.

Against the Victorians, Farmer did not want another ruckman who would fly and contest along with him, as he and Clarke had done in the interstate games of the '50s. He wanted a partner, and Dempsey was his man. "Virtually I was Polly's man who did all the shit work, stepping in front of fellows, or jumping on their feet or whatever." Nicholls and company were big men to be stepping in front of, but "I knew how to complement him, so it didn't matter. The old code—as long as we're winning, as long as we're getting the ball."

And winning the ball they were. Geoff Christian in the *West Australian* wrote:

Farmer led a winning ruck and his efforts were backed up resolutely by Bradley Smith, Bill Dempsey and Peter Burton. WA were able to win on the ball because of the solid roving of Bill Walker ... and the mature performance of interstate newcomer Bruce Duperouzel ... WA took firm control on the ball after half-time and, for the first time in 11 years of watching interstate football in Melbourne, I saw Victoria's following division forced to play a minor role.[2]

Farmer was still very much able to assert his authority, as Newman recalls with feeling:

I went up for a ruck throw-in, and I think I back-handed him. This is the pupil giving back to the master, you know. I mean he did that, he used to up and throw his arm back and hit the ball with his other hand. I did it once to him, and the very next time we went for a ball he broke my nose. He just went bang, straight back, and it went numb. I thought it was marvellous.

Farmer was playing the game hard, but not quite with the give-no-quarter attitude of the 1969 finals. His other former teammate, Billy Goggin, who was starring for Victoria in the first half remembers that: "He could have cleaned me up in that game. I marked the ball, and he could have just kept rolling and it would have been a split decision, you know. He didn't step aside, he just grabbed me [and] said: 'I could have.' He just grabbed me and he smiled. I said: 'It wouldn't have hurt anyhow.'" Goggin reckons that one of the reasons he was doing so well against a beaten ruck, was that he was still able to read Farmer's moves. "I knew him, I knew what he was going to do. It was good to be on the ground with him again ... I felt good about the game. Even though I was playing against him, it was good to see him."

Goggin's teammates would have been feeling a bit less chuffed though:

> Farmer left no doubt that he ranks as football's greatest ruckman when he provided the inspiration that lifted his team to the brink of victory at the MCG yesterday. Farmer ... reserved one of his best performances for the crowd who saw Victoria scramble to a six-point victory.[3]

It was a case of a team display from the Sandgropers being counterpunched by flashes of brilliance from the Victorian superstars like Jesaulenko and Hart. Western Australia led by four points at quarter-time, trailed by 19 at half-time, and still by 11 at the last break. There was an early goal each in the last quarter, after which Western Australia absolutely dominated the game, but could not break through.

With the Victorians' counter-attacking play, Farmer's tactics were to go to all lengths to lock the ball in his forward line, desperately seeking the goal that would put them in front and lift them. He had himself and Dempsey forward of the centre, Mal Brown at centre half-forward, and pulled his resting ruckman Peter Burton out to join them, forming a wall. But the ball just rebounded between this wall and the full-forward line, with the occasional point, and mark after mark to the unmarked Gary Dempsey.

All acknowledged it as a great contest, and a virtuoso performance from Farmer. The Victorian press acknowledged the West as a better team on the day, unlucky to lose. Everyone chose Farmer as the best man on the ground. And the West Australian press acclaimed the players as heroes for their brave attempt.

Nineteen seventy should have been Farmer's last year as a player. He had promised Marlene that he would stop at the age of 35. She saw more than anybody else what he went through to get himself onto the field and perform each Saturday. By now his back was playing up on a regular basis. Every week there was this to contend with as well as the fluid on the knee and the heel soreness flaring up from time to time, plus whatever new aches and knocks were received from week to week.

Marlene did not class herself as a football widow. She spoke of how she loved the game almost as much as he did, and how it would be strange when he finally stopped playing, as she had never known him to do anything else. But she felt that he should stop torturing himself, and she did not want him to be remembered as a champion who played a couple of seasons too many.

Early that year there had been press stories quite definite about the fact that it would be his last season. Farmer had suggested that he was looking forward to getting a small farm and breeding horses on his retirement. But it was not long before he had begun to hedge his bets. Early in the season he squashed a rumour that his children were enrolled in colleges in Geelong for the 1971 year, and insisted that it was too early to make any decisions. And as the year went on the talk died down, and there were no preparations to mark a departure at the end of the season.

Farmer had nothing to prove to anybody by now. His performance as a player, a captain and a coach of the state team had held at bay any criticism that might have begun building as a result of West Perth's performance. But then, he had never really worked to anyone's standards and judgements except his own. And by his own standards, 1970 had been a disaster. The ultimate criterion for judgement was always the performance of his team, and West Perth's sixth position was in fact his worst finish ever. Even in the three unsuccessful years with Cronin at the outset of his career, East Perth had finished fifth on the ladder each time.

If West Perth's performance had been more creditable, he probably would have bowed out. This factor was certainly uppermost in his mind, but no doubt he considered his own strong finish to the season as a player, and the fact that at the close of the year, with 335 club games under his belt he was only three short of Jack Sheedy's All-Australian record. When he sat down with his family and then with the West Perth committee to make a decision, he decided to gird his loins for one last effort. He signed on as playing coach for the 1971 season. He told the West Perth committee that if they were to make a success of it, a boost was needed to the club's playing strength.

Nineteen seventy-one was the year of Farmer, even from New Year's day, when football was normally far from the public consciousness. The front-page lead, as always, was devoted to the most prominent among those on the New Year's honours list. This year in Melbourne and Perth the feature pictures and stories were of Graham Farmer, Member of the British Empire, the first footballer to receive a decoration from the Queen. Farmer, as always, was phlegmatic about such things. He thinks the nomination was initiated by Mick Cronin, but is not sure:

> It's a question of do you accept it or don't you. Now, I had no reason not to accept it, but it didn't make one bit of difference to my lifestyle. I didn't take advantage by becoming a member of the Royal Society. I didn't use it as a means of identification. I did not alter my outlook on life by having it. In fact, I'd find it difficult [now] to find it. I don't think I'm one for knocking back some special privilege, but I don't go out of my way to use it to my advantage.

No doubt it was the cause of some jokes and ribbing during the summer social gatherings and the early season training of the West Perth squad, and no doubt he took it in fun. He was pleased with the team that he had to work with for the year ahead, and acknowledges the committee for having done a great job in response to his demand for extra players.

The only significant loss to the squad was Laurie Richards, who left to play with Fitzroy, ultimately with considerable success. But a ready-made replacement was found in Phil Smith, who had spent three years at Geelong as the understudy full-forward to Doug Wade, and was a similarly strong mark and kick, if not quite in the Wade class. From Darwin, presumably through the services of Jack Larcombe, they picked up Leon O'Dwyer. He was a small man who had played junior football with Collingwood, but not gone on; a "quality player", says Farmer, pencilled in for a back flank or pocket. Bill Valli was back on the playing list, and expected to be a boon to the side, though as it turned out injuries would restrict his appearances. But two youngsters who had played a handful of games in 1970 were emerging from the ranks to boost the following division. Steve Arnott became a useful ruckman and utility player, and Shane Sheridan exploded on to the scene as a rover, releasing Smeath back to his specialist position of half-forward flank.

Although he was not officially on the list at the start of the season, the coup de grâce though was Peter Steward. Steward was an out-an-out champion at full-back, or more often, centre half-back for North Melbourne. "One of the best players in Victoria at the time," according to Farmer. He had been the local recruit of the year in 1962 in the VFL, though outshone by the imports Farmer and Baldock, and had fought back from terrible knee injuries in the mid-'60s to become a regular Victorian representative at centre half-back. He had captained North through 1970 when skipper John Dugdale broke down, and they did not want to let him go. A prolonged and bitter clearance wrangle held up his debut until a few weeks into the season, and cost West Perth $12,000 in transfer fees, but he was undoubtedly a solid gold investment.

Despite coming off sixth placing, West Perth was tipped by some of the pundits prior to the season as the possible premiers. After the first three games though, in their fickle way, the experts were already starting to wonder aloud again. In another shaky start it was one win and two losses leading into the fourth game against reigning premiers, South Fremantle, which had shocked everyone under Hassa Mann's guidance by beating Perth twice in the final round of 1970 to take the flag.

This was the game in which Farmer broke Jack Sheedy's record by playing his 339th senior club game. Ted Whitten, the only player who might have threatened to overhaul him, had retired in 1970 after 20 seasons and 321 games, breaking Dick Reynolds' VFL record by one.

It was the occasion for eulogies, ceremonies and many a feature article. The official *Football Budget* took the unprecedented step of shifting its editorial to page three, voicing the opinion that: "there comes the rare time when the player is greater than the game—relatively."[4] There were presentations before and after the game, and he ran on to the ground through a guard of honour formed by the players and official cheer squads for both sides. More importantly to him though, his players rose to the occasion, and West Perth led all day and recorded a five-goal win that put it back in the four.

The next day he relaxed by watching youngest son, Dean, nine years old, playing in his first competitive game of football at a local oval. Brett was also playing by now. As he watched his boys out on the field, perhaps the thought occurred to him that there were a handful of youngsters now playing in the WANFL competition who had not yet been born at the time he made his debut for East Perth.

The high of the record-breaking game did not last. By the end of the first round of games West Perth was in the same position as the previous year, in the bottom half of the ladder on three wins and four losses, and needing to turn things around if it was to maintain its finals hopes. Farmer admitted to being worried, and spoke of getting the players to spend more time with each other, and the need to build team spirit. There were whispers in the ever-busy rumour mill of the footy world that the man who had been 'greater than the game' three weeks earlier might have his head on the chopping block. The qualifying 'relatively' of the *Budget*'s editorial was not misplaced.

In contrast to the previous year, West Perth came to the party in the crucial second round of matches. It started by avenging the first-up loss to Perth in a high-standard, high-scoring game. Perth were sitting in second place and coming off a win over leaders Claremont, and was fired in the first half by the absolute brilliance of the little master Barry Cable, back with his old side after just one very successful season with North Melbourne. But the Cardinals withstood the blitz and came from behind in the last quarter for their most impressive performance to date.

After this point both Claremont and Perth fell into holes, while West Perth followed up with another four consecutive victories that carried it to second place on the ladder behind East Perth. One key factor was the impact of Steward at centre half-back. He was a casual-looking, casual-seeming character, but deceptively tight and coolly creative in this critical position that marshalled the backline. Smith at full-forward was also doing well, chasing Austin Robertson at the head of the goalkicking list. And the evergreen Whinnen, who like Dempsey had always put in for every one of his 200-plus games, was having a particularly good year in the centre.

While Farmer was away for a week along with Dempsey, Steward and Astbury, coaching the state team to a four-goal loss against South Australia, West Perth's winning run came to a very sticky end—a 16-goal loss to East Perth. This was followed by another loss to East Fremantle, before there was a week's break while the West played host to a visiting Victorian team. Farmer was a last-minute inclusion as a player when two of his big men were injured the week before. It was his 36th and last interstate match. Once again he made the best player lists, but his side went down by six goals to the Vics.

He got West Perth back on the winning track the next week against Perth, and was set to make a new milestone all of his own—his 350th game—when things went awry. On the eve of the game he was laid low by kidney stones. Whinnen went to the hospital to see him on the Saturday morning to get instructions for the day's game: "Polly said: 'Gee, I've had pain in my life, but I've never had pain like this.' It really knocked him at that stage."

There is a photograph of him supervising training at Leederville Oval after coming out of hospital. It is perhaps the only one of many hundreds of Farmer in which he does not look like an athlete. In others, even when relaxed, when grimacing with pain, or being carried off a field, there is the Farmer aura of fitness and determination, and that big square frame. Here he looks pale, his shoulders droop, and he does not seem to fill his jacket. Yet he only missed two games, coming back for the final four matches of the qualifying round. There was too much at stake for the luxury of a prolonged recovery. The Cardinals still held second place, but it was potentially under threat from East Fremantle and Claremont, with a remote chance if they went through a real slump at the end of slipping out of the four behind Subiaco.

They won the next two against South Fremantle and Swan Districts to ensure a finals berth, but East Fremantle still threatened them for the coveted double chance. Then their third loss of the season to East Perth put the acid on. Coming to the last game they only held second position on percentage from East Fremantle, the next team they were due to play.

East Fremantle had made a dramatic recovery from the turmoils of the 1970 sacking of coach Eric Sarich and a seventh-place finish. It had taken the unusual step of importing a non-playing coach from Victoria, Allan Joyce, who would later go on to prove an astute and successful deputy and then successor to Allan Jeans at Hawthorn. He had left Hawthorn as a player at the young age of 22 to coach successfully in the second Victorian competition, the VFA, from where the East Fremantle brains trust had snaffled him.

He had quickly moulded the East Fremantle side into a team, bringing about the dramatic improvement. As part of the climb up the ladder, it had already defeated West Perth in both of their meetings so far that year. There was no doubt it was the game of the round, with some spice added by the fact that Phil Smith had brought his goal tally for the season to 97, just three behind Austin Robertson sitting on the ton.

Four weeks out of hospital, "Farmer took complete charge [and] dominated from the outset."[5] By half-time the Cardinals led 11.8 (74) to 1.5 (11), and they ran out winners by seven goals. Smith got seven to go to 104, but as usual Austin Robertson finished in front, with 11 on the last day.

Thirteen wins and eight losses in the eight-team competition was usually about the quota for third position on the ladder, and sometimes was the final tally of the team in fourth spot. But this year, with a clear leader, a long last and the middle six relatively close, it got West Perth the double chance. As in 1969 they secured it well behind East Perth, which had emerged as the dominant team with a 16-five record. But as in 1969, the prime objective had been achieved. There was a real chance for one last shot at glory.

The second semi-final at Subiaco got underway with a little scene that said much about the approaches of the rival captain-coaches. At the toss of the coin Mal Brown tried the old trick of moving off before the coin had come to rest, pointing to indicate that he would kick with the wind. "Farmer grabbed Brown, forced him to return to the scene of the toss and in front of one of the boundary umpires made it clear that the coin had fallen [the other way]."[6] Having made his point he then chose as usual to go against the wind, giving the same outcome.

The game was played under shocking conditions of fickle wind and rain squalls described as some of the worst seen in a football match, and the contest became a fierce, slogging affair. West Perth was 11 points down at the last change. It was one goal each in the last quarter, and a 10-point win to East Perth. Best for the Cardinals were the veterans, in order, Farmer, Steward and Dempsey, then young rover Sheridan ahead of Whinnen.

East Fremantle had disposed of Claremont in the first semi to set up a return clash. Farmer and his side went into the game realising that if they went down it would be his last. For the first three quarters it seemed they were safe. But in the last quarter both the Cardinals' system and their run seemed to disappear, and a fierce East Fremantle whittled away at their lead, and by time on had got within three points. Two minutes from the end of the game, Easts' ruck-rover Gary Fenner could have put an end to the Farmer career when he marked close to goal in the forward pocket. His shot went across the face of goal, West Perth cleared, and lived to fight another day. Farmer was named as their second best player after Smith. The old master was still providing more than just leadership on the field.

East Perth's form coming into the Grand Final was impeccable. Its record for the year against West Perth stood at four nil, with two of these coming in their last three games of football. It was the fresher, younger and stronger team, according to most. West Perth, on the other hand, seemed to have stumbled its way to the Grand Final. This would be its fifth hard game in a row against the two other top sides. In each of the previous four the Cardinals had put in bad last quarters. They were seen as brittle under pressure.

Their centreline of Pleitner, Whinnen and Watling had the 1969 look. The defence, led by Steward and Astbury, was solid. Smith was a trump card at full-forward. But Dyson at centre half-forward, though always a goer, was definitely a stopgap out of position, and his flankers Smeath and Miller were in patchy form. Farmer and Dempsey were still a great first ruck, but their support level was nowhere near the same, with Knell battling injuries all year, and their opposition of Brown, McCulloch, Hayes and Alexander was formidable.

Bill Dempsey insists it was a good West Perth side, but concedes: "We seemed to struggle a lot more. Maybe the other teams worked us out ...

plus the fact that Pol and I were getting a bit bloody old and had to cheat a lot more to compete. It seemed to be a harder year."

A dispassionate analysis had to have the Royals as warm favourites. In any other year they would have been firm sentimental favourites, too, with the cruel record of four Grand Final losses in five years, another two before that, and their last pennant now 12 years old. But this was the year of Farmer. The build-up to the game centred less on the possibility of the Royals overcoming the hoodoo that seemed to have enveloped them than on the final farewell of the great man, and the fascinating possibility that he may inspire an underdog's victory as his last achievement.

West Perth president, Len Roper, made a public appeal to the players to win it for Farmer. Mal Brown countered by saying that East Perth had to win for three men: Derek Chadwick, who was set to break Kilmurray's club record of 257 games in the Grand Final—he had debuted in 1959 but not made that year's premiership side, and had since played in six losing Grand Finals; back pocket specialist, Bob Graham, who was playing his 211th and last game, in a similar situation; and Fred Book, "a great club president who has suffered many disappointments in the last 12 years."[7]

Perhaps it was because these comparisons did not quite work, and Brown wanted to get the attention away from Farmer, perhaps it was the stinging memories of two years ago, or perhaps it was just his eternal impetuosity, but something prompted Brown to an outburst that the West Perth camp remember as his greatest mistake that year. He came out with a statement remembered by Mel Whinnen as being along the lines of: "We'll fight them behind the grandstand, we'll fight them on the oval, we'll fight them everywhere." Whinnen reckons that if anything it put the East Perth players off, and perhaps got them wondering who would get taken out of the game this time around, while it merely served as an additional spur to the West Perth players.

'Do it for Polly' was certainly a factor in the West Perth camp, but not the overriding one according to the players. And it was certainly not a theme that he played on. The training and build-up followed the usual routines, culminating once again in the Thursday night players' tea. Though Dempsey always remembers the 1969 speech as Farmer's most powerful, it is the one on the eve of the 1971 Grand Final that others cite as his great piece of oration. Some of the West Perth people seemed to get a shiver up their spine as they referred to it, and wish ruefully that it had been recorded. Farmer suggests that:

> The commitment of coaches is to provide enough positive remarks that will make a person want to be successful for his own reasons. The people who succeed on a football field are the ones who want to succeed. When someone else is providing the stimulus, they have got to take up the challenge to make it their own ... It was a committed, emotional speech on bringing out that little bit extra in players, that little bit of adrenalin that would make them perform to their absolute best, or better. And the players responded to it ... It began as a general conversation. I suppose in the heat of the moment you relate a little of things that happened in the past, in different circumstances, and try to encourage the players to get a mental picture of success in their minds, and what they have to do to be successful ... If they make it a personal commitment where they are going out to fight for their lives, then no matter what, they can't be stopped. The whole basis of my talks with players is to sell them on the idea that they are going to be responsible for their own success.

All this preparation and psychology is put to the test in the opening minutes of a Grand Final. For Farmer, it worked:

> The team's second-string players rose magnificently to the occasion. Their champions all played well, as expected, but it was the full-blooded efforts of the lesser lights that gave West Perth a stranglehold on the game.[8]

The Cardinals bounced out of the blocks, with Farmer and Dempsey in control in the ruck. At quarter-time they had 6.6 (42)—with three of the behinds having been shots that hit the post—to East Perth's 2.1 (13).

From that point it was a matter of maintaining the pressure and guarding against a fade-out or an East Perth comeback. Brown rang the positional changes but none of them came off. Chadwick had been East Perth's one clear winner on his wing, but then lowered his colours to Whinnen when moved to the centre. By three-quarter time it was 80 points to 40. There was a flurry at the start of the final quarter when East Perth got three early goals, but its brief run died. Farmer not only marshalled his troops, but garnered 27 possessions along the way, to be listed as West Perth's number two player after his rover Sheridan. West Perth held firm for a 32-point victory.

Barry Cable, the small man who would come closer than any other West Australian to Farmer in football stature, had this to say of his final game:

> Football's ageing maestro bowed out at the end of a magnificent career when he led rank underdogs West Perth to a crushing victory over East Perth in the Grand Final. I thought it was a fantastic triumph, both as a player and a coach, for Farmer, who despite his 36 years was one of the best players on the field … West Perth were far too dedicated and disciplined and Farmer's great influence was blatantly obvious.[9]

Farmer was chaired to the victory dais on the shoulders of his players. When he held the Premiership Trophy aloft he received what was said to be the greatest ovation ever heard at Subiaco Oval. There had been appeals before the game for the crowd to stay off the oval to allow a lap of honour from the winning side, but it seemed that every one of the 50,000 spectators surged on to the ground, eager to be close to the sense of history in the making. Farmer, smiling and exhausted, could only make his way off the ground for the last time with the aid of a police escort as the fans reached out to touch him. It was over. Nineteen years of playing the game he loved was over in the best possible way.

The West Perth club had made plans early in 1971 to stage a testimonial match for Farmer's benefit at the end of the season. The original intention had been to put together two invitation teams for a Western Australia versus the rest match. However, it was discovered that Swan Districts was also well advanced with plans for an end-of-season carnival, with a commercial sponsor bringing in interstate clubs.

The two ideas were brought together, and so were the top four teams from WA, plus Hawthorn, Richmond, Port Adelaide and North Adelaide. They gathered on the weekend after the Grand Final. There were further speeches and presentations. A choir of boys from the Clontarf and

Castledare Homes adapted 'Hello Dolly' into a tribute sung as 'Goodbye Polly'. And there was a lightning carnival of half-length games held over three days. Farmer played in the carnival, pulling on his guernsey for the last time for a competitive, though not too serious, game in a play-off for third and fourth with Port Adelaide.

A guarantee from the carnival organisers and sponsors negotiated by West Perth, plus a sportsmen's dinner and donations netted the testimonial fund about $10,000 as a parting gesture to the titan of the game.

Perhaps the most ironic tribute of the year though came from his first club East Perth. At its annual general meeting in December, East Perth made him a life member. There is no question that he was entitled to the honour in terms of his contribution to the club, but it is hard to imagine another circumstance where the Grand Final conqueror of a club twice in three years would be rewarded with such a prize. It was a fitting end to the year of Farmer.

Bill Dempsey was never the sentimental type. He wanted to keep the ball rolling. "We were on a high again. I said to him: 'You're still playing good footy. West Perth's still got not a bad side.'" He tried to talk Farmer into another season.

Certainly his last four games in the crucible of finals football had shown that he was capable still, not just of holding his own, but of dominating and controlling a game. He had been in West Perth's best two players on each occasion. And this a month after being in hospital with kidney stones. Over the full year he finished as runner-up to Mel Whinnen in the club best and fairest.

He believes himself that he had one more year of good football left in him. There was one thought that played on his mind: the idea of playing two full decades of senior football—as he says, you could count on the fingers of one hand the number of players who have achieved that milestone. Jack Sheedy and Ted Whitten had already done it. Only Michael Tuck, Kevin Murray, Robert Harvey and Dustin Fletcher have since. But he did not seriously consider continuing. Had he tried, Marlene probably would not have let him this time. But he had the clarity to see that he had achieved the perfect finish to his career, that to keep going could hardly add to it.

18

THE COACH

Retirement from football, for Farmer, was not unlike retirement from the work force, which comes to most people in their '60s. Since his teenage years, the rhythms and requirements of training and playing had been the dominating factor in his life. While he had always held a job, he had never made a career; the job was always secondary to the football. His personal training program of workouts and running, plus the club training, the playing, and in latter years the demands of coaching, had consumed at least the amount of time most people put into their full-time job, with the sales work being more in the nature of a part-time sideline. Yet unlike the average retiree, Farmer had half a lifetime or more still ahead of him, and a young family to support.

While he had been well paid over his football career in comparison to most of his peers, the recompense had not really amounted to a lot more than a substitute for the income from a regular job, allowing him to make the choice to devote his time to football. When interviewed in 1970, Farmer had said:

> From a football point of view I was born 20 years too early. Australian football is just entering an era of all-out professionalism. If I started my career this season and had the same success in the next 18 years as I have had in the past 18 I could expect to retire at 35 a rich man.[1]

He could perhaps have retired richer than he did in 1971, had he tried more vigorously to exploit the sponsorship and business opportunities that were available to a person of his prominence. But he had never altered the outlook on life that had arisen in the wake of his near death from electrocution just after his marriage, of living for the day and letting the morrow take care of itself. He told the footballers under his charge that they had to plan for success if they wanted to achieve. He did not see this as applying to his own life off the football field—at least not in material terms. More than once he was reported as saying that as one door closes, another one will open.

His priorities were lifestyle and family:

> I love my family and being at home. I want to be an ordinary man who walks down the street and enjoys it when the weather is bright and sunny, or goes home and sits by the fire with his wife and children when it is cold and raining.[2]

The plans that he did have centred around these thoughts. He wanted his children to be at good private schools, and after this, the main thing in his mind was to acquire a small rural property, and to indulge his fascination in horse breeding. The question was where to do it, Perth or Geelong.

The rumours of early 1970 turned out to be correct, just a year premature. The Farmer family packed their bags to move back to Geelong. The family had always been comfortable there, with a network of friendships that included both he and Marlene, and the children. He still preferred the small-town atmosphere, and in geographic terms it offered all he needed. He could live in Geelong itself, and be close to the beaches, and there were small properties available close to the town, "whereas in Perth I was looking at a 20- or 30-mile drive" to such a smallholding. One also suspects that football was still something of a consideration. Having experienced both competitions, to watch the VFL as an outsider would be more interesting and satisfying than watching the WANFL.

To finance the move and the plans for his new life, Farmer cashed in his one nest egg. When he sold his first house, at the time of the move from East Perth to Geelong, against the advice of all except Kevin McGill, he had used his remaining equity and some borrowed funds to buy four acres of low-lying land on what was then the fringes of Perth. By 1971 the swamps had been drained, and when the council resumed part of the land for a new thoroughfare they compensated by bearing the cost of subdividing the land into new building blocks. The four acres of swamp had become 15 prime suburban blocks, which were sold along with the home at Trigg to provide him with some capital. With this start Farmer was able to buy a house in the Geelong suburbs, and a 25-hectare block five minutes away.

There were some early reports that he would belatedly take up the 1967 offer of employment with Lou Rocka. There was an offer, but "it was up in the city, too far away for me." Instead, he put the balance of his capital into a business partnership with another former Perth man, John Buckenara, whose son, Gary, would later become a football superstar. 'Polly Farmer's Tyre Service' in Geelong West became his first venture into the world of small business. He was no man of leisure. He was the front man and active manager of the tyre service. But it was a more relaxed life than he had led until then. His time revolved around home, work, and daily visits to the farm to feed the horses.

He had purchased three unfashionable but carefully selected brood mares in Perth, and brought them across to Geelong. He could not afford to put the mares to the best stallions in the state, but nor did he want to. His leisure time was consumed with his reading and research into the bloodlines of his own mares and the available and affordable stallions in order to make the best selection possible:

> The thing that I did do a lot of was investigation of the likelihoods and probabilities and variabilities of breeding. I researched the best bred horses and who they came from, and researched the best breeders and what they did. I got a fairly good understanding of what was required.

He was influenced by the theories of the great Italian breeder, Frederico Tesio. Tesio had produced two outstanding horses in Nearco and Ribot, which had gone on to become champion stallions whose bloodlines were dominant factors in thoroughbred racing around the world. But it was nowhere near as simple as just looking for these lines in your mare and stallion. It was a matter of intense examination and interpretation, looking for the right 'nicks', or links between the individual horses on the mare's and the sire's lines, and "inbreeding to the right ancestors. Often the best to the best doesn't produce the best ... It's like a bottle full of hundreds and thousands—that's how many genes are shaken around." Ever the individual, he ignored the advice and suggestions of his racing mates, and made his choices for his mares. Horse breeding though, is a long-term business, in which only time and fortune will tell the result.

He remained a semi-public figure in Geelong, and as the 1972 football season approached, it seemed odd to people that the great man was there in town, but not set to participate. A rumour spread that he would play with Geelong West in the VFA, where Goggin had been appointed captain-coach after retiring from the VFL at the end of the previous season. Goggin was always game, and probably put the question to him, or even started the rumour to see what it might produce. But Farmer quickly quashed any such suggestions, saying that if he was fit enough to play football, he would be playing with Geelong, not Geelong West—not for Farmer the indignity of turning out in the secondary competition.

He says that one of the best things about 1972 was simply giving his body a rest from the punishment it had endured for so long, and taking a break from the gym work and the running he had done every morning before work, whatever the winter weather held. "I was ready for a spell," he says, using the racing terminology. However, he did maintain his connections with the game. He became the special comments man for the local radio station that broadcast all of Geelong's games, and wrote a newspaper column. In this capacity, he witnessed Geelong's sorry performance through the 1972 season.

Since Farmer's departure at the end of 1967, Geelong had undergone a steady decline. It had made the 1968 preliminary final after upsetting St Kilda in the first semi; in 1969, it was eliminated in the first semi by the eventual premiers, Richmond; in 1970, it finished fifth, missing the finals for the first time since 1961. Pianto resigned at the end of the 1970 season. It was also the last year in the long reign of Jack Jennings as club president. He was beaten in the end of year election by Vern Johnstone, the man who had joined him in criticising Farmer three years earlier.

Pianto's replacement, Bill McMaster, had no success, with the club slipping to 10th place in 1971, and staying there in 1972, with a seven-win, 15-loss record. His basic problem was lack of players. Since 1965—the year after Marshall, Newman and Closter had started with the club—the quality of the players recruited from outside or nurtured through the ranks had not matched the standard of those who left year by year.

It is said that in unsuccessful football clubs the natural order of things is to blame first the coach, then the committee, and last of all the players. Among the coaching fraternity there is an even more pointed truism: that there are two kinds of coaches, those who have been sacked, and those who are waiting to be sacked. As the 1972 season progressed, Bill McMaster was certainly a man in the latter category.

With the team in the doldrums, and the coach under fire, there was a man in town who, in football terms, was sitting twiddling his thumbs. He was not only regarded as the greatest player in the club's history and as the inspiration behind their last premiership, but he had recently coached a League team to two premierships in four years. The logic of the situation was inevitable, and seemed to gather a momentum of its own. Almost throughout 1972 there was constant speculation that Farmer would replace McMaster. Once the season was over the axe came quickly. The committee held a special meeting on the Thursday after the last game, which resulted in Johnstone ringing McMaster to tell him he was finished, and then announcing the appointment of Farmer.

Farmer had remained publicly and privately aloof from the speculation about McMaster, and did not discuss the coaching position with anyone until club officials approached him a couple of days before McMaster was sacked. In his years at West Perth, when asked about the likelihood of continuing on in football as a coach after his playing days, he had frequently said that he was not keen on the idea. He knew that all coaches are expected to be miracle workers, and that he in particular would have even higher than usual expectations placed on his shoulders.

Of Geelong at the time, he says: "I didn't want to coach them, because I knew what was going to happen to me before it started, I'd seen it happen at other clubs." Nevertheless, when the invitation came, he did not decline.

The whole situation seemed to just develop without any real analysis or direction. The committee offered him the job because the club was in decline, because he was there, and because it seemed the obvious thing to do; but it did not think through the reality of what else was needed beyond a change of coach.

In a sense Farmer had seemed destined to coach Geelong one day—there had been talk of it as long ago as the beginning of 1964. Despite his real reservations, the lure of coaching must have exercised his mind from time to time. It was the only challenge left to him now in football. If there was any club he would want to coach it would be Geelong. When offered the position, it was too great a temptation and too great a challenge to walk away from.

Given his assessment of the club and the team at the time, he was certainly setting himself up for a fall:

> A team completely out of touch with reality in football—what I mean by that is, just turning up for a game is all that was happening ... At that time they were rapidly slipping into oblivion. From my point of view, I made no promise whatsoever. How could you make a promise with a side that wasn't certain of winning a game? ... The problem when I took them over was that to win games our best 20 players had to be available. If anyone of those got injured, we were going to be in trouble—no depth whatsoever. There wasn't only no depth, there was no plan within the club at the time to get the players.

In this situation, it was even more of a blow when captain Doug Wade pulled the pin on Geelong after 12 years and 834 goals. Farmer's arrival at Geelong as coach coincided with the introduction of the 10-year rule, that gave long-serving players virtually automatic clearance rights. Wade was one of a number of big name players who accepted the very lucrative carrots being dangled by North Melbourne in their dollar-driven quest for their first premiership. By contrast, whenever Farmer raised the issue of recruiting, he was told the club hardly had enough to pay the existing list of players. There was a recruiting committee, headed by Bill McMaster, who had accepted the conciliatory gesture of appointment as a full-time recruiting officer. But McMaster and his team could do little more than hopefully tour the local and rural competitions for likely lads. Gone were the days when there was any chance that players of quality could be attracted without appropriate payment.

As well as Wade's departure, Bill Ryan and Hugh Strahan retired at the end of 1972, meaning that the two key forwards and a utility player who often filled a third key position were gone. Wade and Ryan, as Farmer would point out, were worth considerably more than 100 goals a year between them. From Farmer's playing days those still around were 1967 debutant Geoff Ainsworth, who replaced Wade as captain, Gareth Andrews, Wayne Closter, Terry Farman, Ken Newland and John Newman. Newman, although he would continue for another eight seasons, was running on heart, not on his legs. "John did remarkably well to play, he's a credit to himself. His ankles were that bad he spent half his time having them strapped, locked up so they wouldn't move." The club's star player by now was David Clarke, a versatile forward who won the best and fairest in his debut season of 1971.

Farmer's first step was to seek to get the players to an acceptable level of fitness. At the first players' meeting in October he introduced them to a new fitness adviser, and handed each player a monthly chart. They were told to run five miles a day and record their times on the chart. Over the summer there were camps and fitness and skills competitions between teams of eight players. Then, as the season approached, the hard physical stuff was introduced. Pianto had been a demanding coach, but this was certainly a significant change from the regime under McMaster.

He also had to educate the team to the style of play he wanted. Apart from the fact that it was a very average bunch of players, he felt that he was handicapped by the fact that there were few natural ball-getters in the side, players in his own mould who would win the hard balls, and get the plays happening. This meant that the players had to cover more ground to be at the ball in numbers, and then work it out until one could be put in the clear to move the ball down field with a modicum of system. This in turn required the players to be fit enough and willing to run up and down the ground all day. Two who would have understood what he was driving at missed most of the pre-season recovering from operations—Newman to an ankle, and Closter to a cartilage.

The early season draw for Geelong was a new coach's nightmare. The first game was against the premiers, Carlton, then he faced the other Grand Finalist, Richmond, followed by Collingwood, which had finished third. Geelong stayed with Carlton until fading in the last quarter, finished within a creditable three goals of Richmond in a high-scoring game, but collapsed to a thrashing against the Magpies, before recording their first win against cellar-dwellers South Melbourne. After that though, it was six straight losses that put the club well and truly out of consideration for the season.

Within the Geelong camp, a move began to convince Farmer to attempt a comeback. He was ambivalent, but said he would consider it if Marlene could be convinced. Bob Davis and chairman of the match committee, John Hyde, were deputised to approach her, but she refused to give the idea her support. Farmer had submitted himself to the same training regimen that he demanded of the players. Perhaps like a horse fresh back in work from a spell, he even felt a bit frisky. Even so, he could not have been anywhere near match fit. Even if he had survived physically to play out the season, it would have been a lost cause, and an unfortunate footnote to the playing career that ended so happily.

There were players in the side who, given half a chance, Farmer would have dropped, whether for lack of fitness in a couple of cases, for disciplinary reasons, or for either refusal or inability to follow on-field instructions or obey such basics as picking up their man. But they survived because there were no ready replacements, and "you have to pick your best 20 each week." He never relented the pace at training, for he did not believe that relaxation was the answer. "I made it hard for them [and] they resented me. I just did it to have them fit. If you can't win the games, you can fight it out. And that's what they did do—they put up, they did their best."

The record at the end of the season was not encouraging. The score stood at six wins and 16 losses—one worse than the previous season, and the team finished in 11th place, one position down. There were some signs of hope though, in the improvement shown in the latter part of the season, when they won four of their last seven games, including victories over final five teams Essendon and St Kilda. Towards the end of the year Farmer was making positive, though heavily qualified, comments:

We're not a team of champions and it has taken a long time to develop it as
a team of triers ... but the players are now prepared to put their heads down
and go in after the ball. We are playing football with a lot of strength. They
have learned to maintain their concentration in tight finishes, which is why
we have won three by less than a goal.[3]

But in the same interview he stressed that there would not be much
improvement the following year without fresh blood.

If the off-season recruiting efforts had produced some results, there
would have been good reason to hope for significant improvement in 1974,
but without the cash to back it up, the search proved fruitless. In the 1973
annual report, John Wynne of West Perth and Norwood was listed as a
recruit, but he did not show. There were 14 players who played their first
game with Geelong in 1974, and none of them made an immediate impact.
The only one who would go on to a career of any note was Michael Turner,
who was still a raw, young winger.

Despite the fact that the playing personnel was much the same, there was
a marked improvement in the team's performance in 1974. They held their
own in a steady year-long performance, in the sense that they won as many
games as they lost. Throughout the season they sat about the middle of the
ladder, and finished up with an 11-11 record in sixth spot, just one position,
but two and a half games, out of the final five. During the course of the year
they defeated each of the five finalists once.

As at West Perth, the second year had been better than the first. He had
got the players fit and hard. Importantly, the team had a relatively injury-
free year. And he began to instil the style he wanted into their play. There
was one piece in the press late in the year suggesting that Geelong was
playing the football of the future. But unlike at West Perth, there was no
reward at the end.

He was to say later that what he did in his time at Geelong was prevent
them from finishing on the bottom of the ladder, which is where the team
belonged in comparison to the rest of the competition. In 1974, he extracted
the maximum from the material at his disposal. He did it by squeezing it out
of them, and some found the pace too hard. Farmer was not the only hard

taskmaster in the coaching ranks at the VFL. Tom Hafey at Richmond was renowned for punishing his players, but in his team there were a number of champion players, and between them they produced results. John Kennedy was back at Hawthorn, Ron Barassi was now at North Melbourne. All these teams trained as hard as Farmer's charges.

But for such an uncompromising style to bear fruit, for the players to participate willingly—as they must if there is ultimately to be success—there must be a sense of achievement along the way, and a sense of purpose that the team and the club as a whole is heading somewhere, that there might be the sweet reward of a premiership at the end. A combination of the knowledge that the team did not have this capability—that the 1974 result probably represented its peak—and the continuing bickering, political manoeuvring, and changing of faces at committee and administrative level meant that the sense of purpose was clearly lacking at Geelong.

Nineteen seventy-five got off to a shocking start. David Clarke did a leg before the season got underway, and was effectively put out for the year. Clarke was not Farmer's version of the ideal player—he would not handball—"but he was my best player." He was good enough, Farmer believes, to have made the two or three goal difference that was critical in a number of their early games. With such a turn around they could have won three of the first five games, and been in the top five on seven wins and four losses at the halfway mark of the season, instead of struggling again at four and seven.

Farmer attributes the slippage of the team simply to the injuries to Clarke and others, compared to the good run of the year before. This view is also expressed in the annual report, which notes: "Injuries and suspensions accounted for the loss of in excess of 200 man playing weeks."[4] He was desperate for players. Halfway through the year, full-forward Phil Baker was obtained from North Melbourne, through the efforts of Bob Davis. Rex Hunt had also come to the club from Richmond halfway through the previous season, in a swap with Gareth Andrews. Farmer says:

> They were better than not having anyone at all, but they weren't the answer
> to our problems, they were playing in the forward line. The problem for us

was the ball was going in the other direction. The players we wanted were
the ones who were going to get the ball and set the play.

Farmer defends his team as a bunch of triers who were simply outclassed.
But others are not so kind. Bill Goggin believes that by 1975 the players
were cheating on their coach: "To put it bluntly, they were dogging it
on him. He was too hard for them." In Goggin's eyes though, this was a
shortcoming of the players and the club, not of Farmer. Goggin spent a
lot of time with Farmer in these years talking about football in general,
coaching in particular, and what Farmer was trying to do with the team:

> He was trying to instil into them professionalism and the correct way to
> play, which now is par for the course ... Guys running into the backline—the
> wingmen running into the backline, getting the ball out and taking it back
> out again, and then going back into position ... His theory was that every
> guy should be able to run up and down the ground all the time. Guys do it
> now. He felt that would have developed the handpassing more and the team
> play more than ever...
>
> He got stuck with poor players and a lack of knowledge in the people
> around him. He was very hard because he knew what he wanted ... But if
> they had waited they would have got the success. He would have been
> an innovator. In my view he was an innovator ... The club didn't have the
> patience, and he didn't tolerate people. I suppose if you are urgent about
> something, you don't stand fools do you? ... I don't see it as a criticism [of
> him]. I see the criticism as of the people who were supposed to help him ...
> I think he was absolutely right, because when you get down to it, it's only
> the strong succeed at the end. I think people didn't fully understand him.
> I think that he was quite brilliant—what his theories were. They only had to
> follow him, but they were cheating—most of them were cheating on him.

In the second half of the season it proved impossible to turn the team's
fortunes around. Geelong finished on seven wins for the season, once again
back in 11th place. At the first meeting of the committee after Geelong's
season had ended they decided to defer the matter of appointment of the
1976 coach for a month. It was a weak decision. Clearly Nipper Trezise,
who by now had replaced Vern Johnstone as president, did not relish the

prospect of ringing Farmer, as his predecessor had rung McMaster three years earlier. A few days later Farmer attended a function at the club. "Nobody said anything to me about the coaching position, but I think I could see in their faces that I wouldn't be coach next year."[5]

The committee were saved the trauma of having to sack him. First to get the news was a reporter who bailed him up at the airport on the way to a function in Tasmania:

> Farmer reached the decision yesterday after discussing the matter with his wife Marlene. He has not told the Geelong committee. "They can read about it in the *Australian*," a despondent Farmer said.[6]

He did not spare the committee in his comments at the airport to the *Australian's* reporter:

> I was originally approached to coach Geelong. Now I have lost the desire to continue. Others have suffered the same fate as me at Geelong in the past. Unfortunately there are a lot of people connected with the club who don't know much about football ... I told the committee at the start of the year not to expect too much this year, but obviously they didn't take any notice of me. They apparently expected bigger things than we were capable of ... They don't know what needs to be done to lift a club from the depths of the League ladder and to ensure that it stays up. When they don't get results they blame the coach ... We didn't have the players this year, it was as simple as that.[7]

It must have seemed ironic to Farmer to watch the North Melbourne side that had been put together in 1973 take the club to its first ever premiership in 1975. For by now it had become known that Farmer was approached by the North Melbourne committee in 1972 to take on the coaching position there, and only after he turned it down did the job go to Ron Barassi. It was the North Melbourne experience that turned Ron Barassi into a coaching legend. It is interesting to speculate how Farmer might have gone with a team that contained the stars of the Kangaroos, a committee with drive and professional attitudes, and a clearly mapped out plan for success. One suspects that the environment would have suited him perfectly.

19

BACK HOME

After losing the coaching job Farmer could have chosen to stay on in Geelong, concentrating on his business and his horse breeding. The option of working again in the media as a commentator and writer would also have been open to him. Certainly his family were well settled at home and at school, and would have been happy to stay. But when East Perth officials contacted him to ask if he would be interested in returning to Perth as their coach, he decided to try his hand once more.

He held a liquidation sale at which he sold and fitted $50,000 worth of tyres. He sold the house, but not the farm, which he put into the care of some people he knew who ran sheep on it while looking after his horses. And once again the Farmers made the trans-Nullarbor journey, this time from east to west. The prodigal son was returning home to Perth Oval. It created a neat symmetry to his career: from East Perth to Geelong to West Perth, back to Geelong, and now back to the place where he had started his football career.

After losing seven Grand Finals in a row, the Royals had finally broken through in 1972, with Mal Brown as captain, coach and club best and fairest. Brown had left at the end of 1973 to play his one and only season in Victoria, where a suspension cost him a place in the Richmond premiership side. Kevin Murray accepted a three-year contract to come back to East Perth to replace Brown, but came under enormous pressure from Fitzroy, and after a messy few weeks, pulled out of the arrangement on the eve of the 1974 season to stay in Melbourne, where he played his 20th and last year of senior football. East Perth found a last-minute replacement in former player Ray Giblett. He was living in Broken Hill, but just happened to be in town on holidays when the Murray crisis came to a head. Given the circumstances it is not surprising that the club slipped back to sixth place that year, but Giblett did manage to get the team to the first semi-final in 1975 before resigning from the job.

The team Farmer took over had some remarkably talented players and good depth. In 1975, East Perth players Alan Quartermaine, Peter Spencer and Ross Glendinning had taken the first three positions in the Sandover Medal. From the 1975 side it lost brilliant defender, Ken McAullay, forced out of the game by injuries, and ruckman, Ron Alexander, to Fitzroy. But Gary Malarkey, a class full-back, stayed on, and the big man department was taken care of by the return of Bradley Smith and Ian McCulloch from Victoria. These two, along with small men Verstegen and Bygraves, gave experience to the side, backed by a core of competent players and some up-and-comers from the 1975 Colts premiership side. Further depth was added by the acquisition of fringe VFL players Neville Taylor and Gerald Betts.

The team was well poised to progress in an open competition that had seen six clubs win the flag in the previous seven years. The only multiple winner had been West Perth, which had staged a last-to-first performance under new coach Graham Campbell to take the 1975 flag. John Todd was now coaching at East Fremantle, where he had tasted premiership success for the first time in 1974. Mal Brown held the reins at Claremont where he had made a disastrous start in 1975, being suspended for 15 weeks after a practice match incident, then, when he finally got on to the field, incurring a further six-week suspension late in the season.

As at Geelong in 1973, in 1976 Farmer's first-up assignments were against the two Grand Finalists of the previous year. This time though his side leapt out of the blocks, recording a 14-goal win over West Perth, then keeping their noses in front of South Fremantle all day in a high-class game to win by a goal. "It was a nice way to start off as coach," was Farmer's comment after the initial victory:

> East Perth played well and I'm sure we can continue this style of football. It is nice to have the talent available ... At Geelong, the players did what I asked them to do, but they didn't really have the ability to win more games. At Perth Oval we have players who have that ability.[1]

The Royals did continue to play in good style. Through the first round of games they were in the top two. Their second win over South Fremantle in the ninth game—this time by 11 goals—put them in top spot, where they remained until the end of the season with a two-game break. This was achieved despite a rash of injury problems. Only five members of the team were able to play all games. Glendinning was in and out trying to overcome an injured neck and missed nine games. Quartermaine missed 10. Classy winger John McGuire was plagued with ankle troubles, and sharp-shooting forward Larry Kickett broke his hand mid-season, just after a five-goal performance. Farmer earned plaudits for the way he had the team playing, and the manner in which he improvised and shuffled players to cover the injury problems.

The improvisation during the season proved to be good practice for the final round to come. In the second semi-final against South Fremantle, some of the team were carrying injuries into the game, a situation compounded early on when Betts and McCulloch were forced off. Spencer and Martin were then injured, and propped in the two forward pockets for most of the game.

By rights East Perth should have been gone, with only 16 'fit' players, and some of them struggling. But the Royals fought their way magnificently to a five-goal win, to gain a place in the Grand Final. Spencer was the particular hero of the day with six goals playing on one leg in his forward pocket. The coach was pleased with his charges, describing their performance as "one of the best I've seen from East Perth against the odds. But also it set them up. I think it knocked the stuffing out of them." The annual report describes it as:

> ...a team decimated in victory. The respite of two weeks produced an urgency of "repair and maintenance" on bruised and broken limbs ... The

doctors and trainers worked days, nights and weekends to try to repair what, in some cases, proved to be impossible in the short time available.[2]

As always in such situations, the club threw up a smokescreen to hide the extent of the problems they had:

East Perth, despite the injury clouds that have hovered over the club for a fortnight, have the capacity to beat Perth in today's Grand Final ... They are, perhaps, the best equipped side to go into a Grand Final since West Perth in 1969 and it is no coincidence that Graham Farmer was coach of that side too ... East Perth have thrived under the Farmer influence this year and he has produced one of the best teams in the club's history. Farmer's great depth of knowledge and understanding of the footballer's make-up have been evident at East Perth since the start of this season. He has produced a tough, skilful team that has plenty of courage.[3]

Perth, which had occupied second spot on the ladder for most of the year before losing it in the last round of qualifying games, came through the preliminary final. On Grand Final day, Perth won the toss and kicked with what was described as a seven-goal breeze, but was held to a narrow lead. The advantage that should have been with East Perth in the second quarter disappeared when heavy rain swept over the ground, and Perth held the lead throughout over a Royals side that had run out of spark.

The general consensus was that East Perth was clearly the best side in the competition, but played its Grand Final two weeks early. Farmer was never one to take defeat lightly, but he seemed to accept this one with relative equanimity as one in which the fates were against them. In his contribution to the annual report he stated:

The 1976 season was, and always will be, a great year for East Perth, spoilt by one game ... Given the same support from members and directors, we will be a force again next season.[4]

East Perth had a team that was capable of going on to dominate the WANFL if it could be held together, but by the mid-1970s that task was becoming harder and harder in the Perth competition. The trickle of top players from Perth across to Melbourne after each season had steadily increased to the point where the cream was being skimmed each year by the VFL. Player payments had escalated in the wake of the North Melbourne drive that started in 1973, the competition for players there was keener, and the incentives being offered to West Australian stars greater. The success of Farmer and Marshall in the 1960s, and John McIntosh, Barry Cable and Graham Moss in the 1970s, in establishing themselves as champions in Victoria, set precedents and provided encouragement to other West Australian players. Also, with the passage of the years, the psychological distance between Perth and the Eastern States had shrunk. It seemed more natural and less daunting for a player to make the transition.

The regular loss of top-line players was one of the reasons why it had become harder for a single club to stamp its authority on the competition. Opinions varied in WA about the trend. Many accepted that it was the players' right to test themselves against the best and seek greater rewards in Melbourne. But as ever in Perth there was also a strong sentiment against the Eastern States, with diehards and traditionalists opposed to letting players go.

Each club of course tried to protect its own interests and playing strength, by hanging on to its top players, negotiating swaps, or at least seeking the top dollar in transfer fees with which to acquire replacements. It was not unknown for financially troubled clubs to sell a top player to the highest bidder to solve a problem or two with the bank. Perth had established a trend with the deal that allowed Barry Cable to play with North Melbourne for a year in 1974. North were required to post a massive bond that would be forfeited if Cable was not cleared back when the year was up. At the end of 1975 East Perth had let Ron Alexander go on a type of lease arrangement.

After the 1976 season three quality players, all defenders, sought to leave East Perth to try their luck in the big time. Gary Malarkey was released to Geelong under a similar arrangement to that made for Alexander. But East Perth drew the line at George Michalczyk and Ross Glendinning. Malarkey was 100-game player with six years' service, but the other two had been with the Royals for only three seasons—not enough service, it was deemed, to warrant clearances. Glendinning in particular was extremely keen to go, and desperately wanted by North. He moved to Melbourne, much as Farmer had in 1961, and waited there on the assumption or the hope that the dispute between the clubs would be resolved. But heels were dug in on both sides. At the same time East Perth were in dispute with South Melbourne, which were refusing to clear Ian Thomson, a former East Perth player, back to the club.

The Royals began the season reasonably well, with three wins from their first four. Neither Glendinning or Michalczyk were in the first losing game against West Perth. Michalczyk was persuaded to return, and was in and out of the side, but not performing, due to injury problems, and perhaps, one is forced to wonder, lack of desire.

But then the team slumped to three consecutive losses, including one to bottom side Subiaco, to end the first round of seven games with a three-win, four-loss score, clinging to fourth place. Clearly the team had been unsettled by the off-field problems with players, and had lost the cohesion and spirit of the previous year, and this was being reflected in the on-field performance.

East Perth won five out of seven in the second round of games, but actually slipped out of the four despite the relative improvement. Subiaco, Swan Districts and Claremont had dropped right out of contention, and the other five clubs were locked in a close battle for the four spots. The field was open, but East Perth was at the tail, trailing the third and fourth clubs on percentage.

At this point in the season, Glendinning and Michalczyk came back into the side. A deal had been done with North Melbourne—without the knowledge of the coach. Barry Cable was approaching the end of his playing days, and was known to want to finish as a captain-coach. If Ross Glendinning would come home and play out the year with the Royals, he would be cleared to North Melbourne for the 1978 season—in return for Cable. For obvious reasons the details of the deal were kept quiet. It would seem that Cable himself did not know of it at the time.

It is hard to imagine in the circumstances that young Glendinning felt terribly committed to the East Perth cause, or that either he or Michalczyk were happy at the club. Their return coincided with the playing of the

Ardath Cup, a short-lived competition that was intended as a national interclub series, but ignored by the VFL. It was played between Western and South Australia and VFA sides as a knockout series of night games midweek, as an addition to the regular weekend domestic games. East Perth won its way through to the Grand Final with a couple of very good performances. In what was probably their best effort of the year, the Royals were narrow losers to Norwood in the Grand Final in extremely adverse circumstances—flying midweek to Adelaide to play Norwood on their home ground under lights, with a South Australian umpire, and a free kick count running heavily against them, they led until well into the last quarter. It was an indication of what the team was capable of.

In the third round of games, East Perth again had a five-two record to secure a first semi-final berth. The game that probably finished up costing the club a second semi-final spot, in spite of all the troubles it was going through, was an inexplicable loss on a day on which it had every incentive. East Perth was in third position, but level on points with the second and fourth teams, with the finals in sight. Hans Verstegen was playing his 200th game for the club. Full-forward Archie Duda was poised on 99 goals for the season, set to bring up the ton, and the Royals were playing at home against lowly Claremont. Yet they slumped to a two-goal loss. Played only a week and a half after the game against Norwood, it was an indication of something else—a team that was lacking spirit as well as consistency.

East Perth's last game of the qualifying round, three weeks after the Claremont debacle, was an astounding 19-goal win over ladder-leader Perth. Form clearly meant nothing this season, but if it had, the Royals should have come into the first semi-final as favourites against West Perth, which on the same day had lost second place by going down to East Fremantle by 12 goals. But in a performance that reflected all the internal problems of the club, the team failed to score a goal until the last minute of the first half of the game. The Royals went down 10.5 (65) to 14.13 (97).

Within a week the football press was running the story that the East Perth directors had demanded Farmer's resignation. He describes it as being called in and given the big A. His contract was terminated with a year still to run. The "ethics and principles" of East Perth, that made it impossible to replace Chadwick mid-term with Farmer exactly 10 years earlier, according to Hec Strempel, had clearly changed. The list of possible replacements for Farmer listed in the press included Kevin Sheedy, Kevin Murray, Grant Dorrington and Mal Brown. The Glendinning-Cable deal was still well under wraps, and did not emerge until later.

Once again, Farmer showed his feelings about those who had appointed him, then withdrawn their support:

> I'm the unfortunate victim. It's very unreasonable, an unbelievable decision
> ... When the going gets tough a club should stick together and fight to beat
> it. But some people chip and chip at the ground underneath you in trying
> to find someone to blame. I do my best in football and I have no time to
> protect my back, so it's left wide open. Maybe that's a lot of my trouble.[5]

Comment in the *Football Budget* had a similar theme. "Farmer's major fault seems to have been in the area of Public Relations and communication with the committee and the club's many members."[6] The *Daily News* writer, Rod Easdown, concluded an article on the events with the opinion: "I thought the East Perth decision was arrogant. Polly told me he would not be affected by it, but I know he's disappointed. So am I, and so, I think, are a great deal of West Australians."[7]

Farmer's feelings on the matter have remained strong:

> Ross Glendinning wanted to go to North and Barry Cable was the swap,
> but he wanted to come back as a coach ... If I'd had that last year with the
> idea that Barry would have been coach the following year, it probably would
> have been all right. But to tip me out just to do that, to me seemed terribly
> wrong. It didn't show any loyalty ... I was hurt at the time. The people who
> did it, I resented, and probably haven't and won't speak to them for the rest
> of my life—but they're not at the club now.

Cable was never one of the people he held responsible, and there was no ill-feeling between the pair. In years to come, when they found themselves working together, they would become friends.

The experiences as coach at Geelong and East Perth have left Farmer with a distrust for football administrators and powerbrokers as a type—though many individuals who fill such roles have been and are personal friends. But apart from a few particular people whom he will never forgive, he has buried his differences with the clubs in the years since, and is always keen to stress that the club itself is a stronger and longer lasting institution than the people who inhabit it from time to time. He remains an East Perth man, and a Geelong man.

There was a footnote to the 1977 season that provided Farmer with a distraction to the turmoil created by his sacking, and that would ultimately be remembered as a far more significant event. His very last role in senior football as either player or coach would prove to be a ground-breaking one.

Nineteen seventy-seven was the year of the first interstate match to be played on a state-of-origin basis. It was the brainchild of Subiaco promotions director Leon Larkin, and had taken almost two years to put together. Players were eligible for selection for the state in which they played their first senior League game, meaning that the West Australians playing in the VFL—Cable, Alexander, Miller, Balme, Magro and others—could play for their home state.

Farmer had been appointed the West Australian coach. When sacked from East Perth he offered to withdraw, but was told to continue in the position. The game was scheduled for Subiaco on the weekend after the two state Grand Finals, but was forced back by a week when North Melbourne and Collingwood played a draw in the VFL Grand Final and had to hold a replay. Four of the West Australian team were in the VFL Grand Finals, including Cable in his farewell appearance for North Melbourne.

The game seized the public imagination in Perth, where people saw it as the first ever chance for a true test between the two states, after decades of seeing their home-grown boys wearing the big V in sides that beat them. Premier Sir Charles Court invited his Victorian counterpart, Dick Hamer, across to watch the game. Western Australia's pride was on the line.

As coach, Farmer's task was not easy. He had a squad from all corners, and in all stages of condition. Some, like his captain Graham Moss, whose clubs had not made the finals, had not played for five weeks. Others were coming straight off one of the most gruelling finals campaigns in VFL history:

> I had half a dozen of them for two weeks, and the rest I had for two training sessions. It wasn't very much at all. We had a very good meal together, where all the players had the opportunity to get up and have a talk and make a personal commitment. [They] talked of all the times in the past—here was an opportunity to make up for them. So they not only played for all the people that went to the game, but they also played for all the people who'd played for Western Australia and been soundly beaten ... There was a great feeling. It was a feeling that was probably far superior to what the Victorians could generate. That was the difference. We had quality players and a great feeling.

In the first quarter of the game, to the absolute delight of the crowd, the West held the Victorians scoreless while kicking 6.5 (41). Farmer used the three reserves and interchange system that had been adopted for the game to protect those of his players who had dropped off peak playing condition, putting them on for concentrated bursts. Cable was the star of the game, as the West ran away to a 94-point win.

In home town eyes it was a vindication and a triumph, and the jubilation in the dressing-rooms was almost finals-like in its atmosphere, with the Premier and other dignitaries crowding in to offer their congratulations and be a part of it all. For a West Australian there was nothing sweeter than beating the Victorians. Farmer and his players were heroes.

The state-of-origin concept revived interstate football, as well as evening it out. In the years to come, Western Australia would win a fair share of games—the record stood at seven out of 19 when the state-of-origin era came to an end in 1999.

The 1977 match was a significant moment in the historical context of football. The victory did much to boost football morale in WA. In the years to come the continuing games meant that the Perth stars playing in Melbourne seemed less like exiles or traitors, as they donned the home colours once a year. On both sides of the Nullarbor, it all contributed to an increasingly national perspective on the game, that eventually would culminate in the creation of the West Coast Eagles and the formation of the Australian Football League.

That first game was not the cause of what followed, but it was a large contributor. It was a fitting end point for the man who had started as a lad in a competition dominated by returned soldiers, in the days when a packet of chewies and a pat on the back was the reward for the effort on the field.

20

OUT OF THE LIMELIGHT

"It was getting to the stage in life where it suited me more to be a spectator watching the passing parade than participating in it," says Farmer of the period that followed his last coaching job. "As you get a little bit older, your expectations of what you want to do aren't anywhere near as great as they were when you were younger. I was happy to watch the boys playing and watch the passing parade."

In the 10 years from 1977 his official involvement in the football world was very limited. Initially the family moved back to Geelong. He took on a small role at the football club as a specialist ruck coach under his replacement Rod Olsson, and eldest son, Brett, started playing with the under 19s. He got work as a car salesman, and took charge of his horses again.

For one with such a small-scale involvement in the chancy world of horse breeding, he had shown himself to be a canny judge. His brood mares produced one very good horse in Grey Sapphire, which he leased out. It won races on city tracks in four states, and was a leading sprinter and miler of its day, winning at weight for age, and being placed in a number of major handicap races, despite problems with the feet that limited its racing. Another called Hydroskia, which Farmer raced himself in partnership with a syndicate that included former teammates Terry Callan and John Brown, won in Melbourne. Farmer points out with pride that in all, his three brood mares dropped horses that won more than 80 races.

Early in the 1978 season, when Carlton coach Ian Stewart retired suddenly after suffering a heart spasm, there were reports that Farmer headed a shortlist of possible replacements. He did not entirely rule out the possibility, but damped down the speculation, saying that he was well entrenched at Geelong, adding that Marlene would certainly not be keen on the idea. The Farmer family had had enough of coaching.

Throughout the year they were living in a flat, waiting to sell the house they had bought in Perth at the time of the last move, before buying in Geelong. At the end of the year a flash flood burst through a retaining wall and coursed down a former creek bed, right through the flat, wiping out many of their possessions. The family decided to move back to Perth to regroup. Initially the intention was to go west for a year at the most, to sell the house at Trigg and then reestablish themselves in their own home in Geelong. But back in Trigg, with Dean and Kim in school, and Farmer getting a job, they decided that they had had enough of the continual moving back and forth, and dropped anchor for the last time.

Farmer joined the sales team at McInerney Ford, where he would stay for some years. Dennis McInerney was a sponsor of the Subiaco club, and as part of his employment Farmer did some ruck coaching there, where young giant Laurie Keene was emerging as a big man of real potential. But by now the club whose fortunes he was most interested in was neither Subiaco, nor his old clubs of East and West Perth, but Claremont, where both Brett and Dean were playing.

Brett established himself in the Claremont senior team in 1981, playing mainly as a half-forward and second spearhead in the forward pocket alongside Warren Ralph. He was a member of that year's Claremont premiership side, captained by Graham Moss and including the Krakouer brothers, in their last season before leaving the west to play with North Melbourne. In 1981, Dean was still at school, and by the time he joined Claremont the following year Swan Districts had become the dominant club, winning the first of a hat-trick of premierships under John Todd.

Farmer had by no means disappeared from public sight. A couple of times each winter, for one reason or another, a feature article appeared in the sporting press recalling his past deeds. He would be asked to comment from time to time on developments in the game, and various honours and accolades continued to come his way. In 1983, as part of the celebrations of 125 years of football, a panel of Victorian experts named him as the lead ruckman in 'The Greatest Team Of All Time', with Barassi as his ruck-rover, and Gary Dempsey and Jack Dyer as the second ruck. Ten years later another similar selection was made, but, reflecting the contemporary trend, it included only one specialist ruckman, and the one named was still Farmer, again with Barassi as his ruck-rover.

In 1984, the VFL commissioned a huge glass tile mosaic for VFL Park at Waverley. Each club was asked to nominate two retired players to be included on the mosaic. The selections were a cause of much debate in Melbourne, and some could have been excused at being miffed at their non-inclusion. But no one questioned the nomination of Farmer as one of Geelong's pair, along with Doug Wade, nor his rightful place among the elite 24. Of those included, only Ron Todd of Collingwood and John Coleman of Essendon had played fewer games in the VFL than Farmer.

In 1985, the Western Australian Institute of Sport announced 14 foundation members of a hall of champions that would form the entry to the new state sports centre. Half of the 14 came from the two high-profile sports of football and cricket. The other half were all world champions or Olympic gold medallists in their particular fields. The cricketers were Dennis Lillee, Rod Marsh and Graham McKenzie. The footballers were Farmer and Cable, and from earlier eras, George Moloney and Nipper Truscott. To mark the occasion, bronze busts of the 14 were unveiled at a formal dinner. The honour was repeated on a national scale when Farmer also became a member of the Australian Sporting Hall of Fame.

In 1986, though came publicity of a very different nature that devastated the whole Farmer family; an experience that Farmer and Marlene describe as their worst in football. Playing for the Perth reserves team, both Dean and Brett, along with a teammate, were reported for offences against the umpires. Perth's senior coach, none other than Mal Brown, was also reported for pulling the team from the field. In three Tribunal hearings over the next nine days, events seemed to spin out of control, just as they had on the field. Brown's case was heard first, and he was fined $5000, with the Tribunal chairman Bernie O'Sullivan making comments afterwards about the actions of the players that seemed highly prejudicial given that he was yet to hear their cases.

Despite confusing evidence from the umpire concerned, Dean was found guilty of interfering with an umpire over an incident that had brought laughter from the crowd—a collision that seemed purely accidental. Brett was accused and convicted of threatening umpire Hearne when he conceded nothing more than calling him a cheat during the heat of the chaotic last quarter of the game. Outside the Tribunal rooms Brett's emotions boiled over. He had words with Hearne, then pushed him. Farmer ushered Brett away, but in the meantime the incident was reported to O'Sullivan. "Hearne did not want to proceed with the matter. 'Just forget it,' he said. But a stern-faced Mr O'Sullivan told Perth advocate Mick Moylan: 'I want Brett Farmer with his brother Dean at 5 o'clock next Monday for further Tribunal action'."[1] This seemed to indicate that he was both laying and planning to hear further charges. When they appeared again before O'Sullivan, Dean was suspended until the end of the 1987 season—effectively 27 games. At this, Brett left the Tribunal without waiting for the further charge against him to be heard. In his absence he was suspended for 10 seasons.

Press reaction to the sentences imposed on the Farmers seems to have been unanimously of the opinion that Dean had been unfairly treated. Brett, it was agreed, whatever the rights and wrongs of the original decision, had brought trouble on himself by laying hands on umpire Hearne outside the Tribunal. Though even in his case, many thought the 10-year ban, which effectively amounted to life, was extremely excessive. But the general consensus was that the Farmer version of the collision between Dean and Hearne was correct, it had been an unfortunate accident originally, that had got blown out of all proportion, and then judged not in its own right, but in the light of subsequent events.

Gary Stocks in the *West Australian* drew the parallel to other cases involving players and umpires. Earlier the same season Swan Districts rover Barry Kimberley was found guilty of pushing a field umpire in the chest with an open hand, and was fined $500 dollars. At the beginning of the 1975 season Mal Brown had been found guilty of deliberately tripping an umpire and had received 15 weeks. Both of these cases had been heard under O'Sullivan. In Melbourne in 1980, the controversial Phil Carmen of Collingwood, with a record of offences behind him already, headbutted and pushed an umpire, and received a 20-week suspension—seven games fewer than Dean's amounted to.

As these events had unfolded Farmer had remained silent. In fact he was shattered, and not talking to anyone at all, until he contacted Stocks at the *West Australian*. In a lengthy interview with Stocks he made a passionate defence of his sons. "Throughout their careers there was not one shred of evidence to suggest that they were angry footballers or showed malice ... Until now, both had been reported only once—Brett for a striking charge last year, which was dismissed, and Dean for wasting time and he was reprimanded ... Brett and Dean have done nothing that warrants their character being assassinated throughout Australia."[2] He gave a detailed account of what had taken place on the field that day, and said: "Before the first hearing, at no stage did Dean, Brett or I consider they would be suspended. I am still stunned ... They don't deserve this treatment."[3] He also went on, by way of trying to explain what went on on the football field, to say:

> Dean and Brett through no fault of their own, have had to suffer from being sons of Graham Farmer. They have also had to suffer for being the descendants of Aborigines ... I'll give you a couple of classic examples from my career. In 1971 I was playing for West Perth against East Fremantle and a prominent East Fremantle player called out: "They're only bloody boongs and dings; they're no bloody good". Every time I played against another chappie—he was one of the state's great players—his only words to me were "you bloody nigger; you boong". And that goes on all the time.[4]

The latter reference was to Jack Clarke of course. It was the first time Farmer had ever referred publicly to the racial abuse he had copped himself on the field. In December, three weeks after the Farmers requested a rehearing of the cases, the League's directors made a surprise announcement of clemency.

Mal Brown's fine was halved. Brett's suspension was reduced from 10 years until the end of the 1987 season, and Dean was made eligible to resume after seven games of the next season. The cited reason for the clemency was "to mark W.A.'s entry next year into the expanded VFL competition. The directors decided the reduction in penalties was an appropriate gesture at the start of a new era in football".[5]

Farmer was not mollified, saying at the time:

> If they had done something wrong these reductions would be great news. What I would like is to have the whole business reviewed completely ... There was nothing Brett and Dean did at Lathlain Park that should have led to their suspension.[6]

He says now of the clemency: "I assume by doing that even the League recognised how wrong it was." He believes the whole episode was a grave miscarriage of justice, in which egos, personalities and preconceptions got in the way of fair consideration of the evidence. "At least there should be set penalties if they are going to find people guilty of these sorts of offences. Then it is not up to one man, for his own reasons, to take matters into his own hands."

The new era that the League directors referred to when granting clemency to Brown and the Farmers—whether it was a reason or an excuse—was the entry of the West Coast Eagles into what was then still called the Victorian Football League. The birth of the Eagles changed the face of West Australian football in a way that no other event ever had. A few diehards held out against the move to enter the national competition, but it was overwhelmingly embraced by the football public of the state, who, almost to a person, swung their support behind the new team. 'The west against the rest' was a theme that would always arouse the passions of the people.

The press collectively fell over itself in the competition to become the Eagles' greatest supporter and provide the most extensive coverage. The centrepiece of the *Daily News*' effort was to strike a special medallion to be awarded to the Eagles' best player each year. The medal was called the Farmer Medal. For the first time since 1972, Farmer was enticed back to the football media, as a special comments man for one of the stations broadcasting West Coast games.

Ron Alexander, who had coached East Fremantle (from 1982 to 1986) after six seasons at Fitzroy, was not to last beyond the first season as coach. He obtained a creditable 11-win, 11-loss record in a year in which everything was new and experimental, from the player list to travel arrangements. But the directors decided he was not the man to take the club further. In October, the Board replaced him with John Todd, a man acknowledged by then as the master coach in Western Australia, but also one with no experience of the VFL.

On the day that Todd was appointed, he announced that his first move would be to get Farmer on to his staff and to upgrade the role that Cable was playing at the club. The two were made assistant coaches to Todd. With Graham Moss on the administrative team, and Glendinning on the field as captain, the Eagles certainly had the greats of the game in the west on their side.

Farmer's particular role was as a ruck coach and working with the big men of the side. But in Todd's eyes, he and Cable had another equally important role: "He was mainly there to try to help the young guys, and just impart some of his knowledge and reinforce them when things weren't going all that well; to give them a direction."

Todd's first year was a success, with the Eagles making the final five. But in the second year injuries struck with a vengeance—especially to the big men Farmer worked with—and they slipped down the ladder. In the eternal story, the sniping soon got underway internally and externally. It was not, according to Todd, a happy year, and he cites Farmer as one of the few who gave him absolute support in the job he was trying to do.

At the end of 1989, after the team finished 11th of 14, Todd was replaced by Mick Malthouse. From the club's point of view the appointment was an unqualified success. Malthouse brought his own support team with him—which Farmer acknowledges as his right—and Farmer's role was reduced specifically to that of ruck coach. After a year he quietly left the club.

By the time the Eagles played in their second Grand Final, against Geelong in 1992, Farmer was able to happily declare his allegiance to his old team when pictured in Grand Final week with the other West Australian Cats, Denis Marshall, John Watts and John O'Connell.

> Farmer admitted he had split loyalties, except when it comes to the crunch. "I support the West Coast Eagles and I support Geelong. But if it comes to a clash I support Geelong."[7]

The assistant coaching stint at the Eagles under John Todd was Farmer's last active involvement with a football team. By 1992 he and Marlene had invested in the lease of a motel near the zoo in South Perth, and were putting their time and energy into running the business. But it did not turn out as they had hoped, with the downturn in the Asian economy leading to a huge drop in visitors to Perth from their main customer base, and by 1998 they were forced to walk away from the business. At the time Farmer was quoted as saying: "We have nothing and we are back to square one. But we didn't borrow money to keep the business going. All my life I have helped myself and there is no reason why I can't still do that."[8]

A year earlier it had been announced by the State Government that a major new piece of Perth infrastructure under construction would be named the Graham Farmer Freeway. The new freeway, though short, would incorporate a new bridge over the Swan River, and Perth's first (and thus far only) underground road, the Northbridge Tunnel. It would provide the first realistic bypass to the city proper for the ever-increasing through traffic, and, as the Transport Minister pointed out, it would link Farmer's two old stomping grounds of East and West Perth. The Graham Farmer Freeway has become a crucial part of Perth's transport network, and the tunnel has become colloquially known to locals as 'the Polly Pipe'.

When the Farmers had to give up the motel business, they were temporarily accommodated in a flat supplied by the Main Roads Department, and Farmer undertook publicity work for Main Roads associated with the freeway project, and once again picked up the special comments work with radio station 6PR's football coverage.

His old Geelong mates, Bob Davis, John Watts and Sam Newman, assisted with a couple of fundraising events that brought in enough for him and Marlene to buy a small villa in Innaloo. But in 2000 he had to put his Sandover Medals and his MBE up for sale to help fund their retirement.

Although the 1990s was not a good decade for the Farmers, as the years went by, Farmer's status as one of the unique heroes of the game continued to grow. The accolades that have continued to come his way are of the type beyond Sandovers and Brownlows, and even royal decorations. They are recognition of the kind that can only be bestowed on the game's very elite.

Perhaps the most significant in its symbolism was the decision in 1991 to create the Polly Farmer Cup as the prize for victory in state-of-origin matches between Victoria and Western Australia.

In formal terms the final seal of recognition from his home state came in 1993. The President's Lounge, the main function room of the West Australian Football Commission at its headquarters at Subiaco Oval—with the prime view of the ground where the best football action in the state takes place, and where the honour boards hang—was renamed the Polly Farmer Room. A portrait of Farmer was commissioned to watch over the room. A dinner was held to mark the occasion, with Graham and Marlene, Brett, Dean and Kim all present, along with friends from all eras of his football career, right back to Steve Jarvis of Maddington days. There were speeches from Jack Sheedy, John Watts, and Bob Davis, who flew over for the occasion.

Then in 1993, in the Year of Indigenous people—though it could equally have been in any other year—Farmer was asked by the Australian Football League to undertake one of the sacred duties of the year: the presentation of the Premiership Cup to the winning team out there in the middle of the MCG at the conclusion of the Grand Final between Essendon and Carlton.

Nineteen ninety-six marked the 100th anniversary of the VFL/AFL competition, and as such was big on commemorations and symbolism. Farmer figured prominently in two aspects of this. When the AFL appointed a panel to select an official 'Team of the Century', Farmer was named as first ruck, with his great rival, Carlton's John Nicholls as his back-up, starting out of the back pocket. The consensus of the 1960s that these two titans were the best ruckmen the game had seen was vindicated. An official Australian Football Hall of Fame was also established, with 136 initial inductees made up of players, coaches, officials and media figures. Of these, an elite 12, including Farmer, were officially declared to be Legends of the game

The accolades did not stop when the clock ticked over into a new century.

One of the most notable features of football in the 1990s had been the changing role and status of Indigenous players at the AFL level, as more and more were recruited to club lists. The unforgettable catalyst for change was that moment in 1993 when Nicky Winmar lifted his St Kilda jumper and defiantly pointed at his black skin in front of the Victoria Park stands from where rabid Collingwood fans had been hurling racial abuse at him all day. Michael Long of Essendon was the torch carrier; his poise and skill as a generational footballer matched by his dignity and eloquence as a spokesman.

Long was the man who changed the unspoken rule that Farmer and Indigenous players before and after him had had to play by: cop the racial abuse and don't complain, it's all part of the game. In 1995, Long refused to stay silent, and took on the system when Collingwood ruckman Damien Monkhurst abused him in a match at the MCG.

It was a game changer. And not only in terms of what is acceptable between players on the field. Long and his Indigenous brothers created a change in attitudes in the halls of power and, more importantly, among the game's huge supporter base, to the point where football can genuinely claim to be a leader in acknowledging and celebrating Indigenous Australia and forging better race relations.

The high point in this tectonic shift came in 2005, when an official AFL Indigenous Team of the Century, selected by an eminent panel chaired by Pat Dodson, was announced at a gala event with Prime Minister John Howard as guest of honour and principal speaker. First ruck and captain of the team was none other than Graham 'Polly' Farmer. Of the 24 players named, only five had not played in the VFL/AFL. One of these was Farmer's oldest friend from Sister Kate's days, Ted 'Square' Kilmurray. Another was his colleague in arms from West Perth, the inimitable Bill Dempsey. At the urging of the Kilmurrays, the Farmers somewhat reluctantly headed over to Melbourne for the announcement of the Indigenous Team of the Century, and by all reports had a fine old time, including a lengthy one-on-one chat with Prime Minister Howard.

That event was virtually the last public appearance for Farmer. As the new century rolled on he effectively dropped out of sight, as far as the public was concerned.

The reason was that dementia had begun to take hold of the great man. It is a cruel disease that creeps up quietly, as the mind gradually, randomly shuts down, losing more and more function. One of the great football brains was slowly losing touch with the world around him.

The development of Alzheimer's disease is perhaps even more cruel to the family and loved ones than to the sufferer. They must bear witness to the slow disintegration, and must continue to love and care for someone who remains physically present, but increasingly dependent, while ever more remote; a mere shell of the spirited soul that once inhabited the body.

Marlene and the children have cared for Pol throughout his decline, and will continue to do so, even as Marlene faces her own struggle with recurring bouts of breast cancer. They have, on the whole, chosen to treat it as a family matter and a private affair. But for someone of Farmer's stature, the world insists on intruding.

In 2012, Perth's *Sunday Times* ran an article under the headline 'My Beautiful Man in his Bravest Fight'. Farmer's old mate John K Watts was also part of the story, talking about his own struggle with cancer as he kept up the old shtick about being the man who made "Pol" the player he was. But at its heart, the article was about a romance:

> For nearly 55 years, Marlene has been married to Graham 'Polly' Farmer, perhaps the greatest Australian Rules footballer of all time. Years ago, the man who changed football with his ruckwork ... started losing his memory.
>
> Marlene didn't want to make it public, wanting to keep it in the family and preferring countless fans all over Australia to remember Polly, 'The Big Cat,' as they saw him star on footy grounds wherever he went. Now she has come

out to talk about "the centre of my life" and dementia ...

"It's an awful, awful thing. I saw it get my mum. And now my Graham, my Polly, has it. It's still the same Graham that everyone knows. But he's just lost his memory. He has to be watched all the time ...

"We don't have any other relatives here, so it makes it hard. Don't make me out to be an angel, don't make people feel sorry for us. We're happy, we're living good lives." ...

Misty-eyed, Marlene Farmer listens intently to Watts, while looking adoringly at her husband. The year before they married, she came to Perth on a working holiday from Tasmania. "I met Pol, fell in love, and haven't left," she said. "He's like no man I have met, he's the centre of my world. And he's still good. We have our good days—he washed the dishes and hung out the clothes this morning. I might mollycoddle Pol, but he's so special."[9]

The first edition of this biography in 1994 closed with the observation that:

Graham Farmer will never be far away from football in one capacity or another. Whether it is the local teams in which his sons now play and coach, or the AFL, he can sit and watch the footy, as he does, making judgments and observations as keen as ever, knowing that it is a game that he shaped and influenced as perhaps no other individual in its history has.

Twenty years on, the reality has changed, but the sentiment remains absolutely valid.

AFTERWORD

It is fair to say that Graham Farmer did not particularly rate Gareth Andrews as a footballer, as Andrews himself acknowledges below. If Farmer could read Andrews' tribute with a clear mind, he would probably comment drily along the lines of: 'Typical, no discipline, no respect for team rules.'

But Andrews certainly rated Farmer. He played 136 games for Geelong, under Farmer as first his captain, and later his coach. In 1974, in a swap for Rex Hunt, he had moved across mid-season to play for Richmond, and played in their premiership team. Eventually he returned to the fold at Geelong, joining the board in 1998, and serving as vice-president during their triple premiership era. His piece, published in *The Age* in August of 2013 after the team had made the trip west for a match against the West Coast Eagles, under the headline 'Precious Moments with a Legend', is an appropriate tribute to Farmer's enduring legacy, especially at the Geelong Football Club.

That article (following pages) is reproduced with permission.

CLOSE TIES: Farmer with Gareth Andrews, Perth 2013 (GARETH ANDREWS)

PRECIOUS MOMENTS
WITH A LEGEND

BY GARETH ANDREWS

Polly Farmer was my hero as a kid. He was my first captain when I went to Geelong and my last coach when I left the Cats. I was not his favourite player in either of his roles but it's fair to say I never exactly fitted his mould.

He was a perfectionist as much as I was an imperfectionist. Polly was a beautifully balanced athlete with exquisitely honed skills, whereas I was a left-sided person in a right-sided body forever struggling to marry the two. He was co-ordinated while I was gawky. When Polly lined up for goal, the fans would mark it in the *Record* before he kicked; when I had a shot, they shut their eyes and hoped for the best. Fortunately I had an innate ability to get the ball and this served me well.

In 1974 we went our separate ways; I headed to the Tigers to be part of their mighty team and Polly finished his Victorian period and returned to the west. We would meet each other occasionally at football functions and the banter was always friendly and respectful. Whatever we might have felt about each other, I was always able to rationalise that I had played with one of the greatest players to have played our game. Polly was a legend even before he came to Geelong in 1962—and when I travelled to his home in Perth last Saturday along the Graham Farmer Freeway I knew where he sat in the mind of his home town.

I had rung his wife Marlene a couple of days earlier to see whether Polly would like to come across to Geelong's team hotel and watch the boys have a light stretch on the lawns in front of the hotel—standard before the game. I promised to look after him and, with a bit of reluctance in her voice, Marlene agreed to the plan. Marlene has been Polly's rock over the past half a dozen years or so since dementia has crept insidiously into his life. She is a remarkable woman.

I had gone through the exercise four years earlier. Then, Marlene had driven Polly to the hotel. He looked healthy but his mind wandered. I heard subsequently that Polly didn't leave home very often, a few laps around a local park and a visit to the shops being his usual excursion. This time around I agreed that I would collect him and bring him home.

On my arrival, Marlene apologised but thought the outing would be beyond Polly. Since my phone call, the big fella had slipped in the house and smashed his forehead on the tiled floor. He had spent time in hospital and when he walked into the room he had a blackened left eye and about five stitches to show for it. He was much slower and had become a man of fewer words. He was looking slightly dishevelled, but at 78 years of age he had a right to look like a prize fighter post-bout. He had heard Marlene lovingly protecting him but I just had the feeling that Polly wasn't a party to this plan.

"Poll," I said, "we are taking you to the Crowne Plaza in a lovely Range Rover and you can watch the boys from the car. Marlene, I promise he won't leave the car and I promise I'll have him back in an hour." As Polly started to head to the door, I knew that he had won the day. A quarter-hour drive there and another quarter of an hour back wasn't going to give us much time, but we headed off. Polly sat in the front seat with my friend Rob, owner of the car, while I sat in the back seat trying to explain to Rob's six-year-old who Mr Farmer was. I think Ollie got the drift when we arrived at the stretching session.

I broke the first promise. When I pointed to a bench outside, Polly almost fell out of the car to get to it. He wanted to be closer to the action. The boys were only metres away and even to the youngest members of the team this ageing man with brooding eyes was instantly recognisable. Matty Stokes was the first to break from the training drill and race over to introduce himself. It was a big day for him—playing his 150th game—made even bigger now by sharing it with this Aboriginal legend and hero of the game. He shook his hand and plonked himself next to Polly, talking to him about stuff and not expecting anything in return.

These modern-day stars and superstars all wanted photos with Polly. A group gathered around him and Stevie Johnson was as chatty as ever. When I asked Poll what he thought about Stevie Johnson, Polly quietly stated, "I don't know much about him." Stevie was mortified, while his mates went into fits of laughter. I'm sure Stevie's 36 possessions later that night were his way of rebuilding his dented ego!

Travis Varcoe and Steven Motlop then joined Stokes just to hang out with Polly for a while. The moment was priceless. Varcoe, the proud wearer of the No. 5 jumper which had been worn by Farmer and Gary Ablett snr. Varcoe promised to dedicate all his goals that night to Polly and, at my suggestion, promised to kick 10. None were forthcoming but you had the feeling early in the game that something special had rubbed off from the meeting.

"Time to go, Polly," I said. We packed him back in the car and drove into the hotel driveway. I said I'd get Brian Cook to come outside to say hello. I headed inside only to look behind and find Polly following me. He was having too much fun. Cooky was halfway through a hamburger and chips and I asked Polly whether he wanted to eat. "No," was the response, but coach Chris Scott joined us and while we were having a chat we suddenly found Poll eating all of Cooky's chips. When these were finished he accepted Cooky's offer and proceeded to gulp down the remains of his hamburger.

Promises had been broken all around when I finally got Polly home, 40-odd minutes overtime, to find Marlene and daughter Kim beginning to mount a search party. Polly had a wry smile. He had broken all the rules because he wanted to. He wanted to be back with the Geelong boys. Shaking his hand a couple of times, I left him inside and headed off. When I looked back at the house, he had come to the gate to wave. Goosebumps. It was only then that I realised what an important part Polly had played in my football life. We have travelled different journeys but come to the same place. Our shared love of the Cats.[1]

APPENDIX

PLAYMAKER, TEAM MAKER:
RATING THE GREATS

To review and summarise the career of a player such as Graham Farmer is not a simple task, for there are too many angles of approach. The starting point should be the bare statistics, though even here, choice and editing are involved.

A basic career summary reads as follows:

NINETEEN SEASONS OF LEAGUE FOOTBALL, 1953-71.

356 SENIOR LEAGUE GAMES COMPRISED OF:

- 176 with East Perth, 1953-61.
- 101 with Geelong, 1962-67. (Captain 1965-67.)
- 79 with West Perth. (All as captain-coach.)
  - Three with West Perth.

- Appeared in League finals rounds in 14 years:
  - Six with East Perth.
  - Five with Geelong.

PLAYED IN 10 GRAND FINALS:

- Six with East Perth.
- Two with Geelong.

- Two with West Perth.

350

PLAYED IN SIX PREMIERSHIP TEAMS:

- Three with East Perth.
- One with Geelong.
- Two with West Perth.

CLUB BEST AND FAIREST 10 TIMES:

- Seven times at East Perth.
- Twice at Geelong.
- Once at West Perth.

LEAGUE BEST AND FAIRESTS:

- Winner of two Sandover Medals, in 1956 and 1960.
- Runner-up in the Sandover Medal three times, in 1955, 1957 (on count back) and 1969.
- Runner-up in the Brownlow Medal in 1963.

WINNER OF FOUR SIMPSON MEDALS:

- 1956 for Western Australia against South Australia.
- 1958 for Western Australia against Victoria.
- 1959 as best player in the Grand Final.
- 1969 as best West Australian player at the national championships.

INTERSTATE CAREER:

- Thirty-six interstate matches: 31 for Western Australia, five for Victoria.
- Played in four Australian Championship carnivals, all for Western Australia, in 1956, 1958, 1961 and 1969.
- Winner of the Tassie Medal as best player of the championships in 1956.
- Named in the All-Australian team three times, 1956, 1958 and 1961.

It is a career in three distinct phases. There are three clubs, with a move interstate with each change. There is a graduation from player, to captain, to captain-coach with each new club. It is true that only a third of his time was spent in the very best competition in the land, a fact that he quietly regrets. But there is no doubt that except for his first year, he was a player of the very highest class.

There is often debate over whether he played his best football with East Perth or with Geelong, with the balance often coming down, even among Victorians, that it came in his East Perth days, before the crippling knee injury that came in his first VFL game. John Watts, who saw more of him than anyone else in all three phases of his career, vigorously denied this conventional wisdom, arguing that he developed and refined his game, and was even more effective in the tougher VFL competition.

It is probably true that he was more graceful, looked more athletic, took more truly spectacular high marks, and was even better to watch in his phase at East Perth. But by force of will, physical effort and clever adaptation he was able to ensure that his effectiveness as a player and as a contributor to his team was never reduced.

Even in his third and final phase at West Perth he was able to play football that convinced committee member Les Day—admittedly a partisan—to change his opinion as to the best footballer he had seen. In the '50s Day had only seen Farmer during East Perth-West Perth matches. He still maintained at that stage that Haydn Bunton snr of Fitzroy and Subiaco was the best footballer he had seen. Watching Farmer in his last four years he changed his mind, partly on the basis of Farmer's skills and individual displays, but largely because of what he was able to contribute to the team.

Table One shows some of the statistical information on his career on an annual basis, with additional aspects designed to show, as well as such things can, the quality and consistency of his performance. In particular, his ranking in team best player listings are collated week by week over each year, and his finishing position in the club best and fairest award is shown.

Ultimately such rankings and voting are value judgments, subject to the prejudices one way or another of observers who in many cases are anonymous. Many would argue that they mean little. But over such a prolonged period they show an undoubted pattern and a consistency.

Farmer was officially judged his club's best player in more than half of his playing years. Excluding his debut year in which he did not play a full season, and the injury-plagued years of 1958 and 1962, he did not finish lower than fourth in the best and fairest awards. When one takes into account the allusions of his teammates—especially at Geelong—that he did not always receive the votes he deserved, this record perhaps should be even better.

On a regular basis over his time with each club, Farmer is named as their best player on the day in a quarter of his games—96 times in all. He is on the team's best players list in three-quarters of his games. Many of the remaining games can be accounted for by occasions when he left the field or was known to be carrying particular injuries. Once these are considered, the listings show that there was hardly a game he played in which he was not a major contributor to his side. Here we have the quality that the insiders of the game—the other champions, and above all the great coaches—most admire. Not just the capacity for brilliance, but the ability to reproduce it week after week and year after year.

TABLE ONE

Year	Games played	Games missed	Finished in club best & fairest	Best Player listing[1]						Total games listed	Games played but not listed
				1	2	3	4	5	6		
East Perth[2]											
1953	12	8	18th	–	–	3	–	–	–	3	9
1954	19	1	1st	5	1	2	1	1	3	13	6
1955	19	1	1st	6	2	3	1	2	2	16	3
1956	21	–	1st	6	2	2	1	1	5	17	4
1957	23	–	1st	6	3	3	2	1	7	22	1
1958	18	6	7th	3	2	–	1	4	4	14	4
1959	20	3	1st	6	–	3	1	7	1	18	2
1960	22	2	1st	10	3	1	3	1	1	19	3
1961	22	1	1st	9	2	–	1	2	2	16	6
Total	176	22		51	15	17	11	19	25	138	38
%				29	9	10	6	11	14	78	22
Geelong[3]											
1962	6	18	9th	2	2	–	–	–	–	4	2
1963	19	1	1st	5	3	4	–	2	1	15	4
1964	19	1	1st	5	1	2	4	2	1	15	4
1965	18	1	4th	4	3	2	–	–	3	12	6
1966	18	1	2nd	3	4	3	–	1	2	13	5
1967	21	–	2nd	5	1	–	3	2	3	14	7
Total	101	22		24	14	11	7	7	10	73	28
%				24	14	11	7	7	10	72	28

TABLE ONE CONTINUED.

Year	Games played	Games missed	Finished in club best & fairest	Best Player listing[1]						Total games listed	Games played but not listed
				1	2	3	4	5	6		
West Perth[4]											
1698	18	5	3rd	5	3	1	1	1	1	12	6
1969	21	2	1st	7	2	2	2	1	4	18	3
1970	19	2	3rd	4	3	3	1	1	–	12	7
1971	21	3	2nd	5	3	2	1	–	2	13	8
Total	79	12		21	11	8	5	3	7	55	24
%				27	14	10	6	4	9	70	30
Career											
Total	356	56		96	40	36	23	29	42	266	90
%				27	11	10	6	8	12	75	25

Notes—Table One

1. Most best player listings name six players from each team. Occasionally seven or eight are named. In the few instances where Farmer was named seventh or eighth, this has been converted to a sixth.

2. East Perth listings are taken from the *Football Budget*, published by the WANFL. The only exceptions are some of the six Grand Finals, where no *Budget* was published the following week. In these case the ranking is taken from the *West Australian*.

3. Almost all the Geelong listings are taken from the *Geelong Advertiser* match reports. In a few cases where these were not available, *The Age* was used.

4. West Perth listings for 1968-70 are taken from the *Football Budget*. The *Budget*'s 'prominent player' listings were discontinued in 1971, so the listings for that year are taken from the *West Australian*'s match reports.

(Thanks are due to the late Geoff Christian for the *Football Budget*s and to AFL historian and statistician Col Hutchinson for access to his *Geelong Advertiser* clippings.)

Comparisons, it is said, are odious. Ruckmen cannot be judged in comparison to rovers, or forwards, or defenders. Players cannot be compared across eras, because they never clashed, and times and playing styles were different. Nevertheless, from bar-room debates through to officially sanctioned 'Team of the Century' style lists, endless efforts to compare are made by all means from statistics, through straightforward opinion and assertion, through to supposedly scientific analysis.

As a ruckman, Farmer is almost unanimously acknowledged within Western Australia to be without peer in the history of the game. In Victoria it nearly always boils down to an argument between he and Nicholls, in which case there are good grounds for direct comparison. They were close, there is no doubt about it. They had many similar strengths, and each had some unique to himself. When they clashed it was nearly always a draw or a narrow points decision either way, with just the occasional clear-cut victory for one or the other.

The argument for Farmer is strongest in two particular respects. One is in the broader historical context of the game: both the unique contribution he made to the arts and sciences of ruckwork, which Nicholls, among others, learned from; and the role he played in the development of handball in the game. The other is in terms of the role he played in a team; Nicholls perhaps had greater inspirational qualities, but not even he could make a team zing and hum and play in the way Farmer could.

When analysing great ruckmen, Tom Outridge, a veteran West Australian ruckman who won the first Sandover Medal in 1921, used descriptive terms rarely heard in the sporting world, but nevertheless highly appropriate:

> Farmer was a dynamic ruckman with an abundance of football intellect. Not only did he perform tremendously himself, he also assisted other players in the side to play well ... To me, he was always the master of the situation. Any rovers roving to him had things made easy for them ... [No one could] measure up to Farmer's brilliance intellectually as a ruckman.[1]

A 1970 poll of Victorian commentators on the game asked to vote for the best ruckman of the previous 20 years placed Farmer on top with 41.5 votes, ahead of Nicholls on 36. The man perhaps best placed to make a direct comparison was the 1960 Brownlow medallist from Footscray, John Schultz, who played third fiddle to the pair. He gives the nod to Farmer as well. No one has suggested that any of the hundreds of ruckmen who have come since could seriously rival these two.

In terms of trying to compare and rank players of all types, the most scientific effort is one applied only to West Australian players. Published in 1984, it commissioned four judges to give marks out of 10 in 10 different categories of skill and achievement to top players of the previous 40 years.[2] Out of a possible 400 points, Farmer was ranked first with 353, ahead of Barry Cable on 344, with a gap to Ross Glendinning and Graham Moss in the next two places. Farmer being just ahead of Cable was an outcome that reflects the general opinion of the football world when the same question is assessed in a less rigorous manner.

In the Victorian context the field is more open. The closest parallel to the West Australian exercise was *Football's 50 Greatest*, published in 1976.[3] Football writers Greg Hobbs and Scott Palmer did not use a panel of judges or a points system, but claimed rigorous analysis and extensive consultation, while conceding that ultimately everyone should stick to their own opinions. Nevertheless, the ranking they came up with had Ted Whitten first, Farmer second, then John Coleman, Dick Reynolds, Haydn Bunton snr, and Alex Jesaulenko. On this list Nicholls came in at 24. Cable, with only four seasons in the VFL at the time, snuck in at number 40. Of Farmer, they wrote:

> Who could deny the select placement of this giant who changed the face of football in the '60s. He brought a touch of wizardry to ruck play and every player around him was caught up in the pure joy of it.[4]

In the years since 1976 there have been a number of players who would now claim a place in this top 50, with Leigh Matthews and Wayne Carey foremost among them. Whitten has maintained his reputation as the best of all, although Mike Sheahan, commissioned to create his top 50 as part of the AFL's official 150th birthday publication, preferred Wayne Carey as the game's best, with Farmer a slot behind Nicholls, in eighth spot.[5] One of Whitten's greatest assets, and the one constantly referred to in this type of discussion, was his incredible versatility; but who would play Farmer anywhere else except the ruck? He could have filled any key position—but what a waste of the special part of his talent.

Two factors that usually enter consideration when assessing a player's contribution to the game are longevity and finals performance. The case could be argued that had Farmer played even 200 games in the VFL compared to Whitten's 300-plus, he would have created a legacy that put him clearly at the top of the tree. And if Geelong had won the two or three premierships that they should have in his time with them, it might also be a different story.

On the score of longevity, a handful of players have subsequently gone on to break Farmer's record for the number of games played: Whinnen in Western Australia; Cable, like Farmer, in both states; Michael Tuck, Kevin Bartlett, Simon Madden, Bernie Quinlan and Bruce Doull in Victoria. In more recent times, the Harveys, Robert and Brent, Dustin Fletcher, Brad Johnson and John Blakey have gone past Farmer's 356-game mark. They are all champions of the game, with many achievements in addition to longevity.

Many of the hard men of the game, like coach Mick Malthouse, cite performance at the crunch level in finals football as the ultimate yardstick of both team and individual. Ron Barassi is the great example most often cited in this context. But Farmer holds his own with the best. Only Tuck, with seven, played in more premiership teams. Barassi, Cable, and others have achieved the next best, along with Farmer, at six.

The following table compares some of the greats, and some of the most successful players in these areas of longevity and success. Three players from the past 20 years have been added to the original list: Wayne Carey and the Gary Abletts, snr and jnr.

TABLE TWO

Player	Years	Seasons	Seasons in finals	League games	Finals games	Grand Finals	Premierships
Farmer	1953-71	19	15	356	30	10	6
Ablett Snr	1982-96	14	6	248	16	4	0
Ablett Jnr	2002 to end 2013	12	6	253	17	3	2
Barassi	1953-68	16	12	253	23	8	6
Bartlett	1965-83	19	10	403	27	7	5
Cable	1962-79	18	12	382	34	9	5
Carey	1989-2004	16	10	272	23	3	2
Collier, H	1926-40	15	13	253	27	9	6
Doull	1969-86	18	15	359	29	6	4
Madden	1974-92	19	10	378	19	4	2
Matthews	1969-85	17	10	332	29	7	4
Nicholls	1957-74	18	9	328	23	6	3
Reynolds	1933-51	19	11	320	27	10	4
Sheedy, J	1942-63	21	18	338	28	8	4
Tuck	1972-91	20	15	426	39	11	7
Whinnen	1960-77	18	13	371	23	5	4
Whitten	1951-70	20	5	321	10	2	1

Notes—Table Two

1. The listed players have been selected on the basis of length of career, finals record and reputation. Some who perhaps should have been included as well are Albert Collier, Gordon Coventry, Bill Dempsey, Jack Dyer, Graham Moss, Bernie Quinlan and Wayne Schimmelbusch.

2. Details are taken from official statistics. The only area of doubt is where players may have missed final-round matches in which their club participated, through non-selection, injury or suspension. This does not apply to Grand Finals and premierships, for which full team lists were available. Where it is known that games were missed, or there were other unusual circumstances, this is taken into account, with instances listed below:

Farmer: Missed the 1962 finals through injury.
Ablett Snr: Not selected for Hawthorn finals teams in debut season of 1982.
Barassi: Missed the 1963 finals through suspension.
Cable: Includes a Grand Final replay in 1977.
Collier: Missed the 1938 finals through suspension.
Doull: Career commenced in 1969, but not included in the Carlton Grand Final team of 1969, or premiership team of 1970.
Reynolds: Includes a Grand Final replay in 1948.
Sheedy: Includes games played for East Fremantle in 1942-3 when the WANFL became an under-age competition; did not play in the 1945 season; missed the 1958 premiership through suspension; missed the 1960 Grand Final through injury.

Even here there is a particular feature of the nature of Farmer's success that makes him stand out. Football by definition is ultimately about the team not the individual. The only real aim is to take a team and either turn it into, or keep it as, a premiership team. In all three phases of Farmer's career he joined a team that was sitting around the middle of the competition, that became a premiership team with a prolonged period as a power side of its League. And in each case he was universally recognised by his teammates as the reason for, and the critical factor behind this lift. He was a team-maker.

Throughout the second half of his career parallels were drawn at various times and in various ways between Farmer and Sir Donald Bradman. Many of these were to do with aspects of personality and dedication to their sport, as well as ability. It cannot be claimed that Farmer is the undisputed Australian king of his sport in the manner that Bradman is, but the other great footballers did not inspire the same type of comparison. There was an aura of uniqueness and distinction about Farmer the footballer. As Whitten and others have commented, it seemed to mesmerise others on the field in the heat of combat. It inspired observers to talk about nobility and statuary. Somehow he seemed to stand in a class of his own, as Bradman did in the world of cricket.

Farmer is keenly aware of his own place in the history of the game of football, and his own special skills and contributions. But to get him to talk directly about this is not easy. He would prefer to let the record speak for itself, and to let others make their judgments. In many hours of conversation he did make one comment—tricked unintentionally by another context, and he was not actually speaking about himself—but it stands as an appropriate assessment:

> You've got your average players. Then you've got players of outstanding ability. And then you have the absolute pinnacle, the player who is the playmaker, because he playmakes everyone around him. And there are not many players like that.

ACKNOWLEDGEMENTS

T his book would never have come to life without extensive support from many individuals and organisations. Twenty years down the track, I feel no less obliged to provide my thanks for this assistance, as per my acknowledgements in the 1994 edition:

> The list of those whose assistance in one form or another has contributed to this book seems almost endless, and cannot be reproduced in full here. First and foremost thanks go to Graham and Marlene Farmer, for their cooperation, their time and their patience with me. Secondly, to Alex Popescu and Eric Kornhauser, whose support made it possible.

> The photographs and illustrations in the book come from many sources. Particular thanks are due though to the following organisations for their generosity in donating photographs without the usual permission fees: West Australian Newspapers Ltd, The Herald and Weekly Times Ltd, the *Geelong Advertiser*, and Harry Beitzel, for the *Footy Week* photographs. Thanks also to Ted Whitten, Max Eastwood and Paul Tatz for supplying photographs from personal collections.

> For their kind assistance with the mammoth task of transcribing taped interviews: the Oral History Department of the Battye

Library, Dean Cannon and staff of Spark and Cannon, Jeni Lewington and Jan Pieters. For making available their personal collections of records and information: Geoff Christian, Col Hutchinson, Dave Clements, Hec Strempel, Len Branch, Ted Kilmurray and Steve Jarvis. For their hospitality and support during my research in Victoria: Marie Davidson and the Geelong Football Club, with special thanks to Russ Stephens. For their cooperation and the information provided from club records: the East Perth and West Perth Football Clubs. And finally, all those people from the football world who kindly submitted themselves to my rather rambling interviewing style.

I acknowledge the passing of the one and only Bob Davis. He was a key figure in the Farmer story, and it was a joy to get to know him when writing the book. The years roll on, and many others who contributed with interviews, and in other ways, have passed on since the early 90s, including Alex Popescu, Ted Whitten, Geoff Christian and Russ Stephens mentioned above. I remember them all fondly.

To have the chance to give the book another life is a dream come true for a writer. I think it is the enduring power of the Farmer name that I have to thank more than anything else. But I would like to thank Ken Spillman, who chose to include an extract in his and Ross Fitzgerald's footy anthology *Australia's Game* (2013), also published by Slattery Media Group, and then assisted in the discussions that led to this new edition. Thanks also to Lesley Corbett for the grunt work of proofreading the scans from the first editions; a life saver—or at least a major time saver!

ABOUT THE AUTHOR

Steve Hawke grew up in Melbourne barracking for Geelong, though unfortunately he is just too young to remember the 1963 premiership. He found his way to the Kimberley as a young man, and worked for many years with Indigenous communities and organisations. Writing the original edition of the Polly Farmer biography was a welcome reintroduction to the world of footy after the Kimberley years, when scratchy shortwave broadcasts and week-old papers were the only access to the game. In the years since he has become an avid armchair follower.

Steve's other writings include two histories, *Noonkanbah* and *A Town Is Born*, a children's novel, *Barefoot Kids*, and the stage play, *Jandamarra*, which he has also recently adapted as a libretto.

ENDNOTES

ABBREVIATIONS:

EPFC-AR: East Perth Football Club Annual Report.
GFC-AR: Geelong Football Club Annual Report.
WPFC-AR: West Perth Football Club Annual Report.
FB: The Football Budget (Official publication and weekly guide of the Western Australian National Football League. Followed, where available, by volume, issue and page numbers, and date.)

CHAPTER ONE

1. Unless noted otherwise, or explained in the body of the text, quotes attributed to Farmer and others come from interviews with the author in 1992-93.
2. Joan Leaming, *Nearly White: Assimilation Policies In Practice In Western Australia At Sister Kate's Home From 1933-1964*, BA (Hons) dissertation, University of Western Australia, 1986, p20. (I am indebted to Ms Leaming's work for much of the historical background and information on Sister Kate's, as well as for the quotes attributed here.)
3. ibid., p19.
4. ibid., p23.
5. ibid., p24.
6. ibid., p28.
7. *Australian Women's Weekly*, source undated, March or April 1949.
8. Leaming, p21-22.
9. ibid., p32-33.
10. Ron Davidson, 'Graham Farmer, The Footballer', in Lyall Hunt (ed.) *Westralian Portraits*, University of Western Australia Press, 1979, p266.
11. The school reports and some of the other information concerning Farmer was acquired directly from Sister Kate's Childrens Home archival records held at the Battye Library

CHAPTER TWO

1. *Sunday Times*, 18 May 1952.
2. ibid.
3. ibid.
4. ibid.

CHAPTER THREE

1. FB, Vol. 18, No.6, pp20-21, 23 May 1953.
2. *West Australian*, 12 Apr. 1954.
3. ibid.
4. FB, Vol. 19, No.3, p12, I May 1954.
5. FB, Vol. 19, No.4, p12, 8 May 1954.
6. *West Australian*, 17 May 1954.
7. FB, Vol. 19, No.7, p8, 29 May 1954.
8. FB, Vol. 19, No. 23, p8, 4 Sept. 1954.
9. EPFC-AR, 1955.
10. FB, Vol. 20, No.2, p2, 23 Apr. 1955.
11. *West Australian*, 23 May 1955.
12. FB, Vol. 20, No.7, p8, 28 May 1955.
13. *Daily News*, 23 May 1955.
14. *West Australian*, 7 June 1955.
15. *West Australian*, 27 June 1955.
16. FB, Vol. 20, No. 25, p9, 17 Sept. 1955.
17. *Herald*, Melbourne, 12 Oct. 1955.
18. *Daily News*, 12 Oct. 1955.
19. ibid., 13 Oct. 1955.
20. ibid., 14 Oct. 1955.

CHAPTER FOUR

1. Garrie Hutchinson, 'Days When The Big Men Flew High And Hard', in Fitzgerald & Spillman (eds.), *The Greatest Game*, Melbourne, 1988, pp134-5.
2. *Sunday Times*, 3 July 1955.

CHAPTER FIVE

1. *To Members and Players of East Perth Football Club*, election pamphlet published by M W Stirling, R C Hull & T L Reynolds, 1955.
2. ibid.
3. Jim Main & Russell Holmesby, *The Encyclopedia o/League Footballers*, Wilkinson Books, 1992, p381.
4. *Sunday Times*, 11 Sept. 1955.
5. EPFC-AR, 1956, p8.
6. *Sunday Times*, 10 June 1956.
7. *Sunday Times*, 17 June 1956.
8. *Sunday Times*, 24 June 1956.
9. ibid.
10. FB, Vol. 21, No. 23, p24, 25 Aug 1956.
11. *West Australian*, 21 Sept. 1956.
12. FB, Vol. 21, No. 28, p20, 6 Oct. 1956.
13. *West Australian*, 1 Oct. 1956.
14. EPFC-AR, 1956, p23.

CHAPTER SIX

1. FB, 18 May 1957, p8.
2. Interview with Bob Hawke on *The Sattler File*, radio 6PR, 14 Aug. 1992.
3. *Sunday Times*, 25 Aug. 1957.
4. *West Australian*, 30 Sept. 1957.
5. EPFC-AR, 1956.
6. *Sunday Times*, 13 Oct. 1957.
7. ibid.
8. EPFC-AR, 1957, p12.
9. *Sunday Times*, 5 Oct. 1958.
10. EPFC-AR, 1958, p15 (Note: Marsh did in fact play one more game in 1960, when coaching East Fremantle, after four of his players came down with the flu.)
11. *Sunday Times*, 12 Oct. 1958.
12. FB, 11 July 1959, p12.
13. *West Australian*, 12 Oct. 1959.
14. EPFC-AR, 1957, p21.
15. *Sporting Globe*, 5 Mar. 1960.
16. *West Australian*, 16 May 1960.
17. *West Australian*, 25 July 1960.
18. *Sunday Times*, 2 Oct. 1960.
19. *West Australian*, 10 Oct. 1960.

CHAPTER SEVEN

1. Leonie Sandercock & Ian Turner, *Up Where Cazaly?: The Great Australian Game*, Granada, Sydney, 1981, p222.

CHAPTER EIGHT

1. *Sunday Times*, 16 Apr. 1961.
2. *Sunday Times*, 11 June 1961.
3. *Sunday Times*, 18 June 1961.
4. Clipping in Farmer's possession, possibly *Courier Mail*, 24 July 1961.
5. ibid.
6. *Sunday Times*, 30 July 1961.
7. *West Australian*, 3 Oct. 1961.
8. *Sunday Times*, 8 Oct. 1961.
9. *West Australian*, 18 Jan. 1962.
10. Unsourced clipping in Fanner's possession.

CHAPTER NINE

1. Melbourne novelist and journalist George Johnston, quoted in Sandercock &.Turner, p155.
2. Bruce Dawe. "Life Cycle" reproduced in Sandercock & Turner.
3. Sandercock & Turner.
4. *Jack Dyer's Football Heroes*, magazine, Southdown Press, 1974, p21.
5. G Atkinson, *The Courage Book of VFL Finals, 1897-1973*, Wren Publishing, 1974, p199.
6. *Sporting Globe*, undated clipping.
7. *Sun*, Melbourne undated clipping.
8. *Sun*, 21 Apr. 1962.
9. *Geelong Advertiser*, 23 Apr. 1962.
10. *Sun*, 23 Apr. 1962.
11. *Sun*, 30 Apr. 1962.
12. *Geelong Advertiser*, 7 May 1962.
13. *Truth*, undated clipping, probably 2 May 1962, clipping in Farmer's possession.
14. Unsourced clipping in Farmer's possession.
15. *Geelong Advertiser*, 14 May 1962.
16. *West Australian*, 16 May 1962.
17. *Geelong Advertiser*, 25 June 1962.
18. *Sun*, 20 Aug. 1962.

CHAPTER TEN

1. *Truth*, undated clipping, Apr. 1963.
2. *Geelong Advertiser*, 20 May 1963.
3. *Truth*, undated clipping, probably 21 May 1993.
4. *Sporting Globe*, undated, probably midweek edition, approx. 29 May 1963.
5. *Sporting Globe*, 29 June 1963.
6. *Geelong Advertiser*, 5 Aug. 1963.
7. ibid.
8. ibid.
9. *Geelong Advertiser*, 2 Sept. 1963.
10. *Geelong Advertiser*, 9 Sept. 1963.
11. ibid.
12. *Sun*, 21 Sept. 1963.
13. *Sun*, 23 Sept. 1963.
14. ibid.
15. *West Australian*, 7 Oct. 1963.
16. *Herald*, 5 Oct. 1963.
17. *Sporting Globe*, 5 Oct. 1993.
18. *Herald*, 5 Oct. 1963.
19. *Geelong Advertiser*, 7 Oct. 1963.
20. *Sun*, 7 Oct. 1963.
21. ibid.
22. *West Australian*, 7 Oct. 1963.
23. *Sun*, 7 Oct. 1963.
24. ibid.
25. *Geelong Advertiser*, 7 Oct. 1963.

CHAPTER ELEVEN

1. *Daily News*, 7 Oct. 1963.
2. *West Australian*, 12 Oct. 1963.
3. *Sun*, 20 Apr. 1964.
4. Jack Dyer, *Jack Dyer's Football Heroes*, magazine published by Southdown Press.
5. *Sun*, 31 Aug. 1964.
6. *Sporting Globe*, midweek edition, probably 15 Sept. 1964.
7. *Geelong Advertiser*, 14 Sept. 1964.
8. Dyer.
9. *Geelong Advertiser*, 14 Sept. 1964.
10. Quoted in an article in the *Herald*, 31 Mar. 1965.
11. *Herald*, 31 Mar. 1965.
12. ibid.
13. *Herald*, 24 Apr. 1965.
14. *Geelong Advertiser*, 26 Apr. 1965.
15. ibid.
16. *Geelong Advertiser*, 25 July 1965.
17. ibid.
18. *Sun*, 5 Sept. 1965.

CHAPTER TWELVE

1. *Sporting Globe*, undated clipping of Farmer's, probably 21 Apr. 1964.
2. GFC-AR, 1964, p5.
3. *Sporting Globe*, undated clipping of Farmer's, probably 21 Apr. 1964.

CHAPTER THIRTEEN

1. *Geelong Advertiser*, 9 May 1966.
2. *Geelong Advertiser*, 6 June 1966.
3. ibid. •
4. ibid.
5. *Geelong Advertiser* 13 June 1966.
6. *Geelong Advertiser*, 29 June 1966.
7. *Geelong Advertiser*, 22 Aug. 1966.
8. ibid.
9. ibid.
10. *Geelong Advertiser*, 5 Sept. 1966.
11. *Geelong Advertiser*, 1 May 1967.
12. *Geelong Advertiser*, 22 May 1967.
13. ibid.
14. *Sporting Globe*, 26 Apr. 1967.
15. *The Age*, 29 May 1967.
16. *The Age*, 5 June 1967.
17. *The Age*, 28 Aug. 1967.
18. *The Age*, 4 Sept. 1967.
19. *Geelong Advertiser*, 18 Sept. 1967.
20. *Geelong Advertiser*, 25 Sept. 1967.
21. ibid.

CHAPTER FOURTEEN

1. *Truth*, undated clipping, probably 12 July 1967.
2. *Herald*, undated clipping, thought to be 1 Dec. 1967.
3. ibid.
4. *Sun*, 5 Dec. 1967.
5. *Sun*, 7 Dec. 1967.
6. Jack Dyer in *Truth*, 9 Dec. 1967.
7. ibid.

CHAPTER FIFTEEN

1. WPFC-AR, 1967, p21.
2. FB Vol. 33, No.10, p13, 15 Apr. 1968.
3. *West Australian*, 13 May 1968.
4. *West Australian*, 26 Aug. 1968.
5. *West Australian*, 16 Sept. 1968.
6. *West Australian*, 23 Sept. 1968.
7. WPFC-AR, 1968, p4.
8. Brian Atkinson, *West Perth Football Club 1885–1985*, Action Press, Perth, 1985, p128.

CHAPTER SIXTEEN

1. *West Australian*, 28 July 1969.
2. ibid.
3. Geoff Christian, *The Footballers*, St. George Books, Perth, 1988, p97.
4. *Ross Elliott's West Australian Football Register*, 1969, Mt Lawley Print, 1969, pl33.
5. *West Australian*, 15 Sept. 1969.
6. ibid.
7. ibid.
8. *Weekend News*, 27 Sept. 1969.
9. *Independent*, 28 Sept. 1969.
10. ibid.

CHAPTER SEVENTEEN

1. *West Australian*, 15 June 1970.
2. ibid.
3. ibid.
4. FB, Vol.36, No.5, p3, 1 May 1971.
5. Atkinson, p135.
6. *West Australian*, 20 Sept. 1971.
7. *West Australian*, 2 Oct. 1971.
8. *West Australian*, 4 Oct. 1971.
9. *Sunday Independent*, 3 Oct. 1971.

CHAPTER EIGHTEEN

1. 'Football 70', *Weekend News*, 1970, p6.
2. ibid.
3. *Sun*, Undated clipping, around Aug. 1973.
4. GFC-AR, 1975, p7.
5. *Australian*, 13 Sept. 1975.
6. ibid.
7. ibid.

CHAPTER NINETEEN

1. FB, 10 Apr. 1976.
2. EPFC-AR, 1976, p3.
3. FB, 25 Sept. 1976.
4. EPFC-AR, 1976, p15.
5. *Daily News*, undated clipping, Sept. 1977.
6. FB, 17 Sept. 1977.
7. *Daily News*, undated clipping, Sept. 1977.

CHAPTER TWENTY

1. *West Australian*, 11 July 1986.
2. *West Australian*, 19 July 1986.
3. ibid.
4. ibid.
5. *West Australian*, 8 Dec. 1986.
6. ibid.
7. *Herald-Sun*, 12 Sept. 1992.
8. *Herald Sun*, 18 Jun. 1998.
9. *Sunday Times*, 25 Mar. 2012.

AFTERWORD

1. *The Age*, 24 Aug. 2013.

APPENDIX

1. *Daily News*, 3 Apr. 1967.
2. *WA.'s Fabulous 40*, Alan East editor, Commonwealth Bank, Perth, 1984.
3. *Football's 50 Greatest*, Greg Hobbs & Scott Palmer, Melbourne, 1976.
4. ibid., p5.
5. *The Australian Game of Football*, Slattery Media Group for the AFL, Melbourne, 2008.